William A. Herri

# The Powers, Duties, and Liabilities of To.... and Parish Officers in Massachusetts

## Second Edition

William A. Herrick

**The Powers, Duties, and Liabilities of Town and Parish Officers in Massachusetts**
*Second Edition*

ISBN/EAN: 9783337845872

Printed in Europe, USA, Canada, Australia, Japan

Cover: Foto ©Suzi / pixelio.de

More available books at **www.hansebooks.com**

THE

# POWERS, DUTIES,

AND

## LIABILITIES

OF

# TOWN AND PARISH OFFICERS

## IN MASSACHUSETTS;

WITH FORMS AND PARLIAMENTARY RULES FOR CON-
DUCTING TOWN AND OTHER MEETINGS.

BY

### WILLIAM A. HERRICK.

**SECOND EDITION.**

### BOSTON:
LITTLE, BROWN, AND COMPANY.
**1880.**

UNIVERSITY PRESS: JOHN WILSON & SON,
CAMBRIDGE.

# ADVERTISEMENT

## TO THE SECOND EDITION.

THIS second edition of the "Town Officer" has been prepared upon the same plan, and in the same manner, as the former edition, and states the law as it exists at the present time. Such of the Acts of the Legislature of 1879 as pertain to the duties of Town and Parish Officers are given in the Addenda. The chapter on "State Aid to Soldiers and Sailors, &c." has been omitted, as the provisions of law with reference to granting such aid expire with this year. It is almost needless to add, that the changes in the law since the former edition have been very numerous, affecting almost every subject. A great deal of labor has been expended to state the law accurately and intelligibly.

W. A. H.

BOSTON, April 10, 1879.

# PREFACE.

I HAVE endeavored in the following pages to bring together in a convenient order, for the use of Town and Parish Officers and all citizens interested in the administration of town affairs, all the statutes now in force in this Commonwealth pertaining to the duties, powers, and liabilities of towns, parishes, and their officers. To these statutes have been added such comments, drawn from the decisions of the Supreme Judicial Court, as I thought would serve to explain or illustrate them to such as were called upon to act under them as officers of towns or parishes. The matter in the larger type, except that enclosed in brackets, consists of the statutes printed verbatim, so that any one may rely on them without the necessity of reference to the originals. The matter in the smaller type consists of the comments mentioned above, and in some instances of statutes, abridged, where this could be done without danger of mistake, and the entire statute contained matter unnecessary to town officers. I earnestly hope, and I believe from the care bestowed upon it, that the book will be found trustworthy. In the Appendix are brief rules

for conducting town and other meetings, and forms
for drafting the papers to be made by town officers.
The *Addenda* contains the statutes enacted by the
Legislature of 1870, since the body of the book was
printed. The larger part of the legislation of this
year will be found, in connection with the subjects
affected by it. The law of the duties of town officers
relating to the sale of intoxicating liquors is so liable
to change, and so readily found in the statutes usually
of one year, that it was thought best to omit it.

W. A. H.

Boston, June 24, 1870.

# TABLE OF CONTENTS.

## CHAPTER X.

# TOWN AND PARISH OFFICER.

---

## CHAPTER I.

### GENERAL POWERS AND DUTIES OF TOWNS.

1. Towns shall continue to be bodies corporate with all the powers heretofore exercised by them, and subject to all the duties to which they have heretofore been subject.[1] The word "town" may be construed to include cities and districts, unless such construction would be repugnant to the provisions of any statute specially relating to such cities or districts.[2]

They are *qua* corporations with limited powers coextensive with the duties imposed upon them by statute or usage, but deficient in many of the powers incident to the general character of corporations.[3]

2. The boundary lines of towns shall remain as now established.

3. There shall be a perambulation of town lines, and they shall be run and the marks renewed, once in every five years, by two or more of the selectmen of each town. or such substitutes as they in writing appoint for that purpose. After every such renewal the proceedings shall be recorded in the records of the respective towns.

Selectmen have no authority to change the boundaries or to adjudicate upon the limits of towns, but only to ascertain existing lines and renew old marks and monuments.[4]

---

[1] Gen. Stats. ch. 18, § 1.

[2] Gen. Stats. ch. 3, § 7, cl. 17, and ch. 18, § 77.

[3] Rumford *v.* Wood, 13 Mass. 193; Hill *v.* Boston, 122 Mass. 349:

Linehan *v.* Cambridge, 109 Mass. 212.

[4] Commonwealth *v.* Heffron, 102 Mass. 151.

4. Towns may in their corporate capacity sue and be sued by the name of the town, and may appoint all necessary agents and attorneys in that behalf.[1]

But selectmen are not such agents without special authority.[2] Towns may submit suits to arbitration.[3]

5. They may hold real estate for the public use of the inhabitants, and may convey the same, either by a vote of the inhabitants, or by a deed of their committee or agent; may hold personal estate for the public use of the inhabitants, and alienate and dispose of the same by vote or otherwise; may hold real and personal estate in trust for the support of schools and for the promotion of education within the limits of the town; may make contracts necessary and convenient for the exercise of their corporate powers; and may make orders for the disposal or use of their corporate property as they may judge necessary or expedient for the interest of the inhabitants.[4]

They may take and hold devises and bequests for appropriate charitable uses,[5] and in certain cases take, hold, and sell tax titles.[6] They may also purchase water rights for the purpose of supplying their inhabitants with pure water.[7]

6. When a town is required to enter into a recognizance, the selectmen may by an order or vote authorize any person to enter into the recognizance in the name and behalf of the town, and it shall be binding like any other contract made by such town. No surety shall be required in such recognizance.

7. They may, at legal meetings, grant and vote such sums as they judge necessary for the following purposes: —

For the support of town schools;

For the relief, support, maintenance, and employment of the poor;

[1] Gen. Stats. ch. 18, §§ 2, 3, 8.

[2] Walpole v. Gray, 11 Allen, 149.

[3] Campbell v. Upton, 113 Mass. 70.

[4] Gen. Stats. ch. 18, § 9.

[5] Drury v. Natick, 10 Allen, 169; Hill v. Boston, 122 Mass. 349.

[6] Stats. 1862, ch. 183.

[7] Stats. 1870, ch. 94. See chapter concerning this subject hereafter.

For laying out, discontinuing, making, altering, and repairing highways and town-ways, and for labor and materials to be used thereon;

For procuring the writing and publishing of their town histories;

For burial-grounds;

For encouraging the destruction of noxious animals;

For all other necessary charges arising therein; [1]

8. The foregoing seems not to have been intended to be an enumeration of objects and purposes for which towns may raise money, but the expression of a few leading and prominent objects, by way of instance, and a general reference to others under the term "other necessary charges." [2] But these "other necessary charges" are limited to objects of a like character with those previously specified. [3]

9. And courts have held such charges to embrace building a market-house; [4] repairing a meeting-house as compensation for its use for town meetings, and paying a sexton for services; [5] repairing fire-engines, whether belonging to the town or private owners; [6] repairing a public clock; [7] constructing reservoirs for water to supply fire-engines; [8] and raising money to indemnify the officers of the town against liabilities incurred or damages sustained in the *bona fide* discharge of their duties, and sometimes even when in good faith they exceed their authority; [9] and making additional compensation to a person for labor done by him in building a town-house, although as a contractor under another person with whom the town had contracted to build it for a fixed sum. [10]

10. But towns cannot legally raise or appropriate money to celebrate anniversaries, such as the fourth of July, or the surrender of Cornwallis. Upon this point Bigelow, C. J., says: "The appropriation is neither necessary to the exercise of any power expressly granted to the city; nor is it incidental to any right or authority, which, though not expressly granted, has its origin in well-settled usage, and is founded upon the necessities, convenience, or even the comfort, of the inhabitants. This is the extreme limit, of the power of towns and cities to grant money, as settled by repeated adjudica-

[1] Gen. Stats. ch. 18, §§ 10, 18.

[2] Shaw, C. J., Willard v. Newburyport, 12 Pick. 227.

[3] Allen v. Marion, 11 Allen, 108; Coolidge v. Brookline, 114 Mass. 594.

[4] Spaulding v. Lowell, 23 Pick. 71.

[5] Woodbury v. Hamilton, 6 Pick. 101.

[6] Allen v. Taunton, 19 Pick. 485.

[7] Willard v. Newburyport, 12 Pick. 227.

[8] Hardy v. Waltham, 3 Met. 163.

[9] Bancroft v. Lynnfield, 18 Pick. 568; Fuller v. Groton, 11 Gray, 340.

[10] Friend v. Gilbert, 108 Mass. 408.

tions of this court." [1] Nor can towns appropriate money to pay the expenses incurred by individuals in procuring an act of the legislature incorporating the town; [2] nor in opposing before the legislature the annexation of the whole or a part of its territory to another town; [3] nor in petitioning the legislature to annex the town to another town; [4] nor in purchasing uniforms for a military company; [5] nor to distribute money upon those liable to pay a poll-tax, or in payment of poll-taxes.[6] *Cities* are now allowed by a late statute to appropriate a certain sum for celebrating holidays, and "other purposes of a public nature," upon a certain vote,[7] and cities and towns are required in certain cases to provide armories,[8] and any town may appropriate money to be expended by the school committee in their discretion in providing for the conveyance of pupils to and from the public schools.[9] A town may at its annual meeting raise by taxation a sum of money not exceeding one tenth of one per cent of its assessed valuation, for the year last preceding, for the purpose of celebrating any centennial anniversary of its own incorporation, or for the purpose of celebrating the one hundredth anniversary of the declaration of independence.[10]

11. "Legal meetings" include special meetings called after the annual meeting.[11] The purposes for which money is raised should be expressed in the vote, though it has been held sufficient when the objects were stated in town meeting by the chairman of the selectmen, where the parties afterwards objecting to the appropriation were present and made no objection.[12]

12. Towns may appropriate money for erecting monuments in memory of their soldiers who have died, or may die, in the service of our country in the present war.[13] Towns may at any legal meeting vote such sums of money as they judge necessary, for the purpose of erecting headstones or other monuments at the graves of persons who served in the military or naval service of the United States in the war of the Rebellion: provided, that no town shall expend money raised under this act, except in cases where the soldier or sailor shall have been accredited to the quota of said town.[14] The inhabitants of any town on the coast of Massachusetts are authorized to raise money and expend the same in defending such city or town against the public enemies of the United States; but no such expen-

---

[1] Hood *v.* Lynn, 1 Allen, 105, and cases cited.

[2] Frost *v.* Belmont, 6 Allen, 152.

[3] Coolidge *v.* Brookline, 114 Mass. 592.

[4] Minot *v.* Roxbury, 112 Mass. 3.

[5] Claflin *v.* Hopkinton, 4 Gray, 502.

[6] Allen *v.* Marion, 11 Allen, 108; Cooley *v.* Grantville, 10 Cush. 56.

[7] Stats. 1861, ch. 165.

[8] Stats. 1878, ch. 265, §§ 88–91.

[9] Stats. 1869, ch. 132.

[10] Stats. 1874, ch. 112.

[11] Freeland *v.* Hastings, **10 Allen,** 570.

[12] Ibid.

[13] Stats. 1864, ch. 100.

[14] Stats. 1873, ch. 335.

ditures shall be made without the approval of the governor and council, nor any thing done in contravention of the constitution and laws of the United States.[1]

13. Any town may, at a legal meeting, grant and vote a sum not exceeding twenty-five cents for each of its ratable polls in the year next preceding that in which such appropriation is made, to be expended under the direction of the selectmen in premiums, or in any such manner as they may deem most effectual to encourage the planting of shade-trees by the owners of real estate, upon the public squares, or highways, adjoining such real estate.[2]

14. The inhabitants of any town, and the city council of any city, are hereby authorized to raise money and expend the same for the purpose of procuring the detection and apprehension of persons committing any felony in such place.[8]

15. Every town containing more than three thousand inhabitants shall, and every town may, keep and maintain a secure and convenient lock-up or place of security, to which such persons as may be arrested or detained by an officer without a warrant may be committed; and a police court or justice of the peace may commit, upon continuation for further examination, any prisoner charged with a bailable offence, and not recognizing, to the lock-up in the town in which the court is held, whenever in his opinion it may be deemed safe and commodious and costs may be saved thereby.

16. For the expenses of detention and support in cases provided in the above section, there may be charged upon the warrant, or other precept, if any, fifty cents a day, or at that rate for the fractional part of a day, and no more, which shall be paid to the town or city maintaining the same.[4]

No charge shall be made for the detention and support of persons committed to any lock-up, except as above provided.[4]

[1] Stats. 1863, ch. 118.
[2] Stats. 1869, ch. 381.
[8] Ib. 1869, ch. 206. By statute in this State, any crime punishable by death or imprisonment in the State prison, and no other, is a felony. Gen. Stats. ch. 168, § 1.
[4] Stats. 1862, ch. 216, §§ 16, 17; Stats. 1876, ch. 159.

17. The city council of any city and the inhabitants of any town, at a town meeting duly held for that purpose, may select and take any parcel or parcels of land within the limits of such city or town, not appropriated to public uses, as a place for the erection of a city or town hall, for the use of such city or town, or for the enlargement of any existing city or town hall lot; but no lot so taken or enlarged shall exceed in extent one acre. The city or town shall, within sixty days after such taking, file for record in the registry of deeds for the county or district in which the land is situated, a description of the lands so taken, as certain as is required in a common conveyance of land, and a statement of the purpose for which such lands were taken, which description and statement shall be signed by the mayor of the city or by the selectmen of the town, or a major part thereof; and the title of land so taken shall vest in such city or town from the time of the filing of said description and statement.

18. All damages sustained by any person by reason of the taking of any land for the purposes aforesaid, shall be paid by the city or town; and if the mayor and aldermen or the selectmen shall fail to agree upon such damages with the owner of such land, the same may be assessed and determined by a jury in the manner provided by law in the case of the laying out of city or town ways, respectively; and application for a jury may be made at any time within three years after said description and statement shall be recorded as above provided. If the damages so awarded shall exceed the amount which the city or town may have tendered him as compensation before the filing of his application for a jury, the owner shall recover his costs in the proceedings for such assessment; otherwise the city or town shall recover costs.

19. Any parcel of land, taken under authority of this act, shall revert to the owner, or his heirs or assigns, unless a city or town hall shall be erected thereon, or unless the same shall be enclosed and devoted to the enlargement of an existing city or town hall lot, within three years

after the recording of the description and statement above provided.[1]

20. Cities and towns may construct for their own use lines of electric telegraph upon and along the highways and public roads within their respective limits, subject to the provisions of chapter sixty-four of the General Statutes, as far as the same are applicable.

21. The board of aldermen of cities and the selectmen of towns may authorize any person, upon such terms and conditions as they may prescribe, and subject to the provisions of chapter sixty-four of the General Statutes, as far as applicable, to construct for private use a line of electric telegraph upon and along the highways and public roads of the city or town. After the erection of such line, the posts and structures thereof within the location of such highways and roads shall become the property of the city or town, and shall be subject to the regulation and control of the board of aldermen or selectmen, who may at any time require alterations in the location or erection of such posts and structures to be made by the parties using the same, and may order the removal thereof, having first given such parties notice and an opportunity to be heard. The city or town may, at any time, attach wires for its own use to such posts and structures, and the board of aldermen or selectmen may permit other persons to attach wires for their private use thereto or to posts and structures established by the city or town, and may prescribe such terms and conditions therefor as they shall deem reasonable.

22. Whoever unlawfully and intentionally injures, molests, or destroys any wires, posts, structures, or fixtures of any line of electric telegraph, established or constructed under authority of this act, shall be punished by a fine not exceeding five hundred dollars, or by imprisonment not exceeding two years, or by both said penalties.[2]

23. When a town votes to raise by taxation or pledge

---

[1] Stats. 1869, ch. 411, §§ 1, 2, 3.  See chapter concerning Telegraph
[2] Stats. 1869, ch. 457, §§ 1, 2, 3.  Companies.

of its credit, or to pay from its treasury, any money, for a purpose other than those for which it has the legal right and power, the supreme judicial court may upon the suit or petition of not less than ten taxable inhabitants thereof, briefly setting forth the cause of complaint, hear and determine the same in equity. Any justice of said court may in term time or vacation issue injunctions and make such orders and decrees as may be necessary or proper to restrain or prevent any violation or abuse of such legal right and power, until the final determination of the cause by said court.[1]

24. Each town and city may establish and maintain a public library therein, with or without branches, for the use of the inhabitants thereof, and provide suitable rooms therefor, under such regulations for its government as may from time to time be prescribed by the inhabitants of the town, or the city council.[2]

25. Any town may, at a legal meeting, grant and vote money for the establishment, maintenance, or increase of a public library therein, and for erecting or providing suitable buildings or rooms therefor; and may receive, hold, and manage any devise, bequest, or donation for the establishment, increase, or maintenance of any such library.[8]

The selectmen of the several towns in this commonwealth, in which may now or hereafter be public libraries, owned and maintained by said towns, are authorized to place in the public libraries, for the use of the inhabitants, such books, reports, and laws, as have been or may be received from the commonwealth.[4] Any town may appropriate and pay such sum annually as it may see fit, toward defraying the expenses of maintaining any library within such city or town to which the inhabitants are allowed free access for the purpose of using the same on the premises.[5] Whoever wilfully and maliciously or wantonly and without cause writes upon, injures, defaces, tears or destroys any book, plate, picture, engraving or statue belonging to any law, town, city or other public library, shall be punished by a

[1] Gen. Stats. ch. 18, § 79.
[2] Gen. Stats. ch. 33, § 8.
[8] Stats. 1866, ch. 222, § 1.  Section 2 of this chapter repeals section 9 of chapter 33 of Gen. Stats.  As this section seems to cover the whole subject, it is possible that the repeal of section 8, of chapter 33, was omitted by mistake.
[4] Stats. 1871, ch. 26.
[5] Stats. 1873, ch. 306.

fine of not less than five dollars nor more than fifty dollars, or by imprisonment in the jail not exceeding six months for every such offence.[1] So long as any corporation formed under chapter 217 of the Acts of 1872 shall allow the inhabitants of the city or town wherein the same is located free access to and use of its library, such city or town may annually appropriate and pay to the said corporation established therein money to aid in supporting its library.[2]

26. They (towns) may make such necessary orders and by-laws, not repugnant to the laws of the state, for directing and managing the prudential affairs, preserving the peace and good order, and maintaining the internal police thereof, as they may judge most conducive to the welfare of the town ; and may affix penalties for breaches of such orders and by-laws not exceeding twenty dollars for one offence.[3]

27. The term "by-law" has a peculiar and limited signification, being used to designate the orders and regulations which a corporation, as one of its legal incidents, has power to make, and which is usually exercised to regulate its own action and concerns, and the rights and duties of its members amongst themselves.[4] By-laws must be reasonable, and it is for the court to decide whether they are unreasonable or not. If unreasonable, they are void. If necessary for the good government of society, they are good.[5] "*Prudential concerns*" of a town embrace that large class of miscellaneous subjects affecting the accommodation and convenience of the inhabitants, which have been placed under the municipal jurisdiction of towns by statutes or by usage. Such as public hay-scales, burying-grounds, wells, and reservoirs, one or more public clocks for the common regulation of time, in all large towns and populous villages.[6]

28. But the usage must be what the law terms a good usage. "An unlawful expenditure of the money of a town cannot be rendered valid by usage, however long continued. A casual or occasional exercise of a power by one or a few towns will not constitute a usage. It must not only be general, reasonable, and of long continuance, but, what is more important, it must also be a custom necessary to the exercise of some corporate power or the enjoyment of some corporate right, or which contributes essentially to the necessities and convenience of the inhabitants."[7]

[1] Stats. 1872, ch. 42.
[2] Stats. 1872, ch. 217.
[3] Gen. Stats. ch. 18, § 11.
[4] Shaw, C. J., Commonwealth v. Turner, 1 Cush. 496.
[5] Commonwealth v. Worcester, 3 Pick. 472; Vandine's Case, 6 Pick. 191; City of Boston v. Shaw, 1 Met. 130.
[6] Willard v. Newburyport, 12 Pick. 231.
[7] Hood v. Lynn, 1 Allen, 106.

29. Cities and towns may make by-laws to prevent the falling, and to provide for the removal of snow and ice from the roofs of buildings, in such portions of their limits, and to such extent, as they may deem expedient, and may annex penalties not exceeding twenty dollars, for any violation of such by-laws by the owner of any such building, or his agent having the care thereof.[1]  Cities and towns may make ordinances and by-laws, with appropriate penalties for the violation thereof, requiring owners of buildings near the line of streets and public ways to erect barriers or take other suitable measures to prevent the falling of snow and ice from such buildings upon persons travelling on such streets and ways, and to protect such persons from any other dangers incident to the maintenance, occupation, or use of such buildings.[2]

30. Towns which have adopted or shall adopt the provisions of sections seven and eight of chapter forty-five of the General Statutes may, at their annual town meetings, establish by-laws to provide for the removal of snow and ice, to such extent as they may deem expedient, from sidewalks which have been or shall be established, constructed, or graded, in accordance with the provisions of said sections.

31. Said by-laws shall determine the time and manner of such removal, and annex penalties, not exceeding ten dollars, for each violation of their provisions by any owner or tenant of the estate abutting upon the sidewalk from which the snow and ice are required to be removed; and such penalties shall be recovered in an action of tort, in the name and to the use of the town.[3]

32. Said sections of chapter forty-five are as follows: —

§ 7.   In cities in which the city council, and in towns in which the inhabitants, have adopted the provisions of this and the following section, the mayor and aldermen or selectmen may establish and grade sidewalks in such streets as in their judgment the public convenience may require, and may assess the abutters on such sidewalks one half the

---

[1] Stats. 1863, ch. 86.     [2] Stats. 1878, ch. 91.     [3] Stats. 1863, ch. 114.

expense of the same, the residue being paid by such city or town. All assessments so made shall be a lien upon the abutting lands in the same manner as taxes are a lien upon real estate.

§ 8. No sidewalk constructed or graded in a city or town shall be dug up or obstructed in any part thereof, without the consent of the mayor or aldermen of the city, or of the selectmen of the town, in which such sidewalk is established.

33. Cities and towns may, by ordinance or by-law, prohibit persons from riding or driving horses or other beasts of burthen, carriage, or draught, in or upon any of the streets or ways for public travel therein, at a rate of speed which they deem inconsistent with the public safety or convenience, under such penalties as they are authorized to impose for breaches of other ordinances or by-laws.

34. A person violating a provision of such ordinance or by-law may be apprehended by a sheriff, deputy sheriff, constable, police officer, or watchman, without a written warrant, and kept in custody in a convenient place, not more than twenty-four hours, Sunday excepted; at or before the expiration of which time he shall be brought before a justice of the peace or police court, and proceeded against according to law.[1]

35. Any city or town shall have power to regulate, by suitable ordinances or by-laws, to be made in the manner now provided by law, the passage and driving of sheep, swine, and neat cattle through and over the public streets, ways, causeways and bridges within the limits of such city or town, and to annex penalties not exceeding fifty dollars for each violation thereof.[2]

36. Any city or town in which a draw for the passage of vessels through a bridge used as a public highway and maintained at the public expense is situated, shall have

---

[1] Stats. 1865, ch. 31. For the authority of towns to make by-laws, &c., in reference to truant children, neglected children, and absentees from school, see chapter on that subject.

[2] Stats. 1876, ch. 20.

power to make ordinances or by-laws regulating the passage of vessels through such draw, and to annex penalties not exceeding fifty dollars for each violation thereof: *provided*, such ordinances or by-laws shall be approved by the harbor commissioners.

37. In all cases where such ordinances or by-laws are made applicable to any draw, it shall be the duty of such city or town to place said draw under the direction of a suitable person or persons, as draw-tender or superintendent, and to post in some conspicuous place near by a written or printed copy of such ordinances or by-laws.

38. Such draw-tender or superintendent shall have full control of the passing of all vessels through the draw, shall furnish all facilities for such passing, shall allow no detention, having due regard for the public travel, and shall enforce the ordinances or by-laws aforesaid.

39. If any vessel shall, through the negligence of the master or others having charge of her, or their neglect to comply with such ordinances or by-laws, or disregard of the directions of such draw-tender or superintendent, injure any bridge, draw, or pier or wharf connected therewith, the owner or owners thereof shall likewise be liable to pay for such damage, to be recovered by such city or town in an action of tort.

40. Such draw-tender or superintendent shall likewise have authority to remove any vessel obstructing such draw, or interfering with the passage of other vessels through the same, or made fast to such draw or bridge or pier or wharf connected with the same, without the consent of such draw-tender or superintendent, or wilfully violating any ordinance or by-law, and the expense of such removal shall be recovered in the manner set forth in the foregoing section.[1]

41. Any city or town may regulate by suitable ordinances or by-laws, to be made in the manner now provided by law, with penalties not exceeding fifty dollars for each

[1] Stats. 1876, ch. 122.

violation thereof, the use of reservoirs and land and drive-ways appurtenant thereto, forming a part of its system of water supply within its limits.[1]

No person, except on military duty in the public service of the United States or of this commonwealth, shall keep, have or possess, in any building, place, vehicle, ship or other vessel, within one rod of a dwelling-house in any city or town, any explosive compound in quantity exceeding one fifth of a pound in any way or manner prohibited by this act or by any ordinance or by-law, which may be made in accordance with section two of this act. Section two is as follows : —

"The city council of any city may make ordinances necessary for the protection of life and property, in regard to the keeping, storage, use, manufacture, or sale of explosive compounds, and may regulate the transportation thereof through the streets or highways of such city, and affix penalties, not exceeding fifty dollars for each offence. Towns may make like by-laws for the same purpose, to be approved in the manner prescribed in section fourteen of chapter eighteen of the General Statutes, and affix penalties not exceeding twenty dollars for each offence : *provided*, such by-laws and ordinances shall not prohibit the transportation of explosive compounds from one place to another, nor be otherwise repugnant to the provisions of this act and the rules made thereunder by the railroad commissioners."

The selectmen of any town may license, upon such terms as may be prescribed in the ordinances or by-laws mentioned in section two, the keeping, storage, transportation, use, manufacture, or sale of explosive compounds, within the limits of the city or town.

Any person duly authorized by the by-laws of any town may enter the building or premises of any person or persons licensed to sell explosive compounds, to examine and ascertain if the laws, rules, and regulations relating thereto are strictly observed ; and on an alarm of fire may cause the explosive compounds there deposited to be removed or destroyed, as the case may require.

By the words "explosive compound" shall be understood either gun-cotton, nitro-glycerine, or any compound of the same ; any fulminate, or generally any substance intended to be used by exploding or igniting the same, to produce a force to propel missiles or to rend apart substances, except gunpowder.[2]

42. All penalties for breaches of the orders and by-laws of a town may be recovered on complaint before a police court or a justice of the peace, and shall inure to the town, or to such uses as the town may direct.[3]

---

[1] Stats. 1876, ch. 130.

[2] Stats. 1877, ch. 216, §§ 1, 2, 3, 9, 12.

[3] Gen. Stats. ch. 18, § 12.

43. When a town in a by-law imposes a duty and affixes a penalty for refusal or neglect to perform the same, they may therein provide that in case of such refusal or neglect the duty may be performed by officers therein named, at the expense of the party liable to perform the same, and such expense may be recovered of him by the town in an action of contract in the name of the treasurer, but the amount recovered shall not exceed the penalty fixed in the by-law.

44. Before any by-law takes effect, it shall be approved by the superior court, or in vacation by a justice thereof, and shall with such approval be entered and recorded in the office of the clerk of the courts in the county where the town is situated, or in the county of Suffolk in the office of the clerk of the superior court for civil business.

45. Such by-laws shall be binding upon all persons coming within the limits of the town, as well as upon the inhabitants thereof.

46. All by-laws made by a town shall be published in one or more newspapers printed in the county where the town is situated.

47. Each town shall provide at its own expense some suitable cabinet or bookcase for the safe preservation of such books, reports, and laws, as they receive from the commonwealth, and for every month's neglect shall forfeit ten dollars to the use of the commonwealth.[1]

48. One copy or more of the annual report, or of any special report relating to income, expenditures, or other municipal affairs of any city or town, shall be returned by the clerk thereof, on or before the last day of April in each year to the state librarian, to be deposited and preserved in the state library.

49. If any city or town shall neglect or refuse to make the return required in the preceding section, such city or town shall thereby forfeit its share of the publications hereafter to be distributed by authority of the commonwealth,

---

[1] Gen. Stats. ch. 18, §§ 13, 14, 15, 16, 17.

and said publications shall be withheld until the provisions of this act are complied with.[1]

50. The secretary shall furnish annually a complete set of the public series (of documents) in a bound volume to each city and town in the commonwealth, to be preserved in some public place therein, which volume shall have a title-page bearing the date of the year, and a brief index to the title of the several documents.[2]

Also one copy of a volume containing all the acts and resolves passed during the preceding session of the legislature, with the governor's address and messages, the constitution of the commonwealth, a list of names changed and returned during the preceding year by the probate courts, and a list of the officers of the civil government, with an index.[3]

And also immediately after the close of the session of the general court to each town its proportionate part, according to the census, of thirty-five thousand copies of the general laws enacted at said session.[4]

### *Limits of Municipal Indebtedness.*

51. The assessors of cities and towns shall each year assess taxes to an amount not less than the aggregate of all sums appropriated, granted, or lawfully expended by their respective cities or towns since the last preceding annual assessment and not provided for therein; and of all sums which are required by law to be raised by taxation by the said cities or towns during said year; and of all sums which are necessary to satisfy final judgments recovered against the said cities or towns; but such assessments shall not include sums for the payment of which cities or towns have voted to contract debts according to the provisions of the third section of this act; and the assessors may deduct from the amount required to be assessed the amount of all the estimated receipts of their respective cities or towns (except from loans or taxes) which are lawfully applicable to the payment of the expenditure of

---

[1] Stats. 1866, ch. 195, §§ 1, 2.
[2] Gen. Stats. ch. 4, § 8.
[3] Gen. Stats. ch. 3, §§ 1–2.
[4] Stats. 1866, ch. 65.

the year, but such deduction shall not exceed the amount of such receipts during the preceding year; and such assessments shall be made in the manner provided by law for the assessment of taxes; and any assessor wilfully neglecting to make an assessment required by this act shall be subject to the penalties provided by law for neglecting to assess taxes.

52. No debts shall hereafter be incurred by any city or town except debts for temporary loans in anticipation of the taxes of the year in which such debts are incurred, and of the year next ensuing and expressly made payable therefrom by vote of the said city or town; and except as hereinafter provided.

53. Debts, other than those authorized by the second section of this act, shall hereafter be incurred by a town only by a vote of two thirds of the legal voters present and voting at a legal meeting, and by a city only by a vote of two thirds of all the members of each branch of the city council, taken by yeas and nays, and, in any city where the mayor has the veto power, approved by the mayor; or, if he disapprove said vote, by another like vote taken after notice of such disapproval, which notice shall be given within ten days from the time in which the vote of the city council shall have been laid before the mayor; and if the mayor shall fail to give such notice to the branch of the city council in which said vote was first taken, he shall be deemed to have approved said vote of the city council.

54. Any debt contracted by a city or town, as provided by the third section of this act, shall be payable within a period not exceeding ten years from the time of contracting the same, and said city or town shall annually raise by taxation an amount sufficient to pay the interest thereon as it accrues, and shall also annually raise by taxation a sum not less than eight per centum of the principal thereof, until a sum is raised sufficient with its accumulations to extinguish the debt at maturity, which sum shall be set apart for that purpose and shall be used for no other pur-

pose ; and any balance required to extinguish said debt shall be raised by taxation at the annual assessment next preceding its maturity : *provided, however*, that debts incurred in constructing general sewers may be made payable at a period not exceeding twenty years from the time of contracting the same, and that debts incurred in supplying the inhabitants with pure water may be made payable at a period not exceeding thirty years from the time of contracting the same ; and *provided, also*, that when the debt is, under the authority of this act, made payable at a period exceeding ten years from the time of contracting the same, said town or city shall, and when it is made payable at a period not exceeding ten years, said town or city may, besides paying the interest, as it accrues, from taxes assessed for the purpose, establish, at the time of contracting the debt, a sinking fund, and contribute thereto from year to year an amount raised annually by taxation, sufficient, with its accumulations, to extinguish the debt at maturity ; and said sinking fund shall remain sacred and inviolate and pledged to the payment and redemption of said debt, and shall be used for no other purpose.

55. Any town establishing a sinking fund under the provisions of this act shall, at the time of establishing the same, elect, in the manner in which selectmen are by law required to be elected, three or six suitable persons as commissioners of its sinking funds, and any city establishing such a fund shall elect such commissioners by a concurrent vote of both branches of the city council.   One third of the number shall be elected for one, two, and three years respectively.   And annually thereafter there shall be elected for a term of three years a number equal to the number whose term of service then expires.   Vacancies occurring in the board of commissioners shall, in towns, be filled by the remaining member or members and the selectmen, by a majority of ballots of the officers so entitled to vote, at a meeting called for the purpose by the selectmen ; and in cities such vacancies shall be filled by

the city council in the manner above provided for the election of the commissioners. The remaining member or members shall, in case of a vacancy, exercise the powers of the board till the vacancy is filled. The city or town treasurer shall not be eligible as a commissioner of sinking funds; and the acceptance of the office of treasurer by a commissioner already elected shall work a resignation of the office of commissioner. But the foregoing provisions as to the mode of electing commissioners and filling vacancies shall not apply to boards of sinking fund commissioners already established.

The commissioners shall choose a treasurer, who may be the city or town treasurer; and if the city or town treasurer shall be chosen, his bond shall apply to and include duties performed under this act. If any other person shall be chosen as treasurer, he shall give a bond, with sureties, to the satisfaction of the commissioners, for the proper discharge of the duties of his office.

The commissioners shall receive all sums contributed to a sinking fund, and invest and reinvest the same, and the income thereof as it shall accrue, in the name of the board, in the particular scrip, notes, or bonds for the redemption of which such sinking fund was established, or in other bonds of said town and city which are secured by sinking funds, or in the securities in which by law the funds of savings banks may be invested, except personal securities, although guaranteed by sureties; but no portion of the same shall be loaned to the city or town except as herein provided; and the commissioners may sell and reinvest such securities when required in their judgment for the good management of the fund. They shall keep a record of their proceedings; and shall annually, at the time when other municipal officers are required to make an annual report, make a written report to the city or town of the amount and condition of said funds and the income thereof, for the then preceding financial year. The record, and the securities belonging to said funds, shall at all times be open to the inspection of the selectmen, mayor, and aldermen, or any committee of said city or town duly authorized for the purpose. The necessary expenses of the board shall be paid by said city or town ; and the treasurer and secretary thereof shall receive such compensation as shall be fixed by the city or town, but no commissioner shall receive compensation for his services.

When any securities issued by the city or town become a part of a sinking fund, the commissioners shall cause to be stamped or written on the face thereof a notice that they are a part of such sinking fund, and are not negotiable ; and the coupons thereof, as they become due and are paid, shall be cancelled.

56. No city or town, except as hereinafter provided, shall become indebted to an amount (including existing indebtedness) exceeding in the aggregate three per centum on the valuation of the taxable property therein, to be ascertained by the last preceding city or town valuation for the assessment of taxes. In determining the amount of indebtedness under this act, the amount of the sinking funds shall be deducted from the gross indebtedness.

57. Cities or towns indebted when this act takes effect, to an amount not less than two per centum on their valuation as aforesaid, may increase such indebtedness to the extent of an additional one per centum on their valuation, but no more ; and, when such indebtedness of any city or town exceeds five per centum on its valuation as aforesaid, such city or town shall raise annually by taxation a sum sufficient to pay the interest on its whole indebtedness, and to make the necessary contributions to a sinking fund which shall be established for the redemption of the same at a period not exceeding thirty years from the time this act takes effect in the manner provided in the fourth and fifth sections of this act ; and any city or town indebted when this act takes effect to an amount less than five per centum, and more than one per centum on its valuation as aforesaid, shall make like provision for the payment of the interest on its whole indebtedness, and for the extinction of such indebtedness within a period not exceeding

twenty years from the time this act takes effect, but it shall be sufficient to make such provision for the extinction of indebtedness contracted in supplying the inhabitants with pure water within a period not exceeding thirty years from the time this act takes effect, and to make like provision for the extinguishment of any existing funded debts, when the same mature.

58. Nothing contained in this act shall be construed as prohibiting the inhabitants of towns, or city councils, from paying or providing for the payment of any municipal debts at earlier periods than is herein required, or from renewing the same in securities payable within the period required for the final payment of the debt, or from adding to any sinking funds, or funds for the extinguishment of any debt, the excess of municipal appropriations over the amounts required for the purpose thereof, or any sums derived from taxation or special assessments, or other sources, which are not required by law to be otherwise expended; and such additions may be made for the purpose of reducing the entire debt for the redemption of which the sinking fund was established, or of reducing the amount to be raised by taxation for such fund.

59. No part of the sinking funds of the commonwealth shall hereafter, except for the renewal of existing loans, be loaned to any city or town the indebtedness of which shall exceed five per centum of its valuation as aforesaid, or which shall not comply with the provisions of this act; but the certificate of the treasurer of any city or town as to the percentage of its indebtedness, and as to such compliance, shall be deemed satisfactory evidence thereof, for the justification of the treasurer of the commonwealth in making any such loan, unless he has reasonable cause to suppose that the statements of such certificate are not true.

60. The restrictions of this act shall not exempt any city or town from its liability to pay debts contracted for purposes for which cities or towns may lawfully expend money; and the limits of municipal indebtedness pre-

scribed by this act shall be exclusive of debts created for supplying the inhabitants with pure water, and its provisions shall not apply to subscriptions lawfully made to the capital stock or securities of railroad corporations.

61. The supreme judicial court may, upon the suit or petition of the attorney-general, or of one or more taxable inhabitants of any city or town, or of any creditor to whom the said city or town appears to said court indebted in an amount not less than one thousand dollars, compel the said city or town and its assessors, collectors, treasurers, commissioners of sinking funds, and other proper officers, to enforce the provisions of this act by mandamus or other appropriate remedy, and hear and determine any cause of complaint in equity, where such remedy is more appropriate ; and any justice of said court may in term time or vacation issue injunctions and make such orders and decrees as may be necessary or proper to enforce the provisions of this act, and to restrain or prevent any violation thereof.[1]

### 4. *Town Subscriptions.*

62. Any town and any city having by the census of the year eighteen hundred and seventy less than thirty thousand inhabitants, within which the road of any railroad corporation hereafter organized, or the roads of any existing railroad corporation not now constructed shall be located or terminate, may subscribe for and hold shares of the capital stock or the securities of such railroad corporations, or either of them, to an amount not exceeding, for the aggregate in all such corporations, two per centum of the valuation of such town or city for the year in which the subscription is made ; and towns having a valuation not exceeding three millions of dollars may subscribe for and hold the securities of such corporation or either of them to an amount not exceeding three per centum of the valuation of such town in the year in which the subscription is made, in addition to the two per centum herein

---

[1] Stats. 1875, ch. 209.

before provided : *provided*, that two-thirds of the legal voters, present and voting by ballot and using the check-list, at legal meetings called for the purpose in such town or city, and held in like manner as the meetings for the choice of municipal officers are now held by law in such town or city respectively, shall vote to subscribe for such shares or securities in such corporation.

63. Any town or city may vote, in accordance with the provisions of the preceding section, to become an associate for the formation of a railroad corporation in compliance with section nineteen of this act, and by virtue of such vote, may become an associate in such corporation, with all the powers and privileges enjoyed by any individual associate.

64. The form in which the matters provided for in the two preceding sections shall be submitted to the voters of any town or city, shall be determined, in cities by a concurrent vote of both branches of the city council, and in towns by the selectmen ; and whenever a town or city has voted to subscribe to the stock or securities of a railroad corporation, or to become an associate for the formation of such corporation, the mayor and aldermen, in cities, and the selectmen, in towns, shall select some person who shall be authorized, in behalf of said city or town, to execute its vote.

65. If any subscription, authorized under section thirty-five (section thirty-five of this chapter) by vote of any town or city, is not actually made, by the persons authorized, within twelve months from said vote, such vote shall be void ; and unless, within the said period part of said subscription shall have actually been paid, or unless some proceeding is commenced, by such corporation to enforce payment thereof, and unless at least twenty per centum of the capital stock of the corporation to which the subscription is made shall have been actually paid in, in cash, and at least ten per centum of such capital stock is actually expended by such corporation in the construction of its road, said subscription shall be void ; but nothing in this

act contained shall invalidate the action of any town which may have already subscribed for shares or securities of any railroad corporation before the expiration of the time limited by section thirty, or by the charter of such corporation, as now existing, for the construction of its railroad.

66. Towns and cities subscribing for stock or securities under this act, may raise money to pay for the same by tax or loan, and may issue their notes or bonds for such loan; they may hold and dispose of such stock and securities in like manner as other town property, and the selectmen of towns, and such persons as may be authorized by vote of the city council of cities, may at all meetings of the corporations in which the stock or securities are held, represent their respective municipalities and vote upon each and every share of stock owned by them respectively.[1]

67. No town or city shall hereafter increase its indebtedness for the purpose of subscribing to the stock or securities of railroad corporations, to an amount which, with the existing net indebtedness of such town or city, incurred for any purpose, shall exceed the limit of three per centum of the valuation of the taxable property therein, to be ascertained by the last preceding town or city valuation for the assessment of taxes; but the limitation of this act shall not apply to temporary loans in anticipation of the taxes of the year in which such debts are incurred, and the year next ensuing, and expressly made payable therefrom by vote of the said town or city.[2]

68. Any town or city owing debts incurred to obtain funds for one or more subscriptions for the capital stock and securities of any railroad corporation may, for the purpose of paying the same, establish a sinking fund, which shall be subject to the provisions of section five of chapter two hundred and nine of the acts of the year eighteen hundred and seventy-five (section forty-eight of this chapter) and may contribute thereto any sums which it may receive from the sales of such stock or securities,

---

[1] Stats. 1874, ch. 372, §§ 35–39.    [2] Stats. 1876, ch. 175.

or from any dividends or interest upon the same, or from taxes which it may vote to raise for the payment of such indebtedness; and such town or city may transfer the custody and management of such stock and securities to the commissioners of the sinking fund provided for by this act.

69. Any town or city having a sinking fund for the payment of its general indebtedness, under the provisions of said chapter two hundred and nine,[1] may, by a vote of the inhabitants of said town, or of the city council of said city, provide that the commissioners of sinking funds elected under said act shall be the commissioners of the sinking fund under this act.

70. Any town or city owing debts described in section one of this act (section fifty-six of this chapter) shall annually raise by taxation a sum sufficient to pay the interest on the same, or, if there is any income derived from the capital stock or securities owned by such town or city as aforesaid, a sum sufficient to pay the excess of such interest payable by said town or city over such income; and the assessors thereof shall assess such sum in the manner provided by section one of said chapter two hundred and nine,[1] and shall also assess, in the manner aforesaid, such further sum as the inhabitants of said town or city council of said city may vote to raise by taxation for the purpose of paying the principal of the indebtedness incurred by such subscriptions; and the remedies provided by sections one and eleven of said chapter shall be applicable to proceedings under this act (this and two preceding sections).[2]

71. Every county, city, and town in this commonwealth, and every corporation incorporated or organized, or hereafter incorporated or organized, by or under the laws or authority of this commonwealth, which has issued or shall hereafter issue any bond, promissory note, or certificate of indebtedness payable to bearer, and either with or without coupons or interest warrants attached, may, at the request

---

[1] Chapter 209 of the Stats. of 1875 is sections 44 to 54 of this chapter inclusive.  [2] Stats. 1876, ch. 133.

of the owner or holder, at any time while more than one year remains before the principal of such bond, promissory note, or certificate of indebtedness shall be due and payable, issue in exchange for the same a registered bond, promissory note, or certificate of indebtedness of the same effect, except that it shall be payable to the holder by name, and not to bearer.

72. Any person to whom any registered bond, promissory note, or certificate of indebtedness shall be transferred by assignment acknowledged before any officer authorized to take acknowledgments of deeds conveying real estate in this commonwealth, and any trustee, executor, administrator, assignee in bankruptcy or insolvency, or any other person, not the person named therein, in whom the title to any registered bond, promissory note, or certificate of indebtedness shall be vested by operation of law, shall be entitled to a new registered bond, promissory note, or certificate of indebtedness of the same effect, except that it shall be payable to him by name, in exchange for the bond, promissory note, or certificate of indebtedness so transferred or the title to which is so vested in him.

73. Every county, city, and town in this commonwealth, and every corporation incorporated or organized by or under the laws or authority of this commonwealth, shall keep a register showing the number, date, amount, and rate of interest of every registered bond, promissory note, or certificate of indebtedness issued by it, and when the same is payable and the name of the person to whom the same is payable, and what bonds, promissory notes, or certificates of indebtedness, if any, were received in exchange therefor; and shall be entitled to a fee of fifty cents for every registered bond, promissory note, or certificate of indebtedness issued in exchange for any other bond, promissory note, or certificate of indebtedness.

74. Any city or town may, by the exercise of any rights reserved by the terms of any of its securities heretofore created or hereafter to be created, recall and pay said securities, or any portion thereof, and issue other securi-

ties in place of those so recalled and paid ; said new securities to be payable at periods within the maturity of those originally issued. But such new securities shall, for debts heretofore created, be made payable at a period not more remote than thirty years from the time of the taking effect of chapter two hundred and nine of the acts of the year eighteen hundred and seventy-five, and shall, for debts hereafter created, be made payable at a period not more remote than thirty years from the time of contracting the same.[1]

75. Any city or town may raise money by taxation and appropriate the same in order to purchase or lease suitable lands and erect any buildings suitable for public baths and wash-houses, either with or without open drying grounds, and may make open bathing places, and convert any buildings into public baths and wash-houses, and may from time to time alter, enlarge, repair, and improve the same, and fit up and furnish the same with all requisite furniture, fittings, and conveniences, and may raise and appropriate money therefor.

76. Any city or town may establish such rates for the use of said baths and wash-houses, and appoint such officers as are deemed proper to carry the provisions of this act into effect, and may make such by-laws or ordinances for their government as they from time to time deem necessary, and may authorize them to make such rules and regulations for the management of the baths and wash-houses as may seem to them expedient : *provided*, that such by-laws or ordinances, rules or regulations shall be subject to alteration or repeal at any time.

77. This act (this and two preceding sections) shall not take effect in any city or town until it has been accepted by the council of such city, by a two thirds vote, or by two thirds of the legal voters of such town present and voting at any annual meeting.[2]

78. Any city or town may by ordinance or by law regulate the transportation of the offal of slaughtered cattle,

---

[1] Stats. 1876, ch. 238.      [2] Stats. 1874, ch. 214.

hogs, sheep, or other animals, over, along, or through any of the public streets or highways in such city or town ; and may impose fines for the violation of such ordinance or by-law, not exceeding one hundred dollars for each offence.[1]

79. The board of mayor and aldermen in any city may grade and construct sidewalks, and complete any partially constructed sidewalk in any street of such city, as the public convenience may require, with or without edge-stones, as said board shall deem expedient, and may cover the same with brick, flat stones, concrete, gravel, or other appropriate material, and may assess upon the abutters on such sidewalks, in just proportions, not exceeding one half of the expense of the same ; but all assessments so made shall constitute a lien upon the abutting land, and be collected in the same manner as taxes on real estate are now collected, and such sidewalks, when constructed, with edge-stones and covered with brick, flat stones, or concrete, shall afterwards be maintained at the expense of such city. When any such sidewalk shall be permanently constructed with edge-stones, and covered with brick, flat stones, or concrete, as aforesaid, there shall be deducted from the assessment therefor any sum which shall have been previously assessed upon the abutting premises, and paid to the city for the expense of the construction of the same in any other manner than with edge-stones and with brick, flat stones, or concrete as aforesaid ; and such deduction shall be made *pro rata,* and in just proportions from the assessments upon different abutters, who at the time of such assessments are owners of the estate which at the time of such former assessments was the estate of the abutters who had previously paid such former assessments.

80. In estimating the damage sustained by any party by the construction of sidewalks as aforesaid, there shall be allowed, by way of set-off, the benefit, if any, to the property of the party by reason thereof.[2]

81. Chapter three hundred and three of the acts of

[1] Stats. 1874, ch. 225.     [2] Stats. 1872, ch. 303.

eighteen hundred and seventy-two (two preceding sections) is amended so as to provide that no abutter shall be assessed for the expense of any sidewalk a sum exceeding one per cent of the valuation of his estate abutting on such sidewalk as fixed by the annual assessment last preceding the construction of such sidewalk.

82. The provisions of chapter three hundred and three of the acts of eighteen hundred and seventy-two, as amended by the first section of this act, are extended to any town accepting the same at an annual meeting; and the authority conferred by said act upon the mayor and aldermen of cities is conferred upon the selectmen of such town.

83. The provisions of this act (this and two preceding sections) shall not apply to any sidewalk now constructed according to the provisions of chapter three hundred and three of the acts of eighteen hundred and seventy-two, nor to any city unless accepted by the city council thereof.[1]

84. No building exceeding six hundred square feet in superficial area upon the ground shall be erected in or upon any public common or public park which has been dedicated to the use of the public, without leave of the legislature previously obtained.

85. Any violation of this act may be restrained by the supreme judicial court or any justice thereof in the manner provided in section seventy-nine of chapter eighteen of the General Statutes.[2]

For the powers and duties of towns in relation to other subjects, see the chapters and sections on these subjects hereafter.

[1] Stats. 1874, ch. 107.　　　　[2] Stats. 1877, ch. 223.

# CHAPTER II.

## TOWN RECORDS.

1. ALL matters of public record in any office shall be entered or recorded on paper made wholly of linen, of a firm texture, well sized, and well finished; and the clerks and registers of said offices shall give a preference to linen paper of American or domestic manufacture, if such paper is marked in water line with the word "linen," and also with the name of the manufacturer.

2. The county commissioners, city governments, and selectmen, of the respective counties, cities, and towns, shall have all books of public record or registry belonging thereto substantially bound, and other papers and documents within their respective departments duly filed and arranged conveniently for examination and reference, and shall also cause such of said public records as are left incomplete by any clerk or register to be made up and completed by his successor from the files and usual memoranda as far as practicable, and certified and preserved in the same manner and with the same effect as is provided for other cases in sections seven, eight, and ten of this chapter (being sections six, seven, and nine below).

3. City governments and selectmen shall provide at the expense of their respective cities and towns fire-proof safes of ample size for the preservation of books of record or registry, and other important documents or papers belonging thereto; and the clerk of each city and town shall keep all such books, papers, and documents, in the safe so provided, at all times, except when they are wanted for use.

4. A city or town may cause to be carefully transcribed such of its records as relate to grants of lands, or the

grants or divisions and allotments of land made by the original proprietors of the township, or to any easements, private rights, or ways, or any records of births and marriages kept by such city or town, or by any parish within the same.

5. A city or town whose territory in whole or in part has been set off from any other city or town may cause to be carefully transcribed such records named in the preceding section as relate to lands, easements, rights, or ways, situated in the territory so set off.

6. When the records of a county, city, or town, are becoming worn, mutilated, or illegible, the county commissioners, city government, or selectmen, shall have fair legible copies seasonably made ; and when the interests of any county, city, or town require, the county commissioners, mayor and aldermen, selectmen, or overseers of the poor, may have copies of any records or parts of records, or of any papers or documents, in the legal custody of any other county, city, or town, so made at the expense of their respective counties, cities, or towns ; which copies shall be certified by the register or clerk of the office where they are taken to be true copies of the originals, and they shall be preserved in like manner as the original records, papers, and documents of the place for which they are made.

7. A transcript made in pursuance of the provisions of the preceding sections, and compared and certified under oath by the clerk or register having the custody of the original to be a true copy, shall have the same force and effect when deposited among the records of the place for which it is made as if the same were an original record, or an original paper, or document, deposited there.

8. Registers of deeds, registers of courts, and the registers and clerks of courts, cities, and towns, shall keep all records and documents belonging to their offices in their sole custody, and shall in no case, except upon summons in due form of law, or when the temporary removal of records and documents in their custody is necessary or

convenient for the transaction of the business of the courts or the performance of the duties of their respective offices, cause or permit any record or document to be removed or taken away.

9. Under the direction of the officers having the custody of the county, city, and town records and files, the same shall be open for public inspection and examination, and any person may take copies thereof. And the several clerks and registers shall, on payment of a reasonable fee therefor, compare and certify, in the manner herein mentioned, all transcripts properly and correctly made for any county, city, or town, in pursuance of the provisions of this chapter.

10. The legal custody of the books of record and other documents of the ancient proprietors of townships or of common lands, when they have ceased to be a body corporate, shall, unless they have made other legal disposition thereof, be vested in the clerk of the city or town in which such lands or the larger portion of them are situated; who, if such records and documents are in the possession of any other person, shall demand the same, and may make and certify copies thereof in the same manner as the clerk of the proprietors might have done.

When any church or religious society ceases to have a legal existence, and the care of its records and registries is not otherwise provided for by law, the person having possession of the same shall deliver them to the clerk of the city or town in which such church or society was situated, who may certify copies thereof.

11. Every county, city, and town, for each month it neglects or refuses to perform any duty required by this chapter, shall forfeit twenty dollars; a register or clerk who neglects or refuses to perform any duty required of him shall forfeit for each offence ten dollars; whoever takes and carries away any book of record, paper, or written document, belonging to the records or files of any county, city, or town, except as is provided in section nine (section eight above), or defaces, alters, or mutilates, by

mark, erasure, cutting, or otherwise, any such record, paper, or written document, shall forfeit a sum not exceeding fifty dollars ; and whoever, after demand made by the clerk of the city or town entitled by law to have possession of the books of record and other documents mentioned in sections eleven and twelve (section ten above), wrongfully detains the same, shall forfeit fifty dollars.[1]

[1] Gen. Stats. ch. 29, §§ 1, 2, 3, 13.

# CHAPTER III.

## TOWN MEETINGS.

1. THE annual meeting of each town shall be held in February, March, or April; and other meetings at such times as the selectmen may order. Meetings may be adjourned from time to time, and to any place within the town.[1]

2. The words " annual meeting," when applied to towns, shall mean the annual meeting required by law to be held in the months of February, March, or April.[2]

3. The governor, lieutenant-governor, counsellors, secretary, treasurer, and receiver-general, auditor, attorney-general, and senators and representatives in the general court, shall be elected annually on the Tuesday next after the first Monday of November, as prescribed in the constitution.[3]

4. Every town meeting shall be held in pursuance of a warrant under the hands of the selectmen, directed to the constables or some other persons appointed by the selectmen for that purpose, who shall forthwith notify such meeting in the manner prescribed by the by-laws or a vote of the town. The selectmen may by the same warrant call two or more distinct town meetings for distinct purposes.[4]

5. The warrant must be signed by a majority of the selectmen, otherwise the meeting will not be legal.[5] And it is the law of the construction of statutes in Massachusetts that "words purporting to

[1] Gen. Stats. ch. 18, § 20. The adjournment should be to a fixed future time. Reed *v.* Acton, 117 Mass. 391.

[2] Gen. Stats. ch. 3, § 7. See chapter hereafter on the Duties of Town Officers in reference to Jurors; for

meetings in certain cases for drawing jurors.

[3] Gen. Stats. ch. 8, § 1.

[4] Gen. Stats. ch. 18, § 21.

[5] Reynolds *v.* New Salem, 6 Met. 340.

give a joint authority to three or more public officers or other persons, shall be construed as giving such authority to a majority of such officers or persons."[1]  But seals to the warrant are not necessary.[2]

6. It is sufficient for the constables or persons to whom the warrant is directed to return that "pursuant to the warrant they have notified," &c., or that they have notified the inhabitants "as the law directs," or "agreeable to the within warrant they have notified the inhabitants of, &c., of the time, place, and purpose, of the within meeting,"[3] but this indefiniteness is not allowable in the return of a sheriff of his service of a writ, and it would undoubtedly be better that the return to the warrant should specify how and when the service was made.

7. As to the manner of notifying meetings, the court say,[4] the time that shall elapse between the notification of the meeting and the holding of the same must, of course, be a reasonable one. In the absence of any vote of the town on the subject, usage would aid in deciding the legality of the notice. If there had been an entirely uniform practice of notifying a certain number of days before the meeting, for a considerable length of time, and such meetings thus called had been sanctioned by the silent acquiescence of the inhabitants, and their adoption of the meetings, &c., as properly called by transacting at them their ordinary business, a meeting so called would be reasonably notified in point of time, that where no vote of the town exists as to the time of posting up notice, and such return is posted up seven days before the meeting, and in proper places and manner in every other respect, and due return of the service of such warrant made by the constable, the votes passed at such meeting are not to be held invalid upon the ground that the meeting was not legally notified. The period of seven days seems a reasonable period. It is that prescribed by the constitution for meetings for choice of senators, ch. 1, § 2. It is that prescribed for the first meeting of corporations.

8. The mayor and aldermen and selectmen of the several cities and towns shall, as provided in chapter seven,[5] call meetings to be held on the Tuesday next after the first Monday in November in the year one thousand eight hundred and sixty, and thence afterwards biennially, on the Tuesday next after the first Monday in November, for the voters to give their votes for representatives in congress.

---

[1] Gen. Stats. ch. 3, § 7.

[2] Colman v. Anderson, 10 Mass. 105.

[3] Briggs v. Murdock, 13 Pick. 305.

[4] Rand v. Wilder, 11 Cush. 296.

[5] The provisions of chapter seven, though repealed, are incorporated in chapter 376 of the Stats. of 1874, which will be found in Chapter IV. of this book.

9. In case of no choice in a congressional district, the governor shall cause precepts to issue to the mayor and aldermen and selectmen of the several cities and towns in the district, directing them to call a new meeting on the day appointed in such precept, for the voters to give their votes for a representative in congress. The precept shall be accompanied with a list of all the persons voted for in the district who received fifty votes or more according to the next preceding return, and shall show the number of votes for each of such persons; similar proceedings shall be had thereon and the same returns made as in an original election; and the like proceedings shall be repeated as often as occasion may require.

10. When a vacancy happens in the representation of this commonwealth in congress, the governor shall cause precepts to issue for a new election in the district where the vacancy exists; and similar proceedings shall be had thereon as in an original election.

11. The several sheriffs, upon receiving precepts from the governor for the election of a representative in congress, shall seasonably transmit them to the officers of the towns or cities within their respective counties to whom they are directed.[1]

If a town officer wilfully neglects or refuses to perform any duty required of him in the four preceding sections, he shall forfeit for each offence a sum not exceeding two hundred, nor less than thirty dollars.[2]

12. The warrant shall express the time and place of the meeting, and the subjects to be there acted upon; the selectmen shall insert therein all subjects which may, in writing, be requested of them by any ten or more voters of the town, and nothing acted upon shall have a legal operation, unless the subject-matter thereof is contained in the warrant.[3]

13. But it is sufficient if the warrant gives intelligible notice of the subjects to be acted upon. An article in the warrant " to hear

[1] Gen. Stats. ch. 9, §§ 3, 5, 6, 7.    [3] Gen. Stats. ch. 18, § 22.
[2] Gen. Stats. ch. 9, § 8.

the report of any committee heretofore chosen, and pass any vote in relation to the same," is a form of notice for action on reports of committees of common use and sanctioned by authority, and it is sufficient to enable the town to grant money upon it, if the subject is one that is likely to require money.[1] Whenever practicable, however, a more definite specification of the committee or the objects to be voted on would be better.

Under an article in the warrant "to elect town officers for the ensuing year," the town may invest such officers with any special authority in the discharge of their duties which it is authorized by statute to confer upon its officers.[2]

14. If the selectmen unreasonably refuse to call a meeting, any justice of the peace of the county, upon the application of ten or more legal voters of the town, may call such meeting by a warrant under his hand directed to the constables of the town, if any, otherwise to any of the persons applying therefor, directing them to summon the inhabitants qualified to vote in town affairs to assemble at the time and place and for the purpose expressed in the warrant.

15. If by reason of death, resignation, or removal from town, a major part of the selectmen thereof originally chosen vacate their office, those who remain in office may call a town meeting.[3]

---

[1] Fuller v. Groton, 11 Gray, 340; Grover v. Pembroke, 11 Allen, 88. In Torrey v. Milbury, 21 Pick. 68, the warrant was "to see if the town will make an appropriation towards purchasing a fire-engine." The vote was "to raise and appropriate $400 for the purchasing of a fire-engine, and necessary apparatus, provided," &c. The court were of opinion that under this warrant the town were authorized to pass the vote which they did. Shaw, C. J., says: "The object of a warrant is to give previous notice to the inhabitants of the subjects to be acted on, and, if this is done substantially, it is sufficient. In such a body as a town, which ordinarily has no funds, and no sources of revenue but taxation, to consider the subject of appropriating money to a particular object seems necessarily to involve the consideration of the means of raising the money, unless there is something in the warrant itself which indicates that the word 'appropriate' is used in a more limited sense. For instance, if a warrant were to see if the town would appropriate to a specific object money already in the treasury, or under the control of the town, it might well be contended, that under such a warrant it could not be understood that the town could be called on to consider the question of laying a tax for the same object."

[2] Sherman v. Torrey, 99 Mass. 472.

[3] Gen. Stats. ch. 18, §§ 23, 24.

16. (In each year when the election of president and vice-president of the United States takes place) the mayor and aldermen and selectmen of the several cities and towns shall, in the manner provided in section three of chapter seven (of the General Statutes), call meetings to be held on the Tuesday next after the first Monday in November of such year, for the voters to give their votes for the whole number of electors to which the commonwealth is entitled. All laws in relation to the duties of sheriffs, city and town officers, and voters, in the election of civil officers, shall, as far as the same may be applicable, apply to the meetings and elections held respecting the choice of electors of president and vice-president of the United States ; and like penalties shall be incurred for the violation thereof.[1]

[1] Gen. Stats. ch. 9, §§ 10, 18.

## CHAPTER IV.

### VOTERS. THE MANNER OF CONDUCTING ELECTIONS AND RETURNING VOTES.

1. EVERY male citizen of twenty-one years of age and upwards (except paupers, persons under guardianship, and persons excluded by article twenty of the amendments to the constitution), who has resided in the state one year, and within the city or town in which he claims a right to vote, six months next preceding any election of city, town, county, or state officers, or of representatives to congress, or electors of president and vice-president, and who has paid, by himself, his parent, master, or guardian, a state or county tax assessed upon him in this state within two years next preceding such election, and every citizen exempted from taxation but otherwise qualified, shall have a right to vote in all such elections ; and no other person shall have such right to vote.

The amendment to the constitution above mentioned is : —

ART. XX. No person shall have the right to vote, or be eligible to office under the constitution of this commonwealth, who shall not be able to read the constitution in the English language, and write his name: *provided, however*, that the provisions of this amendment shall not apply to any person prevented by a physical disability from complying with its requisitions, nor to any person who now has the right to vote, nor to any persons who shall be sixty years of age or upwards at the time this amendment shall take effect.

2. In any election of representatives to congress, no person shall be allowed to vote for the same until he shall have resided in the congressional district where he offers to vote six months next preceding such election, and shall

be otherwise qualified according to the constitution and laws: *provided*, that when the state shall be districted anew for members of congress, he shall have the right so to vote in the district where he is located by such new arrangement; and *provided*, *also*, that no voter residing in any city which now is, or hereafter may be, divided by the line between congressional districts, shall be deprived of his vote in the district in which he was assessed, or liable to assessment, on the first day of May next preceding such congressional election, if he be otherwise qualified.

3. The collectors of state and county taxes in each city and town shall keep an accurate account of the names of all persons from whom they receive payment of any state or county tax, and of the time of such payment; and, upon request, shall deliver to the person paying the same a receipt specifying his name, and time of payment; and such receipts shall be admitted as presumptive evidence thereof.

4. The collectors, whether the time for which they were chosen has expired or not, shall twice in each year, namely, once not more than twenty nor less than fifteen days before the annual city or town elections, and once not more than twenty nor less than fifteen days before the Tuesday next after the first Monday in November, return to the mayor and aldermen and selectmen of their respective cities and towns an accurate list of all persons from whom they have received payment of any state or county tax subsequently to the time appointed for making their last preceding return.

5. Every collector neglecting to make such return shall forfeit one hundred dollars for each neglect; and twenty dollars for every name in respect to which he makes a false return.

6. When any person, on or before the fifteenth day of September, in any year, gives notice in writing, accompanied by satisfactory evidence, to the assessors of a city or town, that he was on the first day of May of that year an inhabitant thereof, and liable to pay a poll-tax, and

furnishes under oath a true list of his polls and estate, both real and personal, not exempt from taxation, the assessors shall assess him for his polls and estate; but such assessment shall be subject to the provisions of chapter one hundred and twenty-one of the acts of the year one thousand eight hundred and sixty-five; and the assessors shall, on or before the first day of October, deposit with the clerk of the city or town a list of the persons so assessed. The taxes so assessed shall be entered in the tax list of the collector of the city or town, and he shall collect and pay over the same in the manner specified in his warrant.

7. The mayor and aldermen of cities and selectmen of towns shall, at least fifteen [1] days before the annual city and town elections, and at least fifteen days before the Tuesday next after the first Monday in November annually, make correct alphabetical lists of all the persons qualified to vote for the several officers to be elected at those periods, and shall at least fifteen days before said elections cause such lists to be posted up in two or more public places in their respective cities and towns.

8. The selectmen of towns shall be in session at some convenient place for a reasonable time, within forty-eight hours next preceding all meetings for the election of town, county, or state officers, or of representatives in congress, or of electors of president and vice-president; for the purpose of receiving evidence of the qualifications of persons claiming a right to vote in such elections and of correcting the lists of voters. Such session shall be holden for one hour at least before the opening of the meeting on the day of the election, and notice of the time and place of holding the sessions shall be given by the selectmen upon the lists posted up as provided in the preceding section.

9. In every town where the number of qualified voters exceeds one thousand, a session of the selectmen for like purpose to that mentioned in section eight of this act (pre-

[1] Stats. 1878, ch. 233, § 1.

ceding section) shall be holden on the day immediately preceding the meeting, and for as much longer time previous to said day as they judge necessary for the purpose aforesaid. When the day immediately preceding such meeting is Sunday, such session shall be holden on the Saturday preceding.

10. The selectmen shall also enter on such lists the name of any person known to them to be qualified to vote, and shall erase therefrom the name of any person known to them not to be qualified.

11. The mayor and aldermen and selectmen before entering upon the lists the name of a naturalized citizen shall require him to produce for their inspection his papers of naturalization and be satisfied that he has been legally naturalized; but they need not require the production of such papers after they have once examined and passed upon them.

12. Whoever gives a false name or a false answer to the mayor and aldermen or selectmen when in session for the purposes aforesaid shall forfeit the sum of thirty dollars for each offence.

13. The mayor and aldermen and selectmen, if they have duly entered on said lists the names of all persons returned to them by the collectors, shall not be answerable for any omissions therefrom.

14. A city or town officer who wilfully neglects or refuses to perform any duty required of him by the provisions of this act shall for each offence forfeit a sum not exceeding two hundred dollars.

15. Meetings for the election of national, state, district, and county officers may be opened as early as seven o'clock in the forenoon, and shall be opened as early as two o'clock in the afternoon of the election day, and the mayor and aldermen and selectmen shall decide whether such officers shall be voted for on one ballot or at the same time on separate ballots, and shall give notice thereof in the warrant calling the meeting.

16. Such meetings in towns shall be called by the select-

men in the manner ordered by the towns, and the warrant
for notifying such meetings shall specify the time when the
polls for the choice of the several officers shall be opened,
and the hour at which the polls may be closed. The polls
in towns shall be kept open at least two hours, and for such
longer time as a majority of the voters present shall by
vote direct, but they shall not be closed until the hour
named in the warrant has arrived; and in no case shall
the polls be kept open after the hour of sunset.

17. At town meetings for the election of national, state,
district, and county officers, the selectmen shall preside;
and shall have all the powers which are vested in moderators.

18. The presiding officers at meetings held for the election of town or other officers shall be provided with a
complete list of the persons qualified to vote at such election; and no person shall vote at an election whose name
has not been previously placed on such list, nor until the
presiding officers find and check his name thereon: *provided, however*, that in the election of town officers it shall
not be necessary to find and check the name of the voter,
except in the cases where the election is, or may be, required by statute to be by ballot; and, in all other cases,
the check-list shall be used or not, as the town, at its
meeting, may determine, except that in the election of
moderators of town meetings, held for the choice of town
officers, the check-list shall be used.

### *Representatives to the General Court.*

19. Warrants for meetings for the election of representatives to the general court shall direct that the voters in
towns, cities, and wards, be notified to bring in their votes
on one ballot for the representatives to which their several
districts are entitled, and shall specify the number thereof.
And such elections shall be conducted, and the results
thereof determined, as provided in chapter seven of the
General Statutes, except as otherwise provided in this act.

20. In towns, cities, and wards, composing a part of a representative district, the selectmen and town clerks and ward officers, in open town and ward meetings, and the mayor and aldermen and city clerks, shall forthwith, upon the vote for representative being recorded, make out under their hands and seal up and deliver to their respective clerks a true transcript of such record.

21. The county commissioners, mayor and aldermen, or board of aldermen, or such special commissioners as are authorized to apportion the representation assigned to the several counties, at their meeting for such purpose, shall designate a place in each representative district, not contained in or consisting of one town or city, at which the clerks of towns, cities, and wards, composing such district, shall assemble for the purpose of ascertaining the result of elections. Due notice of such appointment shall be given by said commissioners or mayor and aldermen to every town, city, and ward in the district. Such place of meeting may be changed once in two years by the same authority, after a hearing on the petition of two of such clerks.

22. The clerks of cities, towns, and wards, composing such districts, shall meet at noon on the day following an election for representatives, at the place so designated, and shall examine and compare such transcripts and ascertain what persons have been elected. If any error appears in a transcript or return, the clerks shall forthwith give notice thereof to the officers required to make the return, and such officers shall forthwith, in conformity with the truth and under oath, make a new return, which, whether made with or without such notice, shall be received and examined by said clerks within two days after the time appointed for the meeting; and for that purpose the meeting may be adjourned not exceeding two days. No return shall be rejected when the number of votes given for each candidate can be ascertained.

23. Such clerks shall at such meeting make out under their hands a complete return of the names of all persons for whom votes were given in the district, and the number

of votes for each person, and a record of the return shall be made in the book of records of their respective cities, towns, and wards, within four days after the day of the meeting.

24. When it is ascertained who is elected representative in a district, composed of one town or city, or one or more wards of a city, the selectmen or mayor and aldermen shall make out duplicate certificates thereof, one of which they shall transmit to the office of the secretary of the commonwealth on or before the first Wednesday in January following, and the other by a constable or other authorized officer to the person elected, within ten days after the day of election.

25. When the clerks of cities, towns, and wards composing a district, at their meeting for the purpose, ascertain that a representative is elected in their district, they or a majority of them shall make out duplicate certificates thereof, one of which they shall deliver into the office of the secretary of the commonwealth, on or before the first day of January following, and the other by a constable or other authorized officer transmit to the person elected, within ten days after the day of election.

26. Such certificates of election shall be in substance as follows : —

Commonwealth of Massachusetts, county of          . Pursuant to a law of this commonwealth, the qualified voters of representative district number          , in their several meetings on the day of November instant, for the choice of representatives in general court, did elect          , being inhabitants of said district, to represent them in the general court to be holden on the first Wednesday of January next

Dated at          the          day of          in the year one thousand eight hundred and          .

Such certificate shall have a return thereon, signed by the officer authorized to give such notice, and stating that notice of the choice was given to the persons therein mentioned, and that said persons were summoned to attend the general court accordingly.

27. If it shall appear that no choice of representative

has been effected by reason of two or more persons having the same number of votes so that no person has a plurality, a certificate of the fact shall be transmitted to the secretary of the commonwealth by the same officers and in the same manner as is provided in sections twenty-nine and thirty of this act for one of the certificates of election in cases when an election is made.

28. When a vacancy occurs in a representative district, the speaker of the house of representatives shall, in the precept which he may issue by order of the house giving notice of such vacancy, appoint a time for an election to fill the same. Upon the reception of such precept, the mayor and aldermen of a city and the selectmen of the towns comprising the district, shall issue their warrants for an election on the day named in the precept; and similar proceedings shall be had in filling such vacancy as in the original election of representatives.

29. The secretary of the commonwealth shall furnish to cities and towns blank forms for certificates, transcripts, and returns required under this act. Such blanks for returns shall have printed thereon sections twenty-nine, thirty, thirty-one, and thirty-two of this act, and the first four sections of chapter two of the General Statutes.

30. In all returns of elections, the whole number of ballots given in shall be distinctly stated in words at length; and blank pieces of paper shall not be counted as ballots: *provided*, that the omission to state the whole number of ballots shall not make the return invalid in any case in which the true result of the election can be ascertained from the other parts of the return (or by a recount made in conformity with the provisions of law).[1]

31. Selectmen giving a certificate of election to a person voted for as representative to the general court, not in accordance with the declaration of the vote in open town meeting at the time of the election, shall forfeit three hundred dollars.

32. Clerks wilfully signing a certificate not in conformity

[1] Stats. 1876, ch. 188, § 8.

with the result of an election, as apparent by the transcripts and returns, shall forfeit a sum not exceeding three hundred dollars.

33. Towns and cities may provide suitable compensation to clerks and selectmen for services performed by them under the requirements of this act.

34. In case of a vacancy in the office of town, city or ward clerk, or any disability in such clerk to perform the duties required by this act, the selectmen, mayor and aldermen, or board of aldermen, or warden, may appoint a clerk *pro tempore*, who shall be sworn and perform such duties.

35. At every election in towns for officers other than town officers, the selectmen shall cause all ballots given in, after having been counted, declared, and recorded, to be secured in an envelope and sealed, and they shall indorse on such envelope for what officers the enclosed ballots were cast, and at what election, and the same shall be sealed, indorsed, and delivered to the town clerk, before the adjournment of the meeting at which the ballots were cast.[1]

36. The clerk of each town shall receive the envelopes containing the ballots thrown at any election, sealed as provided in the preceding section, and shall retain them in his care until the requirements of this section, or of any act which may hereafter be passed in amendment hereof, have been complied with; and as soon as may be thereafter the said clerk shall cause such ballots to be destroyed without examining them or permitting them to be examined by any person whatsoever, and shall make an entry in the records of the city or town that they have been so destroyed.

If within thirty days next following the day of an election a person who received votes for any office at said election shall serve upon the clerk of any city or town, by himself, his agent or attorney, a statement in writing claiming an election to such office, or declaring an intention to controvert or dispute the election of any other person who has received, or who may receive, a certificate of election for the same, the clerk of such city or town shall retain the envelope containing the ballots thrown at such election, sealed as provided by law, subject to the order of the body to which either of said persons may claim or be held to have been elected, or until such claim shall have been withdrawn or such election shall have been decided by the authority competent to determine the same.

[1] Stats. 1874, ch. 376.

Whenever a district for the election of a representative or representatives to the general court is composed of one or more wards of a city, together with one or more towns, the meeting of clerks prescribed by section twenty-seven of said chapter (twenty-two of this chapter) shall be held on the Tuesday next following the day of election, instead of being held on the day prescribed in said section ; and all provisions of law relative to the meeting of the clerks shall apply to their meeting so held on said Tuesday, continued by adjournment not exceeding two days, if need be.[1]

37. In all elections in towns in which a check-list is required by law to be used (except elections for town officers), the selectmen shall cause the check-list so used to be enclosed and sealed in an envelope in the same manner, but not in the same envelope, as the ballots cast at said election are required by law to be secured by section forty-six of this act (thirty-five of this chapter) ; and a majority of the selectmen shall certify on such envelope to the identity of the check-list so enclosed : *provided*, that nothing in this act shall be construed to prevent the selectmen from furnishing a copy of a check-list after it has been used in any election, upon the application of not less than ten legal voters, resident therein ; and immediately upon such copy being furnished, the check-list shall be again sealed up, with a new certificate attached, by which the identity and original condition shall be certified by a majority of the selectmen.[2]

38. When the right of a person offering a ballot at any election in towns, for officers other than town officers, is challenged for any cause recognized by existing laws, the selectmen, if they receive the same, shall require the name and residence of the voter to be written thereon, either by himself or by some one in his behalf, and they shall add thereto the name of the challenger and the cause assigned for challenging. And if such ballot shall be offered sealed, the writing as aforesaid may be upon the envelope covering the same, and the selectmen shall mark and designate such ballot by writing thereon the name of the person by whom it was cast, before it is counted, and at the close of the election the same shall be returned to the envelope in which it is deposited.

Whoever wilfully or negligently violates the provisions of this section shall be punished by a fine of not less than twenty or more than

1 Stats. 1876, ch. 188, §§ 1, 2, 3.     2 Stats. 1874, ch. 376, § 48.

two hundred dollars, or by imprisonment in the county jail for a term not exceeding one year.[1]

39. Whoever wilfully or negligently violates any provision of the preceding sections thirty-five and thirty-seven shall be punished by a fine not exceeding two hundred dollars, or by imprisonment in the county jail not exceeding one year.[2]

40. The selectmen of each town shall make and keep a record of all persons entitled to vote therein at any election for town, county, state, or national officers, which shall be known as a register of voters.

41. Said register shall contain the names of such voters written in full, the street or place in the town where each resides at the time of registration, each voter's occupation, and such other specifications as may be necessary to fully identify the persons named, and the date of registration.

42. No name shall be added to a voting list in any town until it has been recorded in said register, and none shall be added to a list of voters in use at any election after the opening of the polls, except to correct a clerical error or omission; and all names on voting lists shall be written or printed in full.

43. The secretary of the commonwealth shall furnish to each town, at cost price, on or before the first day of July in the current year, suitable blank books for said registration, and thereafter said registers shall be uniform in character, and such books shall contain seven blank columns with uniform headings in the following form:[8] —

| When registered. | NAME. | Residence. | Occupation. | When ceased to be a voter. | Why ceased to be a voter. | Remarks. |
|---|---|---|---|---|---|---|
| | | | | | | |

[1] Stats. 1877, ch. 206.
[2] Stats. 1874, ch. 376, § 50.
[8] Stats. 1877, ch. 208.

44. In the registers of voters in towns, it shall be sufficient if the first christian name of each voter, or that name by which he is generally known, is written or printed in full, with the initial or initials of any other name or names which he may have in addition to his surname.

45. It shall be the duty of the selectmen, in making said registers, to cause proper notices to be published or posted, and proper opportunity given, at least two weeks before any annual election in said town, to all persons to present themselves for registration ; and before registering any person hereafter, they shall inquire into his qualifications to vote, and shall require such person to write his name before they place it in said register, unless such person is exempted by article twenty of the amendments to the constitution, or unless his name is upon the register or voting list of the preceding year.[1]

46. The selectmen shall not be answerable for refusing the vote of any person whose name is not on the list of voters, unless such person before offering his vote furnishes them with sufficient evidence of his having the legal qualifications of a voter at such meeting, and requests them to insert his name on said list.[2]

47. The moderator of a town meeting shall receive the votes of all persons whose names are borne on the list of voters as certified by the selectmen ; and shall not be answerable for refusing the vote of a person whose name is not on said list.

48. No vote shall be received by the presiding officers at any election provided for in this chapter, unless presented for deposit in the ballot-box by the voter in person, in a sealed envelope, or open and unfolded, and so that such officers can know but one ballot is presented.

49. Votes for different persons for the same office found in one envelope shall not be counted ; and if more than one vote for the same person for the same office is found in one envelope, but one such vote shall be counted, and no vote shall be counted which does not clearly indicate in

[1] Stats. 1878, ch. 251.    [2] Gen. Stats. ch. 7, § 10.

writing the office for which the person voted for is designed, except when but one office is voted for.

50. In all elections of civil officers by the people, the person or persons having the highest number of votes shall be deemed and declared to be elected; but no persons receiving the same number of votes shall be deemed to be elected, if thereby a greater number would be elected than required by law.

51. The votes in elections for national, state, county, and district officers shall be received, sorted, and counted by the selectmen, and by the ward officers, and public declaration made thereof in open town and ward meetings. The names of persons voted for, the number of votes received for each person, and the title of the office for which he is proposed, shall be entered in words at length by the town and ward clerks in their records. The ward clerks shall forthwith deliver to the city clerks certified copies of such records, who shall forthwith enter the same in the city records.[1]

52. In each year when the election of president and vice-president of the United States takes place, there shall be chosen as many electors of president and vice-president as the commonwealth is at such time entitled to.

53. The names of all the electors to be chosen shall be written on each ballot; and each ballot shall contain the name of at least one inhabitant of each congressional district into which the commonwealth shall be then divided; and shall designate the congressional district to which he belongs.

54. Votes for electors shall be counted, recorded, certified, sealed, and transmitted to the secretary of the commonwealth, as provided in sections fifteen, sixteen, and seventeen of chapter seven.[2]

55. Whoever knowing that he is not a qualified voter at

---

[1] Gen. Stats. ch. 7, §§ 11, 15.
[2] Gen. Stats. ch. 9, §§ 9, 11, 12. The sections in the above section 55 refer to those of Gen. Stats. ch. 7.

Section 16 applies only to cities. Sections 15 and 17 are sections 6 and 7 of Chapter VII. hereafter.

an election wilfully votes for any officers to be then chosen shall forfeit a sum not exceeding one hundred dollars for each offence.

56. If a voter knowingly gives more than one ballot at one time of balloting at an election, he shall forfeit a sum not exceeding one hundred dollars.[1]

57. Whoever wilfully gives a false answer to the selectmen or moderator presiding at an election shall forfeit for each offence a sum not exceeding one hundred dollars.

58. Whoever by bribery, or threatening to discharge from his employment, or to reduce the wages of, or by a promise to give employment or higher wages to, a person, attempts to influence a qualified voter to give or withhold his vote in an election, shall be punished by fine not exceeding three hundred dollars or by imprisonment in the county jail or house of correction for a term not exceeding one year, or both, at the discretion of court.

59. Whoever wilfully aids or abets any one, not legally qualified, in voting or attempting to vote at an election, shall forfeit a sum not exceeding fifty dollars for every such offence.

60. Whoever is disorderly in a meeting held for an election mentioned in this chapter shall forfeit a sum not exceeding twenty dollars.

61. If a city or town officer wilfully neglects or refuses to perform the duties required of him respecting elections by the provisions of this chapter (ch. 7, Gen. Stats.), he shall for each offence forfeit a sum not exceeding two hundred dollars.[2]

62. All laws in relation to the duties of sheriffs, city and town officers, and voters, in the election of civil officers, shall, as far as the same may be applicable, apply to the meetings and elections held respecting the choice of electors of president and vice-president of the United States; and like penalties shall be incurred for the violation thereof.[3]

[1] See other provisions on same subject in this chapter.

[2] Gen. Stats. ch. 7, §§ 28–34.

[3] Gen. Stats. ch. 9, § 18.

63. Whoever votes, or attempts to vote upon any name other than his own at any national, state, or municipal election, or whoever knowingly gives more than one ballot at one time of balloting at an election, shall be punished by imprisonment in the house of correction for not less than three months nor more than one year.

If any person shall pay, give or bestow, or directly or indirectly promise, any gift or reward to secure the vote or ballot of any person for any officer to be voted for at any national, state, or municipal election, the person so offending, upon conviction before the court having jurisdiction of such offence, shall be punished by a fine of not less than fifty nor more than one thousand dollars, or by imprisonment in the house of correction not less than three months nor more than one year, or by both, at the discretion of the court.

Whoever aids and abets any person in the commission of either of the offences described in this section shall be punished by a fine not exceeding one thousand dollars or by imprisonment in the house of correction not exceeding one year.[1]

64. Whoever in an assembly of people, met for a lawful purpose, at which an alphabetical list of voters is used in voting, votes, or attempts to vote, under any name other than his own, shall be punished by a fine not exceeding fifty dollars, or by imprisonment in the jail not exceeding thirty days, on complaint in any court of competent jurisdiction.[2]

[1] Stats. 1876, ch. 172.          [2] Stats. 1874, ch. 344.

# CHAPTER V.

## MODERATORS.

1. AT every town meeting, except for the election of national, state, district, and county officers, a moderator shall first be chosen.

2. During the election of a moderator, the town clerk, if present, shall preside; if he is absent, or there is no town clerk, the selectmen shall preside; and the town clerk and selectmen respectively shall in such case have the powers and perform the duties of a moderator.[1]

3. The moderator shall preside in the meeting, may in open meeting administer the oaths of office to any town officer chosen thereat, shall regulate the business and proceedings of the meeting, decide all questions of order, and make public declaration of all votes passed. When a vote so declared by him is immediately upon such a declaration questioned by seven or more of the voters present, he shall make the vote certain by polling the voters or dividing the meeting, unless the town has by a previous vote or their by-laws otherwise provided.

4. No person shall speak in the meeting without leave of the moderator, nor while another person is speaking by his permission; and all persons shall at his request be silent.

5. If a person behaves in a disorderly manner, and after notice from the moderator persists therein, the moderator may order him to withdraw from the meeting; and, on his refusal, may order the constables or any other persons to take him from the meeting and confine him in some convenient place until the meeting is adjourned. The person so refusing to withdraw shall for such offence forfeit a sum not exceeding twenty dollars.

[1] Gen. Stats. ch. 18, §§ 25, 26.

6. A moderator or other presiding officer who at a town meeting, before the poll is closed and without the consent of the voter, reads, examines, or permits to be read or examined, the names written on such voter's ballot, with a view to ascertain the candidate voted for by him, shall forfeit a sum not exceeding fifty dollars.[1]

[1] Gen. Stats. ch. 18, §§ 27–30.

## CHAPTER VI.

### ELECTION AND APPOINTMENT OF TOWN OFFICERS.

1. At the annual meeting every town shall choose from the inhabitants thereof the following town officers, who shall serve during the year, and until others are chosen and qualified in their stead : —

A town clerk, who if present shall be forthwith sworn, either by the moderator, or a justice of the peace ;

Three, five, seven, or nine selectmen ;

Three or more assessors, and, if the town deems it expedient, three or more assistant assessors ;

Three or more overseers of the poor ;

A town treasurer ;

One or more surveyors of highways ;

Constables, who shall also be collectors of taxes unless other persons are specially chosen collectors ;

Field drivers ;

Two or more fence-viewers ;

One or more surveyors of lumber ; except that surveyors of lumber shall not be so chosen in towns included in the district established by chapter forty-nine, section one hundred twenty-[six] [one] ; [1]

Measurers of wood and bark, unless the town authorizes the selectmen to appoint them ; and

All other usual town officers.

All the town officers designated by name in this section shall be sworn.

2. The election of town clerks, selectmen, assessors, treasurer, constables, and the moderator of the meetings held for the choice of town officers, shall be by written

[1] Gen. Stats.

ballots ; (also fence-viewers) ; [1] and the election of all other town officers in such mode as the meeting determines, except in cases otherwise provided by law. [2]

3. In the election of moderators of town meetings, held for the choice of town officers, the check-list shall be used. In the election of other town officers, it shall not be necessary to find and check the name of the voter in the list of voters, except in the cases where the election is, or may be, required by statute to be by ballot; and in all other cases the check-list shall be used or not, as the town, at its meeting, may determine. [3]

4. Where a town chose three assessors, two of whom were sworn, and the third did not refuse to accept the trust, but omitted to take the oath of office, and when called upon by the other two declined to act, and the town did not choose another in his stead, it was held that the other two had authority to assess a tax. Upon this point, Shaw, C. J., said : "The court are of the opinion, that when three assessors are duly chosen by the town, there is a board of assessors. Each is an assessor. But, until qualified, by taking the oath, he is not legally competent to act. If a majority do qualify, by taking the oath, and the third has not taken the oath, still, if he has notice of their proceeding to execute the office, and declines to take the oath and act with them, their acts will be good, in the same manner as if he had taken the oath, and declined to act with them, because he is an assessor, and the office is full. He may, at any time, take the oath, and thus be a qualified assessor ; unless he has legally expressed his non-acceptance, or unless the town, in consequence of his neglecting or declining to take the oath of office, has filled the vacancy by electing another in his place. Whether the town may thus proceed to make his mere neglect to take the oath, as a non-acceptance, and thereupon fill the vacancy, it is not now necessary to decide. Probably, from the necessity of the case, especially if a majority of those chosen should thus neglect, they might do so to avoid penalties to which they might be otherwise liable. Rev. Stats. ch. 15, §§ 35, 36, 42. But, until the town has so done, and filled the vacancy, the office is still full ; there is a board, and of these, by force of the statute as well as by long usage, the majority may act." [4]

5. A selectman and assessor of taxes may be chosen collector of taxes also.

A collector of taxes may be sworn at any time before entering upon the duties of his office ; and his oath need not be matter of record, but may be proved by other evidence.

---

[1] Stats. 1862, ch. 93, § 3.
[2] Gen. Stats. ch. 18, §§ 31, 32.
[3] Stats. 1874, ch. 376, § 23; ch. IV. of this book, § 18.
[4] George v. Mendon, 6 Met. 511.

A town record of the election of a collector of taxes need not show a determination by the town of the manner in which he should be chosen.[1]

6. Every person chosen constable shall, if present, forthwith declare his acceptance or refusal of the office. If he does not accept, the town shall proceed to a new election until some one accepts the office and takes the oath.

7. A town which neglects to make choice of selectmen or assessors shall forfeit to the use of the commonwealth a sum not exceeding five hundred nor less than one hundred dollars, as the county commissioners shall order.

8. If a town, at the annual meeting, fails to elect a full board of selectmen, or if any of the persons chosen refuse to act or omit to be qualified according to law, the selectmen or selectman chosen and qualified may sign warrants for town meetings until a full board is elected.

9. If a town neglects to choose selectmen or assessors, or if the persons chosen do not accept the trust, or, having accepted it, shall not perform the duties, the county commissioners may appoint three or more suitable persons within the county, to be assessors of taxes for such town, who shall have the powers, perform the duties, and receive the compensation of assessors chosen by a town.

10. The selectmen of each town shall annually, in March or April, appoint the following town officers, unless the inhabitants at their annual meeting choose them : —

One sealer of weights and measures, and as many more as the inhabitants at their annual meeting determine ; and they may also appoint a gauger of liquid measures ; and the selectmen may at any time remove such sealers or gaugers, and appoint others in their places.

One measurer of wood and bark, and as many more as the inhabitants at their annual meeting determine.

And in every town which has town scales for the weighing of hay, one or more persons to have the superintendence thereof.[2]

---

[1] Howard *v.* Proctor, 7 Gray, 128.     [2] Gen. Stats. ch. 18, §§ 33–37.

The mayor and aldermen or selectmen of any city or town where boilers and heavy machinery are sold, shall appoint one or more persons not engaged in the manufacture or sale thereof, to be weighers of boilers and heavy machinery, who shall be sworn to the faithful discharge of their duties, and shall receive such fees as may be ordered by the board appointing them, which shall be paid by the seller, and shall be removable at the pleasure of the appointing power.[1]

11. They may at any time appoint police officers, with all or any of the powers of constables, except the power of serving and executing civil process, who shall hold their offices during the pleasure of the selectmen by whom they are appointed.[2]

12. An appointment "to superintend the police of the town" is sufficient to give the person appointed all the power conferred by this section, and this includes under section sixty-nine, ch. 18, Gen. Stats. authority to apprehend in any place within the commonwealth a person on a warrant issued against him for an offence alleged to have been committed within the town for which the officer was appointed.[3] Also an appointment "on police duty," and the officer need not be sworn.[4] An appointment of a police officer by the selectmen of a town, "to continue in said office till the next annual town meeting," is a valid appointment during their pleasure.[5]

13. After the election or appointment of town officers who are required to take an oath of office, the town clerk shall forthwith make out a list, containing the names of all such persons not sworn by the moderator, and a designation of the offices to which they are chosen, and deliver the same with his warrant to a constable, requiring him within three days to summon each of such persons to appear and take the oath of office before the town clerk within seven days after such notice; and the constable

[1] Stats. 1863, ch. 173.
[2] Gen. Stats. ch. 18, § 38. Sections 10 and 11 above are repeated in chapter on General Powers and Duties of Selectmen, as they are equally applicable to both chapters.

[3] Commonwealth v. Martin, 98 Mass. 4.
[4] Commonwealth v. Cushing, 99 Mass. 592.
[5] Commonwealth v. Higgins, 4 Gray, 34.

shall within seven days make return of the warrant to the town clerk.[1]

14. A constable duly chosen and sworn is qualified to act as collector of taxes, without any further oath, if another person duly chosen collector does not accept the office, although that person is not summoned in writing to accept the office, and his refusal to accept does not appear of record.[2]

15. If a person so chosen and summoned, who is not exempt by law from holding the office to which he is elected, shall not within seven days take the oath of office before the town clerk, or before a justice of the peace, and file with the town clerk a certificate thereof under the hand of such justice, he shall, unless the office to which he is chosen is that of constable or some other for which a different penalty is provided, forfeit five dollars.

16. A person removing from the town in which he holds a town office thereby vacates such office.

17. When the office of treasurer or collector of taxes is vacant by reason of death, removal, or other cause, or when the treasurer or collector is prevented from performing the duties of his office, the selectmen of the town may by writing under their hands appoint a treasurer or collector *pro tempore*, who shall be sworn and give bonds in like manner as treasurers and collectors chosen by towns, and hold his office until another is chosen.[3]

18. "Removal" here means a removal from town.[4]

19. It is not necessary that the limitation "until another is chosen" be expressed in the appointment.[5]

20. When a collector fails to give the bond required by section seventy-two of chapter eighteen of the General Statutes, the selectmen may appoint another collector in the manner and subject to the provisions set forth in section forty-two in said chapter.[6]

21. Whenever a vacancy occurs in the office of highway surveyor, fence-viewer, constable, or field driver, in any

---

[1] Gen. Stats. ch. 18, § 39.
[2] Hays v. Drake, 6 Gray, 387.
[3] Gen. Stats. ch. 18, §§ 40–42.
[4] Barre v. Greenwich, 1 Pick. 134.
[5] Blackstone v. Tuft, 4 Gray, 250.
[6] Stats. 1865, ch. 234.

town, the selectmen thereof may, in their discretion, appoint some suitable person to fill the vacancy.[1]

22. When a vacancy occurs in a town office by reason of the non-acceptance, death, removal, insanity, or other disability of a person chosen thereto, or by reason of a failure to elect, the town may fill such vacancy by a new choice at any legal meeting.

23. No person shall be obliged to serve in the same town office two years successively; and no person in commission for any office of this state or of the United States, or who is a minister of the gospel, or a member of the council, senate, or house of representatives, or an engineman or member of a fire department, or who has been a constable or collector of taxes of a town within seven years next preceding, shall be obliged to accept the office of constable.[2]

24. Any town in this commonwealth which shall have accepted the provisions of this act (this and the four following sections) in regard to selectmen at any annual meeting thereof, may, at such or any annual meeting thereafter, elect its selectmen for the period of three years, in the following manner, namely: if the selectmen be three in number, the inhabitants may elect one person for the period of one year, one person for two years, and one person for three years; and thereafter at each annual meeting may elect one selectman to serve for three years. If the selectmen be five in number, then they may elect one person for a period of one year, two persons for two years, and two persons for three years; and thereafter, at each annual meeting, they may elect one or two selectmen, as the term of office of one or two may expire in that year, to serve for three years. If the selectmen be seven in number, then they may elect two persons for a period of one year, two persons for two years, and three persons for three years; and at each annual meeting thereafter they may elect two or three selectmen as the term of office of two or three may expire in that year, to serve for three

---

[1] Stats. 1864, ch. 174.          [2] Gen. Stats. ch. 18, §§ 43, 44.

years.    If the selectmen be nine in number, then they may
elect three persons for a period of one year, three persons
for two years, and three persons for three years; and at
each annual meeting thereafter they may elect three persons to serve for three years.

25. Any town which shall have accepted the provisions
of this act, in regard to assessors at any annual meeting
thereof, may elect at such or any annual meeting thereafter three or five assessors for the term of three years in
the manner hereinbefore provided for electing three or five
selectmen, or it may elect four assessors, two for the period
of one year, and two for two years; and at each annual
meeting thereafter the inhabitants may elect two assessors
to serve for two years.

26. If any town votes at any annual meeting thereof to
increase or diminish the number of its selectmen or assessors, it may do so by electing or omitting to elect such a
number at that or any annual meeting thereafter as will
make the board of the required number with terms of office
expiring in the manner provided in the first two sections
hereof: *provided, however*, that the number shall not be
diminished in such a manner as will prevent one member
being elected in every year.

27. Vacancies in either the board of assessors or of
selectmen may be filled in the manner now provided by
law, and the person chosen to fill any vacancy shall hold
office during the unexpired term of the member whose
place he fills.

28. The acceptance of this act by any town may, at any
subsequent annual meeting thereof, be revoked by such
town, and thereupon this act shall cease to be operative
in such town: *provided, however*, that such a revocation
shall not affect the term of office of selectmen or assessors
previously chosen.[1]

[1] Stats. 1878, ch. 255.

# CHAPTER VII.

## GENERAL DUTIES OF TOWN CLERKS.

1. THE town clerk shall record all votes passed at the meeting, at which he is elected, and at the other meetings held during his continuance in office.[1]

2. This does not include the reports of committees, but only the votes passed by the town. Such reports should, however, be put on file, so that reference may be made to them, otherwise the record in relation to them would be unintelligible.[2] It is competent and proper for the town clerk to make a record of his own election and qualification; and whenever the oath of office is administered to a town officer in open town meeting by a justice of the peace in presence of the town clerk, the clerk's record of the fact is competent evidence of the administration of the oath.[3]

3. He shall administer the oaths of office to all town officers who appear before him for that purpose, and shall make a record thereof, and of oaths of office taken before justices of the peace, of which certificates are filed.

4. When at a town meeting there is a vacancy in the office of town clerk, or he is not present, the selectmen shall call upon the qualified voters present to elect a clerk *pro tempore*, in like manner as town clerks are chosen. The selectmen shall sort and count the votes and declare the election of such clerk, who shall be sworn to discharge the duties of said office at such meeting; and be subject to like penalties for not discharging them as town clerks are for neglect of the like duties.

5. When other duties than those mentioned in the preceding section are required to be performed by the town clerk, and by reason of death, removal, or other cause, there is a vacancy in such office, or such clerk is prevented

---

[1] Gen. Stats. ch. 18, § 45.          [3] Briggs *v.* Murdock, 13 Pick. 305.
[2] Howard *v.* Stevens, 3 Allen, 409.

from performing such duties, the selectmen may in writing under their hands appoint a clerk for the performance thereof, who shall be sworn, and immediately after entering upon the duties of his office make a record of such election or appointment.[1]

6. The votes in elections for national, state, county, and district officers, shall be received, sorted, and counted by the selectmen, and by the ward officers, and public declaration made thereof in open town and ward meetings. The names of persons voted for, the number of votes received for each person, and the title of the office for which he is proposed, shall be entered in words at length by the town and ward clerks in their records. The ward clerks shall forthwith deliver to the city clerks certified copies of such records, who shall forthwith enter the same in the city records.

The fourth section of chapter nine of the General Statutes provides that the clerks in making their returns of votes for representatives to Congress under section fifteen of chapter seven of the General Statutes, shall transmit them in envelopes expressing on the outside the district in which the votes were given. It would seem that section seventeen instead of fifteen of said chapter was intended, which is section seven hereafter.

7. City and town clerks shall within ten days from the day of an election for governor, lieutenant-governor, councillors, senators, secretary, treasurer and receiver-general, auditor, attorney-general, representatives in congress, commissioners of insolvency, sheriffs, registers of probate and insolvency, district-attorneys, or clerks of the courts, transmit copies of the records of the votes, attested by them, certified by the mayor and aldermen or selectmen, and sealed up, to the secretary of the commonwealth; they shall in like manner within ten days after an election for county treasurer or register of deeds transmit such copies of the records of the votes to the county commissioners of their several counties; and within seven days after an election for county commissioners transmit such copies of the records of the votes to the clerks of the courts for their

[1] Gen. Stats. ch. 18, §§ 46–48.

several counties; but in Suffolk the return of votes for register of deeds shall be made to the board of aldermen of Boston, and in Chelsea, North Chelsea, and Winthrop, the returns of votes for county commissioners shall be made to the clerk of the courts for the county of Middlesex. Or within three days after such elections, such clerks may deliver such copies, sealed up, to the sheriffs of their several counties, who within seven days after receiving them shall transmit them to the office of the secretary, and to the county commissioners, board of aldermen, and clerks of courts, as severally above designated.[1]

It should appear by the certificate that the "return" is a true copy of the town record, and the clerk should add to his name the designation of his office.[2]

8. Proof that a return of votes was properly directed to the person to whom it was required to be transmitted or delivered, and mailed within forty-eight hours after closing the polls, shall be a bar to any complaint for delinquency.[3]

9. It shall be the duty of the clerk of every city and town of this commonwealth, as soon as may be after the passage of this act,[4] to make out a full and complete record of the names of all the soldiers and officers who compose his town's quota of the troops furnished by the commonwealth to the United States during the present rebellion, stating the place of residence, the time of enlistment of each, and the number and designation of his regiment and company; also the names of all who have resigned or been discharged, and at what time and for what cause; and all who have died in the service, and stating, when practicable, at what time and place and the cause of death, whether by disease, accident, or on the field of battle; and the promotions of officers and from the ranks, and the date thereof; and the names of all absentees, if any; and all such other facts as may relate strictly to the military career of each soldier and officer.[5]

[1] Gen. Stats. ch. 7, §§ 15, 17.
[2] Luce v. Mayhew, 13 Gray, 83.
[3] Gen. Stats. ch. 7, § 18.
[4] March 7, 1863.
[5] Stats. 1863, ch. 65, § 1.

10. (The foregoing is amended as follows, so that the record) shall, as far as practicable, state the time and place of birth, names of parents, previous occupation, term of enlistment, time of entering the service, and whether married or single, of all such soldiers and officers.

11. The clerk of each city and town shall also keep a full and complete record of the names of all seamen and officers, residents of such cities and towns, engaged in the naval service of the United States, during the present rebellion, which record shall, as far as practicable, state the time and place of birth, name of parents, the date at which he entered such service, his previous occupation, whether he was married or single, the vessel or vessels on which he served, the battles or kind of service in which he was engaged, whether he resigned, or was discharged or deserted, and the date of such resignation, discharge, or desertion, the cause of such discharge or resignation, his promotions, and the dates, occasions, and nature of the same; and, if he died in the service, it shall state the date and cause of his death; and such record shall contain any and all such other facts as relate to the naval career of such seamen or officers during such rebellion.

12. The adjutant-general shall prepare suitable blank books, in conformity with the requirements of this act, with proper blanks for marginal notes, and furnish the same to the several cities and towns at cost, on the application of the clerk thereof.

13. All the expenses incurred in making said records, with the cost of the record-books, shall be paid by the several cities and towns, and the records, when completed, shall be deposited and kept in the city and town clerk's office.[1]

14. City and town clerks, upon payment of their fees, shall record all mortgages of personal property delivered to them, in books kept for the purpose, noting therein, and on each mortgage, the time it is received; and such mortgages shall be considered as recorded at the time

[1] Stats. 1863, ch. 229, §§ 1-4.

when left for the purpose in the clerk's office. The fees for recording, and all other services relating thereto, shall be the same as are allowed to registers of deeds, for like services.[1] (That is) for entering and recording a deed or other paper, certifying the same on the original and indexing it, and for all other duties pertaining thereto, twenty-five cents; and if it contains more than one page, at the rate of twenty cents for each page after the first; to be paid when the instrument is left for record:

For all copies, at the rate of twenty cents a page:[2]

They shall also record notices to foreclose, with the affidavits of service, and notices to pledgers of property of intention to foreclose, with affidavits of service, and notices of liens on ships.[3]

15. Persons intending to be joined in marriage shall, before their marriage, cause notice thereof to be entered in the office of the clerk or registrar of the city or town in which they respectively dwell, if within the state. If there is no such clerk or registrar in the place of their residence, the entry shall be made in an adjoining city or town.[4]

Persons living without the commonwealth, and intending to be joined in marriage within the commonwealth, shall, before their marriage, cause notice of their intention to be entered in the office of the clerk or registrar of the city or town in which they propose to have the marriage solemnized; and no marriage between such parties shall be solemnized until they shall have delivered to the justice of the peace or minister in whose presence the marriage is to be contracted, a certificate from such clerk or registrar, specifying the time when notice of the intention of marriage was entered with him, together with all the facts in relation to the marriage required by law to be ascertained and recorded, except those respecting the person by whom the marriage is to be solemnized.[5]

16. The clerk or registrar shall deliver to the parties a

---

[1] Gen. Stats. ch. 151, § 3.
[2] Gen. Stats. ch. 157, § 12.
[3] Gen. Stats. ch. 151, §§ 7, 9, 13.
[4] Gen. Stats. ch. 106, § 7.
[5] Stats. 1867, ch. 58.

certificate under his hand, specifying the time when notice of the intention of marriage was entered with him, together with all facts in relation to the marriage required by law to be ascertained and recorded, except those respecting the person by whom the marriage is to be solemnized. Such certificate shall be delivered to the minister or magistrate in whose presence the marriage is to be contracted, before he proceeds to solemnize the same.

17. If a clerk or registrar issues such certificate to a male under the age of twenty-one years, or a female under the age of eighteen years, having reasonable cause to suppose the person to be under such age, except upon the application or consent in writing of the parent, master, or guardian of such person, he shall forfeit a sum not exceeding one hundred dollars; but if there is no parent, master, or guardian in this state competent to act, a certificate may be issued without such application or consent.

18. The clerk or registrar may require of any person applying for such certificate an affidavit sworn to before a justice of the peace for the county where the application is made, setting forth the age of the parties; which affidavit shall be sufficient proof of age to authorize the issuing of the certificate.

19. Whoever, applying for such certificate, wilfully makes a false statement in relation to the age or residence, parent, master, or guardian of either of the parties intending marriage, shall forfeit a sum not exceeding two hundred dollars.

20. When a marriage is solemnized in another state, between parties living in this state, and they return to dwell here, they shall, within seven days after their return, file with the clerk or registrar of the city or town where either of them lived at the time a certificate or declaration of their marriage, including the facts concerning marriages required by law, and for every neglect they shall forfeit ten dollars.[1]

21. For entering notice of an intention of marriage and

[1] Gen. Stats. ch. 106, §§ 8–12.

issuing the certificate thereof, and for entering the certificate of marriage filed by persons married out of the state, fifty cents, to be paid by the parties:

For a certificate of a birth or death, ten cents:

For copies of town records and other documents furnished to any person at his request, if containing less than one page, ten cents, and if more, at the rate of twelve cents a page.[1] (And a page means two hundred and twenty-four words.) [2]

22. Whoever finds lost money or goods of the value of three dollars or more, the owner whereof is unknown, shall within seven days give notice thereof in writing to the town clerk, and pay him twenty-five, cents for making an entry thereof in a book to be kept for that purpose; and whoever takes up a stray beast shall cause to be entered with the town clerk in a book kept for that purpose a notice thereof, containing a description of the color and natural and artificial marks of the beast.

Every finder of lost goods or stray beasts of the value of ten dollars or more shall also within two months, and before any use is made of the same, procure from the city or town clerk, or from a justice of the peace, a warrant directed to two disinterested persons, to be appointed by the clerk or justice, and returnable into said clerk's office in seven days from the date, to appraise the same at their true value, upon oath to be administered by the clerk or justice.

If no owner appears within one year, the lost money or goods shall remain to the finder, he paying to the treasurer of the city or town one half of the value thereof according to said appraisement (all lawful charges being first deducted), and upon his neglect or refusal to pay the same it shall be recovered by the city or town treasurer.[3]

23. Whenever the commissioners on inland fisheries shall determine to occupy and improve a pond, among other duties, they shall file a notice of such purpose in the office of the town clerk of the town or towns in which such pond is located.[4]

24. It shall be the duty of the city or town clerk of any city or town which now is, or hereafter may be, authorized to subscribe for the stock of any railroad company, or to loan its credit or grant aid to the same, to transmit to the

[1] Gen. Stats. ch. 157, § 9.
[2] Gen. Stats. ch. 157, § 15.
[3] Gen. Stats. ch. 79. For other duties of the finder and rights of the owner of lost money, goods, or beasts, see ch. 79 Gen. Stats.
[4] Stats. 1876, ch. 62.

secretary of the commonwealth and to the board of railroad commissioners a certified copy of any vote of such city or town, under such authority, within thirty days from the day on which said vote shall be taken ; and also within sixty days from the passage of the act (March 8, 1870) to transmit a certified copy of any vote heretofore passed by such city or town under such authority, unless the same has already been transmitted to the secretary as aforesaid ; and any city or town clerk who shall neglect to comply with the requirements of this act shall be liable to a fine of not less than five and not more than fifty dollars.[1]

25. When an attachment is made of articles of personal estate which by reason of their bulk or other cause cannot be immediately removed, a certified copy of the writ (without the declaration), and of the return of the attachment, may at any time within three days thereafter be deposited in the office of the clerk of the city or town in which it is made ; and such attachment shall be equally valid and effectual as if the articles had been retained in the possession and custody of the officer.

26. The clerk shall receive and file all such copies, noting thereon the time when received, and keep them safely in his office, and also enter a note thereof, in the order in which they are received, in the books kept for recording mortgages of personal property ; which entry shall contain the names of the parties to the suit and the date of the entry. The clerk's fee for this service shall be twenty-five cents, to be paid by the officer and included in his charge for the service of the writ.[2]

[1] Stats. 1870, ch. 64.  [2] Gen. Stats. ch. 123, §§ 57, 58.

# CHAPTER VIII.

## GENERAL POWERS AND DUTIES OF SELECTMEN.

1. EVERY person elected selectman, who enters upon the performance of his duties before taking the oath of office, shall forfeit for each offence a sum not exceeding one hundred dollars.

2. The selectmen shall be assessors of taxes and overseers of the poor in towns where other persons are not specially chosen to those offices, and when acting as assessors they shall take the oath required of assessors.[1]

3. " The powers and duties of selectmen are not very fully defined by statute. Many of the acts usually performed by them in behalf of towns, and which are recognized as within their appropriate sphere, have their origin and foundation in long continued usage. The management of the prudential affairs of towns necessarily requires the exercise of a large discretion, and it would be quite impossible by positive enactment to place definite limits to the powers and duties of selectmen to whom the direction and control of such affairs are intrusted. Speaking generally, it may be said that they are agents to take the general superintendence of the business of a town ; to supervise the doings of subordinate agents, and the disbursement of moneys appropriated by vote of the town, to take care of its property and perform other similar duties. But they are not general agents. They are not clothed with the general power of the corporate body for which they act. They can only exercise such powers and perform such duties as are necessarily and properly incident to the special and limited authority conferred on them by their office. They are special agents empowered to do only such acts as are required to meet the exigencies of ordinary town business."[2]  They are not authorized to institute or defend suits where the town is a party without special power given by the town.[3]  Nor are they authorized by virtue of their office merely to make a contract, in behalf of a town, for the hiring of a building for the purpose of holding town meetings in it.[4]

[1] Gen. Stats. ch. 18, §§ 49, 50.
[2] Smith v. Cheshire, 13 Gray, 319.
[3] Walpole v. Gray, 11 Allen, 149.
[4] Goff v. Rehoboth, 12 Met. 26.

4. The selectmen of each town shall annually in March or April appoint the following town officers, unless the inhabitants at their annual meeting choose them : —

One sealer of weights and measures, and as many more as the inhabitants at their annual meeting determine, and they may also appoint a gauger of liquid measures ; and the selectmen may at any time remove such sealers or gaugers, and appoint others in their places :

One measurer of wood and bark, and as many more as the inhabitants at their annual meeting determine :

And in every town which has town scales for the weighing of hay, one or more persons to have the superintendence thereof.

5. They may at any time appoint police officers, with all or any of the powers of constables, except the power of serving and executing civil process, who shall hold their offices during the pleasure of the selectmen by whom they are appointed.[1]

Whenever a vacancy occurs in the office of highway surveyor, fence-viewer, constable, or field driver, in any town, the selectmen thereof may, in their discretion, appoint some suitable person to fill the vacancy.[2]

6. The mayor and aldermen of any city, and the selectmen of any town, may make such rules and regulations in relation to the passage of carriages, wagons, carts, trucks, sleds, sleighs, horse-cars, or other vehicles, or to the use of sleds or other vehicles for coasting in and through the streets or public ways of such city or town as they shall deem necessary for the public safety or convenience, with penalties for violations thereof, not exceeding twenty dollars for one offence.[3]

7. The mayor and aldermen or selectmen of any city or town where boilers and heavy machinery are sold shall appoint one or more persons, not engaged in the manufacture or sale thereof, to be weighers of boilers and heavy machinery, who shall be sworn to the faithful discharge of

---

[1] Gen. Stats. ch. 18, §§ 37, 38.    [3] Stats. 1875, ch. 136.
[2] Stats. 1864, ch. 174.

their duties, and shall receive such fees as may be ordered by the board appointing them, which shall be paid by the seller, and shall be removable at the pleasure of the appointing power.[1]

8. There shall be a perambulation of town lines, and they shall be run and the marks renewed, once in every five years, by two or more of the selectmen of each town, or such substitutes as they in writing appoint for that purpose. After every such renewal the proceedings shall be recorded in the records of the respective towns.

9. Previously to a perambulation, the selectmen of the most ancient of the contiguous towns shall give ten days' notice, in writing, to the selectmen of the adjoining town, of the time and place of meeting for such perambulation; and selectmen who neglect to give such notice, or to attend either personally or by their substitute, shall severally forfeit twenty dollars, to be recovered on complaint to the use of the commonwealth, or by action of tort to the use of the town whose selectmen perform their duty.

10. The selectmen of the contiguous towns shall erect at the joint and equal expense of such towns permanent monuments to designate their respective boundary lines at every angle thereof, except where such lines are bounded by the ocean or some permanent stream of water. The monuments shall be of stone, well set in and at least four feet high from the surface of the ground; and the initial letter of the respective names of such contiguous towns shall be plainly and legibly cut thereon; but it shall not be necessary to erect a new monument in a place where a permanent stone monument two feet in height above the surface of the ground already exists.

11. The selectmen of towns bordering on another state, where the lines between the states are settled and established, shall once in every five years give notice to the selectmen or other proper municipal officers of such towns in the other state as adjoin their towns, of their intention to perambulate the lines between their adjoining towns.

[1] Stats. 1863, ch. 173.

Where such state lines are in dispute, the perambulations shall be made once in every five years after the lines are settled and established. If such notice and proposal are accepted by the officers to whom they are made, a perambulation shall be made in the same manner as between towns in this state. No boundary erected by authority of this state and an adjoining state shall be removed by such selectmen or other municipal officers. .

12. A selectman who refuses or neglects to perform any duty required of him by the three preceding sections shall forfeit twenty dollars to the use of the commonwealth.[1]

13. It shall be the duty of the selectmen of the several towns in this commonwealth to cause a stone monument with the initials of the name of the towns engraved thereon, to be placed on town lines wherever a highway crosses said lines, the expense of which shall be paid equally by the adjoining towns.[2]

14. The mayor and aldermen or selectmen of any city or town, when in their opinion the public good requires it, may offer a suitable reward, to be paid by such city or town, not exceeding five hundred dollars in one case, to any person who in consequence of such offer secures any person charged with a capital crime or other high crime or misdemeanor committed in such place; and such reward shall be paid by the treasurer upon the warrant of the mayor and aldermen or selectmen.[3]

Under this section it has been held that the person for whose arrest a reward is offered must have been charged by a complaint or indictment.[4]

15. When more than one claimant appears and applies for the payment of such reward, the mayor and aldermen or selectmen shall determine to whom the same shall be paid, and if to more than one person, in what proportion to each; and their determination shall be final and conclusive.[5]

---

[1] Gen. Stats. ch. 18, §§ 3–7.
[2] Stats. 1861, ch. 84.
[3] Gen. Stats. ch. 170, § 7.
[4] Day v. Otis, 6 Allen, 477.
[5] Gen. Stats. ch. 170, § 8.

16. The mayor and aldermen of any city, or the select-men of any town, when in their opinion the public good requires it, may offer a suitable reward, to be paid by such city or town, not exceeding five hundred dollars in one case, to any person who, in consequence of such offer, detects and secures any person who has committed a capital crime, or other high crime or misdemeanor in such place; and such reward shall be paid by the treasurer upon the warrant of the mayor and aldermen or select-men.

17. When more than one claimant appears and applies for the payment of such reward, the same shall be deter-mined in the manner provided in the eighth section of the one hundred and seventieth chapter of the General Stat-utes. (Section fifteen above.) [1]

18. There is no statute provision in reference to the amount of compensation selectmen shall receive for the performance of their general duties, and it is therefore left to the town to determine the same.

In addition to the management of the prudential affairs and gen-eral superintendence of the business of a town not imposed by law upon particular officers, selectmen are authorized and required by statute to perform specific duties in reference to very many subjects. These are treated of in connection with those subjects.

[1] Stats. 1866, ch. 9.

## CHAPTER IX.

### ASSESSORS OF TAXES.

1. THE assessors' oath of office shall be in substance as follows : —

> You, being chosen assessors [or an assessor], for the town of for the year ensuing, do swear that you will impartially, according to your best skill and judgment, assess and apportion all such taxes as you are during that time directed to assess, and that you will faithfully discharge all other duties of said office.

2. Assistant assessors, when chosen, shall be sworn, and shall in their respective wards or districts assist the assessors in taking a list of the ratable polls, in estimating the value of the real and personal estate in said wards or districts, and in making out lists of persons qualified to vote at elections.

3. If a person chosen assessor, having notice of his election, neglects to take the oath of office, he shall forfeit a sum not exceeding fifty dollars.[1]

4. The secretary of the commonwealth shall furnish to each of the cities and towns in the state, on or before the first day of May in each year, suitable blank books for the use of the assessors of said cities and towns in the assessment of taxes, which books shall contain blank columns numbered from one to twenty-seven, inclusive, with uniform headings for a valuation list, and blank tables for aggregates, in the following form : —

[1] Gen. Stats. ch. 18, §§ 51–53. For mode of election, see Election and Appointment of Town Officers.

*Valuation List for the     of     May 1, 187 .*

| NAMES OF PERSONS ASSESSED. | Number of polls. | Total cash tax on polls. | Value of each person's whole stock in trade. | Description of taxable cash assets. | Value of cash assets. | Value of machinery used in manufacturing establishments. | Number of live stock, each kind specified separately. | Value of each kind of live stock. | Description of all other ratable personal estate not before named. | Value of same. | Aggregate of each person's ratable personal estate. | Total tax on personal estate. |
|---|---|---|---|---|---|---|---|---|---|---|---|---|
| No. 1 | 2 | 3 | 4 | 5 | 6 | 7 | 8 | 9 | 10 | 11 | 12 | 13 |

| Buildings of all kinds, described by naming their uses. | Value of buildings, exclusive of land. | Description by name or otherwise, of each and every lot of land owned by each person. | Number of acres or feet in each lot of land. | | Value of same. | Superficial feet of wharf. | Value of same. | Aggregate value of real estate. | Total tax on real estate. | Total cash tax on polls, personal and real estate. | HIGHWAY TAX. | | | |
|---|---|---|---|---|---|---|---|---|---|---|---|---|---|---|
| | | | Acres. | Feet. | | | | | | | Tax on polls. | Tax on personal estate. | Tax on real estate. | Aggregate highway tax. |
| 14 | 15 | 16 | 17 | | 18 | 19 | 20 | 21 | 22 | 23 | 24 | 25 | 26 | 27 |

*Table of Aggregates for the     of     of Polls, Property, Taxes, &c., as assessed May 1, 187 .*

| Total number of polls. | Total tax on polls. | Total value of personal estate. | Total value of real estate. | Total tax for state, county, city, and town purposes, including highway tax. | Rate per cent of total tax. | Total valuation, May 1, 18–. | Total number of dwelling-houses. | Total number of horses. | Total number of cows. | Total number of sheep. | Total number of acres of land taxed in the city or town. |
|---|---|---|---|---|---|---|---|---|---|---|---|
| 1 | 2 | 3 | 4 | 5 | 6 | 7 | 8 | 9 | 10 | 11 | 12 |

5. The assessors in each of the several cities and towns shall enter in the books furnished in accordance with the provisions of the preceding section the valuation and assessment of the polls and estate of the inhabitants assessed, in the following order : —

*In column number one.* — The names of the inhabitants or parties assessed for polls or estate.

*In column number two.* — The number of polls for which any person named in the preceding column is taxable.

*In column number three.* — Total amount of cash tax on polls.

*In column number four.* — The amount of each person's whole stock in trade, including all goods, wares, and merchandise, at home or abroad, of ratable estate, whether paid for or otherwise.

*In column number five.* — A description of all ratable cash assets : viz., amount of money at interest more than the person assessed pays interest for, including public securities ; the amount of money on hand, including deposits in any bank or in any savings bank which is not exempted by law from taxation ; the number of shares of stock which are taxable, with the name of the corporation, in any bank, railroad, insurance, manufacturing, or other incorporated company.

*In column number six.* — The true ratable value of the several items enumerated in the preceding column, placed opposite the description of said property or shares.

*In column number seven.* — The true value of machinery used in all kinds of manufacturing establishments, including steam-engines, &c., the value of such machinery to be entered opposite the description of the building in which it is used.

*In columns number eight and nine.* — The whole number of taxable live stock, including horses, mules, asses, oxen, cows, steers, heifers, sheep, and swine ; each kind to be stated separately, with the value affixed to each.

*In columns number ten and eleven.* — Description of all

other ratable personal estate not before enumerated, such as carriages, income, plate, furniture, tons of vessels, &c., with the true value of the same.

*In column number twelve.* — The aggregate of each person's ratable personal estate.

*In column number thirteen.* — The total tax on each person's personal estate.

*In column number fourteen.* — Buildings of all kinds shall be described in the following order : —

Dwelling-houses ; barns ; shops of all kinds, naming their uses ; stores ; warehouses ; distilhouses ; breweries ; tanneries and other manufactories of leather ; ropewalks ; grist-mills ; saw-mills ; steam and other mills not above enumerated ; cotton factories, with the number of spindles and looms used in the same ; woollen factories, with the number of sets of cards used in the same ; linen factories, with the number of spindles and looms ; print works ; bleacheries ; gas works ; paper mills ; card factories ; boot and shoe factories ; India rubber factories ; carriage and car factories ; piano-forte and musical instrument factories ; sewing-machine factories ; chair, pail, tub, and other wooden-ware factories ; oil factories ; glass factories ; all kinds of iron and brass works, and other buildings not above named.

*In column number fifteen.* — True value of buildings enumerated in the preceding column placed opposite the description of the same, including water-wheels ; such value to be exclusive of land and water-power and of the machinery used in said buildings.

*In columns number sixteen, seventeen, and eighteen.* — A description by name or otherwise of each and every lot of land assessed, the same placed opposite the name of the person or party to whom it is taxable, with the number of acres or feet in each lot, the number of quartz sand beds, of stone quarries and ore beds, and the true value thereof.

*In columns number nineteen and twenty.* — The number of superficial feet of wharf, and the total value of the same.

*In column number twenty-one.* — The aggregate value of each person's taxable real estate.

*In column number twenty-two.* — The total tax on real estate.

*In column number twenty-three.* — The aggregate cash tax assessed to each person on polls, personal and real estate.

*In columns number twenty-four, twenty-five, twenty-six, and twenty-seven.* — The amount assessed for highway tax ; on polls ; on personal estate ; on real estate ; and the aggregate of the same.

6. The assessors shall fill up the table of aggregates by an enumeration of the necessary items included in the lists of valuation and assessments required by the preceding section, and shall, on or before the first day of October in each of the first four years of each decade, deposit in the office of the secretary of the commonwealth, an attested copy of the same, containing : —

*First.* — The total number of polls.

*Second.* — The total tax on polls.

*Third.* — The total value of[1] personal estate.

*Fourth.* — The total value of[1] real estate.

*Fifth.* — The total tax for state, county, and town purposes, including highway tax.

*Sixth.* — The rate per cent of total tax.

*Seventh.* — The total valuation of the city or town.

*Eighth.* — Total number of dwelling-houses assessed.

*Ninth.* — Total number of horses assessed.

*Tenth.* — Total number of cows assessed.

*Eleventh.* — Total number of sheep assessed.

*Twelfth.* — The total number of acres of land assessed in the city or town.

The assessors shall make similar returns in the first four years of the last half of each decade ; and in every fifth and tenth year of each decade, they shall deposit in the office of the secretary of the commonwealth, on or before the first day of October, a certified copy, under oath, of the assessors' books of those years ; and said books thus

[1] Stats. 1861, ch. 215.

deposited shall contain an aggregate sheet properly filled in accordance with the provisions of this act, which shall be in like manner certified by the assessors; and in every fifth and tenth year of each decade, the secretary shall furnish duplicate copies of blank books to the cities and towns for the foregoing purpose: *provided*, *however*, that in the case of the city of Boston the returns, required by this section to be deposited in the office of the secretary, may be thus deposited on or before the first day of November, in the several years respectively.

7. The secretary of the commonwealth shall cause to be printed, and bound in the books to be furnished for the use of the assessors, a copy of this act, and such certificates as are required by the same and by the General Statutes, to be signed by the assessors, together with such explanatory notes as may by him be deemed expedient, for the purpose of securing uniformity of returns under the several headings; and he shall compile and cause to be printed annually, for the use of the legislature, the aggregate returns from the cities and towns in the commonwealth arranged by counties, so as to exhibit the total valuation of the towns, cities, counties, and state.

8. If the assessors of any city or town shall neglect to comply with the requirements of the second or third section of this act (sections five and six above), each assessor so neglecting shall forfeit a sum not exceeding two hundred dollars.[1]

9. Whenever it shall have been ascertained by the assessors of any city or town that the aggregate values of their city or town, respectively, have been diminished since the first day of May of the preceding year, they shall return with the table of aggregates, or books, which they are required by the act of the year one thousand eight hundred and sixty-one, entitled "An act to secure a uniform description and appraisal of estates in the commonwealth, for the purposes of taxation" (being the five preceding sections), and the several acts in addition thereto, to deposit

[1] Stats. 1861, ch. 167, §§ 1–5.

in the office of the secretary, a statement in writing, under oath, of the causes which, in their opinion, have produced such diminution.

10. If the assessors of any city or town shall neglect to comply with the requirements of this act (the preceding section), each assessor so neglecting shall forfeit a sum not exceeding two hundred dollars.[1]

11. The assessors of the several cities and towns shall, on or before the first day of September next, and every third year thereafter, return to the secretary of the commonwealth the number and names of the several industrial corporations, and the number and names of the banks and insurance companies established in their respective cities and towns, with the amount of capital stock owned by each, reckoned at the par value thereof, the number of shares issued, and the amount for which the real estate and machinery of manufacturing corporations are taxed in such cities and towns. Also, the number and names of savings banks in such cities and towns, and the whole amount of deposits in each. Also, the number of shares in industrial corporations, railroads, banks, insurance companies, and steamship companies, specifying the number of shares in each company which are taxed in such cities and towns, and the value of such shares as they stand upon the assessors' books. Also, the amount of deposits in any savings banks, specifying the name thereof, taxed in their respective cities and towns.

12. The assessors of each city and town shall, at the same time, return to the secretary the name of any other association or corporation organized for loaning money, and established in their respective cities and towns, with the amount of their capital stock and deposits, if known, and the amount for which they are taxed, for the year eighteen hundred and sixty-one, and for every third year thereafter.

13. The secretary of the commonwealth shall, on or before the first day of June next, and on or before the first

---

[1] Stats. 1864, ch. 210, §§ 3, 4.

6

day of June of every third year thereafter, transmit to the several cities and towns suitable blank forms, to enable the several assessors to make the returns prescribed in the foregoing sections of this act.

14. The secretary shall make a digest of the returns of the assessors, made to him in conformity with the foregoing provisions of this act, in convenient form, for the use of the legislature, and shall cause the same to be printed on or before the first day of January next, and on or before the first day of January of every third year thereafter; and in addition to the number provided for the legislature, shall cause one copy of the same to be sent to the clerk of each city and town in this commonwealth.

15. If any agent or assessor wilfully refuses or neglects to perform any duty required of him by this act (being four preceding sections), he shall forfeit a sum not exceeding three hundred dollars.[1]

16. The assessors of the several cities and towns shall annually, on or before the first Monday of August, return to the tax commissioner (treasurer of the commonwealth), hereinafter named, the names of all corporations, except banks of issue and deposit, having a capital stock divided into shares, chartered by this commonwealth or organized under the general laws, for purposes of business or profit, and established in their respective cities and towns, or owning real estate therein, and a statement in detail of the works, structures, real estate, and machinery owned by each of said corporations, and situated in such city or town, with the value thereof, on the first day of May preceding, and the amount at which the same is assessed in said city or town for the then current year. They shall also, at the same time, return to said tax commissioner the amount of taxes laid, or voted to be laid, within said city or town, for the then current year, for state, county, and town purposes, including highway taxes.[2]

The assessors of each town shall in each year, at the time of making the returns required by this section, return to the tax commis-

---

[1] Stats. 1861, ch. 171, §§ 1–5.    [2] Stats. 1865, ch. 283, § 1.

sioner a statement showing the whole number of steam-boilers located in their respective towns on the first day of May then next preceding; by whom and when built, and the aggregate estimated amount of horse power which such boilers are capable of furnishing. Such return shall also state the number of accidents causing permanent injuries to persons which have arisen from the use of such boilers during the year, with the causes thereof, as far as may be ascertained by the assessors. The tax commissioner shall in due season forward to the assessors blanks suitable for making these returns.[1]

The provisions of this section are extended to apply, so far as applicable, to companies, copartnerships, and other associations having a location or place of business within this commonwealth, in which the beneficial interest is held in shares which are assignable without consent of the other associates specifically authorizing such transfer.

Every company, copartnership, or association to be taxed by this act shall, when required, submit its books to the inspection of the tax commissioner and tax assessors of the city or town in which the same is located; and its treasurer, agent, trustee, superintendent, and business manager shall be subject to examination on oath in regard to all matters affecting the taxation of the same.[2]

17. If the assessors of any city or town shall neglect to comply with the requirements of this act (preceding section), each assessor so neglecting shall forfeit the sum of one hundred dollars.[3]

18. When the collector of taxes of any city or town in this commonwealth shall become satisfied that any poll tax, or tax upon personal property, or any portion of said tax, which has been committed to him or to any of his predecessors in office, for collection, cannot be collected by reason of the death, absence, poverty, insolvency, bankruptcy, or other inability to pay of the person or persons to whom such tax has been assessed, he shall notify the assessors of taxes of the said city or town thereof in writing. stating the reason why such tax cannot be collected, and verifying the same by oath. It shall then be lawful for the assessors of such city or town, after due inquiry into the circumstances, to make abatement of such tax or any part thereof. Upon such abatement being made, the said

[1] Stats. 1873, ch. 321.
[2] Stats. 1878, ch. 275.
[3] Stats. 1865, ch. 283, § 14.

assessors shall certify the same in writing to the collector of taxes ; and said certificate shall discharge the collector from further obligation to collect the tax so abated. But no poll tax shall be abated under the provisions of this act, within two years from the time of its assessment.[1]

When any person, on or before the first day of October, in any year, gives notice in writing, accompanied by satisfactory evidence, to the assessors of a city or town, that he was on the first day of May of that year an inhabitant thereof, and liable to pay a poll tax, and furnishes under oath a true list of his polls and estate, both real and personal, not exempt from taxation, the assessors shall assess him for his polls and estate ; but such assessment shall be subject to the provisions of chapter one hundred and twenty-one of the acts of the year one thousand eight hundred and sixty-five, and the assessors shall, on or before the fifth day of October, deposit with the clerk of the city or town a list of the persons so assessed. The taxes so assessed shall be entered in the tax list of the collector of the city or town, and he shall collect and pay over the same in the manner specified in his warrant.[2]

---

[1] Stats. 1878, ch. 77.

[2] Stats. 1874, ch. 376, § 6; Stats. 1877, ch. 207. This section is also inserted in Chapter IV., section six.

By accident, in that section the first date is September 15th instead of October 1st, and October 1st instead of October 5th.

# CHAPTER X.

## ASSESSMENT OF TAXES.

1. WHEN a state tax is to be assessed, the treasurer shall send his warrants for the assessing thereof by mail to the assessors of the several cities and towns in the commonwealth.[1]

2. The assessors shall assess state taxes for which they receive warrants from the treasurer, according to the rules prescribed in this chapter. They shall in like manner assess all county taxes which are duly certified to them, all city or town taxes voted by their places, and all taxes duly voted and certified by school districts therein.

3. If the assessors of a city or town neglect to obey a warrant so received from the treasurer, or to assess such a county, town, or district tax, each assessor so neglecting shall forfeit a sum not exceeding two hundred dollars ; and the commissioners in the respective counties shall forthwith appoint other suitable persons to assess such tax, according to the warrant of the treasurer. The persons so appointed shall take the same oath, perform the same duties, and be liable to the same penalties, as are provided in the case of assessors of towns.

4. If within five months after the receipt of a warrant from the state treasurer, or a certificate from the county commissioners requiring the assessment of a tax, the same is not assessed and certified as the law requires, the amount of the tax may be recovered of the city or town where the neglect occurs, in an action of contract by the treasurer of the state or county respectively.

5. Keepers of taverns and boarding-houses, and masters and mistresses of dwelling-houses, shall, upon application

[1] Stats. 1867, ch. 166, § 1.

of an assessor in the place where their house is situated, give information of the names of all persons residing therein and liable to be assessed for taxes. Every such keeper, master, or mistress, refusing to give such information or knowingly giving false information, shall forfeit twenty dollars for each offence.

6. Before proceeding to make an assessment, the assessors shall give seasonable notice thereof to the inhabitants of their respective places, at any of their meetings, or by posting up in their city or town one or more notifications in some public place or places, or by some other sufficient manner. Such notice shall require the inhabitants to bring in to the assessors, within a time therein specified, true lists of all their polls and estates, both real and personal, not exempted from taxation.[1]

The assessors of any town, in giving the notice mentioned in this section, may or may not require the inhabitants thereof to include real estate in their lists of property subject to taxation. Unless such requirement is made in said notice, the omission of real estate from the list brought in to the assessors shall not deprive the owner of such real estate of his right to an abatement of the tax thereon: *provided*, he shall file, with his application to the assessors for abatement, a list of the real estate on which the same is claimed, with his estimate of the fair cash value of each parcel thereof, and shall make oath that said list and estimate are true according to his best knowledge and belief.[2]

7. Whoever shall deliver or disclose to any assessor or assistant assessor of taxes, elected or appointed in pursuance of the laws of this commonwealth, any false or fraudulent list, return or schedule of property, as and for a true list of his estates, real and personal, not exempted from taxation, with intent thereby to avoid the lawful assessment or payment of any tax, or with intent thereby to defeat or evade the provisions of law in relation to the assessment or payment of taxes, shall be punished by a fine not exceeding one thousand dollars, or by imprisonment in jail not exceeding one year.[3]

[1] Gen. Stats. ch. 11, §§ 18–22.     [3] Stats. 1869, ch. 190.
[2] Stats. 1877, ch. 160, § 1.

8. Corporations are required to bring in such lists.[1] But it is not intended that such lists should contain an estimated value of the property.[2]

9. The assessors shall in all cases require a person bringing in such a list to make oath that the same is true; which oath may be administered by either of the assessors.

10. The assessors of each place shall at the time appointed make a fair cash valuation of all the estate, real and personal, subject to taxation therein.[3]

11. They shall receive as true the list brought in by each individual according to the provisions of this chapter, unless on being thereto required by the assessors, he refuses to answer on oath all necessary inquiries as to the nature and amount of his property.[4]

They are not to receive as true, under this requirement, any estimate of value contained in the list, as it is not intended that the list should contain such estimate, but to receive as true the description, enumeration of articles, and other description of the property. But note this when the list is shown to be wrong by the answers of the individual to the inquiries of the assessors referred to in the last part of the section above.[5]

12. Any person who in any way directly or indirectly proposes or agrees to an assessment on any specific or limited amount less than he is liable by law to be taxed for, with a view or as an inducement to make any particular place his residence for the purpose of taxation, shall be punished by fine of one thousand dollars; and any assessor guilty of making or assenting to any such proposal shall be subject to a like penalty.

13. They [the assessors] shall ascertain as nearly as possible the particulars of the personal estate, and of the real estate in possession or occupation, as owner or otherwise, of any person who has not brought in such list, and make an estimate thereof at its just value, according to their best information and belief.[6]

[1] Otis Company v. Ware, 8 Gray, 509.

[2] Newburyport v. County Commissioners, 12 Met. 211.

[3] Gen. Stats. ch. 11, §§ 23, 24.

[4] Gen. Stats. ch. 11, § 25.

[5] Lincoln v. Worcester, 8 Cush. 55; Hall v. County Commissioners, 10 Allen, 100.

[6] Gen. Stats. ch. 11, §§ 26, 27.

It is sufficient to make a general estimate of each class of property.[1]

14. Such estimate shall be entered in the valuation, and shall be conclusive upon all persons who have not seasonably brought in lists of their estates, unless they can show a reasonable excuse for the omission.

15. The assessors, when they think it convenient, may include in the same assessment their state, county, and town taxes, or any two of them.

16. In the city of Boston, all taxes assessed for city or county purposes may be assessed separately, as county taxes and as city taxes, or under the denomination of city taxes only, as the city council from time to time directs. Chelsea, North Chelsea, and Winthrop shall not be taxed for county purposes.[2]

17. The assessors shall assess upon the polls, as nearly as may be, one sixth part of the whole sum to be raised; but the whole poll tax assessed in one year upon an individual for town, county, and state purposes, including highway taxes, shall not exceed two dollars; and the residue of such whole sum shall be apportioned upon property, as provided in this chapter.[3]

The omission to comply with this provision renders the whole tax illegal.[4]

18. They may add to the amount of a tax to be assessed such sum, not exceeding five per cent thereof, as any fractional divisions of the amount may render convenient in the apportionment.

19. They shall make a list of the valuation and the assessment thereon, and, before the taxes assessed are committed for collection, shall deposit the same, or an attested copy thereof, in their office, or, if there is no office, with their chairman, for public inspection.[5]

Depositing the list the day before is sufficient.[6]

20. The first part of the list shall exhibit the valuation and assessment of the polls and estates of the inhabitants

---

[1] Tobey v. Wareham, 2 Allen, 594.
[2] Gen. Stats. ch. 11, §§ 28–30.
[3] Gen. Stats. ch. 11, § 31; Stats. 1876, ch. 88.
[4] Gerry v. Stoneham, 1 Allen, 319.
[5] Gen. Stats. ch. 11, §§ 32, 33.
[6] Tobey v. Wareham, 2 Allen, 594.

assessed; and shall contain in separate columns the following particulars, to wit: —

The names of the inhabitants assessed; and opposite to their names,

The number of polls.

The amount of their poll tax.

The description of their real estate.

The true value of their real estate.

The tax assessed on such real estate.

The description of their personal property.

The true value of their personal property.

The tax on their personal property.

The sum total of each person's tax.

The second part shall exhibit the valuation and assessment of the estates of non-resident owners; and shall contain in separate columns the following particulars, to wit: —

The names of the non-resident owners of the property assessed, or such description of them as can be given.

Their places of abode, if known.

The description of their estate.

The true value of such estate.

The tax thereon.[1]

See also in regard to valuation lists, assessors, Chapter X.

21. The tax list committed to the collectors shall be in substance as follows: —

| Names. | No. of Polls. | Poll Tax. | Tax on Real Estate. | Tax on Personal Property. | Total. | Time when paid. |
|---|---|---|---|---|---|---|
| | | | | | | |

**NON-RESIDENTS.**

| Names. | Places of abode, if known. | Tax. | |
|---|---|---|---|
| | | | |

22. The assessors, or other persons empowered to assess the taxes in a city or town, shall, at the close

[1] Gen. Stats. ch. 11, § 34.

of said valuation list, subscribe and take the following oath :

"We (the assessors, or mayor and aldermen, as the case may be, of                ) do hereby solemnly swear that the foregoing list is a full and true list of the names of all persons known to us, who are liable to taxation in                (here insert the name of the city or town) during the present year, and that the real and personal estate contained in said list, and assessed upon each individual in said list, is a full and accurate assessment upon all the property of each individual, liable to taxation, at its full and fair cash value, according to our best knowledge and belief."

23. Any assessor or other person assessing taxes in a city or town, who omits to take and subscribe the oath prescribed in the preceding section, shall be punished by a fine of ten dollars ; but the omission to take and subscribe said oath shall not prevent the collection of a tax otherwise legally assessed.

24. The assessors shall, within a reasonable time, commit said tax list with their warrant to the collector, or if no collector is chosen, to a constable, or if there is no constable to the sheriff or his deputy, for collection.[1]

25. A warrant without a tax list will not authorize a collector to collect by distress, but the two need not be attached together.[2] Where a warrant is directed to a person as "constable or collector," it is sufficient if he is qualified to act at the time of the delivery of the warrant to him though he was not at the time of its date.[3]

26. The warrant shall specify the duties of the collector as prescribed by law in the collection of taxes, the times when and the persons to whom he shall pay them in, shall be substantially in the form heretofore used, and need not be under seal.

27. When a warrant issued for the collection of taxes is lost or destroyed, the assessors may issue a new warrant therefor, which shall have the same force and effect as the original warrant.

28. Towns at their annual meeting, and city councils of cities may allow a discount of such sums as they think expedient to persons making voluntary payment of their taxes within such

---

[1] Gen. Stats. ch. 11, §§ 35–38.
[2] Barnard v. Graves, 13 Met. 85.
[3] Hays v. Drake, 6 Gray, 387.

periods of time as they prescribe. In such case the collectors shall make such discount accordingly.[1]

29. If towns abuse this authority "by making the discounts partial, the remedy is not by resisting the tax, but should be of a more general character. An injunction would seem to be more appropriate."[2]

30. When such discount is allowed, the assessors, at the time of committing their warrant to the collector, shall post up in one or more public places within the city or town notice of the rates of discount.

31. A person aggrieved by the taxes assessed upon him may apply to the assessors for an abatement thereof; and, if he makes it appear that he is taxed at more than his just proportion (or upon an assessment of any of his property above its fair cash value),[3] they shall make a reasonable abatement.[4]

32. But assessors cannot make this abatement after their term of office has expired.[5] When a person is liable to taxation for personal and real estate in a city or town, his *sole remedy* for an over-taxation caused by an excessive valuation of his property, or by including in the assessment property of which he is not owner, or for which he is not liable to taxation, is by an application to the assessors for an abatement; but this does not apply to the case of one who is taxed in a town where he does not reside, upon his poll and personal estate,[6] and upon petition for abatement, taxes upon the same or other property of the petitioner cannot be increased.[7]

33. If legal costs have accrued before making such abatement, the person applying for the abatement shall pay the same.

34. If the assessors refuse to make an abatement to a person, he may, within one month thereafter, make complaint thereof to the county commissioners by filing the same with their clerk, and, if upon a hearing it appears that the complainant is overrated, the commissioners shall make such an abatement as they deem reasonable.

[1] Gen. Stats. ch. 11, §§ 39–41.
[2] Tobey *v.* Wareham, 2 Allen, 594.
[3] Stats. 1877, ch. 160, § 2.
[4] Gen. Stats. ch. 11, §§ 42, 43.
[5] Cheshire *v.* Howland, 13 Gray, 321.
[6] Osborn *v.* Danvers, 6 Pick. 98; Preston *v.* Boston, 12 Pick. 7; Bates *v.* Boston, 5 Cush. 93.
[7] Lowell *v.* County Commissioners, 3 Allen, 546.

35. No person shall have an abatement unless he has filed with the assessors a list subscribed by him of his estate liable to taxation, and made oath that it is full and accurate according to his best knowledge and belief. When such list is not filed within the time specified by the assessors for bringing it in, no complaint from the judgment of the assessors shall be sustained by the county commissioners, unless they are satisfied that there was good cause why such list was not seasonably brought in.[1]

36. This section has been modified by the legislature, as follows : —

When the assessors of a city or town have given notice to the inhabitants thereof to bring in true lists of all their polls and estates, not exempt from taxation, in accordance with the provisions of the twenty-second section of the eleventh chapter of the General Statutes, they shall not afterwards abate any part of the tax assessed on personal estate to any person who did not bring in such list within the time specified therefor in such notice, unless such tax exceeds by more than fifty per centum the amount which would have been assessed to that person on personal estate, if he had seasonably brought in said list ; and if said tax exceeds by more than fifty per centum the said amount, the abatement shall be only of the excess above the said fifty per centum : *provided, however,* that this act shall not affect any person who can show a reasonable excuse for not seasonably bringing in said list.[2]

37. The list must be brought to the assessors before the tax is assessed.[3] The exhibition to the assessors of a plan of the taxpayer's real estate is not the carrying in of a list; nor is a reference by oral communication to a former list, carried in two years before. Nor is the fact that the assessors are satisfied without a list equivalent to bringing in a list.[4] But where a corporation brought in a list in due season, and the only defect was, that it was not sworn to as a full and accurate list until after the time designated for bringing it in, because the assessors told the agent he need not swear to it, — the

[1] Gen. Stats. ch. 11, §§ 44–46.
[2] Stats. 1865, ch. 121.
[3] Porter *v.* County Commissioners of Norfolk, 5 Gray, 365.
[4] Winnisimmet Company *v.* Assessors, &c., 6 Cush. 477.

omission was held to be for good cause. In this case, the law was complied with in all essential particulars. Not so in the case of Winnisimmet Company above, where *no* list was brought in.[1]

38. The omission to tax any particular person who may be liable, does not render the whole tax illegal and void, though in consequence others are taxed more than they ought to be, and it seems a second tax assessed to correct the error would be illegal and void.[2]

39. No abatement shall be allowed to a person unless he makes application therefor within six months after the date of his tax bill.

40. A person having an abatement made shall, if his tax has been paid, be reimbursed out of the treasury of the city or town to the amount of the abatement allowed, together with all charges, except the legal costs provided for in section forty-four.[3]

Charges do not include the petitioner's costs in prosecuting his petition for abatement, nor interest upon the amount abated which had been paid by him under protest.[4]

41. Every person whose tax is abated shall be entitled to a certificate thereof from the assessors, or clerk of the commissioners, or other proper officer.[5]

42. When any person, on or before the (fifteenth day of September)[6] in any year, gives notice in writing, accompanied by satisfactory evidence, to the assessors of a city or town, that he was on the first day of May of that year an inhabitant thereof, and liable to pay a poll tax, and furnishes under oath a true list of his polls and estate, both real and personal, not exempt from taxation, the assessors shall assess him for his polls and estate; but such assessment shall be subject to the provisions of chapter one hundred and twenty-one of the acts of the year one thousand eight hundred and sixty-five; and the assessors shall, on or before the (first day of October),[6] deposit with the clerk of the city or town a list of the persons

---

[1] Lowell *v.* County Commissioners, 3 Allen, 546.

[2] Inglee *v.* Bosworth, 5 Pick. 498; Watson *v.* Princeton, 4 Met. 601.

[3] Gen. Stats. ch. 11, §§ 47, 48.

[4] Lowell *v.* County Commissioners, 3 Allen, 546, 550.

[5] Gen. Stats. ch. 11, § 49.

[6] Stats. 1869, ch. 443.

so assessed. The taxes so assessed shall be entered in the
tax list of the collector of the city or town, and he shall
collect and pay over the same in the manner specified in
his warrant.[1]

43. Whenever any person shall make application to the
assessors of any city or town of this commonwealth to be
assessed a poll tax for the then current year, and it shall
appear that such applicant was on the first day of May
preceding a resident of said city or town, and liable to
pay a poll tax therein, but was not assessed therefor, and
that such applicant is, or has been during any portion of
the two years preceding such application, engaged in the
military or naval service of the United States, it shall be
the duty of such assessors forthwith to assess such tax,
and notify the treasurer of such city or town of the same,
and the person so assessed shall, upon payment of said
tax, be entitled to the right to vote in said city or town to
the same extent as if his taxes had been assessed and
paid in the manner heretofore provided by law.[2]

44. The assessors shall not be responsible for the assessment of a tax in a city, town, parish, religious society,
(fire district) [3] or school district, for which they are assessors, when such tax is assessed by them in pursuance of
a vote for that purpose, certified to them by the clerk or
other proper officer of such city, town, parish, religious
society (fire district),[3] or school district, except for the
want of integrity and fidelity on their own part.[4]

45. Assessors who act with fidelity and integrity in assessing a
tax, in pursuance of a vote duly certified to them, are not responsible in any form of action for accidentally assessing a person not an
inhabitant of the town or liable to be taxed.[5] Nor are they liable for
omitting to tax an individual who is liable to taxation, by which he
lost his right to vote, unless it is shown affirmatively that the omission was caused by want of integrity or fidelity.[6] But they are liable
for assessing and issuing a warrant for the collection of a tax when
the town is not legally organized.[7]

[1] Stats. 1868, ch. 211, § 2.           [5] Baker v. Allen, 21 Pick. 382.
[2] Stats. 1865, ch. 68.                 [6] Griffin v. Rising, 11 Met. 339.
[3] Stats. 1872, ch. 310.        .        [7] Dickinson v. Billings, 4 Gray, 42.
[4] Gen. Stats. ch. 11, § 51.

46. Each assessor shall be paid by his city or town two [1] dollars and fifty cents a day for every whole day that he is employed in that service, with such other compensation as the city or town shall allow. [2]

He is entitled to the statute compensation if it exceeds that provided by the town; but it must appear from the vote of the town that the sum voted is intended to be in addition to the statute compensation, if he is to take both. [3]

47. Every tax, except a poll tax, which is invalid by reason of any error or irregularity in the assessment, and which has not been paid, or which has been recovered back, may be reassessed by the assessors for the time being, to the just amount to which, and upon the estate or to the person to whom, such tax ought at first to have been assessed, whether such person has continued an inhabitant of the same city or town or not.

Taxes re-assessed under the provisions of this section shall be committed to, and collected and paid over by, the collector of taxes for the time being, in the same manner as other taxes, except that the name of the person to whom the taxes were originally assessed shall be stated in the warrant; and the bond of such collector shall apply to such re-assessed taxes. [4]

48. If, through any erroneous or illegal assessment or apportionment of taxes, a party is assessed more or less than his due proportion, the tax and assessment shall be void only to the extent of the illegal excess. [5]

49. Every corporation established within this commonwealth by special charter, or organized under the general laws thereof, which holds on the first day of May in any year shares of stock in corporations other than those subject to taxation under the provisions of chapter two hundred and eighty-three of the acts of the year one thousand eight hundred and sixty-five, and acts in amendment thereof, or bonds of any description, as collateral security for borrowed money, or other liability, shall annually, be-

[1] Stats. 1873, ch. 156.
[2] Gen. Stats. ch. 11, § 52.
[3] Moody v. Newburyport, 3 Met. 431.
[4] Stats. 1870, ch. 394.
[5] Gen. Stats. ch. 11, §§ 53, 54.

tween the first and tenth day of May, return to the tax commissioner the whole number of such shares and bonds so held, the names and residences of the persons pledging the same, and the number, denomination, and the par value, if known, of the shares and bonds pledged by each ; and the tax commissioner shall, on or before the twentieth day of June in each year, transmit to the assessors of the several cities and towns of the commonwealth a true copy of the list furnished by such corporations.

50. Any corporation neglecting or refusing to make the returns required by this act (the preceding section), or wilfully making a return which is materially false or defective, shall forfeit for each offence a sum of not less than fifty nor more than one thousand dollars, to be recovered by an action of tort to the use of the city or town in which a person pledging such stock or bonds resides.[1]

51. The assessors of each city and town in the commonwealth, in addition to the returns which they are now required to make by the provisions of the first section of chapter two hundred and eighty-three of the acts of the year eighteen hundred and sixty-five, shall, at the time specified in said section, return also the aggregate amount of the assets of their respective cities or towns, and the amount of indebtedness of such cities and towns for which notes, bonds, or other similar evidences of debt, the payment of which is not provided for by the taxation of the then current year, were outstanding on the first of May then next preceding, with a concise statement of the various purposes for which such indebtedness was incurred, and the amount incurred for each purpose.[2]

52. When the assessors of any city or town, after the time when their warrant has been committed to the collector of taxes, shall discover that the real or personal estate of any person, to an amount not less than (one[3]) hundred dollars, and liable to taxation, has been omitted from the last annual assessment of taxes in such city or town,

---

[1] Stats. 1870, ch. 144.  
[2] Stats. 1870, ch. 76.  
[3] Stats. 1873, ch. 272.

said assessors shall proceed forthwith to assess such person for such estate in like manner as he should have been assessed in such last annual assessment. The taxes so assessed shall be entered in the tax list of the collector of the city or town, and he shall collect and pay over the same in the manner specified in his warrant: *provided*, that such tax shall not be assessed after the (fifteenth day of September)[1] for any such omission.

53. No tax of any city or town shall be invalidated by reason that, in consequence of the provisions of this act (preceding section), the whole amount of the taxes assessed in such city or town shall exceed the amount authorized by law to be raised.[2]

54. Any inhabitant of this commonwealth who shall escape taxation by wilfully and designedly changing or concealing his residence, or by any other act, with the intent so to escape, shall be liable, upon conviction therefor, to pay a fine of twice the amount of the last tax paid by such person; or if he shall have paid no tax in this commonwealth, a fine of not less than one hundred, nor more than five thousand dollars.[3]

[1] Stats. 1873, ch. 272.
[2] Stats. 1868, ch. 320.
[3] Stats. 1864, ch. 172, § 1.

# CHAPTER XI.

## PERSONS AND PROPERTY SUBJECT TO TAXATION.

1. A POLL tax shall be assessed in the manner hereinafter provided, on every male inhabitant of the commonwealth above the age of twenty years, whether a citizen of the United States or an alien.

2. All property, real and personal, of the inhabitants of this state, not expressly exempted by law, shall be subject to taxation as hereinafter provided.

3. Real estate, for the purposes of taxation, shall include all lands within this state, and all buildings and other things erected on or affixed to the same.

4. Personal estate shall, for the purposes of taxation, include goods, chattels, money, and effects, wherever they are, ships and vessels at home or abroad, money at interest, and other debts due the persons to be taxed more than they are indebted or pay interest for, public stocks and securities, stocks in turnpikes, bridges, and moneyed corporations, within or without the state, the income from an annuity, and so much of the income from a profession, trade, or employment, as exceeds the sum of six hundred dollars a year; but no income shall be taxed which is derived from property subject to taxation.[1]

This section is so far amended that the income subject to taxation shall be only so much as exceeds two thousand dollars, and which has accrued to any person during the year ending on the first day of May of the year in which the tax is assessed.[2]

5. The stock of all corporations chartered under the laws of this state is not now taxable to the shareholders except banks of issue and deposit, including national banks and those yet existing which were chartered by the state, and the mercantile institutions for savings of the city of Boston; but the stock of all corporations chartered by

[1] Gen. Stats. ch. 11, §§ 1–4.      [2] Stats. 1866, ch. 48; 1873, ch. 354.

other states is taxable.[1]   But such proportion of the tax collected by the state under section five of the statutes of 1867, ch. 283, of corporations chartered under the laws of this state as corresponds to the proportion of the stock of such corporation owned by persons residing in this commonwealth, shall be credited and paid to the several cities and towns where it appears from the returns or other evidence that such shareholders resided on the first day of May next preceding, according to the number of shares so held in such cities and towns respectively : *provided*, that in case stock is held by copartners, guardians, executors, administrators or trustees, the proportion of tax corresponding to the amount of stock so held shall be credited and paid to the towns where the stock would have been taxed, under the provisions of chapter eleven of the General Statutes ; and *provided, further*, that when a town owns stock in any corporation taxed under this act, a return to said town shall be made in like manner as is provided in the case of stock held by individuals residing in said town.

Said commissioner shall ascertain and determine the amount due to each city and town, under this section, subject to appeal as hereinbefore provided, and shall notify the treasurer of each city and town thereof, and certify the amount, as finally determined, to the treasurer of the commonwealth, who shall thereupon pay over the same.

6. A clerk in a post-office, who is appointed by the deputy postmaster, and his appointment approved by the postmaster-general, is taxable for the income derived from his appointment as such clerk.[2] This was held on the ground that he is not an officer of the United States, it having been decided in the Supreme Court of the United States that the several states have no authority to tax an officer of the government of the United States for his office or its emoluments.[8] It was admitted in Melcher v. Boston that a postmaster was an officer of the United States ; and it was decided in New Hampshire that a contractor for carrying the mail is not such officer.[4]

---

[1] Stats. 1866, ch. 48; Stats. 1865, chs. 242, 283, § 15; 1866, ch. 291, § 2; 1867, ch. 160, § 1.

[2] Melcher v. Boston, 9 Met. 73.

[8] Dobbins v. Commissioners of Erie County, 16 Pet. 435.

[4] Whitehouse v. Langdon, 16 N. H. 331.

# CHAPTER XII.

## PERSONS AND PROPERTY EXEMPTED FROM TAXATION.

1. THE following property and polls shall be exempted from taxation : —

First. The property of the United States.

Second. The property of the commonwealth, except real estate of which the commonwealth is in possession under a mortgage for condition broken.

Third. The personal property of literary, benevolent, charitable, and scientific institutions incorporated within this commonwealth, and the real estate belonging to such institutions, occupied by them or their officers for the purposes for which they were incorporated.[1]

The real estate of the foregoing institutions, purchased with a view of removal thereto, shall not be exempt from taxation for a longer period than two years until such removal takes place.[2]

Fourth. All property belonging to common-school districts, the income of which is appropriated to the purposes of education.

Fifth. The Bunker Hill Monument.

Sixth. The household furniture of every person, not exceeding one thousand dollars in value, his wearing apparel, farming utensils, and mechanics' tools necessary for carrying on his business.

Seventh. Houses of religious worship, and the pews and furniture (except for parochial purposes) ; but portions of such houses appropriated for purposes other than

---

[1] See chapter on "Associations for Religious, Charitable, Educational, and other Purposes."

[2] Stats. 1878, ch. 214.

religious worship shall be taxed at the value thereof to the owners of the houses.

Eighth. Cemeteries, tombs, and rights of burial, so long as the same shall be dedicated for the burial of the dead.

Ninth. The estate, both real and personal, of incorporated agricultural societies.

Tenth. The property to the amount of five hundred dollars of a widow or unmarried female above the age of twenty-one years, of any person above the age of seventy-five years, and of any minor whose father is deceased: *provided*, that the whole estate real and personal of said persons does not exceed in value the sum of one thousand dollars, exclusive of property otherwise exempted under the provisions of this section.[1]

Eleventh. Mules, horses, and neat cattle, less than one year old; and swine and sheep less than six months old.

Twelfth. The polls and estates of Indians.[2]

Thirteenth. The polls and any portion of the estates of persons who by reason of age, infirmity, and poverty, are in the judgment of the assessors unable to contribute fully towards the public charges.[3]

2. In all cases where lands belonging to the commonwealth are or have been sold by the commissioners of public lands, and agreements for deeds are or have been given by said commissioners, the land shall be free from taxation for the space of three years, unless previously built upon or otherwise improved by the purchasers or their assigns; and upon the expiration of three years from the date of such sale, such lands shall be taxable to the purchasers thereof or their assigns, in the same manner and to the same extent as if deeds of the same had been executed and delivered.[4]

3. A corporation established to manage and apply a fund towards the support of a minister either by paying the same directly, in whole or in part to the minister or to the treasurer of the parish, or otherwise to the use of the parish and for their relief and benefit, is not it seems a "charitable" institution within the meaning of the third clause of section one above.[5]

[1] Stats. 1878, ch. 206.
[2] See Stats. 1869, ch. 463, § 1.
[3] Gen. Stats. ch. 11, § 5. See following sections for amendments and construction of above section.
[4] Stats. 1867, ch. 101.
[5] Trustees of Greene Foundation, 12 Cush. 59.

4. A dwelling-house built by the corporation of Harvard College, one of the institutions included in the third clause of section one above, on land of the corporation within the college yard and leased to one of the professors, to be occupied by him as a residence for himself and family at an annual rent, is not exempt from taxation. But it would be otherwise if the building had been built for one of the professors or officers of the college, and had been occupied by him with the permission of the college and without having any estate therein, or paying any rent therefor.[1]

5. The fifth section of chapter eleven of the General Statutes (section one above) is hereby so far amended in the sixth and seventh clauses, that the tools of a mechanic necessary for carrying on his business are exempted from taxation only to an amount not exceeding three hundred dollars in value; and only such houses of religious worship are exempted from taxation as are owned by a religious society or held in trust for the use of religious organizations.[2]

6. Land taken for public uses is exempt from taxation; that is, where a public duty is imposed upon those taking it or they are charged with a public trust. Under this exemption is included land taken by a railroad company under its location and the buildings and structures erected thereon if they are reasonably necessary to its proper and convenient use as a railroad.[3] But land taken or purchased by a railroad company outside of the limits of its location even for depot or station purposes is not exempt.[4] The limits of its location will be determined by its charter, but it is generally in this state five rods in width. Nor is the property of gas-light companies exempt.[5] But land purchased in fee or otherwise taken by a city by authority of the legislature for the purpose of supplying the city with pure water and used for that purpose only is exempt.[6]

7. All plantations of timber trees in this commonwealth upon land (not at the time of said planting woodland or sprout-land, and not having been such within five years previously), the actual value of which at the time of planting does not exceed fifteen dollars per acre, of any of the following kinds, to wit: chestnut, hickory, white ash, white oak, sugar maple, European larch and white pine, in number not less than two thousand trees to the acre,

---

[1] Pierce v. Cambridge, 2 Cush. 611.

[2] Stats. 1865, ch. 206.

[3] Worcester v. Western R. R. Co., 4 Met. 564; Boston & Maine R. R. Co. v. Cambridge, 8 Cush. 237.

[4] Gen. Stats. ch. 63, § 20.

[5] Commonwealth v. Lowell Gas Light Co., 12 Allen, 75–77.

[6] Wayland v. County Commissioners, 4 Gray, 500.

shall together with the land upon which the same are situated be exempt from taxation for a period of ten years from and after said trees shall have grown in height four feet on the average subsequently to such planting : *provided*, that said exemption shall not extend beyond such time as said land shall be devoted exclusively to the growth of said trees ; and *provided, further*, that the owner or owners of such plantations shall appear before the board of assessors in the towns where the same are located and prove to the satisfaction of such board the herein mentioned conditions.[1]

8. Any town, for the term of ten years next after May 4, 1872, may exempt from taxation for any purpose whatsoever all the machinery, buildings, real estate, and all other property owned by any individual or individuals, corporation or corporations, organized under any law of this state, and used exclusively in the business of manufacturing beet sugar : *provided*, that this exemption from taxation shall not apply to lands upon which beets are raised for the purpose of manufacture.[2]

9. It shall be the duty of the assessors of each city and town in each year to enter upon the valuation list of their respective city or town in the appropriate columns after the enumeration of the taxable persons and estates therein contained a statement and description of all the property and estate and the fair ratable value thereof situate in such city or town or which would be taxable there but for the provisions of the third, seventh, and ninth divisions of section five of chapter eleven of the General Statutes, with the names of the persons or corporations owning the same, and the purpose for which it is used, which are exempted from taxation by the foregoing provisions of law, with a reference to the law by which such exemption is allowed.

10. The assessors of each city or town shall, on or before the first day of October in each year, make and forward to the tax commissioner a statement showing the whole amount of property enumerated in the first section, and

[1] Stats. 1878, ch. 131.　　　[2] Stats. 1872, ch. 327.

the amount in each class, and stating separately the aggregate amount belonging to each of the four classes embraced in the third division of the fifth section of chapter eleven of the General Statutes.[1]

---

[1] Stats. 1874, ch. 227.

## CHAPTER XIII.

### TAXES UPON CERTAIN CORPORATIONS.

1. The tax commissioner shall annually, on or before the twentieth day of June in each year, cause to be forwarded to the assessors of every city and town in this commonwealth a list of all Massachusetts corporations known to him to be taxable on the first day of May next preceding said twentieth day of June under chapter two hundred and eighty-three of the acts of the year eighteen hundred and sixty-five ; and such other information in his possession, as in his judgment will assist the assessors of the cities and towns in the assessment of taxes.[1]

2. All the shares of stock in banks, whether of issue or not, existing by authority of the United States, or of this commonwealth, and located within this commonwealth, including shares in the capital stock of the Mercantile Savings Institution in the city of Boston, shall be assessed to the owners thereof in the cities or towns where such banks are located, and not elsewhere, in the assessment of all state, county, and town taxes imposed and levied in such place by the authority of law, whether such owner is a resident of said city or town or not, at the fair cash value of such shares on the first day of May of the year in which the tax shall be assessed, first deducting therefrom the proportionate part of the value of the real estate belonging to the bank, at the same rate, and no greater, than that at which other moneyed capital in the hands of citizens and subject to taxation is by law assessed. And the persons or corporations who appear from the records of the

---

[1] Stats. 1867, ch. 188, § 2.

banks to be the owners of shares at the close of the business day next preceding the first day of May in each year, shall be taken and deemed to be the owners thereof for the purposes of this section.

3. It shall be the duty of every such bank or other corporation to pay to the collector or other person authorized to collect the taxes of the city or town in which such bank or other corporation is located, at the time in each year when other taxes assessed in the said city or town become due, the amount of the tax so assessed in such year upon the shares in such bank or other corporation. If such tax shall not be so paid, the said bank or other corporation shall be liable for the same ; and the said tax, with interest thereon at the rate of twelve per centum per annum from the day when the tax became due, may be recovered in an action of contract brought by the treasurer of such city or town.

4. The shares of such banks or other corporations shall be subject to the tax paid thereon by the corporation or the officers thereof, and the corporation and the officers thereof shall have a lien on all the shares in such bank or other corporation, and on all the rights and property of the shareholders in the corporate property for the payment of said taxes.

5. Assessors of cities and towns in which any national bank or banking association is located, for the purpose of ascertaining the rate at which taxes shall be assessed, shall omit from the valuation upon which the rate is to be based the value of all shares held by non-residents of said cities and towns, and no tax of any city or town shall be invalidated by reason of any excess of the amount thereof over the amount to be raised in consequence of the provisions of this act.

6. It shall be the duty of the cashier of every such bank to make and deliver to the assessors of the city or town in which such bank is located, on or before the tenth day of May in each year, a statement verified by the oath of such cashier showing the name of each shareholder, with his

residence and the number of shares belonging to him at the close of the business day next preceding the first day of May, as the same then appeared on the books of said bank. In case the cashier shall fail to make such statement, the assessors of the city or town in which the bank is located shall forthwith, upon such failure, proceed to obtain a list of shareholders, with the residence of and number of shares belonging to each.

In either case the assessors of each city and town shall, immediately upon obtaining such list or statement, transmit to the tax commissioner a true copy of the same, and shall further, by notice in writing, inform said commissioner of the rate per centum upon the valuation of the city or town of the total tax in such city or town for the year, immediately upon the ascertainment thereof, and also of the amount assessed upon the shares of each bank located therein, under the provisions of this act.

7. Said commissioner shall thereupon, as soon as may be, determine from the returns provided for by section five of this act, and otherwise, the proportionate amount of the tax so assessed upon the shares in each of said banks which has been assessed upon shares which according to the provisions of chapter eleven of the General Statutes would not be taxable in said city or town, which amounts, as finally determined under the provisions of this act, shall be a charge to said city or town as an offset against any payments to be made from the treasurer of the commonwealth to said city or town.

8. Said commissioner shall, in like manner, determine the proportionate amount of tax so assessed upon shares in each of said banks, which, according to the provisions of chapter eleven of the General Statutes, would be taxable in each city or town in this commonwealth other than that in which the bank is located, which amounts, as finally determined under the provisions of this act, shall become a credit to such city or town.

9. Said commissioner shall, by written or printed notice, delivered at the assessors' office or sent by mail, inform the

assessors of each city or town affected thereby of the aggregate amount of charges and credits against and in favor of such city or town under the seventh and eighth sections of this act, as determined by him, forthwith, upon the determination thereof. From this determination an appeal may be made by said assessors, within ten days from the date of said notice, to the board of appeal created under the thirteenth section of the two hundred and eighty-third chapter of the acts of the year eighteen hundred and sixty-five, which board shall hear such appeal, decide the matter in question, and notify said commissioner and the party appealing thereof, and their decision shall be final.

10. Said commissioner shall, at the expiration of ten days after notice given, as provided in section nine, or upon being informed of the decision of the board of appeal, if an appeal is made, certify to the treasurer and receiver-general the aggregate amount of charges mentioned in section seven against each city and town in the commonwealth, and also the aggregate of credits mentioned in the eighth section in favor of each city or town, as finally determined under the provisions of sections seven, eight, and nine, and the treasurer shall thereupon withhold out of any sums of money which are or may become payable out of the state treasury to any city or town against which a charge is certified, the amount so certified; and shall allow or pay over to each city or town in favor of which a credit is certified the amount so certified.

11. In the adjustment and determination of amounts due under the provisions of this act, an allowance of one per centum upon the amount assessed and collected under this act shall be made for the expenses of assessing and collecting the same, and no city or town shall be entitled to any allowance of credits or payments under this act, or under the two hundred and eighty-third chapter of the acts of the year eighteen hundred and sixty-five, in any year, until the assessors thereof shall have complied with the requirements of this act.

12. Chapter three hundred and twenty-one of the acts of the year eighteen hundred and seventy-two is repealed, but this repeal shall not revive any former acts by said act repealed, or defeat any rights which have already accrued, and no bank, the shares in which are made taxable by this act, shall be subject to taxation under the provisions of chapter two hundred and eighty-three of the acts of the year eighteen hundred and sixty-five, and the acts in addition thereto, nor shall the shareholders be taxable for state, county, or town purposes, except under the provisions of this act in respect to their shares therein.

13. The amount actually paid into the treasury of the commonwealth in each year, under the provisions of this act, on account of shares in banks or banking associations which on the first day of May are the absolute property of any savings bank or institution for savings subject to taxation under the provisions of chapter two hundred and twenty-four of the acts of the year eighteen hundred and sixty-two, and acts in amendment thereof, or of any insurance corporation which is subject to taxation under the provisions of chapter two hundred and eighty-three of the acts of the year eighteen hundred and sixty-five, and acts in amendment thereof, shall be deducted from the tax payable under the provisions of said acts by such savings bank, institution for savings or insurance corporation at the next payment to the commonwealth after the assessment of bank shares as herein provided. The tax commissioner may require a statement of all such shares so owned by any such savings bank, institution for savings or insurance corporation, to be made in a form approved by him, and signed and sworn to by the treasurer or like financial officer thereof. He shall, from such statement and other evidence, and subject to appeal by such corporation, as herein provided in similar cases, determine the amounts to be deducted, and certify the same to the treasurer of the commonwealth upon the final determination thereof.

14. The tax commissioner shall, as soon as may be after the first Monday in December in each year, certify to the

treasurer the amount assessed and collected for that year, in respect of shares in such banks or other corporations owned absolutely by any society, district or institution of any of the classes specified in the third, fourth, and ninth divisions of section five of chapter eleven of the General Statutes, and the treasurer shall thereupon pay over such amounts to the corporations owning such shares.

15. It shall be the duty of the assessors of each city or town, upon request of any person resident in such city or town, who is the owner of any shares in such banks or other corporations which, under the provisions of the tenth and thirteenth divisions of section five of chapter eleven of the General Statutes would be entitled to exemption from taxation, to give such owner a certificate setting forth such fact, and it shall be the duty of the treasurer of such city or town, upon request therefor and the deposit with him of such certificate, to pay over to such owner the amount so collected in respect of such shares, immediately, upon the allowance of the amount which shall be made to such city or town under the provisions of this act.

16. Shares in such banks and other corporations shall be included in the returns required to be made by the provisions of section two of chapter two hundred and eighty-three of the acts of the year eighteen hundred and sixty-five.

17. Whenever it shall be made to appear to the tax commissioner by certificate of the assessors or a majority of them or other satisfactory evidence, that any tax assessed in accordance with the provisions of the seventh section of chapter three hundred and twenty-one of the acts of the year eighteen hundred and seventy-two, which has been paid over or accounted for to the state treasury in conformity with said act, has been assessed in respect to shares in banks upon which the owners have also been specifically taxed for the said year in the city or town in which such owner resides, for state, county, and town purposes, the tax commissioner shall, within a reasonable time thereafter, certify to the treasurer and receiver-general

the name of the person who appears to be the owner of such shares, and the amount so paid or credited in each case, and the treasurer shall thereupon pay over to said person such amount.[1]

---

[1] Stats. 1873, ch. 315, §§ 1–16.

# CHAPTER XIV.

## WHERE POLLS AND PROPERTY SHALL BE ASSESSED.

1. THE poll tax shall be assessed upon each taxable person, in the place where he is an inhabitant on the first day of May in each year, except in cases otherwise provided for by law. The poll tax of minors liable to taxation shall be assessed to, and in the places of the residence of, the parents, masters, or guardians, having control of the persons of such minors; but if a minor has no parent, master, or guardian, within this state, he shall be personally taxed for his poll, as if he were of full age. The poll tax of every other person under guardianship shall be assessed to his guardian in the place where the guardian is taxed for his own poll.[1]

2. It is often a question of great nicety to determine of what place a person is an inhabitant, because, as Chief Justice Shaw says: "It may often occur that the evidence of facts tending to establish the domicile in one place would be entirely conclusive, were it not for the existence of facts and circumstances of a still more conclusive and decisive character which fix it beyond question in another."[2] But there are certain well-established principles or rules which will aid in determining this question. First, "every person has a domicile somewhere, and no person can have more than one domicile at the same time for one and the same purpose." Second, "a man retains his domicile of origin till he changes it by acquiring another, and so each successive domicile continues until changed by acquiring another."[3] It is equally well settled that in order to change the domicile the fact and intent must concur, — neither alone is sufficient, — by which it must be intended that there needs to be a change of residence, with an intention to remain in the new place of residence an indefinite time and without the intention of returning to the former domicile at any particular period or when any particular purpose is accom-

[1] Gen. Stats. ch. 11, § 6.
[2] Thorndike v. City of Boston, 1 Met. 242.
[3] Opinion of the judges of the Supreme Judicial Court of Massachusetts, 5 Met. 587; Otis v. City of Boston, 12 Cush. 50.

plished.[1] But this must be taken with a reasonable limitation as to the time occupied in accomplishing the particular purpose. It often happens in cases of divided residence, that the circumstances of each are so nearly balanced that the *intention* of the party to consider the one or the other to be his domicile will determine it to be so.[2] The place where a corporation is an inhabitant is determined in most cases by its act of incorporation, which fixes its location. And in corporations organized under the general law, the location must be fixed in the articles of association.

3. The poll tax of minors who are in the service of a manufacturing corporation and receiving salaries cannot legally be assessed to such corporation.[3]

4. A taxable person in a city or town on the first day of May who, when inquired of by the assessors thereof, refuses to state where he considers his legal residence to be, shall for the purpose of taxation be deemed an inhabitant of such place. If when so inquired of he designates another place as his legal residence, said assessors shall notify the assessors of such place, who, upon receiving the notice, shall tax such person as an inhabitant of their city or town. But such person shall not be exempt from the payment of a tax legally assessed upon him in the city or town of his legal domicile.

5. Taxes on real estate shall be assessed in the city or town where the estate lies, to the person who is either the owner or in possession thereof on the first day of May. Mortgagors of real estate shall, for the purposes of taxation, be deemed owners until the mortgagee takes possession, after which the mortgagee shall be deemed the owner.[4]

6. The real estate of banks and manufacturing corporations is to be taxed to them in the place where it is situated.[5]

7. When a tenant paying rent for real estate is taxed therefor, he may retain out of his rent the taxes paid by

---

[1] Bulkley *v.* Williamstown, 3 Gray, 495; Holmes *v.* Greene, 7 Gray, 300.

[2] Trustees of Greene Foundation *v.* City of Boston, 12 Cush. 60.

[3] Boston & Sandwich Glass Co. *v.* City of Boston, 4 Met. 181.

[4] Gen. Stats. ch. 11, §§ 7, 8.

[5] Tremont Bank *v.* Boston, 1 Cush. 142; Dunnell Manufacturing Corporation *v.* Pawtucket, 7 Gray, 277.

him, or may recover the same in an action against his landlord, unless there is an agreement to the contrary.

8. The undivided real estate of a deceased person may be assessed to his heirs or devisees without designating any of them by name, until they have given notice to the assessors of the division of the estate and the names of the several heirs or devisees ; and each heir or devisee shall be liable for the whole of such tax, and when paid by him he may recover of the other heirs or devisees their respective portions thereof.

9. The real estate of a person deceased, the right or title to which is doubtful or unascertained by reason of litigation concerning the will of the deceased or the validity thereof, may be assessed in general terms to the estate of the deceased ; and said tax shall constitute a lien upon the land so assessed, and may be enforced by the sale of the same or a part thereof, as provided for enforcing other liens for taxes on real estate.

10. All personal estate within or without this state shall be assessed to the owner in the city or town where he is an inhabitant on the first day of May, except as follows : [1] —

The interest of an inhabitant of this commonwealth, as a partner, in the property of a firm established and carrying on business in another state is taxable here.[2] And where a life-interest in personal property terminates at any time after the first day of May, the life-tenant or his representative is liable for the whole tax.[3]

First. All goods, wares, merchandise, and other stock in trade (except ships or vessels owned by a copartnership), including stock employed in the business of manufacturing or of the mechanic arts, in cities or towns within the state, other than where the owners reside, whether such owners reside within or without this state, shall be taxed in those places where the owners hire or occupy manufactories, stores, shops, or wharves, whether such

[1] Gen. Stats. ch. 11, §§ 9–12.
[2] Bemis *v.* Aldermen of Boston, 14 Allen, 366.
[3] Holmes *v.* Taber, 9 Allen, 246.

property is within said places or elsewhere on the first day of May of the year when the tax is made.[1]

It makes no difference that the property belongs to a firm one of whose partners resides in the town where the property is situated. To constitute an occupation, there must be an actual possession, use, and efficient control of the premises; such an occupation as one who owns or hires would ordinarily have.[2] This clause and the third below do not apply to corporations chartered by this state, as the stockholders are liable to taxation upon their shares in the towns where they dwell, but it is applicable to property owned by a foreign corporation.[3]

Second. All machinery employed in any branch of manufactures, and belonging to a person or corporation, shall be assessed where such machinery is situated or employed; and, in assessing the stockholders for their shares in any manufacturing corporation, there shall first be deducted from the value thereof the value of the machinery and real estate belonging to such corporation.[4]

This clause does not apply to foreign corporations.[5]

Third. Horses, mules, neat cattle, sheep, and swine, kept throughout the year in places other than those where the owners reside, whether such owners reside within or without this state, and horses employed in stages or other vehicles for the transportation of passengers for hire, shall be assessed to the owners in the places where they are kept.

Fourth. Personal property belonging to persons under guardianship shall be assessed to the guardian in the place where the ward is an inhabitant, unless the ward resides and has his home without the state, in which case it shall be taxed to the guardian in the place where he is an inhabitant.[6]

The same rules would seem to be applicable in determining the place where a ward is an inhabitant as in the case of any other citizen.[7]

---

[1] Gen. Stats. ch. 11, § 12, cl. 1.
[2] Lee v. Templeton, 6 Gray, 579.
[3] Middlesex R.R. Co. v. Charlestown, 8 Allen, 333; Blackstone Manuf. Co. v. Blackstone, 13 Gray, 488.
[4] Gen. Stats. ch. 11, § 12, cl. 2.
[5] Dwight v. Mayor, &c., of Boston, 12 Allen, 316.
[6] Gen. Stats. ch. 11, § 12, cl. 3, 4.
[7] Kirkland v. Whately, 4 Allen, 462.

Fifth. Personal property held in trust by an executor, administrator, or trustee, the income of which is payable to another person, shall be assessed to the executor, administrator, or trustee, in the place where such other person resides, if within the state, and if he resides out of the state, it shall be assessed in the place where the executor, administrator, or trustee resides, and if there are two or more executors, administrators, or trustees, residing in different places, the property shall be assessed to them in equal portions in such places, and the tax thereon shall be paid out of said income. If the executor, administrator, or trustee is not an inhabitant of this state, it shall be assessed to the person to whom the income is payable, in the place where he resides.

Whenever personal property belonging to two or more persons under guardianship, or personal property held in trust by an executor, administrator, or trustee, the income of which is payable to two or more persons, or personal property placed in the hands of a corporation or individual as an accumulating fund for the future benefit of two or more heirs or other persons, shall be assessed under section twelve of chapter eleven of the General Statutes (this section), by the assessors of any city or town in whole or in part, they shall, upon being requested in writing within the time specified by them for the bringing in of lists under section twenty-two of said chapter, and being therein informed of the names, domiciles, and proportionate shares of such wards, cestuis que trust, heirs, or other persons, make separate assessments in such manner as to distinguish how much of such personal property is assessed in respect to each. Should any of said several assessments be illegally made, an action at law shall lie to recover back the taxes paid thereon, in the same manner as in other cases of illegal assessment.[1]

Sixth. Personal property placed in the hands of a corporation or individual as an accumulating fund for the future benefit of heirs or other persons shall be assessed to such heirs or persons, if within the state, otherwise to the person so placing it, or his executors or administrators until a trustee is appointed to take charge of such property, or the income thereof.[2]

[1] Stats. 1878, ch. 189.
[2] And after the appointment of a    trustee, to the trustee in the place of his residence to the extent of the por-

Whenever personal property placed in the hands of a corporation or an individual as an accumulating fund for the future benefit of heirs or other persons has been duly assessed to such heirs or persons according to the provisions of this clause six, and the persons so taxed neglect to pay the tax for one year after it has been committed to the collector, the collector may, in his own name, maintain an action of contract therefor against said trustee, in like manner as for his own debt; and the amount thereof paid by said trustee may be allowed in his account as said trustee.[1]

Seventh. The personal estate of deceased persons shall be assessed in the place where the deceased last dwelt. After the appointment of an executor or administrator, it shall be assessed to such executor or administrator until he gives notice to the assessors that the estate has been distributed and paid over to the parties interested therein. Before such appointment, it shall be assessed in general terms to the estate of the deceased, and the executor or administrator subsequently appointed shall be liable for the tax so assessed in like manner as though assessed to him.[2]

A tax is not lawfully assessed to the " estate of " a deceased person after the date of the appointment of the administrator.[8]

Personal property held by an executor or administrator shall be taxable according to the provisions of this seventh clause for the space of three years after the appointment of such executor or administrator, unless the same has been distributed and notice of such distribution has been given to the assessor, stating the name, residence, and amount paid to the several parties interested in the estate who are residents of the commonwealth. After three years from the date of such appointment, such property shall be assessed according to the provisions of the fifth clause of section twelve of said chapter eleven, fifth clause on preceding page, whether the same has been distributed or not.

After personal property shall have been legally assessed in any city or town to an executor, administrator, or trustee, an amount not less than that last assessed by the assessors of such city or town in respect of such property shall be deemed to be the sum assessable, unless a true list of such property is brought in to the assessors, in

tion in his hands belonging to beneficiaries who are non-residents. Davis v. Macy, 124 Mass. 193.

[1] Stats. 1878, ch. 189.
[2] Gen. Stats. ch. 11, § 12, cls. 5–7.
[8] Wood v. Torrey, 97 Mass. 321.

accordance with the provisions of section twenty-two of chapter eleven of the General Statutes.[1]

11. Property held by a religious society as a ministerial fund shall be assessed to the treasurer of the society. If such property consists of real estate, it shall be taxed in the town where it lies; if it consists of personal property, it shall be taxed in the town where such society usually hold their meetings.

12. Personal property mortgaged or pledged shall, for the purposes of taxation, be deemed the property of the party who has the possession.[2]

This section applies only to corporeal, visible, and tangible property of which either party may take open possession; and not of incorporeal hereditaments or rights, which are incapable of such possession — and therefore not to public stocks or securities.[3]

13. Partners in mercantile or other business, whether residing in the same or different places, may be jointly taxed under their partnership name in the place where their business is carried on, for all the personal property employed in such business, except ships or vessels. If they have places of business in two or more towns, they shall be taxed in each of such places for the proportion of property employed therein. When so jointly taxed, each partner shall be liable for the whole tax.[4]

It seems that the terms "place of business" must be understood as a place where business is carried on by the tax-payer under his own control and on his own account.[5]

Ships or vessels owned by a copartnership shall be assessed to the several partners in their places of residence proportionally to their interest therein, if they reside within the commonwealth. But the interest of the several partners who reside without the commonwealth shall be assessed in the place where their business is carried on.[6]

14. When any person liable to be taxed for personal property shall have changed his domicile, it shall be the duty of the assessors of the city or town where he resides to require forthwith of the

---

[1] Stats. 1878, ch. 189.
[2] Gen. Stats. ch. 11, §§ 13, 14.
[3] Waltham Bank v. Waltham, 10 Met. 340; Hall v. Commissioners, 10 Allen, 100.
[4] Gen. Stats. ch. 11, § 15.
[5] Little v. Cambridge, 9 Cush. 301.
[6] Stats. 1870, ch. 328.

assessors of the city or town where such person was last taxed as an inhabitant, such written statement of any facts within their knowledge as will assist in determining the value of the personal estate of such person, and also the amount he was last assessed in such city or town ; and such information shall be furnished by the assessors of the city or town where he was last taxed or assessed.

15. When the assessors of any city or town shall have received notice from the assessors of any other city or town within the commonwealth, of the amount at which a person having been an inhabitant thereof was last taxed on personal property, such notice shall be filed in their office, subject to public inspection; and they shall not assess such person upon any less amount of personal estate than he was last assessed, until he shall have brought into such assessors a list of his personal estate, in accordance with the provisions of the twenty-second and twenty-third sections of the eleventh chapter of the General Statutes.[1]

16. Whenever the assessors of any city or town in this commonwealth have assessed a tax upon real estate, and such real estate has been subsequently divided by sale, mortgage, or otherwise, by the owner or owners thereof, or upon a petition for partition, and record of such division has been made in the registry of deeds for the county in which such real estate is situated, it shall be the duty of the assessors at any time before said real estate has been sold for non-payment of taxes, upon the written request of the owner or mortgagee of any portion thereof, to apportion said tax and the costs and interest accrued thereon, upon the several parcels into which said real estate has been divided in proportion to the value of each parcel thereof, and only the portion of said tax, interest, and costs, so apportioned upon any such parcel, shall thereafter continue to be a lien upon it, and no one of such owners or mortgagees shall thereafter be liable for the tax so apportioned upon any parcel not owned in whole or in part by him at the time of such apportionment.

17. Notice of the request and of the time appointed for such apportionment shall be sent by mail by the assessors to all persons interested in said real estate whose addresses are known to them.

[1] Stats. 1866, ch. 170, §§ 1, 2.

18. Any person aggrieved by any action of the assessors under this act may, within seven days thereafter, appeal to the board to which appeal may be made in case of an over-assessment, and the action of said board upon such appeal shall be final.[1]

19. All reservoirs of water, with the dams connected therewith and the lands under the same, used to maintain a uniform supply of water for mill-power, shall be assessed for the purposes of taxation in the town or towns where located, at a valuation not exceeding a fair valuation of land of like quality in the immediate vicinity.[2] This statute is unconstitutional and void.[3]

All laws which direct and authorize towns to vote sums for the repairs of highways and town-ways, to be paid in labor and materials, and which provide for the assessment and collection thereof, are repealed.[4]

[1] Stats. 1878, ch. 182.
[2] Stats. 1872, ch. 306.
[3] Cheshire v. County Commissioners, 118 Mass. 386.
[4] Stats. 1871, ch. 298.

## CHAPTER XV.

### COLLECTION OF TAXES.

1. Towns may choose suitable persons to be collectors of taxes therein. If the persons chosen refuse to serve, or if no person is elected or appointed, the constables of the town shall be the collectors of taxes.[1]

2. A selectman and assessor of a town may legally be chosen collector of taxes also.[2] The refusal to accept the office need not appear of record. And no further oath is required of a constable, acting as collector, if he has been duly sworn as constable.[3]

3. Every collector shall give bond to the town, in such sum as the selectmen require, and with sureties to their satisfaction, for the faithful discharge of the duties of his office.[4]

4. When a collector fails to give the bond required by the preceding section, the selectmen may appoint another collector in the manner and subject to the provisions set forth in ch. 18, § 42, Gen. Stats.[5]

5. The foregoing provisions of the statute are directory as to the manner of giving bonds by one appointed collector. And the collector may properly refuse to give a bond in any greater sum than the selectmen require. But if a collector voluntarily gives a bond to the town to secure his faithful discharge of the duties of the office of collector, and the same is accepted, it is a good and valid bond without any further evidence of the approval by the selectmen, of the sum or the sureties,[6] but the bond should be given to the town.[7]

6. The removal of the collector from office does not discharge him from liabilities that have already attached for defaults in the duties of his office. In all cases where, by reason of his remissness in enforcing the collections, the tax has been uncollected, and from a

---

[1] Gen. Stats. ch. 18, § 71.
[2] Howard v. Proctor, 7 Gray, 128.
[3] Hays v. Drake, 6 Gray, 387.
[4] Gen. Stats. ch. 18, § 72.
[5] Stats. 1865, ch. 234, § 1.
[6] Wendell v. Fleming, 8 Gray, 613.
[7] Stevens v. Hay, 6 Cush. 229.

change of circumstances is unavailable in the hands of his successor, he will be chargeable therewith.[1]

7. Defects in a warrant or tax list will not excuse a collector from paying over money to the town which he has collected without objection on the part of the tax-payers. He can only avail himself of such defects as have prevented him from performing his duty; and the defects in the warrant or tax list might be a good excuse for not executing the warrant.[2] Nor is a collector excused from paying over money to the town by reason of its being stolen from him without any default on his part.[3]

8. Any town, at a meeting notified for that purpose, may authorize their collector to use all means of collecting the taxes which a town treasurer when appointed collector may use.[4]

9. Every collector of taxes, constable, sheriff, or deputy sheriff, receiving a tax list and warrant from the assessors, shall proceed to collect the taxes therein mentioned, according to the warrant.[5]

If the warrant is good upon its face, it will protect the collector acting under it notwithstanding irregularity in the meetings or votes by which the taxes were authorized.[6]

10. The collector shall, unless removed from office as hereinafter provided, complete the collection of taxes committed to him, although his term of office expires before such completion.

11. Collectors shall, before distraining the goods of a person for his tax, demand payment thereof from such person, either personally or at his usual place of abode, if to be found within their precincts.

12. When the credit of a person taxed is considered doubtful by the assessors, they may (by a special warrant)[7] order the collector forthwith to compel payment by distress or imprisonment, whether the tax is made payable immediately, at a future day, by instalments, or otherwise.

13. If a person claims the benefit of an abatement, he

---

[1] Colerain v. Bell, 9 Met. 499.
[2] Sandwich v. Fish, 2 Gray, 298.
[3] Hancock v. Hazard, 12 Cush. 112.
[4] Gen. Stats. ch. 18, § 73.
[5] Gen. Stats. ch. 12, § 1.
[6] Howard v. Proctor, 7 Gray, 128.
[7] Stats. 1874, ch. 238.

shall exhibit to the collector demanding his taxes a certificate of such abatement, from the assessors or other proper officer, as provided in chapter eleven; and shall be liable to pay all costs and officers' fees incurred before exhibiting such certificate.

14. If, in the assessors' lists or in their warrant and list committed to the collectors, there is an error in the name of a person taxed, the tax assessed to him may be collected of the person intended to be taxed, if he is taxable and can be identified by the assessors.[1]

This section applies to those cases where the error in the name exists as well in the valuation list as in the assessors' warrant to the collector; and it covers all cases of error in the name, and seems intended to apply to a case where the name is mistaken by omitting, as well as by adding or by misnaming.[2]

15. If a person refuses or neglects to pay his tax, the collector shall levy the same by distress or seizure and sale of his goods, including any share or interest he may have as a stockholder in a corporation incorporated under authority of this commonwealth, and excepting the following goods : —

The tools or implements necessary for his trade or occupation; beasts of the plough necessary for the cultivation of his improved lands; military arms, utensils for housekeeping necessary for upholding life, and bedding and apparel necessary for himself and family.[3]

But the distress cannot be made after the death of the person upon whom the tax is assessed.[4]

16. The collector shall keep the goods distrained, at the expense of the owner, for four days at least, and shall, within seven days after the seizure, sell the same by public auction, for payment of the tax and charges of keeping and sale, having given notice of the sale by posting up a notification thereof in some public place in the city or town, forty-eight hours at least before the sale.[5]

---

[1] Gen. Stats. ch. 12, §§ 2–6.
[2] Tyler *v.* Hardwich, 6 Met. 474, Shaw, C. J.
[3] Gen. Stats. ch. 12, § 7.
[4] Wilson *v.* Shearer, 9 Met. 504.
[5] Gen. Stats. ch. 12, § 8.

17. A sale made after seven days is illegal.[1] The notice may be given before the expiration of four days, a proper time for sale being fixed upon.[2] The notice need not state the name of the person whose property is seized, nor the amount of the tax, nor describe the property.[2]

18. The collector may once adjourn such sale for a time not exceeding three days : he shall forthwith give notice of such adjournment, by posting a notification at the place of sale.

19. The seizure of a share or other interest in a corporation may be made by leaving with any officer of the corporation, with whom a copy of a writ may by law be left when the share of a stockholder is attached on mesne process, an attested copy of the warrant, with a certificate thereon, under the hand of the collector, setting forth the tax which the stockholder is to pay, and that, upon his neglect or refusal to pay, the collector has seized such share or interest.

20. The sale of such share or interest shall be made in the manner prescribed by law for the sale of goods by collectors of taxes in like cases, and also subject to the provisions of sections forty-six and forty-seven of chapter one hundred and thirty-three, respecting sales on executions.

21. If the distress or seizure is sold for more than the tax and charges of keeping and sale, the collector shall return the surplus to the owner, upon demand, with an account in writing of the sale and charges.[3]

22. A collector is justified in adding to these charges a commission or percentage on the amount of the tax for his own compensation.[4] And see, as to collectors' fees, section eighty-two of this chapter.

23. If a person refuses or neglects for fourteen days after demand to pay his tax, and the collector cannot find sufficient goods upon which it may be levied, he may take

---

[1] Noyes, Jr. v. Haverhill, 11 Cush. 338.

[2] Barnard v. Graves, 13 Met. 94.

[3] Gen. Stats. ch. 12, §§ 9–12.

[4] Howard v. Proctor, 7 Gray, 132.

the body of such person and commit him to prison, there to remain until he pays the tax and charges of commitment and imprisonment, or is discharged by order of law.[1]

24. This applies to non-residents as well as residents.[2] But the collector has no right to take the body for non-payment of taxes, if sufficient property is shown to him upon which to levy; although fourteen days have elapsed since a demand of payment.[3]

25. When the collector commits a person to prison, he shall give the keeper thereof an attested copy of the warrant, with a certificate thereon, under the hand of the collector, setting forth the sum which such person is to pay as his tax, with the cost of taking and committing him, and that upon his having neglected payment for fourteen days, or otherwise, as the case may be, and for want of goods whereof to make distress, he has taken his body.

26. When a person committed to prison for the non-payment of taxes is unable to pay the same, he shall be entitled to his discharge in like manner as persons committed on execution. The notice required in such case to be given to the creditor may be given to either of the assessors or the collector by whom the party was committed. And the assessors and collector, or any of them, may appear and do all things which a creditor might do in case of arrest on execution.[4]

For further provision as to discharge of persons committed to prison, see section eighty-one of this chapter.

27. If such person is discharged, the collector shall be liable to pay the tax with the charges of imprisonment, unless he arrested and committed the party within one year after the tax was committed to him to collect, or unless he is exonerated therefrom by the city, town, or parish to which the tax is due.[5]

But this does not render the collector liable to pay for the support

[1] Gen. Stats. ch. 12, § 13.
[2] Snow v. Clark, 9 Gray, 192.
[3] Lothrop v. Ide, 13 Gray, 93.
[4] Gen. Stats. ch. 12, §§ 14, 15.
[5] Gen. Stats. ch. 12, § 16.

of the person committed while in jail, although the town may have paid it.[1]

28. A collector when resisted or impeded in the exercise of his office may require any suitable person to aid him therein; and, if such person refuses to render such aid, he shall forfeit a sum not exceeding ten dollars.

29. When a person, after the assessment of a tax upon him, removes out of the precinct of the collector without paying his tax, the collector may demand payment thereof wherever such person is found; and in default of payment the collector may forthwith proceed to collect the tax by making a distress, or by commitment of such person to the prison of the county where he is found; or the collector may issue his warrant to the sheriff of the county or his deputy, or to any constable of the place, where such person is found, directing them to distrain the property or take the body of such person, and to proceed therein in like manner as required of collectors in like cases.[2]

30. To constitute "removal," it is not necessary to change one's domicile, technically speaking, but a change of place of residence for the term of six months, although under the expectation and purpose of returning at the expiration of that time, is a "removal."[3]

31. When a person taxed removes as aforesaid, or dies, or neglects to pay his tax for one year after it is committed to the collector, or, being an unmarried woman, marries before payment of the tax, the collector may, in his own name, maintain an action of contract therefor, in like manner as for his own debt; and he may for that purpose in like manner have a process of foreign attachment against any trustee of such person.[4]

It would be well that the warrant of the collector authorized by this section should recite the facts which are necessary to authorize the collector to issue it because it would then furnish the constable with conclusive evidence for his protection in acting under it. But the recital is not necessary to the validity of the warrant.[5]

---

[1] Townsend v. Walcutt, 3 Met. 152.
[2] Gen. Stats. ch. 12, §§ 17, 18.
[3] Houghton v. Davenport, 23 Pick. 240.
[4] Gen. Stats. ch. 12, § 19.
[5] Cheever v. Merritt, 5 Allen, 565.

32. When a tax is assessed upon the personal estate of a deceased person, the collector may maintain an action of contract therefor in his own name, as for his own debt, against the executor or administrator; and, if a tax is so assessed before the appointment of an executor or administrator, he may enforce it against the estate and its representative after such appointment, in like manner as if the assessment had been made subsequently thereto.

33. When a person is taxed for real estate in his occupation, but of which he is not the owner, the collector, after demand of payment, may levy the tax by distress and sale of the cattle, sheep, horses, swine, or other stock or produce, of such estate, belonging to the owner thereof, which within nine months after such assessment is committed to him shall be found upon the premises, in the same manner as if such stock or produce were the property of the person so taxed; but such demand need not be made if the person on whom the tax is assessed resided within the precinct of the collector at the time of the assessment, and subsequently removes therefrom and remains absent three months.

Any joint tenant or tenant in common of land whose tax shall have been paid by his cotenant shall have the same right in regard to recovering back taxes illegally assessed that he would have had if the tax had been paid under a protest by him in writing.[1]

34. Taxes assessed on real estate shall constitute a lien thereon for two years after they are committed to the collector; and may with all incidental costs and expenses be levied by sale thereof, if the tax is not paid within fourteen days after a demand of payment made either upon the person taxed or upon any person occupying the estate; but the collector may sell real estate for taxes after two years have elapsed, unless the estate has been alienated (prior to the giving of the notice of such sale).[2]

35. Taxes reassessed on real estate shall constitute a lien thereon from the time they are committed to the collector, unless the estate has been alienated between the

[1] Stats. 1875, ch. 236, § 1.          [2] Stat

first and second assessments; and may be levied as provided in the preceding section.

36. If a mortgagee of real estate, situated in the place of his residence, previously to the assessment of a tax, gives written notice to the clerk of such place that he holds a mortgage thereon, with a description of the estate, the collector before proceeding to sell it for non-payment of taxes shall demand payment of said taxes of the mortgagee, as provided in section twenty-two.

37. If a mortgagee or non-resident owner of real estate, previously to the assessment of a tax, gives a written authority to some inhabitant of the place as his attorney, to pay the taxes imposed on such estate, and the authority is filed with, or recorded by, the clerk of the place, the demand of payment shall be made upon such attorney before the estate is sold; otherwise, no demand need be made of payment of taxes assessed on the real estate of non-resident owners.[1]

38. When a demand is made upon the attorney under the preceding section, the collector shall not advertise the sale of the lands, until two months from the time of such demand.

39. The affidavit of a disinterested person, or the collector, who makes a sale of land for the payment of taxes, taken before a justice of the peace and recorded by the clerk of the place where the land lies, before a sale is made, and stating the demand of payment of the tax, the person of whom, and the time and manner in which it was made, shall be competent evidence of the demand.

40. The collector shall give notice of the time and place of sale of real estate taken for taxes, by an advertisement thereof three weeks successively in some newspaper of the county where the real estate lies, if there is such newspaper, and if not, then in a newspaper printed in an adjacent county; the last publication to be at least one week before the time of sale.

41. The advertisement shall contain a substantially

[1] Gen. Stats. ch. 12, §§ 20-25.

accurate description of the several rights, lots, or divisions of the estate to be sold, the amount of the tax assessed on each, the names of all owners known to the collector, and the taxes assessed on their respective lands.[1]

42. The description should be full and satisfactory, so that the owner may know what property is to be sold and especially if the owner's name does not appear in the notice.[2] And the amount of the tax must be stated exactly.[3]

43. The collector shall, three weeks before the sale, post a notice similar to that required by the two preceding sections in some convenient and public place in his precinct, and a like notice on the premises by him advertised to be sold, if any part thereof is bounded by a street, lane, court, or highway.

44. When real estate to be sold under the provisions of this chapter is situated in a place the name of which has been changed by law within three years next preceding the sale, the collector shall in his advertisement and notices of the sale designate such place by its former and present name.

45. The affidavit of a disinterested person, taken before a justice of the peace, of the posting and publishing notifications of the sale of real estate by a collector or other officer for payment of taxes, made upon one of the original advertisements, or a copy thereof, and filed and recorded in the registry of deeds of the county or district where the land lies, within six months after the sale, shall be competent evidence of such notice.

46. If the taxes are not paid, the collector, at the time and place appointed for the sale, shall sell by public auction so much of the real estate, or the rents and profits of the whole estate for such term of time, as shall be sufficient to discharge the taxes and necessary intervening charges ; or he may at his option sell the whole or any part of the land ; and after satisfying the taxes and charges, he shall

---

[1] Gen. Stats. ch. 12, §§ 26–29.   [3] Alexander v. Pitts, 7 Cush. 503.
[2] Farnum v. Buffum, 4 Cush 266.

upon demand pay the residue of the proceeds of the sale, if any, to the owner of the estate.[1]

This section does not authorize the sale of an individual interest in land, and an advertisement of a collector of taxes, which offers for sale a certain parcel of real estate, "or such undivided portions thereof as may be necessary," invalidates a sale thereunder, although, in fact, the whole parcel is sold.[2]

As to amount of fees and as to right of town to purchase, see sections eighty-two and seventy-three of this chapter.

47. The collector may adjourn his sale from day to day not exceeding seven days in the whole ; and he shall give notice of every such adjournment by a public declaration thereof, at the time and place previously appointed for the sale.

48. The collector shall execute and deliver to the purchaser a deed of the real estate, or rents and profits sold ; which deed shall state the cause of sale, the price for which the estate or rents and profits were sold, the name of the person on whom the demand for the tax was made, the places in the city or town where the notices were posted, the newspaper in which the advertisement of such sale was published, and the place of residence of the grantee ; and, if the real estate has been sold, shall convey, subject to the right of redemption provided for in the following section, all the right and interest which the owner had therein at the time when the same was taken for his taxes. Such deed to be valid shall be recorded within thirty days from the day of sale.[3]

49. The deed of a collector, taking effect only as the execution of a statute power, should be construed with some strictness, and the description should be such as to enable the grantee to identify the land and the owner to redeem it.[4] The deed *must* state the cause of sale : it is a condition precedent to the operation of the deed. It is not enough to state that a demand for the tax was made upon the person taxed, but it must also state that payment was not made within fourteen days.[5]

---

[1] Gen. Stats. ch. 12, §§ 30–33.
[2] Wall *v.* Wall, 124 Mass. 65.
[3] Gen. Stats. ch. 12, §§ 34, 35.
[4] Hill *v.* Mowry, 6 Gray, 552.
[5] Harrington *v.* Worcester, 6 Allen, 577.

50. The owner of real estate taken or[1] sold for payment of taxes, or his heirs or assigns, may within two years from the day of (taking or[1]) sale, redeem the estate taken or[1] sold, by paying or tendering to the collector the amount of the tax for which said property was taken, with the charges and fees provided in section eleven of this act, and all intervening taxes, or to the purchaser, his heirs or assigns, the original sum and intervening taxes paid by him, and in each case with ten per cent interest, and the cost of recording the tax deed or evidence of taking, and the sum of five dollars for examination of title;[2] and when the rents and profits are sold for payment of taxes, the same may be redeemed at any time within two years in the manner provided for the redemption of rents and profits taken on execution. And in the following cases real estate so taken or[2] sold may be redeemed, by any person having such title thereto that he might have recovered the same if no such taking or[2] sale had been made, at any time within two years after he has actual notice of the sale : —

First. When no person is named in the tax list as the owner or occupant of the premises, they being taxed as belonging to persons unknown ;

Second. When the person who is named in said list is merely a tenant or occupant of the premises, and not the rightful owner thereof ;

Third. When there is any error in the name of the person intended to be taxed ;

Fourth. Mortgagees of record.[3]

51. A party in possession of land under a contract for its purchase which stipulates that during the continuance of the contract he should remain in possession has such an interest in the land as gives him a right to redeem.[4] "Mortgagees of record" include or extend to assignees of a mortgage.[5]

52. If upon reasonable search the purchaser of real estate sold for non-payment of taxes cannot be found in

---

[1] Stats. 1878, ch. 266.
[2] Stats. 1878, ch. 266.
[3] Gen. Stats. ch. 12, § 36.

[4] Rogers *v.* Rutter, 11 Gray, 413.
[5] Faxon *v.* Wallace, 98 Mass. 45.

the place of which he is described in the collector's deed as resident, the owner of the estate may redeem it as provided in the preceding section, on paying to the treasurer of the place in which it is situated the amount which he would be required to pay to the purchaser; and the affidavit of any disinterested person of the making such search, taken before a justice of the peace and filed in the registry of deeds for the district or county in which the land is situated, within ninety days from the completion of the search, shall be competent evidence of the facts therein stated.

53. Such treasurer shall receive the money and give to the person paying it a certificate of such payment, specifying the estate on which the tax was originally assessed. The certificate may be recorded in the registry of deeds, with a note of reference from such record to the collector's deed; and, when so recorded, shall have the effect to release and discharge all right and title acquired under the collector's deed. The treasurer shall hold all money received by him under the preceding section, for the use and benefit of the persons entitled thereto; and shall pay it over on reasonable demand.

54. After proceedings have been commenced for the (taking or [1]) sale of real estate for a tax assessed thereon, and before the (taking or [1]) sale is made, the holder of any mortgage thereon may pay such tax with all intervening charges and expenses; and when the owner of real estate for three months after demand has neglected to pay such a tax, and the collector has made demand therefor upon a holder of a mortgage thereon, such holder may in like manner pay such tax, charges, and expenses.

55. The holder of a mortgage, upon taking possession of real estate thereunder, shall be liable to pay all taxes due thereon and the expenses of any (taking or [1]) sale for taxes that has been commenced or taken place; to be recovered of him in an action of contract by the collector, or, when a sale has taken place, by the pur-

---

[1] Stats. 1878, ch. 266.

chaser; and upon tender by the mortgagee to the (collector or the [1]) purchaser, within the time provided for owners of real estate to make tender in section thirty-six (section fifty above) (to the collector the amount of the tax for which said property was taken, with the charges and fees provided in section eleven of this act, and all intervening taxes, or to the purchaser, his heirs or assigns, the original sum and intervening taxes paid by him, and in each case with ten per cent interest and the cost of recording the tax deed or evidence of taking, and the sum of five dollars for examination of title [1]), (the city or town or [1]) such purchaser shall at the expense of the mortgagee execute and deliver to him a valid deed of assignment of all interest acquired by virtue of the tax sale. [2]

This applies to mortgages made before the passage of the statute, June 1, 1860, where the mortgagee has taken possession subsequently. [3]

56. For all sums paid to a collector by the holder of a mortgage under either of the two preceding sections, the collector shall upon demand give him a receipt therefor, duly acknowledged; and such sums shall be added to and constitute part of the principal sum of the mortgage; and the mortgage shall not be redeemed, without the consent in writing of the holder, until such sums and interest thereon are paid; and such receipt recorded in the registry of deeds for the district or county where the land lies, within thirty days from its date, shall be notice to all persons of the payment of such sums and the lien upon the estate therefor.

57. In all cases of (taking or [1]) sale of real estate for the payment of taxes assessed thereon, the supreme judicial court shall have equity powers, if relief is sought within five years from the (taking or [1]) sale.

58. When the tax list and warrant of the assessors is committed to the sheriff or his deputy, he shall forthwith

---

[1] Stats. 1878, ch. 266.
[2] Gen. Stats. ch. 12, §§ 37–40.
[3] Andrews *v.* Worcester County Mutual Fire Ins. Co., 5 Allen, 66.

post in some public place in the city or town assessed an attested copy of said list and warrant; and shall make no distress for a tax, till after thirty days from the time of such posting.

59. If a person pays his tax on such list within said thirty days, the officer shall receive for his fees five per cent on the sum assessed; but if a tax remains unpaid after said thirty days, the officer shall proceed to collect the same by distress or imprisonment, in the manner collectors are required to proceed in like cases. The officer may also levy his fees for service and travel, in the collection of each person's tax, as in other cases of distress and commitment.

60. When the city council of a city or the inhabitants of a town vote to appoint their treasurer a collector, he may issue his warrants to the sheriff of the county, or his deputy, or any of the constables of the city or town, returnable in thirty days, requiring them to collect any or all taxes due; and such warrants shall be in substance the same and confer like powers as warrants issued by assessors to collectors.

61. Every collector shall once in two months, if required, exhibit to the mayor and aldermen or selectmen, and where there are no such officers, to the assessors, a true account of all moneys received on the taxes committed to him, and produce the treasurer's receipts for all money paid into the treasury by him.

62. If a collector neglects so to exhibit his accounts, he shall forfeit the sum of two and a half per cent on the sums committed to him for collection.

63. The collector shall be credited with all sums abated according to law, and with the amount of taxes assessed upon any person committed to prison within one year from the receipt of the tax list by the collector, and before paying his tax, and also with any sums which the city or town may see fit to abate to him, due from persons committed after the expiration of a year.

64. If the collector fails to collect a tax without his own

default, and there is a deficiency of the amount due on a state or county tax, such deficiency shall be supplied by him from the proceeds of the collection of city or town taxes, if any in his hands ; and, if he have none, by the city or town treasurer, on the written requisition of the collector.

65. If a collector of taxes neglects to pay, within the time required by law, such sums of money as ought by him to be paid to the state or county treasurer. the city or town by which such collector was appointed shall be liable for such sums, to be recovered in an action of contract by such state or county treasurer respectively.

66. If a collector neglects seasonably to pay a state or county tax committed to him, whereby the city or town is compelled to pay the same, or neglects seasonably to account for and pay in a city or town tax committed to him, the city or town may recover the amount thereof, with all damages sustained through such neglect, and interest, by an action of contract, declaring on his official bond if any has been given.

67. If a collector becomes insane, or in the judgment of the selectmen otherwise unable to discharge his duty, or absconds, removes, or in the judgment of the selectmen is about to remove, from the place, or refuses on demand to exhibit to the mayor and aldermen, or selectmen, or assessors, his accounts of collections, as herein provided. the selectmen may remove him from office and appoint another collector as in case of the death of the collector.

68. If a collector dies before completing the collection of a tax committed to him, the selectmen may appoint some suitable person to complete the collection, who shall receive a reasonable compensation, to be paid by the town, and they may commit the same tax list to him, with their warrant, accordingly ; and when a temporary collector is appointed by the selectmen, the assessors shall commit the tax list to him with their warrant, and he shall have the same powers and be subject to the same duties and liabilities as other collectors.

69. In case of the death or removal from office of a collector, his executors or administrators, and all other persons into whose hands any of his unsettled tax lists may come, shall forthwith deliver the same to the selectmen.

70. Collectors shall be paid such compensation for their services as their cities or towns shall determine. (See this chapter below in reference to fees.)

71. No tax paid to a collector shall be recovered back, unless it appears that it was paid after an arrest of the person paying it, a levy upon his goods, a notice of sale of his real estate, or a protest by him in writing; and the damages awarded in a suit or process based upon any error or illegality in the assessment or apportionment of a tax shall not be greater than the excess of the tax above the amount for which the plaintiff was liable to be taxed. And no sale, contract, or levy shall be avoided by reason of any such error or irregularity.[1]

72. Whenever a town has fixed a time within which taxes assessed therein shall be paid, such town, at the meeting when money is appropriated or raised, may vote that on all taxes remaining unpaid after a certain time interest shall be paid at a specified rate, not exceeding one per centum per month; and may also vote that, on all taxes remaining unpaid after another certain time, interest shall be paid at another specified rate, not exceeding one per centum per month; and the interest accruing under such vote or votes shall be added to and be a part of such taxes.[2]

73. If at the time and place appointed for the sale of real estate taken for taxes, as provided in the thirty-third section of the twelfth chapter of the General Statutes (section forty-six above), no person shall appear and bid for the estate thus offered for sale, or the rents and profits thereof, or for the whole or any part of the land, an amount equal to the tax and charges, and the sale shall have been adjourned from day to day, as provided in the thirty-fourth section of the said chapter (section forty-seven above), a

[1] Gen. Stats. ch. 12, §§ 41-56.    [2] Stats. 1873, ch. 225.

public declaration of the fact shall then and there be made by the collector; immediately after which, provided no bid shall be made equal to the tax and charges, the collector shall give public notice that he shall, and that he then and there does, purchase on behalf of the town or city by which the tax is assessed, the said estate, in one of the forms set forth in the thirty-third section of said chapter (section forty-six above) : *provided, however*, that no sum exceeding the amount of the tax and the incidental costs and expenses of levy and sale shall be offered by him therefor.

74. The deed to be given by the collector in such case shall, in addition to the statements by law required, set forth the fact of the non-appearance of a purchaser at the sale advertised by him, and shall confer upon such town or city the same rights as belong to an individual to whom such a deed may be given. And the several towns and cities of this commonwealth, in their corporate capacity, are hereby authorized, as holders of said deeds, to exercise the same rights and perform the same duties as any individual purchaser of real estate taken for taxes.

75. If within ten days after the sale of real estate for the payment of taxes, any purchaser thereof shall fail to pay to the collector the sum offered by him, and receive his deed, the sale shall be null and void, and the town or city shall be deemed to be the purchaser of the estate according to the provisions of this act. And the deed to be given by the collector in such case shall, in addition to the statements now required by law, set forth the fact of the preceding sale, and the failure of the purchaser to pay the sum offered as aforesaid.

76. The deed given to a town or city under the provisions of this act shall be placed in the custody of the treasurer thereof, to whom all applications for the redemption of the estate sold, under the provisions of law, shall be made. And the several towns and cities of the commonwealth may make such regulations for the custody, management, and sale of such estates, and the assignment of

the tax titles thus obtained, not inconsistent with the laws of the commonwealth, as they may deem expedient. But nothing herein contained shall take from the owner of said real estate, or his heirs or assigns, the right to redeem the same, as provided in section thirty-six, chapter twelve, of the General Statutes (section fifty above).

77. The amount of the tax and all incidental costs and expenses of levy and sale provided for by law, which shall be included in any sale in accordance with the provisions of this act, shall be allowed the collector in his settlement with such town or city.

78. In the deed which the collector shall execute and deliver, as provided in section thirty-five of chapter twelve of the General Statutes (section forty-eight above), there shall also be inserted a special warranty that the sale has in all particulars been conducted according to the provisions of law ; and, if it should subsequently appear that, by reason of any error, omission, or informality, in any of the proceedings of assessment or sale, the purchaser has no claim upon the property sold, there shall be paid to said purchaser, upon his surrender and discharge of the deed so given, by the town or city whose collector executed said deed, the amount paid by him, together with ten per cent interest per annum on the same, which shall be in full satisfaction of all claims for damages for any defect in the proceedings (provided the said purchaser shall, within two years from the date of said deed, in writing, offer to surrender and discharge the same, or to assign and transfer to the town or city all his right, title, and interest therein, as the collector thereof shall elect [1]).

79. If the owner does not redeem the property so purchased by the city or town within the time prescribed by the thirty-sixth section of the twelfth chapter of the General Statutes (section fifty above), said town or city may at any time proceed to sell the said real estate at public auction, after having given the same notice as is required in section twenty-eight, chapter twelve, of the General

[1] Stats. 1878, ch. 266.

Statutes (section forty above), executing and delivering to the highest bidder therefor a quitclaim deed ; and from the money arising from said sale shall be deducted the expenses of making the sale, together with the amount paid at the first sale for tax and charges, with ten per cent interest per annum thereon, and all intervening taxes and necessary charges ; and the balance, if any, shall be deposited in the city or town treasury to be paid to the party legally entitled to the estate if the same had not been sold for taxes, if the same shall be called for within five years ; and if not demanded within that time the same shall enure to the benefit of said city or town.

80. If any estate shall be purchased by any city or town, according to the provisions of this act, taxes shall be assessed upon the same in the same manner as though the same were not so purchased ; and said taxes shall be deducted from the proceeds of the final sale, as provided in the previous section.

81. When a person committed to prison for non-payment of taxes desires to take the oath for the relief of poor debtors, as provided in section fifteen, chapter twelve, of the General Statutes (section twenty-six above), he may represent the same to the jailer, and the jailer shall make the same known to some magistrate named in section one, chapter one hundred and twenty-four, of the General Statutes, and the magistrate shall thereupon appoint a time and place for the examination of the debtor, and shall direct the jailer to cause the debtor to be present at the same, and shall further proceed as directed in said section fifteen of said chapter twelve.

82. The following charges and fees, and no other, shall be allowed to the collector, and shall be added to the amount of the tax, as provided in section thirty-three, of chapter twelve, of the General Statutes : —

For making a written demand, twenty cents ;

For preparing advertisement, fifty cents ;

For advertisement in newspaper, the actual cost of the same ;

For posting up notices in one or more public places, twenty cents for (such service [1]) ;

For posting up notices on each piece of real estate, twenty cents ;

For copy of notice, and the publication thereof, and obtaining affidavit of disinterested person, fifty cents ;

For recording affidavit at registry of deeds, the fees of the register ;

For preparing deed, two dollars ;

And in the event that any delinquent tax-payer offers to pay the tax before the day of sale (or taking [1]), such charges shall be added to the tax as have intervened at the time of said offer to pay.

No sale heretofore made of real estate taken for taxes shall be held invalid by reason of the notice of sale having contained the words " or such undivided portions thereof as may be necessary," or the words " or such undivided portions of them as may be necessary :" *provided, however,* that this act shall not apply to any case wherein proceedings at law or in equity have been commenced involving the validity of such sale, nor to any real estate which has been alienated since the eighth day of February of the current year and before the passage of this act,[2] May sixth, eighteen hundred and seventy-eight.

83. County, city, and town taxes are entitled to the same priority or preference as state taxes are now entitled to, in cases of insolvent debtors.[3]

84. Whenever the collector of taxes in any city or town has reasonable cause to believe that the title created by any deed given in consequence of a sale for non-payment of taxes, or of any assessment, a lien for which is enforceable by sale of real estate, is invalid by reason of any error, omission, or informality in any of the proceedings of assessment or sale, he may, within two years from the date of said deed, or in the case of existing deeds within two years from the passage of this act, give notice to the person who appears by the records in the registry of deeds of the county or district wherein the city or town lies, to be

---

1 Stats. 1878, ch. 266.      3 Stats. 1862, ch. 183, §§ 1–11.
2 Stats. 1878, ch. 229.

the holder of such title, requiring him within thirty days to surrender and discharge the deed so given, and to receive from the city or town the sum due therefor, with interest, as provided by law, or to file with the collector a written statement that he refuses to make such surrender or discharge ; and such statement shall be deemed an absolute release of the city or town from any liability whatever upon the warranty contained in said deed.

85. The notice required by the preceding section shall be served in the manner prescribed by law for the service of summonses for witnesses in civil cases ; but in case the holder has no place of abode in, or cannot be found in, the city or town, it shall be served by mail, or by publication one week in some newspaper published in the county wherein the city or town lies ; or, if there be none such, in some newspaper published in an adjacent county. If the holder fails to comply with such notice the collector shall, upon the expiration of thirty days from the service thereof, cause a copy of the notice, with an affidavit by himself or a disinterested person, of the service thereof, taken before a justice of the peace, to be filed and recorded in the registry of deeds of the county or district wherein the city or town lies. A note of reference to the record of said copy shall be made on the margin of the record of the collector's deed therein referred to ; and from the time of such record the interest payable by law in respect of such deed shall cease, and said copy when so recorded shall have the effect to release and discharge all right and title acquired under such deed. The collector shall notify the treasurer of the city or town, who shall appropriate out of any funds in his hands the amount due in respect of said deed for the use and benefit of the persons entitled thereto, and shall pay it over on reasonable demand.

86. If the invalidity of any deed so recalled by the collector arose by reason of any error, omission, or informality in any of the proceedings of assessment, the collector, after obtaining a surrender and discharge of the deed from the holder, or causing a copy of the notice to be filed and

recorded as provided in the preceding section, shall forthwith notify the board by whom the tax or assessment was
laid, who shall immediately reassess the same as provided
by section fifty-three of chapter eleven of the General Statutes.   If such invalidity, however, arose by reason of any
error, omission, or informality in any of the proceedings of
the collector, he shall, after obtaining a surrender and discharge of the deed, or causing a copy of the notice to be
filed and recorded as aforesaid, forthwith collect the unpaid tax or assessment referred to in such deed by proceedings in conformity to law.

87. In addition to the power now given by law to enforce
the lien for a tax or assessment laid on real estate, with all
incidental costs and expenses by sale thereof, the collector
shall have power to take for the city or town the whole of
the real estate taxed or assessed, if the tax or assessment
is not paid within fourteen days after a demand of payment made as required by sections twenty-two, twenty-four,
or twenty-five of chapter twelve of the General Statutes,
and still remains unpaid at the date of such taking.   The
collector shall give three weeks' notice of his intention to
exercise such power of taking ; which notice may be served
either in the manner prescribed by law for the service of
summonses for witnesses in civil cases, or by advertisement thereof in the manner required by section twenty-
eight of chapter twelve of the General Statutes, and shall
contain the particulars required by section twenty-nine of
said chapter twelve.   He may also post a similar notice in
accordance with the provisions of section thirty of said·
chapter twelve.

The affidavit of the collector, or of a disinterested person, taken before a justice of the peace, of the service
of the demand of payment, and of the notice herein provided, made upon a copy thereof, and filed and recorded
in the registry of deeds of the county or district where the
land lies, shall be competent evidence of such demand or
notice.   But the demand of payment may be made, and
the evidence thereof perpetuated, in the manner provided

by section twenty-seven of said chapter twelve. Said affidavits shall be annexed to the instrument of taking, which shall be under the hand and seal of the collector, and shall contain a statement of the cause of taking, a substantially accurate description of each parcel of land taken, the name of the person to whom the same was assessed, and the amount of the tax thereon, and of incidental costs and expenses to the date of taking. Said instrument shall be filed and recorded in the registry of deeds of the county or district where the land lies ; and the title to the lands so taken shall thereupon vest in the city or town, subject to the right of redemption given by section thirty-six of chapter twelve of the General Statutes as amended by this act.

88. Every city by ordinance, and every town by by-law, may determine and direct which power its collector shall exercise to enforce the lien for a tax or assessment laid on real estate, — that of sale under section twenty-two of chapter twelve of the General Statutes, or that of taking under section five of this act (preceding section) ; and in the absence of any such ordinance or by-law the collector may exercise either power at his discretion.

89. Whenever the collector has reasonable cause to believe that a tax-title, held by a city or town under a sale or taking for non-payment of a tax or assessment, is invalid by reason of any error, omission, or informality in any of the proceedings of assessment, sale, or taking, he may release, disclaim, and annul such title by an instrument under his hand and seal, duly filed and recorded in the registry of deeds of the county or district where the land lies. If the invalidity of such title arose by reason of any error, omission, or informality in any of the proceedings of assessment, he shall forthwith notify the board by whom the tax or assessment was laid, who shall immediately reassess the same, as provided by section fifty-three of chapter eleven of the General Statutes.

90. The treasurer or other disbursing officer of any city or town may, and if so requested by the collector of that place shall, withhold payment of any moneys that may be

made payable from the treasury of that place to any person whose taxes, assessed in that place, are then due and wholly or partly unpaid : *provided*, that no greater sum shall be thus withheld than is necessary to pay the amount of tax then due as aforesaid, with interest and costs. The sum withheld shall be payable to the collector, who shall, if required, give a written receipt therefor. The person taxed may, in such case, have the same remedy as if he had paid such tax after a levy upon his goods. The collector's right as established by this section shall be valid against any trustee process not commenced, or any assignment not recorded, prior to the passage of this act.

91. No person entitled under the provisions of section thirty-six of chapter twelve of the General Statutes to redeem real estate sold for non-payment of a tax or assessment, shall have a right to redeem land held by a city or town under a sale or taking for non-payment of a tax or assessment, unless he pays or tenders to the collector thereof all sums due the city or town in respect of said land by reason of all such sales or takings thereof, and of all subsequent taxes or assessments thereon due and unpaid, with all interest and incidental costs and expenses.

92. If no person, lawfully entitled within the time prescribed by law, redeems the property purchased for and held by a city or town under the provisions of chapter one hundred and eighty-three of the acts of the year one thousand eight hundred and sixty-two, or taken for it under the provisions of this act, the city or town shall forthwith proceed to sell the real estate at public auction, after having given the same notice as is required in section twenty-eight of chapter twelve of the General Statutes, executing and delivering to the highest bidder therefor a quit-claim deed ; and from the money arising from said sale shall be deducted the expenses of making the sale, together with the amount named in the collector's deed or instrument of taking, as the sum due when the same was executed, and all interest and charges thereon fixed by existing law, and also all subsequent taxes and assessments, with all interest and

charges due in respect thereof; the balance, if any, shall be deposited in the city or town treasury, subject to the provisions of section seven of chapter one hundred and eighty-three of the acts of the year one thousand eight hundred and sixty-two.

93. Whenever there is recorded in a registry of deeds a conveyance affecting, by way of assignment, release, partial release, discharge, or disclaimer, a title created by any deed or instrument of taking, executed in consequence of a sale or taking for non-payment of a tax or assessment, the register of deeds shall make a note of reference to the record of such conveyance on the margin of the record of the deed or instrument of taking therein referred to.

94. Whenever the collector exercises the power of taking given by section five of this act (section eighty-seven of this chapter), there shall be allowed to him, and added to the amount of the tax, the same charges and fees as are fixed for similar proceedings by section ten of chapter one hundred and eighty-three of the acts of the year one thousand eight hundred and sixty-two as hereby amended; and when service of the demand of payment, and notice of intention to take, is made in the manner prescribed by law for the service of summonses for witnesses in civil cases, there shall be allowed therefor, and added as above mentioned, fifty cents, together with the fees for travel fixed by section one of chapter one hundred and one of the acts of the year one thousand eight hundred and sixty-five.

95. The owner of any interest in real estate purchased and held by a city or town under the provisions of chapter one hundred and eighty-three of the acts of the year eighteen hundred and sixty-two, having a right to redeem the same, may pay to the treasurer of the town or city all sums required by law for the redemption of such estate; in which case the treasurer shall give to the person so paying a like certificate as that mentioned in section thirty-eight, chapter twelve, of the General Statutes; and the certificate may be recorded in the manner, and with like effect, as that described in said section. If the person so redeeming be the

holder of a mortgage, the sums so paid by him shall be added to, and constitute a part of, the principal sum of the mortgage; and the mortgage shall not be redeemed until such sums, and interest thereon, are paid; and, in such case, the recording of said certificate in the registry of deeds in the district or county where the land lies, within thirty days from its date, shall be notice to all persons of the payment of such sums, and the lien upon the estate therefor.[1]

96. The legal voters of any fire, water supply, improvement or school district, organized under the laws of this commonwealth, may, at the meeting when money is appropriated or raised, fix a time within which all taxes assessed therein shall be paid, and may vote that on all taxes remaining unpaid after a certain time interest shall be paid at a specified rate, not exceeding one per centum per month, and may also vote that on all taxes remaining unpaid after another certain time interest shall be paid at another specified rate, not exceeding one per centum per month; and the interest accruing under such vote or votes shall be added to and be a part of such taxes.

97. The clerk of the district shall certify such vote or votes to the assessors of the town in which said district is situated, together with all sums of money voted to be raised by the district, which shall be assessed and collected by the officers of the town in the same manner that the town taxes are assessed and collected, and be paid over to the treasurer, who shall hold the same subject to the order of the prudential committee or treasurer of the district.[2]

---

[1] Stats. 1878, ch. 266.        [2] Stats. 1878, ch. 185.

# CHAPTER XVI.

## TOWN TREASURER.

1. THE town treasurer shall give bond in such sum as the selectmen require, with sureties to their satisfaction, for the faithful discharge of the duties of his office ; shall receive and take charge of all sums of money belonging to his town, and pay over and account for the same according to the order of such town or the officers thereof duly authorized in that behalf.[1]

2. The bond required in the preceding section should be given to the town and not to the selectmen.[2]

3. A town treasurer is not excused from paying over money collected by him because it has been stolen from him without his fault. And his sureties on his bond will be liable for his failure to pay on that account.[3]

4. He may in his own name and official capacity prosecute suits upon bonds, notes, or other securities, given to him or his predecessors in office, and where no other provision is specially made, shall prosecute for all fines and forfeitures which enure to his town or the poor thereof.

5. He shall prosecute for trespasses committed on any public building or enclosure belonging to his town ; and when a public building is owned partly by the town and partly by the county, such prosecution may be made either by the town or county treasurer, whichever shall first institute the same.

6. A town may at any meeting appoint its treasurer collector of taxes ; and he may appoint deputies, who shall give such bonds for the faithful discharge of their duty as the selectmen think proper. Such collector and

[1] Gen. Stats. ch. 18, § 54.
[2] Stevens v. Hay, 6 Cush. 229.
[3] Hancock v. Hazard, 12 Cush. 112.

deputies shall have the same powers as are vested in collectors of taxes.[1]

7. And such deputies may execute a warrant though it is directed to the collector only.[2]

8. A treasurer so appointed collector may issue his warrant to the sheriff of the county, or his deputy, or to any constable of the town, directing them to distrain the property or take the body of any person who is delinquent in the payment of taxes, and to proceed in like manner as collectors are required to do in like cases.

9. The treasurer shall annually render a true account of all his receipts and payments, and other official doings, to the town, and shall receive such compensation for his services as the town may determine.[3]

[1] Gen. Stats. ch. 18, §§ 55–57.
[2] Aldrich v. Aldrich, 8 Met. 102.
[3] Gen. Stats. ch. 18, §§ 58, 59.

# CHAPTER XVII.

## CONSTABLES, AND THEIR DUTIES.

1. A PERSON chosen to the office of constable, able to perform the duties thereof and not exempt, who refuses to take the oath and to serve in such office, shall forfeit twenty dollars. If he is present in town meeting and declares his refusal or neglects for seven days after being summoned to take the oath of office or to pay such fine, he shall be prosecuted therefor by the treasurer.

2. Any constable who gives to the inhabitants of the town for which he is chosen a bond with sureties in a sum not less than (one thousand[1]) dollars to the satisfaction of the selectmen, with condition for the faithful performance of·his duties in the service of all civil processes committed to him, and causes the same, with the approval of the selectmen indorsed thereon, to be filed in the office of the town clerk, may, within his town, serve any writ or other process in a personal action in which the damages are not laid at a greater sum than (two[1]) hundred dollars, and any process in replevin in which the subject-matter does not exceed in value (two[1]) hundred dollars, and any writ or other process under the provisions of chapter one hundred and thirty-seven; and no constable shall serve any process in a civil action until he gives such bond.

A constable may now serve such writs when the damages are not laid at a greater sum than three hundred dollars, and any process in replevin in which the subject-matter does not exceed three hundred dollars in value, provided he gives a bond with sureties, in a sum not

[1] Stats. 1870, ch. 149.

less than three thousand dollars with condition for the faithful performance of his duties as now provided by law.[1]

3. The town clerk shall note upon every bond given by a constable the time when the same was filed. Any person injured by a breach of the condition of such bond may at his own expense institute a suit thereon in the name of the town, and like proceedings shall be had as in a suit by a creditor on an administration bond. The writ shall be indorsed by the persons for whose benefit the suit is brought; and, if neither of them is an inhabitant of this state, it shall also be indorsed by some other responsible indorser residing in this state. If judgment is for the defendants, execution shall issue for costs against the indorsers, as if they were plaintiffs of record.[2]

To attach the goods of A., on a writ against B., is a breach of the condition of his official bond given for the faithful performance of his duties in the service of civil processes.[3]

4. Constables may serve such writs and processes as are described in section sixty-one (section two above), and warrants and other processes in criminal cases, although their town, parish, religious society, or school district is a party or interested.

5. They may serve by copy by them attested all demands, notices, and citations, and their returns of service thereof shall be *prima facie* evidence; but this provision shall not exclude the service thereof by other parties.

6. They may, like sheriffs, require aid in the execution of their duties. They shall not appear in court or before a justice of the peace as attorney or counsel for any party. The provisions of sections sixty-four and sixty-seven of chapter seventeen shall apply to constables.

7. They shall serve all warrants and other processes, lawfully directed to them by the selectmen of their town, for notifying town meetings or for other purposes.

8. They shall take due notice of and prosecute all vio-

---

[1] Stats. 1872, ch. 268.
[2] Gen. Stats. ch. 18, §§ 60-62.
[3] Greenfield *v.* Wilson, 13 Gray, 336.

lations of the laws respecting the observance of the Lord's day, to prevent profane swearing, and against gaming.

Whoever is found in a state of intoxication in a public place, or is found in any place in a state of intoxication committing a breach of the peace or disturbing others by noise, may be apprehended by any sheriff, deputy sheriff, constable, watchman, or police officer, without a warrant, and kept in custody in some suitable place until he is so far recovered from his intoxication as to render it proper to carry him before a court of justice. The officer may then make a complaint against him for the crime of drunkenness.[1]

Whoever remains upon a street or sidewalk, or elsewhere, in any city or town in wilful violation of an ordinance or by-law, and whoever, upon any street, sidewalk, or in any other public place, accosts or addresses any other person with profane or obscene language in wilful violation of an ordinance or by-law, may be arrested without a warrant by any officer authorized to serve criminal process in the place where the offence is committed, if unknown to the officer making such arrest, and may be kept in custody until he can be taken before a court having jurisdiction to punish such offence.[2]

9. A constable in the execution of a warrant or writ directed to him may convey beyond the limits of his town prisoners and property in his custody under such process, either to the justice who issued it, or to the common jail or house of correction of his county.

10. If a person against whom a warrant is issued for an alleged offence committed within any town, before or after the issuing of the warrant, escapes from or is out of the town, any constable of such town to whom the warrant is directed may pursue and apprehend him in any place in the commonwealth.

11. When an unincorporated place is annexed to a town for the purpose of taxation, the constables of such town shall have and exercise in such unincorporated place the same powers as if it were a part of their town.[3]

12. It shall be the duty of the constables of the several towns and cities, city marshals, chiefs of police and all other police officers, to aid the governor or chief of the state detective force and state detectives in the discharge of their duties, whenever called upon for that

[1] Stats. 1876, ch. 17.       [3] Gen. Stats. ch. 18, §§ 63–70.
[2] Stats. 1878, ch. 181.

purpose : *provided, however*, that said constables of the several towns and cities, city marshals, chiefs of police, and other police officers, shall not be ordered out of their respective cities and towns. And any constable, marshal, or police officer refusing to aid the governor, said chief or detectives, when called upon so to do, shall be punished by imprisonment in the jail not exceeding three months, or by fine not exceeding one hundred dollars.[1]

[1] Stats. 1875, ch. 15.

## CHAPTER XVIII.

### WATCH AND WARD.

1. A CITY or town may establish and keep a watch and determine the number and qualifications of the persons to be employed for that purpose. The mayor and aldermen or selectmen shall appoint a suitable person to be officer of the watch, and direct the manner in which watchmen shall be equipped. The expense of the watch shall be defrayed in like manner as other town charges.

2. The watch shall see that all disturbances and disorders are prevented and suppressed. During the nighttime they may examine all persons abroad whom they have reason to suspect of any unlawful design, demand of them their business abroad and whither they are going; may disperse any assembly of three or more such persons, and enter any building for the purpose of suppressing a riot or breach of the peace therein. Persons so suspected and not giving a satisfactory account of themselves, persons so assembled and not dispersing when ordered, and persons making, aiding, or abetting in a riot or disturbance, may be arrested by the watch, and shall thereupon be safely kept, by imprisonment or otherwise, until the next morning, and then taken before a police court or some trial justice, to be examined and proceeded against.

3. Officers and members of the watch, when on duty, may carry a club of not more than eighteen inches in length; shall wear such badge of office as the mayor or selectmen direct, and shall walk the rounds in and about the streets, lanes, wharves, and principal inhabited parts of the city or town, to prevent danger by fire, and to see that good order is kept.

4. The mayor and aldermen or selectmen of any place

wherein no watch as above provided is established, may from time to time order a suitable watch to be kept in their place, and warn all persons liable to watch and ward duty to perform the same. They may direct the number of the watch, the places and hours for keeping the same, may order in writing any constable or officer of the watch to warn such watch, either by himself or by some person therefor by him appointed, and to see that all persons so warned attend and perform their duty.

5. Every male person of the age of eighteen years or upwards, being able of body, or having sufficient estate to hire a substitute, and not exempt, shall be liable to watch and ward in his city or town, and shall perform the duties, be subject to the liabilities, and have the powers of watchmen as the same are defined in this chapter.

6. Justices of the peace, mayors, aldermen, selectmen, sheriffs, settled ministers of the gospel, and persons living more than two miles from the place where such watch and ward is kept, shall be exempt.

7. Persons liable to watch and ward, and without reasonable excuse neglecting or refusing to appear and do duty personally or by sufficient substitute, and constables or officers or members of the watch refusing to execute and observe proper orders, shall forfeit ten dollars, to be recovered by complaint to the use of the commonwealth, or by action of tort to the use of the city or town.

8. Watch districts may be established and organized in villages containing not less than one thousand persons, for the protection of property against fire, thieves, and robbers, and for keeping the streets quiet in the night-time.

9. The selectmen of a town, upon the application in writing of not less than seven freeholders, inhabitants of such village the limits of which shall be defined in the application, requiring them to notify a meeting of the persons in such district qualified to vote in town affairs, for considering the expediency of establishing such watch district, shall forthwith give notice to such voters, in the manner in which notice of town meetings is given, to assemble at

some suitable place within the district for said purpose, the substance of which shall be expressed in the notification. If the selectmen refuse or neglect to give notice of such meeting, any justice of the peace in the county may so notify the same.

10. When such village belongs to two or more towns, the voters thereof may organize such district at a meeting called and notified as provided in the preceding section by any justice of the peace for the county in which either town is situated, to whom application has been made by at least five voters of each town who are inhabitants of such district.

11. If at any such meeting the voters present determine to establish such district, a clerk shall be chosen, who shall be sworn to keep a true record of the proceedings of all meetings and to perform all duties of clerk of the district so long as he holds the office. He may be removed by the district, or may resign, and in case of a vacancy another may be chosen.

12. A prudential committee of not less than three nor more than five persons shall be chosen by ballot, and shall be sworn.

13. The prudential committee shall annually issue their warrants to the clerk, requiring him to call a meeting in the month of March for the purpose of choosing officers. Such officers shall perform the duties of their offices until others are chosen.

14. Meetings of the district shall be called by the clerk when requested in writing by the prudential committee or seven voters of the district. He shall give notice thereof by posting written notifications in at least six public places in the district, not less than seven days prior to the meeting, which notifications shall contain a brief statement of the purposes of the meeting. At each of the meetings a moderator shall be chosen, who shall have the powers of the moderator of a town meeting. After the choice of a clerk, he shall preside at subsequent meetings with like powers until a moderator is chosen.

15. The district may, at meetings called for the purpose, vote to raise money for the payment of watchmen and other necessary expenses. The prudential committee shall have the superintendence and control of the watchmen, have charge of and be responsible for the property employed, have the custody and management of the money raised, expend the same for the purposes specified in the votes of the district, be accountable to the district for the money received by them, and be liable to a suit for such money or other property of the district, in the name of the inhabitants thereof.

16. The clerk shall certify to the assessors of the town all sums of money voted to be raised, which shall be assessed and collected by the officers of the town in the same manner that the town taxes are assessed and collected, and be paid over to the treasurer, who shall hold the same subject to the order of the prudential committee. The assessors, treasurer, and collector of any town in which such district is organized shall have the powers and perform the duties in reference to the assessment and collection of said taxes which they have and perform in the assessment, collection, and abatement of town taxes; but the sum so voted shall be assessed upon the property real and personal located within such district.

17. When a district is composed of parts of two or more towns, the assessors of such towns shall transmit to the clerk of the district the amount of taxable property in such part of their respective towns as is within the limits of the district; the prudential committee shall thereupon apportion the money voted to be raised by the district among the respective towns according to the returns thus transmitted, and the same shall be collected and held in the manner provided in the preceding section.

18. When the freeholders of a territory adjoining a watch district present to the clerk thereof a petition describing their territory and requesting to be annexed to such district, the clerk shall give notice of the petition at the next annual meeting of the district, when, by a vote

of the meeting, the inhabitants of such territory may be annexed to the district.

19. Watch districts heretofore legally organized shall continue, and be subject to the provisions of this chapter in relation to watch districts.[1]

20. Police officers and officers and members of the watch in any city or town, when on duty, may carry such weapons as the mayor and aldermen of such city or the selectmen of such town shall authorize.[2]

[1] Gen. Stats. ch. 23, §§ 1–19.   [2] Stats. 1864, ch. 110, § 1.

# CHAPTER XIX.

## DUTIES OF OVERSEERS OF THE POOR, AND THE SUP-PORT OF PAUPERS.

1. EVERY city and town shall relieve and support all poor and indigent persons lawfully settled therein, whenever they stand in need thereof.[1]

But they may be supported in another place.[2]

2. In Smith v. Inhabitants of Colerain,[3] Shaw, C. J., in an elaborate opinion, said: "It has been too often decided to be now questioned that the liability of towns to support poor persons is founded upon and limited by statute, and is not to be enlarged or modified by any supposed moral obligation. By this we understand not that there is no moral obligation on all men in society to contribute to the support of the poor; but that towns are corporations, for limited and well-defined purposes, and that the duty of supporting the poor is not more binding upon them than upon parishes, counties, the state, or other organized bodies, further than such duty is created by law." "The first great object of the law, founded on the principle of simple humanity, is, that the party standing in need shall have relief immediately, and at the place where it is required; that is, from the overseers of the town where he is residing, or is found, without regard to their ultimate liability. The person in distress shall not be compelled to wait till notice can be given to a distant town, and whilst, perhaps, a controversy is subsisting as to its liability. And to insure such relief, if the overseers neglect or refuse, on notice, to afford it, any person, not himself liable for such relief, may afford it at the expense of the town."

3. If any person, actually become chargeable as a pauper to any city or town in which he has a settlement, has a settlement subsequently acquired in any place without this commonwealth, the overseers of the poor of such city or town may cause him to be removed to said place of subsequent settlement, by a written order directed to any person therein designated, who may execute the same.[4]

[1] Gen. Stats. ch. 70, § 1.
[2] Smith v. Peabody, 106 Mass. 262.
[3] 9 Met. 492.
[4] Stats. 1868, ch. 328, § 2.

4. It shall be unlawful for the overseers of the poor of any city or town to remove beyond the limits of this commonwealth any minor under their control, or cause or allow the same to be done, or to withhold information concerning the maintenance of such minor, from any person entitled to receive the same : *provided*, that the judges of probate may, upon application of the overseers of the poor of any town in their respective counties, upon a hearing thereon, after due notice to all parties interested, authorize such removal to be made ; and *provided, further,* that this act (this section) shall not apply to minors who have a settlement in other states.

5. Any overseers of the poor violating the provisions of the preceding section shall be punished by a fine not exceeding five hundred dollars.[1]

6. And one who, being in need of immediate relief and support, has received the same from the town of his lawful settlement, is not, in the absence of fraud, liable to an action by the town therefor, although he was possessed of property at the time.[2]

7. Any insane person who is supported by any place as a pauper may be committed by the overseers of the poor thereof to either of the state lunatic hospitals, with the consent of the trustees, and shall be kept for a sum not exceeding the actual expense of his support. And the trustees shall receive into the hospital any other insane person having a settlement or residence in this commonwealth for such compensation as they may determine.

8. The expenses of the state lunatic hospitals for the support of lunatics having known settlements in this state shall be paid quarterly, either by the persons obligated to pay or by the place in which such lunatics had their residence at the time of their commitment, unless other sufficient security is taken to the satisfaction of the trustees for such support. If any place or person refuses to pay whatever sum may be charged and due according to the by-laws of the hospital, on account of the support of such patient therein, or for the removal of any patient

---

[1] Stats. 1868, ch. 279, §§ 1, 2.        [2] Stow *v.* Sawyer, 3 Allen, 515.

whom the trustees are authorized by law to remove, for thirty days after the same has been demanded by the treasurer, in writing, of the mayor and aldermen of the city, or of the selectmen of the town, or of the person liable therefor, the same, with interest from the time of such demand, may be recovered for the use of the hospital in an action to be instituted by the district attorneys, or other prosecuting officers, in the name of the treasurer, against such delinquent city, town, or person.[1] It shall be the duty of the overseers of the poor of any city or town, except the city of Boston, to commit to one of the state lunatic hospitals or the Boston Lunatic Hospital, with the consent of the trustees thereof, any person supported by such city or town who is suffering under recent insanity, and is a fit subject for remedial treatment.[2]

9. The overseers of the poor shall have the care and oversight of all such poor and indigent persons, so long as they remain at the charge of their respective cities or towns, and shall see that they are suitably relieved, supported, and employed, either in the workhouse or almshouse, or in such other manner as the city or town directs, or otherwise at the discretion of said overseers. They may remove to the almshouse such children as are suffering destitution from extreme neglect of dissolute or intemperate parents or guardians.[3]

10. If the municipal authorities of a town have provided supplies for distribution among those out of the almshouse who need relief, upon orders of the overseers of the poor, and have given notice thereof to the overseers, the latter have no authority to contract debts in behalf of the town for the support of the poor; and one who, having knowledge of the facts, furnishes supplies to persons settled in such town, upon order of the overseers, cannot maintain an action against the town to recover the same. But, if he furnishes supplies upon such orders to persons settled elsewhere, he may recover from the town the amount actually received by it on account of such supplies, from the towns which were liable to support the persons who were relieved thereby.[4]

[1] Stats. 1862, ch 283, §§ 9, 10.
[2] Stats. 1864, ch. 288, § 6.
[3] Gen. Stats. ch. 70, § 2.

[4] Ireland, Jr. v. Newburyport, 8 Allen, 73.

11. The overseers of the poor shall have the same power and authority over persons placed under their care which directors or masters of workhouses have over persons committed thereto.

12. The kindred of such poor persons, in the line or degree of father or grandfather, mother or grandmother, children or grandchildren, by consanguinity, living in this state, and of sufficient ability, shall be bound to support such paupers in proportion to their respective ability.[1]

13. The words "poor and indigent persons in need of relief," "persons in distress and in need of immediate relief," "poor person," and "pauper," are used synonymously, except in those instances in which the person termed "pauper" is also described as having been relieved and supported by a town; and in those instances a technical pauper would have been designated if the words "poor person" had been used, instead of the word "pauper." The technical meaning is not evinced by the use of any special word, but by referring to the person, or by describing him as one who has received support from a town; which fact constitutes him a technical pauper.[2]

A town that is obliged by section fifty-eight of chapter one hundred and seventy-eight of the General Statutes to pay not exceeding one dollar per week for the support of a prisoner may recover the same of any parent, master, or kindred, by law liable to maintain him.[3]

14. The superior court in the county where any one of such kindred to be charged resides, upon complaint of any city, town, or kindred who shall have been at expense for the relief and support of such pauper, may, on due hearing, assess and apportion upon such of the kindred as they shall find to be of sufficient ability, and in proportion thereto, such sum as they shall deem reasonable for or towards the support of the pauper to the time of such assessment; and may enforce payment thereof by execution in common form: *provided*, that such assessment shall not extend to any expense for relief afforded more than six months previous to the filing of the complaint.[4]

[1] Gen. Stats. ch. 70, §§ 3, 4.
[2] Hutchings *v.* Thompson, 10 Cush. 238.
[3] Stats. 1876, ch. 148.
[4] Gen. Stats. ch. 70, § 5.

15. The "kindred," who are entitled under the foregoing section to recover their apportionment for support furnished a pauper, are those only who are such by consanguinity.[1]

16. The words "such pauper," when applied to a person whom a town has relieved, means a technical pauper; not because the term "pauper" is used, but because, by being relieved by a town, he becomes a technical pauper. The same words, however, when applied to one whom his kindred have relieved, do not necessarily so mean. As has been already said, they mean one of that class of persons who are designated in sections one and thirteen of this chapter as poor and indigent, and standing in need of relief; including those who have not received relief from a town as well as those who have.[2]

17. Municipal corporations are only authorized to furnish relief to those who, when the relief is furnished, may properly be denominated paupers, either from general poverty or present temporary necessity requiring such aid; and when the town has, in such cases, furnished necessary supplies, through the action of the overseers of the poor, an action will lie at common law against the husband, to recover the amount thus expended for his wife and minor children.[3]

18. The court may further assess and apportion upon said kindred such weekly sum as they shall deem sufficient for the future support of the pauper, to be paid quarter-yearly until the further order of court; and upon application from time to time of the city, town, or kindred, to whom the same is ordered to be paid, the clerk of said court shall issue and may renew an execution for the arrears of any preceding quarter.

19. When the court adjudges two or more of the kindred of a pauper to be of sufficient ability to contribute to his support, they shall tax no more costs against any one respondent than is occasioned by his default or separate defence.

20. The court may further order with whom of such kindred, that may desire it, such pauper shall live and be relieved, and such time with one, and such time with another, as they shall deem proper, having regard to the comfort of the pauper as well as the convenience of the kindred.

[1] Farr v. Flood, 11 Cush. 24.    [3] New Bedford v. Chace, 5 Gray,
[2] Hutchings v. Thompson, 10 Cush.    28.
238.

21. The complaint made as provided in this chapter shall be filed in the clerk's office, and a summons shall be thereupon issued requiring the kindred therein named to appear and answer thereto; which summons shall be directed to any officer qualified to serve civil process between the parties, and served like an original summons, fourteen days at least before the sitting of the court to which it is returnable.

22. Upon suggestion that there are other kindred of ability, not summoned in the original process, they may be summoned, and after due notice, whether they appear or are defaulted, the court may proceed against them in the same manner as if they had been summoned upon the original complaint.

23. The court may take further order from time to time in the premises, upon application of any party interested, and may alter such assessment and apportionment according to circumstances; and upon all such complaints they may award costs to either party as justice requires.[1]

24. Under the preceding section the superior court have power to award costs upon a complaint to compel kindred of a poor person to contribute towards his support. And no appeal lies from their decision.[2]

25. Said overseers, in their respective places, shall provide for the immediate comfort and relief of all persons residing or found therein, having lawful settlements in other places, when they fall into distress and stand in need of immediate relief, and until they are removed to the places of their lawful settlements; the expenses whereof, incurred within three months next before notice given to the place to be charged, as also of their removal, or burial in case of their decease, may be recovered by the place incurring the same against the place liable therefor, in an action at law, to be instituted within two years after the cause of action arises, but not otherwise.[3]

[1] Gen. Stats. ch. 70, §§ 6–11.     [3] Gen. Stats. ch. 70, § 12.
[2] South Reading v. Hutchinson et al., 10 Allen, 68.

26. A town which has furnished relief to a person found therein and standing in need of immediate relief may recover the expenses thereof from the town of his settlement, although sufficient provision may have been made for his general support by his father's will.[1]

27. Notice by one town to another of a claim made by the treasurer of a state lunatic hospital for the past and future support of a pauper is sufficient to support an action for the past expenses (though not actually paid until more than three months after), but not for expenses of the support of the pauper after such notice.[2]

28. A recovery in such action shall bar the place against which it shall be had from disputing the settlement of such pauper with the place so recovering, in any future action brought for his support.

But the action must be prosecuted to final judgment.[3]

29. When a person is supported in a place other than that in which he has his settlement, the place liable for his support shall not be required to pay therefor more than at the rate of two[4] dollars a week : *provided*, that the place so liable shall cause the pauper to be removed within thirty days from the time of receiving legal notice that such support has been furnished.[5]

30. The preceding section does not apply to the case of the removal of a pauper after his decease, though before burial.[6]

31. In computing the thirty days, the day on which notice is received that the support has been furnished is to be excluded.[7]

32. The overseers of the poor of each place shall also relieve, support, and employ all poor persons residing or found therein, having no lawful settlements within this state, until their removal to a state almshouse, and in case of their decease shall decently bury them ; the expense whereof may be recovered of their kindred, if they have any chargeable by law for their support, in the manner hereinbefore provided ; and if, in case of their burial, the

[1] Groveland *v.* Medford, 1 Allen, 23.

[2] Amherst *v.* Shelburne, 11 Gray, 107.

[3] Wenham *v.* Essex, 103 Mass. 119.

[4] Stats. 1873, ch. 213.

[5] Gen. Stats. ch. 70, §§ 13, 14.

[6] Webster *v.* Uxbridge, 13 Met. 198.

[7] Seekonk *v.* Rehoboth, 8 Cush. 371.

expense thereof is not paid by such kindred, there shall be paid from the treasury of the commonwealth (ten dollars [1]) for the funeral expenses of each pauper over twelve years of age, and (five dollars [1]) for the funeral expenses of each pauper under that age.[2]

The provisions of this section are extended to unknown persons found dead, and to all persons without settlement, having died without means of support, notwithstanding such persons may not have applied for public relief during their lifetime.   This however does not affect the following statute.[3]

When a medical examiner views or makes an examination of the dead body of a stranger, he shall cause the body to be decently buried; and if he certifies that he has made careful inquiry, and that to the best of his knowledge and belief the person found dead is a stranger, having no settlement in any city or town of this commonwealth, his fees, with the actual expense of burial, shall be paid from the treasury of the commonwealth.   In all other cases the expense of the burial shall be paid by the city or town, and all other expenses by the county, wherein the body is found.[4]

33. Every city and town shall be held to pay any expense necessarily incurred for the relief of a pauper therein by any person who is not liable by law for his support, after notice and request made to the overseers thereof, and until provision is made by them.[5]

Notice and request made to one member of the board of overseers of the poor, intended for them all collectively and for him to communicate to them, is a sufficient notice and request.[6]

34. The words "necessarily incurred" have been held to mean that "the claim must be proved to have been founded on the absolute necessity of a pauper; that is, it must be for such needful relief or support as the pauper could not otherwise procure or obtain."[7]

35. A town will not be liable unless the pauper was in need of immediate relief at the time when it was afforded.[8]   But an individual cannot recover of the town where a pauper has his settlement, for necessary relief furnished to the pauper in another town, although

---

[1] Stats. 1867, ch. 97.

[2] Gen. Stats. ch. 70, § 15.

[3] Stats. 1878, ch. 256.

[4] Stats. 1877, ch. 200, § 17.

[5] Gen. Stats. ch. 70, § 16;  Wing v. Chesterfield, 116 Mass. 353.

[6] Rogers v. Newbury, 105 Mass. 533.

[7] Chief Justice Bigelow, in Lamson v. Newburyport, 14 Allen, 30.

[8] Shearer v. Shelburne, 10 Cush. 3.

the former town has made provision, which proves inadequate, for the pauper's support in the latter town.[1]

36. "The town is rendered liable for the support of a poor person only after notice and request; not only notice but request importing a distinct call on the town. This provision for notice to the town is of great importance, deeply affecting the interests of towns, and is one to which every person claiming upon the town should be required to give full and complete effect. The terms used in the statute *notice* and *request* clearly import that a party, to hold a town responsible for support furnished to any person, should be required to give express and formal and particular notice to, and make a distinct request of, the town.

"It would alarmingly enhance the burdens and responsibilities of towns, if they were to be held liable to any person who might furnish aid to any one in need, without any other notice than some accidental information, or floating report, which might happen to reach the overseers, and without any request.

"The statute surely does not require the overseers to make inquiry, or to go in pursuit of any reports which may casually reach them. But, on the contrary, it requires that the town shall have notice and request; which clearly must mean formal and express notice and request."[2]

37. The overseers of any place may send a written notification, stating the facts relating to any person actually become chargeable thereto, to one or more of the overseers of the place where his settlement is supposed to be, and requesting them to remove him, which they may do by a written order directed to any person therein designated, who may execute the same.[3]

38. If such removal is not effected by the last-mentioned overseers within two months after receiving the notice, they shall within said two months send to one or more of the overseers requesting such removal a written answer, signed by one or more of them, stating therein their objections to the removal; and if they fail so to do, the overseers who requested the removal may cause the pauper to be removed to the place of his supposed settlement, by a written order directed to any person therein designated,

---

[1] Hawes *v.* Hanson, 9 Allen, 134; Smith *v.* Coleraine, 9 Met. 492.

[2] Walker *v.* Southbridge, 4 Cush.

199; Williams *v.* Braintree, 6 Cush. 399.

[3] Gen. Stats. ch. 70, § 17. See form of notice in Appendix.

who may execute the same ; and the overseers of the place
to which the pauper is so sent shall receive and provide for
him ; and such place shall be liable for the expenses of his
support and removal, to be recovered in an action by the
place incurring the same, and shall be barred from contesting the question of settlement with the plaintiffs in
such action.[1]

But all other questions, such as need of relief, are open to the
defendant.[2]

39. If a notification is sent, by the overseers of the poor of a town
which has incurred expense for the relief of a pauper found therein,
to the overseers of the poor of the town where his settlement is supposed to be, requesting his removal, the answer must be signed by
some one of the overseers; and if it is not so signed, their town will
be barred from contesting the question of his settlement, although the
pauper is not actually removed there ; and the answer will not be
sufficient if signed merely by another person with whom the town has
contracted for the support of its paupers for that year. Overseers to
whom such an answer is sent do not waive the defect by sending a
reply to the overseers of the other town, under the belief that the
answer came from one of them, or by subsequently sending a new
notification to them, for the removal of the same pauper.[8]

40. The notification and answer mentioned in the two
preceding sections may be sent by mail ; and such notification or answer, directed to the overseers of the poor of
the place intended to be notified or answered, postage pre-
paid, shall be deemed a sufficient notice or answer, and
shall be considered as delivered to the overseers to whom
it is directed, at the time when it is received in the post-
office of the place to which it is directed and in which the
overseers reside.

41. Whoever brings into and leaves any poor and indigent person in any place in this state, wherein such pauper
is not lawfully settled, knowing him to be poor and indigent, and with intent to charge such place with his relief
or support, shall forfeit a sum not exceeding one hundred

[1] Gen. Stats. ch. 70, § 18.

[2] New Bedford *v.* Hingham, 117
Mass. 445.

[8] Petersham *v.* Coleraine, 9 Allen,
91.

dollars for each offence, to be recovered in an action of tort to the use of such place.

This applies to public officers bringing paupers into a town.[1]

42. Upon the death of a pauper who at the time of his decease is actually chargeable to any place within this state, the overseers of the poor of such place may take possession of all his real and personal property; and if administration is not taken upon his estate within thirty days after his decease, the overseers may in their own names sell and convey so much thereof as may be necessary to repay the expenses incurred for the pauper. If any part of such property is withheld from said overseers, they may in their own names sue for and recover possession of the real estate, and shall have the same remedy for the recovery of the personal estate or its value that an administrator might have in like case.

43. In all actions and prosecutions founded on the preceding provisions of this chapter, the overseers of the poor of any place or any person by writing under their hands appointed shall appear, prosecute, or defend, the same to final judgment and execution, in behalf of such place.[2]

44. It shall be the duty of overseers of the poor in all the cities and towns of this commonwealth to keep full and accurate records of the paupers fully supported, the persons relieved and partially supported, the travellers and vagrants lodged at the expense of said cities and towns, together with the amount paid for such support and relief.[3]

45. An annual return of the numbers of persons supported and relieved, as enumerated in the previous section, with the cost of such support and relief, and a record of those fully supported, shall be made by the overseers of the poor to the secretary of the board of state charities during the month of April in each year, and shall be for the year ending on the thirty-first day of March preceding. In the year eighteen hundred and eighty-five, and in every tenth year thereafter, the returns provided for in section twenty-three, chap-

---

[1] Palmer v. Wakefield, 102 Mass. 214.

[2] Gen. Stats. ch. 70, §§ 19–22.

[3] Stats. 1867, ch 209, § 1.

ter seventy of the General Statutes, shall be made and transmitted by overseers of the poor to the secretary of the board of state charities during the month of April, and shall be for the year ending on the thirty-first day of March preceding.[1]

46. If the overseers of any town or city shall refuse or neglect to comply with the requirements of this act (the two preceding sections and following section), said town or city shall forfeit the sum of one dollar for each day's neglect, and the amount of such forfeiture shall be deducted from any sum to which said town or city may be entitled in reimbursement for relief of state paupers as provided in chapters one hundred and sixty-two of the acts of the year eighteen hundred and sixty-five,[2] and two hundred and thirty-four of the acts of the year eighteen hundred and sixty-six; and in case no such reimbursement shall be due to said town or city, the forfeiture shall be deducted from any money which may be due such town or city from the state.

47. It shall be the duty of the secretary of the board of state charities to prepare tables from the returns thus made, and to report the most important information thus obtained to the board, who shall cause the same to be printed in their annual reports for the use of the legislature.[3]

48. The several cities and towns may at their own expense send to said state almshouses, to be maintained at the public charge, all paupers who may fall into distress therein, not having a settlement within the commonwealth; that is to say, the cities and towns in the counties of Suffolk, Middlesex, and Essex, may send such persons to the state almshouse at Tewksbury; the cities and towns in the counties of Norfolk, Bristol, Plymouth, Barnstable, Nantucket, and Dukes County, to the state almshouse at Bridgewater; and the remaining cities and towns, to the state almshouse at Monson: *provided*, that the alien commissioners may direct the mayor of any city or the over-

---

[1] Stats. 1875, ch. 216.
[2] §§ 54–56 of this chapter.
[3] Stats. 1867, ch. 209, §§ 3, 4.

seers of the poor of any town to send such paupers to either of the state almshouses; and if any place is so directed to send a pauper to a greater distance than would be required by the preceding provisions of this section, the necessary additional expense shall be paid by the state.

49. No city or town shall send to either almshouse any person who by reason of insanity would be dangerous if at large. And if an inmate of such establishment becomes so insane, the inspectors thereof may apply to the judge of a police court, or any two justices of the peace and of the quorum, in the county in which the institution is situated, who shall have the same power and authority in regard to such application and the commitment of such person to either of the state lunatic hospitals, as judges of probate courts have in regard to lunatics furiously mad: *provided*, that it shall not be necessary to give notice of such application to the officers of any place.[1]

50. No city or town authorities shall be allowed to send to either of the state almshouses any person infected with small-pox or other disease dangerous to the public health, nor any other sick person whose health would be endangered by removal; but all such persons liable to be maintained by the commonwealth shall be supported during such sickness by the city or town in which they are taken sick, and notice of such sickness shall be given to the board of state charities, who shall have authority to examine the case, and order the removal of the patient if they deem expedient.

51. The expense incurred by any city or town under the provisions of the first section of this act (the preceding section) after notice shall have been given as therein required, and the bills for said support having been approved by the agent of the board of state charities, shall be reimbursed by the commonwealth to an amount not exceeding at the rate of the average weekly cost of

---

[1] Gen. Stats. ch. 71, §§ 36, 37.

the support of similar patients at the Rainsford Island Hospital.

52. Any mayor or overseer of the poor who shall knowingly offend against the provisions of the first section of this act (section fifty-five above) shall be subject to a penalty of not less than fifty nor more than one hundred dollars.[1]

53. Guardians and agents of the several tribes of Indians in this commonwealth are authorized to send such Indians to the state almshouses, as they may deem the interest of the state and the welfare of said Indians require ; first obtaining a permit from one of the alien commissioners.[2]

54. Upon complaint (of any one [3]) of the overseers of the poor of any city or town, trial justices and justices of the police and municipal courts may, in their discretion, commit persons, convicted before them of any of the offences enumerated in sections twenty-eight and thirty-five of chapter one hundred and sixty-five of the General Statutes, to the state workhouse at Bridgewater, for a term not less than three months, nor more than two years, there to be governed and subject to the same liabilities as persons sentenced under the provisions of chapter one hundred and ninety-eight of the acts of the year eighteen hundred and sixty-six ; or such offenders may be sentenced as now provided by law.

55. If any person so committed shall have a legal settlement in any city or town in this commonwealth, the said city or town shall pay for his support such sum per week as may be fixed upon by the said board, reference being had to his capacity for labor ; and all moneys so received shall be paid into the treasury in the manner now provided by law : *provided, however*, that upon the written request of said overseers the board of state charities shall permit him to be transferred to the workhouse of his place of settlement, where he shall serve out the remainder of his sentence.[4]

---

[1] Stats. 1865, ch. 162, §§ 1–3.  
[2] Stats. 1863, ch. 159.  
[3] Stats. 1870, ch. 20.  
[4] Stats. 1869, ch. 258, §§ 1, 3.

56. The overseers of the poor in any place where there is no superintendent of alien passengers, or where such superintendent is unable to perform his duties by reason of absence or ill health, shall perform the duties and exercise the authority of superintendents; and shall in like manner render their accounts to the state treasurer, and pay over the money received, deducting therefrom a reasonable compensation for their services.[1]

When a person by excessive drinking, gaming, idleness, or debauchery of any kind, so spends, wastes, or lessens his estate, as to expose himself or his family to want or suffering, or any place to charge or expense for the support of himself or his family, the selectmen of the town of which such spendthrift is an inhabitant or resident, or upon which he is or may become chargeable, may present a complaint to the probate court, setting forth the facts and circumstances of the case, and praying to have a guardian appointed. The court shall cause notice of not less than fourteen days to be given to the supposed spendthrift, of the time and place appointed for the hearing; and if after a full hearing it appears that he comes within the above description, the court shall appoint a guardian of his person and estate.[2]

57. When a woman who has been delivered of a bastard child, or is pregnant with a child which if born alive may be a bastard, refuses or neglects to make a complaint and institute a prosecution against the person whom she accuses of being the father of the child when requested so to do by an overseer of the poor of the place where she resides or has her settlement, such overseer may make the complaint; and when already made, if she refuses or neglects to prosecute the same, such overseer may prosecute the case to final judgment for the benefit of the town. In such case no complaint shall be withdrawn, dismissed, or settled by agreement of the mother and the putative father without the consent of the overseers of the poor of the town in which she has her settlement or residence, unless provision is made to the satisfaction of the court to relieve and indemnify such town from all charges that have accrued or may accrue for the maintenance of the child, and for the costs of complaint and prosecution thereof. But the overseers of the poor may compromise a prosecution on receipt of a fixed sum or security for the payment thereof, for the benefit of the town.[3] Any person arrested upon a warrant issued upon a complaint may be released upon giving a bond, with sufficient sureties, in not less than three hundred dollars, for his appearance before the court or justice having cognizance of said complaint, at a time to be specified in said bond.

[1] Gen. Stats. ch. 71, § 24.
[2] Gen. Stats. ch. 109, § 9.

[3] Gen. Stats. ch. 72; Stats. 1862, ch. 213.

The bond shall be made to the party for whose benefit the complaint is made or prosecuted, and the sureties may be examined, and the bond approved, by a bail commissioner or master in chancery [1] or a justice of a district or police court.[2]

58. No settlement made by the mother and father, before or after complaint is made, shall relieve the father from liability to any city or town, or the state, for the support of a bastard child.

If found guilty on trial, the father shall give bond with sufficient sureties to indemnify and save harmless against all charges of maintenance any town chargeable therewith; and a town may recover by action of contract any sums of money which ought to have been paid to it, if they should not be paid in compliance with any order of the court. The foregoing provisions in relation to bastards do not apply where the child was begotten and born in another state, and neither mother nor child ever had a residence in this state. No statute of limitations applies to prosecutions under these provisions, nor are prosecutions confined to cases where the child is living.[3]

59. The overseers of the poor of each city and town of this commonwealth shall make semi-annual returns to the visiting agent of the board of state charities, concerning all minor children above the age of four years who are supported at the expense of such city or town, in an almshouse or elsewhere, on the first day of January and July. Said returns shall be made in such form, and shall contain such information respecting said minor children as may be prescribed by the board of state charities, and shall be forwarded to said agent on or before the tenth day of each month before mentioned.

60. The provisions of sections two, three, and four of chapter three hundred and fifty-nine of the acts of the year eighteen hundred and seventy, or other acts in addition thereto, in respect to children maintained wholly or in part by the state, and to the indenture of children from the state institutions, shall hereafter apply also to all minor children supported at the expense of any city or town: *provided*, that no such child shall be removed from any city or town without the consent of the overseers of the poor thereof.[4]

[1] Stats. 1871, ch. 42.
[2] Stats. 1875, ch. 109.
[3] Gen. Stats. ch. 72; Grant *v.* Barry, 9 Allen, 459; Wheelwright *v.* Greer, 10 Allen, 389; Meredith *v.* Wall, 14 Allen, 155.
[4] Stats. 1871, ch. 370.

61. Any town in this commonwealth, which shall have accepted the provisions of this act (this and four following sections) at any annual meeting thereof, may, at such or any annual meeting thereafter, elect by written ballot from the inhabitants thereof three persons to be overseers of the poor in such town, one person for one year, one person for two years, and one person for three years, and thereafter at the annual meeting in like manner may elect one person to serve for three years, and these persons so chosen shall constitute the board of overseers of the poor in such town.

62. The members of said boards shall hold office until others are elected and qualified in their stead; vacancies from any cause may be filled by a new choice at any legal meeting, and the person chosen to fill any vacancy shall hold office during the unexpired term, and until another is chosen and qualified in his stead.

63. Said boards shall meet and organize annually within seven days after the annual town meeting, by the choice of a chairman and secretary, which last-named officer may be from their own number or otherwise.

64. Said boards shall cause books to be kept, wherein shall be entered in a neat and methodical style all information in regard to such needy persons as shall have been aided under their direction, that is required by the general laws of this commonwealth; and also all further information in regard to every individual case of relief given, asked for, or refused, as may be of importance to their towns or the commonwealth to preserve, stating the amount and kind of aid given, and the reasons for giving such aid or of refusing the same; such information to be so arranged as to be readily referred to upon the books.

65. The acceptance of this act by any town may at any subsequent annual meeting thereof be revoked by such town, and thereupon this act shall cease to be operative in such town.[1]

66. Any city or town through its authorities, having

1 Stats. 1877, ch. 186.

charge of the execution of the laws for the maintenance of the poor, may, if said authorities deem that the same is for the public interest, furnish temporary aid to poor persons found within its limits, having no settlement within the commonwealth, and the expense thereby incurred, after notice has been sent as hereinafter provided, shall be repaid from the treasury of the commonwealth to such city or town : *provided,* that said authorities shall give immediate notice by mail in each case to the general agent of state charities, who in person or by one of his assistants shall examine the case and direct the continuance of such aid, or removal to the state almshouse or to some place outside the commonwealth, either before or after removal to the state almshouse, in accordance with existing laws ; and *provided, also,* that except in cases of sick state poor such aid shall not be furnished at any one time for a longer period than four weeks, or to a greater amount than one dollar per week for each person, or five dollars per week for each family ; and *provided, also,* that all claims of cities and towns against the commonwealth, for furnishing aid under the provisions of this act, shall be rendered in detail and shall be approved by the general agent of state charities before the same shall be paid.[1]

Nothing contained in this section shall be construed to alter or repeal any of the provisions of law in regard to the sick state poor, or persons ill with contagious diseases.[1]

67. Any new city or town which has been or shall be incorporated, composed of a part of one or more incorporated places, shall be liable for the support of all persons who now do or hereafter shall stand in need of relief as paupers, and have or shall become chargeable to any of said incorporated places by force of chapter three hundred and ninety-two [2] of the acts of eighteen hundred and seventy, and chapter three hundred and seventy-nine of the acts of eighteen hundred and seventy-one : *provided,* the person enlisted, at the time of such enlistment, dwelt,

---

[1] Stats. 1877, ch. 183.    [2] Stats. 1872, ch. 323.

and had his home in the territory embraced within the limits of such new city or town.[1]

68. The overseers of the poor of any town or city, or keepers of almshouses acting under their directions, may require any person, not a resident of said town or city applying to them for and receiving from them food and lodging or either in an almshouse or other place, to perform a reasonable amount of labor in return for such food and lodging and may detain such person until the same is performed, but not beyond the hour of eleven in the forenoon of the day succeeding his application; and if any such person shall refuse or neglect when so required to perform such labor suited to his age, strength, and capacity, or wilfully damage any of the property of such town or city in the charge of such overseers or other officers, he shall be deemed a vagrant within the meaning of the statutes relating to vagrants and vagabonds, and may be prosecuted and punished in the manner provided by chapter two hundred and fifty-eight of the acts of the year eighteen hundred and sixty-nine, or as otherwise provided by law.[2]

If a pauper having a legal settlement in any place becomes an inmate of either of the state almshouses, such place shall be liable to the commonwealth for the expense incurred for him, in like manner as one town is liable to another in like cases; and the same measures shall be adopted by the inspectors and the board of state charities, through their general agent, in regard to notifying towns so liable, the removal of the pauper, and the recovery from towns of expenses incurred for him, as are prescribed for towns in like cases. If any person committed to the state workhouse under chapter two hundred and eighty-eight of the statutes of eighteen hundred and seventy shall have a legal settlement in any city or town in this commonwealth, the said city or town shall pay for his support such sum per week as may be fixed upon by the said board, and all moneys so received shall be paid into the treasury in the manner now provided by law.[3]

---

[1] Stats. 1872, ch. 280.
[2] Stats. 1875, ch. 70.

[3] Gen. Stats. ch. 71, § 49; Stats. 1875, ch. 94.

## CHAPTER XX.

### THE SETTLEMENT OF PAUPERS.

1. LEGAL settlements may be acquired in any city or town, so as to oblige such place to relieve and support the persons acquiring the same, in case they are poor and stand in need of relief, in the manner following, and not otherwise : namely, —

First. A married woman shall follow and have the settlement of her husband, if he has any within the state ; otherwise her own at the time of marriage, if she then had any, shall not be lost or suspended by the marriage.

Second. Legitimate children shall follow and have the settlement of their father, if he has any within the state, until they gain a settlement of their own ; but if he has none, they shall in like manner follow and have the settlement of their mother, if she has any.[1]

But a minor child, having the settlement of its deceased father, does not lose it, and acquire the settlement of its mother, on her gaining a new settlement by a second marriage.[2]

Third. Illegitimate children shall follow and have the settlement of their mother at the time of their birth, if she then has any within the state ; but neither legitimate nor illegitimate children shall gain a settlement by birth in the place where they may be born, if neither of their parents then has a settlement therein.[3]

If the parents of illegitimate children intermarry, and the father acknowledges them as his, the children are made legitimate to all intents and purposes, and thereupon take the settlement of the father.[4]

Fourth. Any person of the age of twenty-one years, having an estate of inheritance or freehold in any place

[1] Stats. 1878, ch. 190, § 1.
[2] Walpole v. Marblehead, 8 Cush. 528.
[3] Stats. 1878, ch. 190, § 1.
[4] Monson v. Palmer, 8 Allen, 551; Gen. Stats. ch. 91, § 4.

within the state, and living on the same three years successively, shall thereby gain a settlement in such place.[1]

But such person does not acquire a settlement in a town, if he receives support as a pauper, during those three years, from the town in which he had his settlement.

And such support granted to such person, as a pauper, by the overseers of the poor of the town in which he has a settlement, will prevent his acquiring a settlement in another town in which he resides, although the act of the overseers, in granting such support, be not ratified by the town of whose poor they are overseers.[2]

And one living three years in any town within this state, on land conveyed to him by a warranty deed, gains a settlement in such town, although his grantor had in fact no title to the land.[3]

Otherwise, however, where a person lives in a town undisturbed for three years in a house built by mistake upon the land of another adjacent to his own land, and having out-buildings upon his own land.[4]

Neither does a tenant by the curtesy initiate in land held by his wife to her sole and separate use gain a settlement after the required residence.[5]

Nor does a person obtain a settlement in a town where he owns a freehold, if before he has lived thereon for three years successively he is committed to the state lunatic hospital and there supported as a pauper; although his family continue to reside on his land for the residue of the three years.[6]

It is now determined that it is not necessary to prove that the deed was recorded, under which land was held, in order to establish a settlement under this clause.[7]

Fifth. Any person of the age of twenty-one years, who resides in any place within this state for five years together, and pays all state, county, city, or town taxes, duly assessed on his poll or estate for any three years within that time, shall thereby gain a settlement in such place.[8]

A person does not acquire a settlement in a town by residing therein ten years together, and paying taxes for five of those years, if he receives aid as a pauper, from such town, before the expiration of the ten years;[9] nor if a town has paid for his support while con-

---

[1] Stats. 1878, ch. 190, § 1.

[2] Oakham v. Sutton, 13 Met. 192.

[3] Boylston v. Clinton, 1 Gray, 619.

[4] Wellfleet v. Truro, 9 Allen, 137.

[5] Leverett v. Deerfield, 6 Allen, 431.

[6] Choate v. Rochester, 13 Gray, 92.

[7] Belchertown v. Dudley, 6 Allen, 477.

[8] Stats. 1878, ch. 190, § 1.

[9] West Newbury v. Bradford, 3 Met. 428.

fined in its workhouse, on conviction of a criminal offence;[1] nor if, during his residence, the assessors omit to tax him, although possessed of real and personal estate; such omission being not on account of his infirmity or poverty, or by mistake, but in order to prevent his acquiring a settlement;[2] nor if, during his residence, he is supplied by the town in which he has a settlement, with money to aid him in supporting his helpless children;[3] nor if his wife is committed to the state lunatic hospital upon his complaint, or with his knowledge, and remains there at the expense of any town, or of the commonwealth, without paying for her support, during part of the time necessary to give him a settlement.[4] It is otherwise, however, if the wife is so supported without the husband's knowledge, and it does not appear that he was ever called upon to pay for such support, or was unable to pay for it.[5]

But insanity occurring after the person has become an inhabitant of a town will not prevent his acquiring a settlement by the requisite residence therein.[6]

And the assessment of a tax on real estate to the occupant, and the payment of the same by him, not as of his own estate, but in right of another, are a sufficient assessment and payment of a tax within the provisions of this clause, for acquiring a settlement as a pauper in the town where such party resides.[7]

A domicile once acquired is presumed to continue until a subsequent change is shown: this is a rule applicable to cases of settlement.[8]

And absence from a town, without a definite purpose at all events to return to it as a home, will not interrupt the residence requisite to a settlement under this clause, until a new domicile is acquired elsewhere.[9]

Sixth. Any woman of the age of twenty-one years, who resides in any place within this state for five years together without receiving relief as a pauper, shall thereby gain a settlement in such place.[10]

But a person does not gain a settlement by paying taxes five years

---

[1] Worcester v. Auburn, 4 Allen, 574.

[2] Berlin v. Bolton, 10 Met. 115.

[3] Taunton v. Middleboro', 12 Met. 35.

[4] Charlestown v. Groveland, 15 Gray, 15; Woodward v. Worcester, 15 Gray, 19.

[5] Berkeley v. Taunton, 19 Pick. 480.

[6] Chicopee v. Whately, 6 Allen, 508.

[7] Randolph v. Easton, 4 Cush. 557.

[8] Chicopee v. Whately, 6 Allen, 508.

[9] Worcester v. Wilbraham, 13 Gray, 586; Lee v. Lenox, 15 Gray, 496.

[10] Stats. 1878, ch. 190, § 1.

successively on real estate, of which he is in possession as tenant at will,[1] or at sufferance.[2]

Seventh. Any person being chosen and actually serving one whole year in the office of clerk, treasurer, selectman, overseer of the poor, assessor, constable, or collector of taxes, in any place, shall thereby gain a settlement therein. For this purpose a year shall be considered as including the time between the choice of such officers at one annual meeting and the choice at the next annual meeting, whether more or less than a calendar year.

Eighth. Every settled ordained minister of the gospel shall be deemed to have acquired a legal settlement in the place wherein he is or may be settled as a minister.[3]

Where a minister who has been regularly ordained in one town is afterwards settled in another, as a pastor, with the full character, rights, and duties of a pastor, but without any new ordination or ceremony of induction, or for a limited time, as for a year, he will by such settlement, as a minister, acquire a settlement as a pauper in the latter town.[4]

Ninth. A minor who serves an apprenticeship to a lawful trade for the space of four years in any place, and actually sets up such trade therein within one year after the expiration of said term, being then twenty-one years old, and continues there to carry on the same for five years, shall thereby gain a settlement in such place ; but being hired as a journeyman shall not be considered as setting up a trade.

Tenth. Any person who shall have been duly enlisted and mustered into the military or naval service of the United States, as a part of the quota of any city or town in this commonwealth, under any call of the President of the United States during the late civil war, or duly assigned as a part of the quota thereof, after having been enlisted and mustered into said service, and shall have duly served for not less than one year, or shall have died, or become

---

[1] Southbridge *v.* Warren, 11 Cush. 292.

[2] Dover *v.* Brighton, 2 Gray, 482.

[3] Stats. 1878, ch. 190, § 1.

[4] Bellingham *v.* West Boylston, 4 Cush. 553.

disabled from wounds or disease received or contracted while engaged in such service, or while a prisoner in the hands of the enemy, and the wife or widow and minor children of such person, shall be deemed thereby to have acquired a settlement in such place; and any person who would otherwise be entitled to a settlement under this clause, but who was not a part of the quota of any city or town, shall, if he served as a part of the quota of this commonwealth, be deemed to have acquired a settlement in the place where he actually resided at the time of his enlistment. But these provisions shall not apply to any person who shall have enlisted and received a bounty for such enlistment in more than one place, unless the second enlistment was made after an honorable discharge from the first term of service, nor to any person who shall have been proved guilty of wilful desertion, or to have left the service otherwise than by reason of disability or an honorable discharge.

Eleventh. Upon the division of a city or town, every person having a legal settlement therein, but being absent at the time of such division, and not having acquired a legal settlement elsewhere, shall have his legal settlement in that place wherein his last dwelling-place or home happens to fall upon such division; and when a new city or town is incorporated, composed of a part of one or more incorporated places, every person legally settled in the places of which such new city or town is so composed, and who actually dwells and has his home within the bounds of such new city or town at the time of its incorporation, and any person duly qualified as provided in the tenth clause of this section, who, at the time of his enlistment, dwelt and had his home within such bounds, shall thereby acquire a legal settlement in such new place: *provided*, that no persons residing in that part of a place, which, upon such division, shall be incorporated into a new city or town, having then no legal settlement therein, shall acquire any by force of such incorporation only; nor shall such incorporation prevent his acquiring a settlement therein within the time and by the means by which he would have gained it there if no such division had been made.

2. No person who has begun to acquire a settlement by the laws in force at and before the time when this act takes effect, in any of the ways in which any time is prescribed for a residence, or for the continuance or succession of any other act, shall be prevented or delayed by the provisions of this act; but he shall acquire a settlement by a continuance or succession of the same residence or other act, in the same time and manner as if the former laws had continued in force.

3. Except as hereinafter provided, every legal settlement shall continue till it is lost or defeated by acquiring a new one within this state; and upon acquiring such new settlement all former settlements shall be defeated and lost.

4. All settlements acquired by virtue of any provision of law in force prior to the eleventh day of February in the year one thousand seven hundred and ninety-four are hereby defeated and lost: *provided*, this shall not apply where the existence of such settlement prevented a subsequent acquisition of settlement in the same place under the provisions of clauses fourth, fifth, sixth, seventh, eighth, ninth, tenth, and eleventh of the first section of this act, or under the same provisions in other statutes existing prior to the passage of this act; and *provided*, *further*, that, whenever a settlement acquired by marriage has been thus defeated, the former settlement of the wife, if not defeated by the same provision, shall be deemed to have been thereby revived.

5. Chapter sixty-nine of the General Statutes, chapter two hundred and eighty-eight of the acts of the year one thousand eight hundred and sixty-six, section one of chapter three hundred and twenty-eight of the acts of the year one thousand eight hundred and sixty-eight, chapter three hundred and ninety-two of the acts of the year one thousand eight hundred and seventy, chapter three hundred and seventy-nine of the acts of the year one thousand eight

hundred and seventy-one, chapter two hundred and eighty of the acts of the year one thousand eight hundred and seventy-two, and chapter two hundred and seventy-four of the acts of the year one thousand eight hundred and seventy-four, are hereby repealed, saving all acts done, or rights accruing, accrued, or established, or proceedings, doings, or acts ratified or confirmed, or suits or proceedings had or commenced, before the repeal takes effect.[1]

6. Any Indian or person of color belonging to any of the Indian tribes specially enumerated in the first section of this act,[2] and to whom the rights of citizenship are not hereby extended, and who desires to possess such rights, may, if residing within the limits of any city or town of this commonwealth, certify his desire to the clerk of said city or town, who shall make record of the same ; and, upon paying a poll-tax, he shall become to all intents and purposes a citizen of the state, and shall not thenceforward return to the legal condition of an Indian. Settlement shall be acquired by those who thus become citizens, in the same manner as by other persons ; and any such citizen becoming a pauper without having acquired a settlement shall be deemed a state pauper.

But by statutes of 1869, ch. 463, all Indians in this commonwealth are made citizens, entitled to all the rights and privileges and subject to all the duties and liabilities of citizens.

7. Any convict who, at the legal expiration of his sentence, is in such condition from bodily infirmity or disease as to render his removal impracticable, shall be provided for and receive such treatment in the state prison, jail, house of correction, or house of industry in which he was confined, as the exigency of the case may require, until he is in a condition to be removed. The expense of such care and treatment of any discharged convict shall be paid, at a rate not exceeding three dollars and fifty cents per week, by the city or town where he may have a legal settlement, after notice upon expiration of sentence shall have been

---

[1] Stats. 1878, ch. 190.  [2] Stats. 1862, ch. 184, § 2.

given by the authorities of the prison to the overseers of the poor of the city or town liable for his support, or to the board of state charities, if he be a state pauper, of the condition of said discharged convict.[1]

[1] Stats. 1874, ch. 170.

## CHAPTER XXI.

### WORKHOUSES AND ALMSHOUSES.

1. A CITY or town may erect or provide a workhouse or almshouse for the employment and support of poor and indigent persons who are maintained by or receive alms from the city or town; persons who, being able of body to work, and not having estate or means otherwise to maintain themselves, refuse or neglect to work; persons who live a dissolute, vagrant life, and exercise no ordinary calling or lawful business; persons who spend their time and property in public houses to the neglect of their proper business, or who, by otherwise misspending what they earn, to the impoverishment of themselves and their families, are likely to become chargeable to the city or town; and other persons sent thereto under any provisions of law.

2. No city or town shall erect or maintain an almshouse or house of correction within the limits of any other place, without the consent of such other place.

3. Every city or town having a workhouse or almshouse may annually choose three, five, seven, or more directors, who shall have the inspection and government thereof, and who may appoint a master and necessary assistants for the more immediate care and superintendence of the persons received or employed therein. Where such directors are not specially chosen, the overseers of the poor shall be the directors.

4. Once in every month, and at other times as occasion may require, the directors shall hold meetings for the purpose of determining the most eligible mode of discharging their duties. At such monthly meetings they may make needful orders and regulations for the house, which shall

be binding until the next meeting of the town or of the city council, when the same shall be submitted to such meeting; and, if approved, shall remain in force until revoked by the town or the city council.

5. Any number of cities or towns may, at their joint charge and for their common use, erect or provide a workhouse or almshouse, and purchase land for the use thereof.

6. The ordering, governing, and repairing of such house, the appointment of a master and necessary assistants, and the power of removing them for misconduct, incapacity, or other sufficient cause, shall be vested in a joint board of directors, who shall be chosen annually by the several places interested.

7. Unless all the places interested in such house shall agree to choose a different number, each of them shall choose three members of the board; and in case of the death of a director, or of his removal from the place for which he was chosen, the vacancy may be supplied by such place. If a place neglects to choose directors, those chosen by the other places shall have the whole charge of the house.

8. Stated quarterly meetings of the board shall be holden on the first Tuesdays of January, April, July, and October, at the workhouse or almshouse under their charge, for the purpose of inspecting the management and directing the business thereof. Meetings of the board may be called at other times by the directors chosen by any place interested, they giving notice of the time and purpose thereof to the other members of the board in such manner as shall have been agreed upon at a stated meeting.

9. The board of directors may choose a moderator; and at their first general meeting they shall appoint a clerk, who shall be sworn and shall record all votes and orders of the board.

10. At a general quarterly meeting, if one half of the members are present, they may make reasonable orders and by-laws not repugnant to the laws of the Commonwealth for ordering and regulating the house under their

charge, and may agree with the master and assistants, and order a suitable compensation for their services.

11. Other matters may be acted upon at any other meeting duly notified, if one third of the members are present; but the doings of such meetings may be altered or revised at any general stated meeting.

12. The yearly compensation of the master and assistants (in addition to the allowance hereafter provided in this chapter for their services), and also the expense of keeping the house in repair, shall be paid by the several places interested, in proportion to their state tax at the time when the expense may have been incurred, or in such proportion as the places interested shall agree.

13. If a place refuses or neglects to advance or reimburse its proportion of the sums of money mentioned in the preceding section, or of any other charges mentioned in this chapter, after the same have been adjusted by the joint board of directors, the same may be recovered of such delinquent place in an action of contract brought by any person whom the board shall in writing appoint for that purpose.

14. No greater number of persons belonging to a city or town shall be received into such workhouse or almshouse than such city's or town's proportion of such house, when the receiving of them would exclude or be inconvenient to such as belong to the other places interested.

15. If any place refuses or neglects to provide its proportion of the necessary expenses of such house, or of the materials, implements, or other means, for performing the work there required, according to its agreement or the directions of the joint board of directors, such place shall be deprived of the privilege of sending any person thither during the time of such neglect or refusal.

16. Each place may furnish such additional materials, implements, and means of work, as the overseers of the poor thereof may choose, for the employment of any person committed to such house; and the master of the house shall receive the same, and keep them separate from those

of the other places, and shall be accountable to each place interested, as well for the cost as for all profits and earnings made by the labor of the persons committed to said house from such place.

17. The master of each workhouse and almshouse shall keep a register of the names of the persons committed or received, the places to which they belong, the dates of their reception and discharge, and of their respective earnings, to be submitted to the overseers of the poor upon their request.

18. Controversies between the masters and the overseers of the poor of any place, respecting the accounts or other official doings of the masters, shall be determined by the directors of the house at their general or quarterly meeting.

19. The profits and earnings arising from the work of persons committed to the workhouse or almshouse, with the stock remaining on hand, shall be disposed of as the overseers of the poor of the several places shall think proper, either to the use of their cities or towns, the persons committed, or their families.

20. No person committed to the workhouse shall be discharged within the time for which he was committed, except by the police court or justice who made the commitment, the directors of the house at their general or quarterly meeting, or by the superior court, at any term held in the county where such house is situated, for good cause shown upon application for that purpose.

21. Every person committed to a workhouse shall, if able to work, be kept diligently employed in labor during the term of his commitment. If he is idle, and does not perform such reasonable task as is assigned, or is stubborn and disorderly, he shall be punished according to the orders and regulations established by the directors.

22. When a person, not having a legal settlement in this state, shall become idle or indigent, he may be committed to the workhouse to be there employed if able to labor, in the same manner and under the same rules as other persons there committed.

23. A workhouse or almshouse may be discontinued or appropriated to any other use, when the place or places interested so determine.

24. Nothing contained in this chapter shall affect any powers or privileges heretofore granted to cities or towns, or the overseers of the poor thereof, by acts specially relating to workhouses or almshouses therein.[1]

25. The secretary of the board of state charities shall furnish, from time to time, to the keepers of the several prisons and workhouses throughout the commonwealth, including the state prison and the houses of industry, reformation, and correction in the city of Boston the following blank schedule for periodical returns, which shall be made weekly from all prisons where the commitments average ten a week and upwards; monthly, from all prisons where the commitments average between two and ten a week; and once in six months from all other prisons: —

ADMISSIONS. — Registered number; name; color; age; sex; birthplace; parents both Americans; parents both temperate; parents both or either convicts; ever married; intemperate; what education; what property; ever in army or navy; ever in reform school; when committed; why committed; number of former commitments; when discharged; how discharged; length of sentence; number of days sick; number of times punished in prison.

DISCHARGES. — Registered number; name; when committed; why committed; when discharged; how discharged; time in prison; number of days sick; number of times punished in prison; number remaining by last report; number committed since last report; number discharged; number transferred from other jails, &c.; number transferred to other jails, &c.; number now in confinement.

26. Every sheriff or prison officer who omits to make and transmit, according to the provisions of this act (preceding section), true answers to the inquiries contained in the schedules, and every director or county commissioner, when his board omits to make and transmit such answers, shall forfeit one hundred dollars.[2]

---

[1] Gen. Stats. ch. 22, §§ 1-24.    [2] Stats. 1864, ch. 307, §§ 1, 4.

# CHAPTER XXII.

## LAYING OUT AND DISCONTINUANCE OF HIGHWAYS.

1. WHEN a new highway, from town to town, or from place to place within the same town, is wanting, or when any highway can with greater public convenience be altered or discontinued, application therefor shall be made, by petition in writing to the county commissioners who have jurisdiction in the place in which such new highway or such alteration or discontinuance is wanted.[1]

The word "highway" may include county bridges; and shall be equivalent to the words "county way," "county road," and "common road."[2]

2. There should be such a description of the bounds of the road prayed for in the petition, as to give substantial notice of what is asked and intended to all persons and corporations interested.[3]

3. No petition for the laying out, altering, or discontinuing, a highway, shall be proceeded upon by the commissioners, until the petitioners cause a sufficient recognizance to be given to the county, with surety to the satisfaction of the commissioners, for the payment of all costs and expenses which shall arise by reason of such petition and the proceedings thereon, if the petitioners shall not finally prevail.

4. The commissioners to whom such petition is presented shall cause a copy thereof to be served upon the clerk of every town within which such new highway, alteration, or discontinuance, is prayed for, thirty days at least before the time appointed for any view or hearing. They shall also cause copies of the petition, or abstracts containing the substance thereof, to be posted in two public places

---

[1] Gen. Stats. ch. 43, § 1.
[2] Gen. Stats. ch. 3, § 7.
[3] Westport v. County Commissioners of Bristol, 9 Allen, 203.

in each of said towns, and shall give notice to all persons interested, by causing a like copy to be published three weeks successively in such newspaper as they shall order; the posting and the last publication of the copy to be fourteen days at least before any view, hearing, or adjudication, on such petition.[1]

5. A town created out of a part of a town already existing, after a highway within that part has been adjudged by the county commissioners to be of common convenience and necessity, and the time for locating it fixed, and notice given to the old town, is not entitled to a further hearing on the questions of the necessity of the way.[2]

6. They shall view the premises, when they deem it expedient or when requested by any party interested; and, before any view, shall give notice in the manner provided in the preceding section (section four above), to all persons interested, of the time and place for commencing the same.

7. They shall hear the parties, either at the time of the view, or at any regular or special meeting, or any adjournment thereof, as they determine; and as soon as may be after the hearing they shall consider and adjudicate upon the common convenience and necessity of laying out, altering, or discontinuing, such highway, as prayed for by the petitioners.

8. When they have adjudicated upon the common convenience and necessity of laying out, altering, or discontinuing a highway, they shall, as soon as may be, proceed to lay out, alter, or discontinue, the same accordingly; first giving such notice[3] thereof as is required before proceeding to view, except that instead of a copy of the whole petition it shall be sufficient to serve and publish an abstract thereof.[4]

9. Personal notice to all the proprietors over whose land the way passes, is not required by the statute.[5] And county commissioners

---

[1] Gen. Stats. ch. 43, §§ 2, 3.

[2] North Reading v. County Commissioners, 7 Gray, 109.

[3] See above, section 4.

[4] Gen. Stats. ch. 43, §§ 4–6.

[5] Taylor v. County Commissioners, 18 Pick. 309.

may lay out a highway at an adjournment of a meeting for that purpose, of which they have given due notice, without giving a new notice of the adjourned meeting.[1]

10. (But) the laying out or alteration of any highway, town way, or private way, shall be void as against the owner of any land over which the same shall be located, unless possession shall be taken of such land for the purpose of constructing such highway, town way, or private way, within two years from the time when the right to take possession for such purpose first accrues by law: *provided, however,* that an entry for the purpose of constructing any part of the laying out or alterations in such way shall, for the purposes of this act, be deemed a taking of possession of all the lands included in the laying or alterations made upon the same petition.[2]

11. They may make such changes between the termini of the highway described in the petition, with regard to the direction, alteration, or discontinuance, thereof, as in their opinion the public convenience requires.

12. If at the time of view, upon a petition for laying out or altering a highway, no person interested shall object, the commissioners may within six months proceed to lay out or alter the same without further notice. If at the time of view upon a petition for discontinuing a highway the commissioners shall decide that the same ought to be discontinued, they may at the same time adjudge and determine that it be discontinued without a further or subsequent meeting therefor, and may estimate the damages caused to any person thereby; and when a return of said proceedings and adjudication is made at the next regular meeting of the commissioners and accepted, it shall be held to be a discontinuance of such highway.

13. If, upon a petition for laying out or altering a highway, the commissioners, after having viewed the same and heard all persons interested, are of opinion that the existing highway between the termini mentioned in the petition

---

[1] Westport *v.* County Commissioners, 9 Allen, 203.    [2] Stats. 1869, ch. 303.

can be so far amended as to supersede the necessity of laying out a new highway or altering the location of existing ways, they may, after due notice to the towns interested, direct specific repairs to be made in the existing ways in such manner as the public convenience requires; and they may apportion the expense of making the same upon the county and towns respectively as in laying out highways.[1]

14. When in the laying out, widening or relocating any highway the county commissioners of any county shall require the making of any culvert, cattle-pass or other passage-way through or under the highway as the commissioners shall direct the same to be made and worked, said commissioners may order and require the town in which such highway is located, to construct such culvert, cattle-pass or other passage-way, and the town shall construct the same as a part of the highway. And the county commissioners may reimburse to said town out of the county treasury, such portion of the cost of the same, if any, as justice and equity may in their judgment require.[2]

15. Where a town has due notice of the application of individuals to the county commissioners for the alteration of a road within the town, alleged in such application and in all the proceedings thereon to be a highway, and also has due notice of the proceedings of the commissioners in directing specific repairs to be made on said road by the town, and does not object that said road is a town way and not a highway, until after the commissioners have caused such repairs to be made, upon the neglect of the town to make them as ordered, and after the town is served with notice, to show cause why a warrant of distress should not issue against the inhabitants of the town for the collection of its proportion of the expense of such repairs, a writ of certiorari will not be granted to remove the records of the commissioners, on the ground that the road was a town way, and that they therefore had no jurisdiction. Nor will a writ of prohibition be granted to restrain the commissioners from issuing such warrant of distress.[3]

16. At the time of ordering specific repairs upon an existing highway, they may direct it to be closed to

---

[1] Gen. Stats. ch. 43, §§ 7-9.
[2] Stats. 1867, ch. 256.

[3] Whately v. County Commissioners of Franklin, 1 Met. 336.

the public travel for such time as they may deem reasonable.

17. Towns in which specific repairs are ordered to be made shall be liable to make the same, and be entitled to a trial by jury in like manner as is provided in laying out highways.

18. When application is made to the commissioners by a town, or by five inhabitants of a town, to locate anew a road within such town, whether the same were laid out by the authority of the town or otherwise, they may, either for the purpose of establishing the boundary lines of such road or of making alterations in the course or width thereof, locate it anew after giving like notice and proceeding in the manner prescribed in laying out highways. The expense shall be assessed upon the (abuttors [1]) or the petitioners, or upon the town or county, as the commissioners order.[2]

19. A party aggrieved by the action of county commissioners in locating a road anew, for the purpose of establishing the boundary line thereof, is entitled to a jury to determine his damages, in the same manner as in an original laying out of such road.[3]

20. The "expenses" arising in the case, which a town applying to the county commissioners to locate anew any road within the town is obliged to pay, include the damages occasioned to the owners of land by such location.[4]

21. When a highway is laid out or altered, the commissioners shall in their return determine and specify the manner in which such new highway or alteration shall be made, and also the time within which it shall be completed ; and shall transmit to the clerks of the several towns in which said highway lies a description of the location and bounds thereof within the limits of such towns respectively, which description shall be recorded within ten days by the clerk in a book of records kept in the town for that purpose. They shall also allow the owner of the land a reasonable time to take off his timber, wood, or trees,

---

[1] Stats. 1873, ch. 165.
[2] Gen. Stats. ch. 43, §§ 10–12. See chapter on Betterments.
[3] Hadley v. County Commissioners of Middlesex, 11 Cush. 394.
[4] Damon v. Reading, 2 Gray, 274.

which shall be expressed in their return. If he shall not remove the same within the time allowed, he shall be deemed to have relinquished his right thereto for the benefit of the town.

The provision applies also to buildings, and parts of buildings, materials of walls and fences, growing crops, and generally every thing valuable to the owner, but inconvenient or unsuitable to be left within the limits of the way.[1]

22. If damage shall be sustained by any persons in their property, by the laying out, altering, or discontinuing, a highway, the commissioners shall estimate the amount, and in their return state the share of each separately; but they shall not order such damages to be paid, nor shall a person claiming damage have a right to demand the same, until the land over which the highway or alteration is located has been entered upon and possession taken for the purpose of constructing it. But when a person so claiming damages has been put to trouble and expense by the proceedings, the commissioners shall allow him full indemnity therefor, instead of the damages awarded, although no entry is made upon his land.[2]

23. The damage to the owner of lands over which a highway is laid out and established is practically equivalent to the whole value of the land. For the public have a right to hold a perpetual easement; and the strong probability and the result usually is, that the easement for the public is of such a nature that substantially it deprives the owner of all, or nearly all, beneficial use of the land, and leaves him a barren fee only. Therefore it is that, in estimating the damages which the public shall pay for such an easement upon the land, the question resolves itself into this, What is the value of the land, the benefit of which is almost wholly lost to the owner by so large and perpetual a lien?[3]

24. When county commissioners, on laying out a highway or ordering specific repairs therein, make no return of damages sustained by a party who has applied to them to estimate his damages, it is equivalent to a return that he has sustained no damage; and the party

---

[1] Commonwealth v. Noxon, 121 Mass. 42.

[2] Gen. Stats. ch. 43, §§ 13, 14.

[3] Harrington, Jr. v. County Commissioners of Berkshire, 22 Pick. 263.

aggrieved must apply for a jury within the same time as if the commissioners had expressly returned that he had sustained no damage.[1]

25. The provision of the statute that "they shall not order such damages to be paid, nor shall a person claiming damage have a right to demand the same, until the land over which the highway or alteration is located has been entered upon, and possession taken for the purpose of constructing it," applies to all public, travelled ways, whether town ways or county ways; but it does not prohibit a person over whose land a town way is laid out by the commissioners, and who is aggrieved by their estimate of his damage from having the damage assessed by a jury before his land is entered upon, and possession thereof taken, for the purpose of constructing the way.[2]

26. The powers of the commissioners extend alike to highways, town ways, and private ways, and are not thereby restricted to highways in the limited meaning of that term; but as it is used in its popular sense, to extend to travelled ways in relation to which they are called upon, under the provision of the statute to direct or adjudicate.[3]

27. But county commissioners have no authority to order a town to pay damages to an individual for land taken for a highway.[4]

28. When specific repairs are ordered to be made in a highway which occasion damage to any person or property, the commissioners shall estimate the same, and make return thereof; and at their first meeting after the repairs are completed, they shall order the damage to be paid. But if the order for repairs does not go into effect, or is rescinded or altered, they shall order only so much of the damage to be paid as in their opinion has been actually sustained.

29. In estimating the damage sustained by laying out, locating anew, altering or discontinuing, a highway, or by an order for specific repairs, regard shall be had to all the damages done to the party, whether by taking his property or injuring it in any manner; and there shall be allowed, by way of set-off, the benefit, if any, to the property of the party by reason thereof.[5]

---

[1] Monagle *v.* County Commissioners of Bristol, 8 Cush. 360.

[2] Harding *v.* Medway, 10 Met. 465.

[3] Jones *v.* Andover, 6 Pick. 59; Commonwealth *v.* Hubbard, 24 Pick.

98; Harding *v.* Medway, 10 Met. 465.

[4] Westport *v.* County Commissioners of Bristol, 9 Allen, 203.

[5] Gen. Stats. ch. 43, §§ 15, 16.

30. In estimating the damage to the land-owner caused by the laying out of a public street over his land, neither the city or town authorities, nor a jury, are confined to the value of the land covered by the street. He is also entitled to the amount of the damage done to his remaining land by the laying out of the street.[1]

31. And the assessment is to be made according to the effect of the taking of the land at the time it was taken. And not as the land then lay unfitted for use as a street, but according to the prospective use of the street when wrought and fitted for use as a part of the street, for a sidewalk or carriage-way; and its effect upon the residue of the land when thus fitted for use as part of the street. Its value for the purpose of building is also to be considered.[2]

32. And if the owner of the land has built a house on a part thereof over which there is a right of way, he may recover, as part of the damage occasioned by the subsequent taking of the land for a highway, the value of the right to have the house remain on the land until its removal be required by the owner of the right of way.[3]

33. In estimating the damages occasioned by taking land for a highway, any direct and peculiar benefit or increase of value, accruing to land of the same owner adjoining or connected with the land taken, is to be allowed by way of set-off; but not any general benefit or increase of value, received by such land in common with other land in the neighborhood.[4]

34. The discontinuance of a highway gives no right to recover damages to the owner of land abutting on the way discontinued, and accessible by other ways.[5]

35. When persons having a claim for damages sustained in their property by the laying out, alteration, or discontinuance, of a highway, have different or separate interests in the property, so that an estate for life or for a term of years in the same, belongs to one person, and the remainder or reversion in fee belongs to another, entire damages. or an entire sum as indemnity, shall be assessed in the same manner as is provided in other cases, without any apportionment thereof; and the amount of such damages or indemnity shall be paid over to or be recoverable by any

[1] First Church in Boston *v.* City of Boston, 14 Gray, 214.

[2] Dickenson *v.* Fitchburg, 13 Gray, 546.

[3] Tufts *v.* Charlestown, 4 Gray, 537.

[4] Meacham *v.* Fitchburg R. R. Co., 4 Cush. 291; Upton *v.* S. Reading Br. R. R. Co., 8 Cush. 600; Farwell *v.* Cambridge, 11 Gray, 413; Dickenson *v.* Fitchburg, 13 Gray, 546. See, in this connection, chapter on Betterment Law, hereafter.

[5] Castle *v.* County of Berkshire, 11 Gray, 26.

person whom the parties owning the several interests may appoint, to be invested by him, when paid over or recovered, in bond, mortgage, or other good securities, and held in trust for the benefit of the parties according to their several interests ; the annual income to be paid over to the person in whom was the estate for life or term of years, for the period such estate might have continued, and the remainder after the termination of such estate to be paid over absolutely to the person that was entitled to the reversion in fee, or to his heirs or devisees.

36. If any of the persons having an interest in such property shall, by reason of legal disability, be incapacitated from choosing a trustee, or if the parties in interest cannot agree upon a choice, the probate court of the county in which the property is situated, upon application, shall appoint some suitable person as trustee.  Said trustee shall before entering upon the duties of his trust give a bond to the judge of probate and insolvency, with sufficient surety or sureties, in such penal sum as the judge directs, conditioned for the faithful performance of his duties as trustee under the provisions of this and the preceding section : which bond upon breach of its condition may be put in suit by order of the probate court for the use and benefit of the persons interested in the trust property, in like manner as is provided in case of bonds given by executors or administrators.[1]

37. In all cases of the assessment of the damages sustained by land-owners by reason of the laying out, alteration, or discontinuance of a highway, whenever it shall appear that the real estate taken or affected is encumbered by any contingent remainder, executory devise, or power of appointment, the assessment of damages shall proceed, and the damages recovered shall be paid over to a trustee or trustees in the manner provided for the assessment of damages where there are different and separate vested interests in the property, in section seventeen of chapter forty-three of the General Statutes.

[1] Gen. Stats. ch. 43, §§ 17, 18.

38. The trustee or trustees to whom such damages are to be paid, as provided in the foregoing section, shall be appointed by the probate court for the county where the land is situated, on petition of the county commissioners or of any person in possession and enjoyment of the land either as tenant of a freehold estate or of a term of years; and in case the commissioners and such tenant in possession shall neglect or refuse to file such petition, then said trustee or trustees may be appointed on petition of any person, filed in behalf of such persons, whether in being or not, as may by any possibility be or become interested in the property, and the trustee or trustees, so appointed, shall hold and invest the funds so received by him or them for the benefit of the persons who would have been entitled to said estate, in the same manner as if such location, alteration, or discontinuance of such highway had not been made, and shall give bond to the judge of probate in such form and amount as the court shall order.

39. In all cases mentioned in section one of this act (thirty-seven of this chapter) the tenant in possession may apply for a jury, as is now provided by law in other cases, to revise the judgment of the county commissioners in the assessment of damages within one year from the adoption of the order of assessment by the commissioners; and if such tenant shall fail to so apply within the first six months of the year so limited, then the trustee or trustees, appointed under section two (preceding section) of this act, may, if they shall see fit, apply for such jury.

40. The provisions of this act (sections thirty-seven to forty-one, inclusive, of this chapter) shall be applicable to all cases of the exercise of the right of eminent domain, in which provision is made that the damages sustained by a land-owner shall be assessed in the manner provided in the laying out of highways; but the limitation as to the time within which proceedings to recover damages shall be commenced, shall be the same as now provided by law in the various cases of the exercise of the right of eminent domain; and the right of the trustee or trustees, named in

this act, to petition in any proceeding to recover damage shall not accrue until the tenant in possession of the estate shall have neglected so to petition for one-half the period so limited in any case.

41. This act shall apply to pending cases whenever the tenant in possession of the property is a party to any proceeding to recover damages, and where no assessment of damages has been made; and the proceedings may be amended, if necessary, on proper terms to confirm trusts; and the trustee or trustees named in this act may, in such cases, be appointed, as though proceedings have already been taken.[1]

42. A party aggrieved by the doings of the commissioners in the estimation of his damages, occasioned either by the laying out, locating anew, altering or discontinuing a highway, or by any specific repairs ordered by the commissioners, or in the sum awarded him as indemnity therefor, may have a jury to determine the matter of his complaint upon written application to the commissioners; unless he agrees with the parties adversely interested to have the same determined by a committee, to be appointed under the direction of the commissioners.[2]

43. As to who may be "a party aggrieved," it has been decided that a town in which a highway is laid out may be one;[3] and a person having only a possessory title of the land over which the highway is located.[4]

44. The county commissioners having estimated the damages, if either party shall be dissatisfied and apply for a jury, they must grant it: their duty here is merely ministerial; they are without discretion, and if they refuse the application of the party, the supreme court will issue a mandate commanding them to grant the proper process for a jury in such a case.[5]

45. Applications for a jury to revise the judgment of the commissioners in the assessment of damages merely,

[1] Stats. 1875, ch. 117, §§ 1–5.

[2] Stats. 1870, ch. 76. See foregoing sections 19, 24, 25.

[3] Lanesborough v. County Commissioners of Berkshire, 22 Pick. 278; Westport v. County Commissioners, 9 Allen, 204.

[4] Trustees of the State Lunatic Hospital v. County of Worcester, 1 Met. 437.

[5] Carpenter v. County Commissioners of Bristol, 21 Pick. 258.

or in the award of indemnity, may be made at any time within one year from the time of the adoption of the order; or, if within that time a suit shall be instituted wherein the legal effect of the proceedings of the commissioners in laying out, locating anew, altering, or discontinuing, a highway, is drawn in question, such application may be made at any time within one year after the final determination of the suit.

46. If two or more persons apply at the same time for joint or several damages or indemnity, they may join in the same petition to the commissioners; and if several applications are pending at the same time before the commissioners for a jury to determine any matter relating to the laying out, alteration, or discontinuance, of a highway, or the assessment of damages or indemnity, they shall cause all such applications to be considered and determined by the same jury; and the costs shall be taxed either jointly or severally, as the court to which the verdict may be returned shall determine to be equitable.[1]

47. In Lanesborough *v.* County Commissioners of Berkshire,[2] Chief-Justice Shaw said: "It is a matter of convenience and economy, that several cases upon the same general subject, shall be determined at once. But if one of the applicants obtains a verdict for his several damages and for his own use, there seems to be no reason why the controversy should not be considered as terminated in regard to him, because the jury in another and distinct case do not agree. If the question were solely upon the subject of alterations, two or more cases might perhaps be connected, that one could not properly be determined without including another. But where the verdict is for several damages, the court are of opinion that where there is a verdict in favor of one, it ought to be received and accepted *pro tanto,* and that the party who thus obtains a verdict for damages, is entitled to the benefit of it, although the jury do not agree as to other subjects committed to them at the same time."

48. No jury shall be ordered, nor committee appointed, until the petitioners give recognizance to the county for the payment of all the costs and expenses which may arise in case the jury or committee shall not alter such highway,

---

[1] Gen. Stats. ch. 43, §§ 22, 23.          [2] 22 Pick. 278.

nor increase the damages or indemnity allowed by the commissioners.

49. No petition for a jury shall abate or be defeated by the death of the petitioner; but the executor or administrator, or the heirs or devisees if they shall be the persons interested, may appear and prosecute such petition, or present a new petition, in the same manner and with the same effect as the original party might have done.

50. If, upon the death of one or more of several petitioners for a jury, the executors or administrators, heirs or devisees, of such petitioners, after due notice that such petition is pending, neglect to appear or to prosecute, the surviving petitioners may proceed in the same manner as if they only had made the application.

51. The warrant for a jury shall be directed to the sheriff of the county or his deputy, who is disinterested, or to a coroner, as the commissioners shall order, requiring him to summon a jury of twelve men to hear and determine the matter of complaint set forth in the petition, and to decide all such matters as shall legally come before them on the hearing.

52. The officer who receives the warrant shall in writing require of the selectmen of the three nearest towns not interested in the question, if there be so many in the county, to return a number of jurors, not less than two nor more than six from any one town unless in case of necessity; and the jurors shall be drawn, summoned, and returned, as in other cases, except that the jurors need not be summoned more than twenty-four hours before the time appointed for their attendance.[1]

In Wyman v. Lexington and West Cambridge Railroad Company,[2] Judge Dewey said that "We are of opinion that the three nearest towns from which a jury is to be summoned, are the three towns nearest to that in which the land is situate, and exclusive of such town. A jury summoned in part from the town in which the land lies that is the subject of damages, would therefore be irregularly summoned, and if seasonably objected to, their verdict would be set aside for that cause."

[1] Gen. Stats. ch. 43, §§ 24-28.    [2] 13 Metcalf, 316.

53. If a person so summoned as a juror fails to attend without sufficient cause, he shall pay a fine not exceeding ten dollars, at the discretion of the court to which the verdict is returned, to be paid into the county treasury.

54. If by reason of challenges or otherwise there is not a full jury of the persons summoned, the officer who summoned the jury, or in his absence the officer attending the jury, shall return some suitable person to supply the deficiency.

55. The jurors shall be sworn to make a just and true appraisement of the damages sustained by the complainant, or of the indemnity to which he is entitled, and well and truly to try all such other matters as shall be lawfully submitted to them under the complaint, and to give a true verdict therein, according to law and the evidence given them; but when no estimate of damages or indemnity is required to be made, that part of the oath shall be omitted.

56. The commissioners, when they issue their warrant for a jury, may at the request of either party appoint some suitable person to preside at the trial, in which case the jury may be attended by a deputy-sheriff; but if no person is appointed, the sheriff of such county shall preside; or, when the sheriff is interested or unable to attend, a coroner of the county shall preside.[1]

57. The person presiding at the trial shall keep order therein, and administer the oath to the jurors and witnesses; shall decide all questions of law arising on the trial which would be proper for the decision of a judge; shall direct the jury upon any question of law, when requested by either party; and shall when requested certify to the court, with the verdict, the substance of any decision or direction by him given.[2]

58. When a petition for a jury is presented, the commissioners shall, on behalf of the county, take notice of the same; and may in behalf of the county agree with the petitioners to substitute a committee in the place of a jury, as before provided. They shall, when they think it neces-

[1] Gen. Stats. ch. 43, §§ 29-32.    [2] Gen. Stats. ch. 43, § 33.

sary, appoint some suitable person to attend upon the jury or the committee, as an agent for the county, who shall be allowed therefor three dollars a day and ten cents a mile travel.

59. The officer by whom a jury is summoned shall give seasonable notice of the time and place of their meeting to the person appointed to preside at the trial, and also to the person appointed agent for the county, if such appointments have been made. When a committee is substituted for a jury, the notice to the agent shall be given by the person first named on the committee.

60. The officer shall receive for summoning the jurors four cents a mile for all necessary travel, and one dollar and fifty cents for each day he attends upon them. He shall certify to the court his own travel and attendance, and also that of each juror.

61. The jury shall view the premises when they think proper, or upon the request of either party, and shall hear and examine all legal evidence laid before them, with the observations of the parties or their counsel thereon. All the jurors shall sign the verdict which may be agreed upon, which shall be enclosed in a sealed wrapper, with an indorsement thereon expressing what it contains, and delivered so indorsed to the officer having charge of the jury.

62. If the interest or right of a complainant in or to the real estate alleged to be damaged by the laying out, locating anew, altering, discontinuing, or making specific repairs upon, a highway, is drawn in question on such hearing, the jury may hear and determine the question of interest or right so far only as respects the damages of such complainant.

63. A jury assessing damages may extend the time allowed by the commissioners for the owner of the land to take off the timber, wood, trees, or other property. If he neglects to take off the same within the extended time, he shall be deemed to have relinquished his claim thereto for the benefit of the town, as before provided.

64. When a jury is ordered, they shall be summoned and

give their verdict within three months next after the date of the order. The verdict shall be returned to the next term of the superior court to be held for the same county, and the court shall receive it, and adjudicate thereon, and may set it aside for good cause. If the matter is determined by a committee, the report of the committee shall be made within three months after their appointment, shall be returned to the next term of the court held after making the same; and like proceedings shall be had thereon as upon the return of a verdict.

65. If the jury do not agree upon a verdict, or if the proceedings are set aside upon a writ of certiorari, the complainant shall be entitled to a new jury from time to time until a verdict is rendered and established; but he may at any stage of the proceedings, upon such terms as the court shall order, waive his right to a trial by jury, and accept the damages assessed by the commissioners.

66. The clerk of the court shall certify such verdict or report, with the adjudication of the court thereon, to the commissioners at their next meeting after the adjudication shall be had: and if the verdict or report has been set aside, the commissioners on application therefor, shall order a new jury, or the parties may agree upon a new committee; and thereupon like proceedings shall be had as are hereinbefore provided.

67. The verdict or report returned to the court as before provided, and accepted and recorded, shall be conclusive upon the parties.

68. If the jury or committee do not alter the highway, nor increase the amount allowed by the commissioners, as damages or indemnity, the costs incurred by reason of the application for the jury or committee shall be paid by the persons who recognize for the payment of costs; otherwise all such costs shall be paid from the county treasury.

69. If a question arises with regard to the taxation of costs, in the proceedings and hearing before a jury or committee, it shall be determined by the court to which the verdict or report is returned; and the court may also

determine the compensation of the committee and of the person who presides at the trial.

70. When the commissioners order a jury, or a committee is agreed upon, to consider and determine with regard to the laying out, alteration, or discontinuance, of a highway, or specific repairs upon an existing highway, the highway so laid out or altered shall not be opened or worked, nor shall the highway so discontinued, or upon which specific repairs are ordered, be shut up, until after the meeting of the commissioners at which the verdict of the jury or report of the committee, with the adjudication of the court thereon, is certified to them as before directed ; and thereupon the commissioners may allow such further time as they think reasonable for making and completing such highway, and for the removal of the timber, wood, trees, or other property, if any, from the premises.

71. When a highway is finally laid out, and established, altered, or discontinued, or specific repairs are ordered, on an existing highway, all the expenses of the proceeding, and also all damages allowed therefor, and all sums awarded as indemnity, shall be paid by order of the commissioners, by the county, except as herein otherwise provided.

72. If a highway is not finally laid out and established, located anew, altered, or discontinued, nor specific repairs ordered, all said expenses shall be paid by the persons who have recognized therefor. If they refuse or neglect to pay such expenses, or to pay the costs incurred by reason of the application for a jury or committee, when required by the commissioners, such expenses or costs shall be ordered by the commissioners to be paid from the county treasury ; and thereupon the commissioners, after giving due notice to the persons who so recognized, shall issue a warrant against them or some of them (unless sufficient cause is shown to the contrary) for the amount ordered to be paid by them, with the further costs of the notice and warrant, and the money shall be collected as in other cases, and paid into the county treasury.

73. After a highway has been established by the commissioners, if a town whose duty it is to make such highway, or a part thereof, shall not make and complete the same within the time and in the manner prescribed, and to the acceptance of the commissioners, they shall, as soon as may be thereafter, cause such highway to be completed as aforesaid ; and at their next meeting they shall direct the expenses and charges of completing the same to be paid out of the county treasury, and shall order notice thereof to be given to each town that is delinquent, stating the proportions which they are respectively required to pay.

74. If a delinquent town does not pay its proportion of the expenses and charges before the next regular meeting of the commissioners, with interest thereon at the rate of ten per cent a year from the time the same is paid from the county treasury, the commissioners, unless sufficient cause is shown to the contrary, shall issue a warrant against such town for the sum it was ordered to pay, with the interest, and the further costs of such notice and warrant ; and the same shall be collected as in other like cases, and paid into the county treasury.

75. When a highway is laid out or altered, the commissioners, after the same is completed, may order the whole or part of the expenses incurred by any town in making or altering the same, to be paid out of the county treasury.[1]

The actual cost, and not the estimated expense, of making and altering highways, is to be divided between towns and the county, by the county commissioners, as they shall decide to be just and reasonable.[2]

76. Upon notice to the commissioners that the part of such highway lying within the limits of a town has been completed according to their directions for making the same, they shall view and carefully examine the same throughout ; and if they find such highway well made, they shall so certify to the county treasurer, who shall thereupon pay to such town the sum so allowed.

[1] Gen. Stats. ch. 43, §§ 34-51.
[2] Lanesborough v. County Commissioners of Berkshire, 6 Met. 329.

77. When there shall be several parties, having several estates at the same time, in land or buildings, other than and different from the estates and interests for which provision is made in section seventeen (section thirty-five above), and the land or buildings are taken or otherwise damaged, in whole or in part, by the laying out, locating anew, altering, or discontinuing, of a highway, or making specific repairs thereon, and one of such parties, by petition as provided in this chapter, applies for a jury to ascertain his damages in the premises, all the other parties so interested may become parties to the proceedings under such petition, and the damages of all of them may be determined by the same jury, in the manner provided in the five following sections.[1]

Under the operation of this section, a tenant in common of land over which the county commissioners have laid out a highway, may apply for a jury to assess his damages, without the joinder of his co-tenants.[2]

78. Upon such application of a party thus interested, the commissioners shall order the petitioner to give notice thereof to all the other parties interested, by serving each of them, fourteen days at least before their next regular meeting, with an attested copy of such petition and the order thereon, that the other parties may, if they see cause, appear at the next meeting, and become parties to the proceedings under the petition ; and at the next meeting a jury shall be ordered as before provided in this chapter, who shall, under the direction of the person presiding at the trial, proceed to hear all the persons who have become parties to the proceedings.

79. If on such hearing the jury find any of the parties entitled to damages, they shall assess the same in the following manner, to wit : they shall first find and set forth in their verdict the total amount of the damages sustained by the owners of such land and buildings, estimating the same as an entire estate and as if the same were the sole property

---

[1] Gen. Stats. ch. 43, §§ 52, 53.
[2] Dwight v. County Commissioners of Hampden, 7 Cush. 533.

of one owner in fee simple ; and they shall then apportion the total amount of damages among the several parties whom they find to be entitled, in proportion to their several interests and claims and to the damages sustained by them respectively, and set forth such apportionment in their verdict ; and if they find any one or more of said parties not to have sustained damage, they shall set forth in their verdict that they award no damages to such party.

80. The verdict, if accepted, shall be conclusive upon all parties interested who shall either have had notice as aforesaid, or by consent have become parties to the proceedings.

81. Each party recovering damages shall recover his several costs ; and each party not recovering damages shall be liable for costs to the town or other corporation of which he shall have claimed damages, in like manner as if the proceedings were had under his several petition ; but if a party shall fourteen days before the trial give notice in writing to the town or other corporation that may be liable for damages, that he relinquishes all claim for damages, and shall also before the trial file in the case a relinquishment of such claim, he shall not be liable for costs in the case.

82. If a person, having notice as aforesaid, neglects to appear and become a party to the proceedings in court, he shall be for ever barred from making an application for damages.[1]

83. The lands now holden, and which may hereafter be holden, by the trustees of any state lunatic hospital, in trust for the commonwealth, for the use of the institution of which they are trustees, shall not be taken for any street, highway, or railroad, without leave of the legislature specially obtained.[2]

84. The county commissioners may, in certain cases, lay out a turnpike road as a common highway. In such cases[3]

The commissioners upon such taking may allow such damages as they think reasonable to the corporation, to be paid out of the county treasury, and they may order a part of such damages, not exceeding one-third thereof, to be re-

[1] Gen. Stats. ch. 43, §§ 54–58.     [3] Gen. Stats. ch. 62, § 14.
[2] Stats. 1862, ch. 223, § 2.

funded to the county treasury by the cities and towns through which the road passes, at such times as they direct. In apportioning the proportions to be paid by each, they shall have regard to the length of way in each, and the advantages to be derived to it.

85. If a city or town refuses or neglects to pay its proportion, the same proceedings may be had to enforce the payment as are provided in case of expenses of making highways by the commissioners where cities or towns neglect to make the same.

86. In the assessment of damages there shall be allowed to persons injured such damages only as they would be entitled to beyond the damages they would have sustained by the continuance of the turnpike road, taking into consideration any advantage which may accrue in consequence of making the same a highway.[1]

[1] Gen. Stats. ch. 62, § 15.

## CHAPTER XXIII.

## LAYING OUT AND DISCONTINUANCE OF TOWN AND PRIVATE WAYS.

1. THE selectmen of the several towns may lay out or alter town ways for the use of their respective towns, and private ways for the use of one or more of the inhabitants thereof; or may order specific repairs to be made upon such ways.[1]

2. "It is quite obvious, that the distinctive character of a road, as a town way or a public highway, must to some extent be indicated by the manner of its creation, or the power which gives it a legal existence. The county commissioners have not only authority to lay out highways from town to town, that is, passing through various towns, but also highways, the termini of which are exclusively within the same town. Hence, to some extent, local roads may be either town ways or public highways. So, also, a town road may be a road of great public travel, from its connection with other roads. The only criterion, therefore, for distinguishing between these different species of roads, is to ascertain whether the proceedings for their location originated with the selectmen, or with the county commissioners. If with the former, they must be town ways; as the jurisdiction of the selectmen is confined to such ways."[2]

3. A majority of the board of selectmen is sufficient to lay out a town way.[3]

4. And they have authority to lay out a town way wholly upon land of citizens, against their consent, entering their land from a highway and returning to it at about the same place where it enters, and leading to no other way or landing-place, and capable of being used for no purposes of business or duty, or of access to the land of any other person; and which is laid out with the design to provide access not for the town merely, but for the public, to points or places in the lands of those citizens esteemed as pleasing natural scenery.[4]

[1] Gen. Stats. ch. 43, § 59.

[2] Monterey v. County Commissioners of Berkshire, 7 Cush. 394; Blackstone v. County Commissioners, 108 Mass. 68.

[3] Jones v. Andover, 9 Pick. 145.

[4] Higginson v. Nahant, 11 Allen, 530.

5. But it seems they have no authority to lay out a town way to be used only during a portion of the year.[1] Nor can they lay out a landing-place on a town way between high-water mark and the channel of a navigable river.[2]

6. A town, at a meeting regularly called for the purpose, may discontinue any town or private way.

7. No town way or private way shall be laid out or altered unless, seven days at least previously thereto, a written notice of the intention of the selectmen of the town to lay out or alter the same is left by them, or by their order, at the usual place of abode of the owners of the land over which such way is proposed to be laid out or altered, or unless such notice is delivered to such owner in person or to his tenant or authorized agent. If the owner has no such place of abode in the town, and no tenant or authorized agent therein known to the selectmen, or if, being a resident in the town, he is not known as such to the selectmen, such notice shall be posted up in some public place in the town seven days at least before the laying out of such way.

8. If damage is sustained by any person in his property by the laying out, alteration, or discontinuance, of a town or private way, or by specific repairs which may be ordered thereon, he shall receive such compensation as the selectmen shall determine, to be assessed and awarded in the manner provided for the assessment and award of damages by county commissioners in laying out highways; which damages shall be paid by the town if it is a town way, but if a private way, then by the person for whose use it is so laid out or altered, or for whose benefit specific repairs are ordered, or on whose application it is discontinued, unless the selectmen deem it reasonable that part of the damage shall be paid by the town and the residue by said persons, in which case they shall make an order specifying the sums to be paid by each.[3]

9. The provision in the foregoing section that the damages shall be assessed and awarded "in the manner provided for the assessment

---

[1] Holcomb *v.* Moore, 4 Allen, 529.     [3] Gen. Stats. ch. 43, §§ 60 – 62.
[2] Kean *v.* Stetson, 5 Pick. 492.     See previous chapter.

and award of damages by county commissioners in laying out highways," "has," said Hoar, J., in a recent case, "reference to the nature
of the damages, the deductions to be made for benefits, and the distribution of damages among different parties in interest." [1]

10. The selectmen of a town may estimate the damages caused to
the owner of land by the laying out of a town way at the same meeting at which the way is located.[1]

11. The damages so awarded shall not be paid until the
land is entered upon and possession taken for the purpose
of constructing such way or alteration, or until the specific
repairs which have been ordered are commenced. And if
possession is not taken, or if the specific repairs are not
made, the party, instead of the damages awarded to him,
shall be entitled to indemnity to be assessed by the selectmen in the same manner that indemnity is awarded by
county commissioners in like cases.

12. If there are separate or different interests in lands or
buildings which are so taken or injured, of the character
and description mentioned in sections seventeen and
eighteen,[2] the damages shall be assessed by the selectmen
in the mode therein provided for an assessment by the commissioners.

13. Except as is hereinafter provided, no town way or
private way laid out or altered by the selectmen, shall be
established until such laying out or alteration, with the
boundaries and admeasurements of the way, is reported to
the town, and accepted and allowed at some public meeting of the inhabitants regularly warned and notified therefor, nor unless such laying out or alteration, with the
boundaries and admeasurements, is filed in the office of the
town clerk seven days at least before such meeting.[3]

Reference to a plan containing the admeasurements and boundaries
is not sufficient unless the plan be filed; and neglect on the part of
the selectmen to file their report seven days before the meeting renders the alteration invalid, though no person applied to the town
clerk during the seven days to inspect the report.[4]

---

[1] Higginson v. Nahant, 11 Allen,
530.

[2] See sections 35 and 36 previous
chapter.

[3] Gen. Stats. ch. 43, §§ 63–65.

[4] Jeffries v. Swampscott, 105 Mass.
535.

14. But a vote of a town that the selectmen shall lay out a particular town way, is unauthorized and improper, it being the intention of the statute that the selectmen shall exercise their own discretion upon the subject.[1]

15. When the location or alteration of a private way is desired in a town for the use of one or more persons, not being inhabitants thereof, or when the location or alteration of a private way lying partly in one town and partly in another is desired, the county commissioners may cause such way to be located or altered, proceeding therein as is provided where the selectmen refuse to lay out a private way.

16. If the selectmen of a town unreasonably refuse or neglect to lay out or alter a town way or private way, when requested in writing by one or more of the inhabitants thereof, the commissioners, on the petition in writing of a person aggrieved presented at any regular meeting within one year, may cause such way to be laid out or altered, ascertain the place and course of the way, and estimate the damages sustained by any person by reason thereof. Such damages with all costs of the proceedings shall be paid by the town, if it is a town way. If it is a private way, the damages and costs, or such part thereof as the commissioners judge reasonable, shall be paid by the persons for whose use it is laid out or altered, and the residue, if any, by the town.[2]

17. But before the commissioners have power to lay out such town way they must determine that the selectmen of the town in which the way is located had unreasonably neglected or refused to lay out the same; and their record should distinctly state such adjudication.[3]

18. The omission of selectmen to make a written report to the town of their alteration of a town way, on a written petition for an alteration, is such a refusal or neglect to alter it as gives jurisdiction of the matter to the county commissioners.[4]

19. But when they refuse to lay out a way, and application is thereupon made to the county commissioners to lay it out, they have

[1] Kean v. Stetson, 5 Pick. 492.

[2] Gen. Stats. ch. 43, §§ 66, 67.

[3] Belchertown v. County Commissioners, 11 Cush. 189.

[4] New Marlboro' v. County Commissioners, 9 Met. 423.

jurisdiction of such application, and may proceed thereon, although the selectmen, in the petition to them, were requested to discontinue an old way (which they had no authority to do) as well as to lay out a new one.[1]

20. And it is a question exclusively within the discretion of the county commissioners to decide whether a town way, for the laying out of which application is made to them on the refusal of the selectmen to lay it out, is for the use of the town within which it is situated.[2]

21. If a town unreasonably refuses or delays to approve and allow a town way or private way laid out or altered by the selectmen, and to put the same on record, any person aggrieved thereby may, within one year thereafter, apply by petition in writing to the commissioners ; and the commissioners, unless sufficient cause is shown against such application, may approve and allow of the way as laid out or altered by the selectmen, and direct the laying out or alteration and acceptance to be recorded by the clerk of such town, which shall have the like effect as if accepted by the town and recorded.

22. If a town in which a town way or private way is laid out, altered, or approved, in pursuance of the three preceding sections,[3] shall not make and complete the same in the manner prescribed by the commissioners, and to their acceptance, within six months from the time when the same is laid out or approved, or within the time directed by the commissioners, they shall, as soon as may be thereafter, cause such way to be completed, and at the next meeting shall direct the expenses and charges of completing the same to be paid out of the county treasury, and order notice thereof to be given to the delinquent town, stating the amount of such expenses and charges. If the town does not before the next regular meeting of the commissioners pay the same, with interest thereon at the rate of ten per cent from the time when the same was paid by the county treasurer, they [shall] cause the same with all

---

[1] Brown *v.* County Commissioners, 12 Met. 208.

[2] Monterey *v.* County Commissioners, 7 Cush. 394.

[3] See sections 15, 16, 21, above.

further costs to be collected in the manner prescribed in section fifty.[1]

23. Upon the application in writing, of any person aggrieved by the refusal of a town to discontinue a town way or private way, the commissioners may order such way to be discontinued.

24. When a town way has been laid out or altered by the commissioners it shall not within two years thereafter be discontinued or altered by the town; and when such way has been discontinued by the commissioners, the town shall not within two years thereafter lay out the same again.

25. When an application is made to the commissioners in consequence of the refusal or neglect of selectmen to lay out or alter a private or town way, or in consequence of the refusal or neglect of the town to accept and allow such way when laid out or altered by the selectmen, or when such application is made for the discontinuance of a private or town way, the commissioners shall cause a like recognizance to be given to the county as is directed in this chapter[2] with regard to applications for highways; and like proceedings may be had on such recognizance. They shall also cause notice to be given, before they proceed to view, or to hear the parties, as in the case of highways.[2]

26. A person aggrieved by the laying out, or by the alteration or discontinuance, of a town or private way, or by an order for specific repairs, or by the assessment of his damages, or compensation by way of indemnity, may have the matter of his complaint determined by a jury, which may be applied for at any time within one year after such laying out, alteration, order for repairs, discontinuance, or assessment of indemnity; or if a suit is instituted within one year wherein the legal effect of the proceedings is drawn in question, such application for damages or indemnity may be made at any time within one year after the final determination of such suit. Upon such application, an order for a jury shall be made by the commissioners (or

---

[1] See section 69, ch. 23.  [2] See preceding chapter.

by agreement of the parties the matter may be determined by a committee to be appointed by the commissioners) ; and the jury or committee shall have the same powers, and the proceedings in all respects shall be conducted in the same manner, as before provided in like case with respect to highways.[1] If the damages are increased or the way is altered, the damages and all charges shall be paid by the town ; otherwise the charges arising on such application shall be paid by the applicant or person recognizing as aforesaid.[2]

27. A town may be an aggrieved party;[3] but when the selectmen of such town, without its authority, apply for a jury to reduce damages estimated by the county commissioners, upon the laying out of a town way, and a warrant is thereupon issued to an officer, requiring him to summon a jury to hear and determine the matter of complaint, and he performs the service so required of him, he may maintain an action against the selectmen to recover therefor and for his disbursements.[4]

28. The aggrieved party's application for a jury must be made to the county commissioners at a regular term, or at an adjourned meeting of the board, held within one year from the time of the laying out of the town way.[5] And his petition should contain a particular description of the land, and the situation of the same in relation to the town way alleged to have been laid out or discontinued, and also an allegation of the injury sustained.[6]

29. Highways and town ways may be laid out, constructed, altered, widened, graded or discontinued under the provisions of chapter forty-three of the General Statutes, and any general laws in amendment thereof, notwithstanding the acceptance by any town of any act authorizing the assessment upon estates benefited of a portion of the cost of such highways or town ways, and every highway or town way hereafter laid out shall be deemed to be laid out under the provisions of said chapter and amendments, unless the order laying out the same expressly declares the same to be laid out under the provisions of law authorizing the assessment of betterments.[7]

[1] See preceding chapter.
[2] Gen. Stats. ch. 43, §§ 68–73.
[3] See section 38, ch. 22.
[4] Baker v. Thayer, 3 Met. 312.
[5] Eaton v. Framingham, 6 Cush. 245.
[6] Perry v. Sherburn. 11 Cush. 388.
[7] Stats. 1874, ch. 275.

30. When a town or private way is laid out or altered by the selectmen or commissioners, they shall in their report or return thereof specify the manner in which such way, location, or alteration, shall be completed, and transmit to the clerk a description of the location and bounds thereof, which shall, within ten days, be recorded by him in a book of records kept for that purpose; and they shall allow the owner of the land through which the way may pass, a reasonable time to take off his trees, fences, and other property, which may obstruct the building of such way. If he neglects to remove the same within the time allowed, he shall be deemed to have relinquished his right thereto for the benefit of the town, if the way be a town way; and if it be a private way, for the benefit of such person as the selectmen or commissioners shall determine.

31. If a jury is ordered to assess the damages done by the location or alteration of such way, they may extend the time for the owner of the land to remove his trees, fences, and other property; and if he neglects to remove the same within such extended time, he shall be deemed to have relinquished his claim thereto.

32. No town shall contest the legality of a way laid out by such town and accepted and recorded as provided in this chapter.[1]

33. The mayor and aldermen of any city, and the selectmen of any town, may make such rules and regulations in relation to the passage of carriages, wagons, carts, trucks, sleds, sleighs, horse-cars, or other vehicles, or to the use of sleds or other vehicles for coasting, in and through the streets or public ways of such city or town, as they shall deem necessary for the public safety or convenience, with penalties for violation thereof, not exceeding twenty dollars for one offence.[2]

34. No highway, town way, street, turnpike, canal, railroad or street railway, shall be laid out or constructed in, upon, through or over any public common or public park which has been dedicated to the use of the public or appro-

---

[1] Gen. Stats. ch. 43, §§ 74–76.    [2] Stats. 1875, ch. 136.

priated to such use without interruption for the period of twenty years or longer, nor shall any part of any such public common or public park be taken for widening or altering any highway, town way or street previously located or constructed, except after public notice, to be given in the same manner as provided in cases of applications for the location and alteration of highways, in which notice shall be specifically set forth, the extent and limits of the portion of the public common or public park proposed to be taken, and unless the consent of the inhabitants of the city or town in which the same is situated is first obtained. Such consent shall be expressed by vote of the inhabitants whenever as many as ten legal voters file a request in writing to that effect, with the selectmen of the town or the mayor and aldermen of the city, within thirty days after the publication of the notice ; in the absence of such request consent shall be presumed to be granted.[1]

35. Whenever any person owning, erecting or maintaining a water-mill, or a dam to raise water for working such mill, upon or across any stream not navigable, under chapter one hundred and forty-nine of the General Statutes, desires to raise, erect or maintain a dam, at such height, or in such manner as to overflow or otherwise injure an existing public way, he may apply by petition to the county commissioners of the county in which such way is located, setting forth the height at which it is desired to maintain such dam, and the ways, which it is expected may be injured thereby, and asking for the alteration, change of grade, or specific repairs of such ways. Said commissioners, after a hearing upon any such petition, may order such alteration, repairs or change of grade of such ways, as will in their judgment, enable the petitioner to raise, erect and maintain such dam without overflowing or otherwise injuring such ways, and they may give written direction and authority to such petitioner to make, at his own expense such alterations, changes of grade and repairs, within a reasonable time. They shall record all such orders and cause

---

[1] Stats. 1875, ch. 163.

certified copies of the same to be filed and recorded in the office of the town clerk of each town in which such alterations, changes of grade or repairs are ordered.

36. Notice of the hearing upon any such petition shall be given to the towns in which the ways are situated, and to the owners or occupants of lands affected thereby, in the same manner as notice of the laying out of highways is given : the commissioners shall assess and order to be paid by the petitioner all damages sustained by any person or corporation (or town or city [1]) by reason of the alterations, changes of grade or repairs ordered by them, and any person or corporation (or town or city [1]) aggrieved by such assessment, may on application within one year from the entry of such order, have the damages assessed by a jury, in the manner provided by law for the assessment of damages occasioned by the laying out or discontinuance of highways.

37. The costs of all proceedings under this act (two preceding and two following sections) shall be paid by the petitioners ; and they may be required by the county commissioners to recognize with sufficient sureties for the payment of the same.

38. The order of the county commissioners, duly issued under this act, shall be deemed to authorize the petitioner to do all acts necessary to be done in compliance therewith ; and if it is shown that the petitioner has substantially complied with such order, no indictment shall be maintained for the flowage or injury by means of the dam of the ways mentioned in such order.

39. Nothing in this act shall impair the right of any person or corporation to maintain any existing water-mill or dam.[2]

40. "The betterment act of 1871, ch. 382, § 1, does not repeal the provision of the highway act (Gen. Stats. ch. 43, § 16), but secures the landowner from being twice charged for the same benefit, by providing that, in assessing betterments under the former, due allowance shall be made for any benefit set off under the latter. The benefit and advantage to be taken into consideration in the assessment

---

[1] Acts, 1876, ch. 117.      [2] Stats. 1873, ch. 144.

under the betterment act may include those shared by the estate in question with other estates in the vicinity, though not bounding on the same street, beyond the general advantage to all lands in the same city. The benefit to be deducted in estimating damages under the highway act is limited to the direct and special benefit to the estate in question, as distinguished from other estates not bounding on the same street." — Gray, C. J.[1]

41. "The benefits which may accrue to any estate from the laying out of a highway are of three kinds: 1. Those directly occasioned to an estate bounding upon the highway, and peculiar to the estate itself, as distinguished from other estates not bounding thereon. 2. Those shared by the estate in common with other estates in the neighborhood. 3. Those which extend to all estates in the same town or city.

"Benefits of the first kind only can be allowed by way of set-off against the damages awarded to the owner under the highway act for taking part of the estate, and injuring it. Gen. Stats. ch. 43, § 16; Dickenson v. Fitchburg, 13 Gray, 546 ; Whitney v. Boston, 98 Mass. 312 ; Allen v. Charlestown, 109 Mass. 243.

"Benefits of the first kind, when no part of the estate is taken or injured by the laying-out of the highway, and of the second kind in all cases, are to be included in the benefit and advantage to be considered in making an assessment under the betterment acts. Stats. 1870, ch. 163, § 3 ; 1871, ch. 382, § 1. The increased value of the estate by reason of benefits of the third kind, being those which its owner receives in common with all other owners of lands in the same municipality, are not subjects of compensation from him to the public in any form of proceeding. Stat. 1871, ch. 382, § 1.

"The bill of exceptions shows that part of the petitioner's land was taken for the highway, and his damages assessed by a committee duly appointed. He now offered to prove that in the estimate of those damages the peculiar benefits to his estate were deducted, and the amount of that deduction.

"But the betterment act of 1870, ch. 163, § 3, under which the present case arose, enacts that in estimating, in accordance with its provisions, the benefit and advantage to any estate by the laying-out or alteration of a highway, 'due allowance shall be made for any benefit set off under the provisions of section sixteen of chapter forty-three of the General Statutes.' If the amount of the peculiar benefit thus set off had been permitted to be given in evidence, the jury must have been instructed not to include it in their verdict ; and the same result was reached more directly and quite as surely by wholly excluding from their estimate all such benefits as could be so set off." — Gray, C. J.[2]

A valid agreement not to assess betterment cannot be made.[3]

---

[1] Green v. Fall River, 113 Mass. 262.
[2] Upham v. Worcester, 113 Mass. 97.
[3] Boylston Market Association v. Boston, 113 Mass. 528.

# CHAPTER XXIV.

## BETTERMENT LAW.

1. AT any time within two years after any street, highway or other way is laid out, altered, widened, graded, or discontinued, when in the opinion of the board of city or town officers authorized to lay out streets or ways respectively therein, any real estate, including that, a part of which may have been taken for such purpose, shall receive any benefit and advantage therefrom, beyond the general advantages to all real estate in the city or town where the same is situated, such board may adjudge and determine the value of such benefit and advantage to any such estate, and may assess upon the same a proportional share of the expense of laying out, alteration, widening, grading, or discontinuance; but in no case shall the assessment exceed one-half the amount of such adjudged benefit and advantage, nor shall the same be made until the work of laying out, altering, widening, and grading is completed or discontinuance made; and in case of laying out a highway or town way by county commissioners, due allowance shall be made for any benefit set off under the provisions of section sixteen of chapter forty-three of the General Statutes.

2. Any such assessment upon real estate which is invalid by reason of any error or irregularity in the making thereof, and which has not been paid, or which has been recovered back, may be re-made by such board, to the amount for which the original assessment ought to have been made, and the same shall be a lien upon the estate, and be collected in the same manner as re-assessed taxes are.

3. The expense to be assessed upon the estates as herein provided shall include all damages for land and

buildings taken; and in estimating such damages all buildings on the land, a part of which is taken, shall be included, and there shall be deducted therefrom the value of the materials removed, and of all buildings or parts of buildings remaining thereon; and the damages for land taken shall be fixed at the value thereof before such laying out, alteration, or widening, and the damage so estimated shall be paid to the persons entitled thereto, in the same manner, and upon the same conditions as are provided by law in other cases of laying out, alteration, widening, grading, or discontinuance of streets and ways.

4. If the owner of any building or materials on land, a part or the whole of which is taken for the purposes named in this act, after reasonable notice in writing from the board authorized to make assessments as aforesaid, shall refuse or neglect to take care of, or remove such buildings or materials, such board may take such care of the same as public safety, or the preservation thereof demands, or may remove such buildings or materials, either upon the adjoining land of such owner, or otherwise; or they may sell the same at public auction, after five days' public notice of such sale, and hold the proceeds of the sale for the benefit of such owner; and the expense incurred by said board, or the value thereof to the owner, shall be allowed in reduction of the damages which said owner is entitled to recover.

5. Any person owning real estate abutting on any street, highway, or other way, which may be laid out, altered, widened, graded, or discontinued, and liable to assessment under this act, may, at any time before the estimate of damages is made, give notice in writing to the board having authority to make the assessment, that he objects to the same, and elects to surrender his estate to the city or town where situated; and if said board shall then adjudge that public convenience and necessity require the taking of such estate, for the improvements named, they may take the whole of such abutting estate, and shall thereupon estimate the value thereof, excluding the benefit or ad-

vantage which has accrued from the laying out, alteration, widening, grading, or discontinuance, and such owner shall convey the estate to such city or town, which shall pay him therefor the value so estimated, and the same may be recovered by an action of contract; and the city or town may sell any portion of said estate not needed for such improvements.

6. All assessments made under this act shall constitute a lien upon the real estate so assessed, to be enforced in the same manner, with like charges for cost and interest, as provided by law for the collection of taxes; and if the owner of the estate shall give notice to the board authorized to make the assessment at any time before demand is made upon him for payment thereof, that he desires to have the amount of such assessment apportioned, said board shall apportion the same into three equal parts, and certify such apportionment to the assessors of the city or town, and said assessors shall add one of said equal parts, with interest thereon from the date of the apportionment, to the annual tax of said estate for the three years next ensuing; and all assessments laid upon real estate, for any of the causes mentioned in this act, which shall remain unpaid after the same become due or payable, shall draw interest from the time when the same became due or payable, until the time of payment thereof.

7. Any party aggrieved by the doings of such board, may apply by petition to the superior court for the county in which the estate is situated (filed in term time, or in the clerk's office in vacation) [1] within one year after the passage of the order or proceedings upon which the application is founded; and after due notice to the city or town against which the petition is filed, a trial shall be had at the bar of the court in the same manner in which other civil causes are there tried by the jury, and if either party request it, the jury shall view the place in question.

8. If the jury shall not reduce the amount of the assessment complained of, the respondent shall recover costs

[1] Stats. 1873, ch. 288.

against the petitioner, which costs shall be a lien upon the estate, and be collected in the same manner as the assessment; but if the jury shall reduce the amount of the assessment, the petitioner shall recover costs, and all assessments shall be a lien on the estate for one year after the final judgment, in any suit or proceeding where the amount or validity of the same is in question, and be collected in the same manner as original assessments.

9. When an assessment is made upon an estate, the whole or any portion of which is leased, the owner of the estate shall pay the assessment, and may thereafter collect of the lessee an additional rent for the portion of the estate so leased, equal to ten per centum per annum on that proportion of the whole sum paid, which the leased portion bears to the whole estate, after deducting from the whole sum so paid any amount he may have received for damages to the estate above what he has necessarily expended on such estate by reason of such damages.

10. This act, except section four, shall not take effect in any town until the same is accepted by such town at a legal meeting called for that purpose, unless the town has passed the vote of acceptance provided for by section four of chapter one hundred and sixty-nine of the acts of the year eighteen hundred and sixty-nine.[1]

11. Any assessment upon real estate, for the benefit and advantage thereto, from the laying out, altering, widening, grading, or continuing any way, made prior to the twenty-sixth day of May, in the year one thousand eight hundred and seventy-one, which is invalid by reason of any error or irregularity in the assessment, and which has not been paid, or which has been paid and recovered back, may be reassessed by the board qualified to make such assessment, to the amount for which the original assessment ought to have been made; and the same shall be a lien upon the estate so assessed, and be collected in the same manner as reassessed taxes are collected.[2] (See sections forty and forty-one of preceding chapter as to assessing betterments.)

[1] Stats. 1871, ch. 382.  [2] Stats. 1872, ch. 246.

## CHAPTER XXV.

### SURVEYORS AND REPAIRS OF HIGHWAYS.

1. If a person chosen surveyor of highways refuses to serve, he shall forfeit a sum not exceeding ten dollars ; but no person shall be obliged to serve oftener than once in three years.[1]

It seems that selectmen may also be surveyors of highways.[2] But selectmen, unless specially authorized, cannot make contracts for repair of highways.[3]

2. A surveyor of highways who neglects the duties of his office shall forfeit ten dollars for each neglect ; and he may be prosecuted by indictment for any deficiency in the highways within his limits occasioned by his fault or neglect.

3. If a town is sentenced to pay a fine for a deficiency in the highways or town ways therein, any surveyor through whose fault or neglect such deficiency existed, shall be liable for the amount of such fine and all costs, to be recovered by the town in an action of tort.[4]

A surveyor is not liable otherwise to the town than as herein provided, and consequently is not liable for damages recovered of the town on account of defects in its highway owing to his neglect.[5]

4. To "repair" a way is to refit, make good, or restore an existing one, not to make a new one or widen the old one by including additional land. The surveyor has no lawful authority to use the money placed in his hands for ordinary repairs on existing roads, in making new structures and additions thereto.[6]

---

[1] Gen. Stats. ch. 18, § 74.

[2] Benjamin v. Wheeler, 15 Gray, 490 ; Bay State Brick Co. v. Foster, 115 Mass. 431 ; but, *quære*, whether the acceptance of office of surveyor incapacitates one to act as selectman. *Ib.*

[3] Clark v. Russell, 116 Mass. 455 ; Hawks v. Charlemont, 107 Mass. 414.

[4] Gen. Stats. ch. 18, §§ 75, 76.

[5] White v. Phillipston, 10 Met. 108.

[6] Todd v. Rowley, 8 Allen, 58 ; Parker v. Lowell, 11 Gray, 355.

5. A bridge would seem to include to some extent the approaches to it as appendages to it. The particular extent must be determined by what is reasonable under the circumstances of each case. This matter becomes important when the bridge is to be kept in repair by a toll company, railroad company, or some party other than the town in which it is situated, which has the care of the roads approaching it also.[1]

6. Towns may bestow labor upon all parts of the located way, and may make such changes in the natural surface of the soil as will add to the convenience or safety of the traveller. If, in consequence of such changes, the water accumulating upon the surface of the way by the fall of rain or the melting of snow pours on to adjoining lands in different places or in somewhat greater quantities in particular places than it otherwise would have done, that is to be considered as one of the natural, probable, or necessary consequences resulting from the establishment and maintenance of the way; and therefore no action will lie for such an injury, as for a tort.[2]

And the owner of the land may raise his land, or may erect upon it a building or other structure which shall prevent this effect.[2]

But see in this connection sections sixteen and twenty-five below.

7. And it is the settled rule of law in this commonwealth that in all cases where a highway, turnpike, bridge, town way, or other way is laid across a natural stream of water, it is the duty of those who use such privilege to make provision by open bridges, culverts, or other means for the free current of the water, so that it shall not be obstructed and pent up to flow back on lands belonging to the riparian proprietors. And it is their duty not only to make such bridge, culvert, or passage for water, but to keep it in such condition that it shall not obstruct the stream.[3]

8. When two or more towns are required by law to maintain or keep in repair a bridge upon a highway or town way, and differ as to the mode or time of doing the same, the county commissioners having jurisdiction to lay out highways in either of such towns to whom application is first made by one of the towns, may, after a hearing upon due notice to all parties interested, pass such orders concerning the maintenance and repair of such bridge as in their opinion the public good may require. Such orders shall be final, and shall be enforced in the same man-

---

[1] Commonwealth v. Deerfield, 6 Allen, 455.

[2] Flagg v. Worcester, 13 Gray,

601; Franklin v. Fish, 13 Allen, 212.

[3] Parker v. Lowell, 11 Gray, 335.

ner as other orders by the commissioners are by law enforced.[1]

9. Towns shall vote to raise such sums of money as are necessary for making and repairing highways and town ways ; and order that the same be assessed upon the polls and estates of the inhabitants, residents, and non-residents, as other town charges are assessed ; and the same shall be collected as other town taxes are collected.[2] (And the said sums so voted shall be carefully and judiciously expended by the surveyors of highways, each in his own district, when the town is divided into highway districts, and in all cases under the direction of the selectmen or by the road commissioners, in making and repairing said ways.[3])

10. The lands of non-resident proprietors shall be taxed for the making and repairing of highways in the same manner as for other town taxes ; and upon default of payment, the same proceedings shall be had as are provided for the collection of other town taxes of such persons.

11. The selectmen of every town having more than one surveyor of highways, shall annually in writing before the first day of May, assign to each surveyor the limits and divisions of the highways and town ways to be kept in repair by him.

12. The surveyor shall give reasonable notice, as directed by the town to each person in his list, of the sum he is assessed to the highways and town ways ; and to the inhabitants within the limits of his district, assessed as aforesaid, seven days' notice of the times and places he shall appoint, extraordinary casualties excepted, for providing materials and working on the highways and town ways ; and each inhabitant shall have an opportunity to work thereon, in person or by his substitute, or with his oxen, horses, cart, and plough, at the prices which the town shall affix to such labor, to the full amount of the sum at which he is assessed ; but if any person so assessed pays to the surveyor in money the sum assessed to him, the

[1] Gen. Stats. ch. 44, § 2.  [3] Stats. 1877, ch. 58.
[2] Stats. 1871, ch. 298.

surveyor shall, according to his best judgment, carefully expend the sum so paid in repairing said ways.

13. Surveyors of highways, except as is provided in the following section, and in sections six and nine of chapter forty-six, may cut down or lop off trees and bushes, and dig up and remove whatever obstructs or encumbers a highway or town way, or hinders, incommodes, or endangers persons travelling thereon ; and when such way is encumbered with snow they shall forthwith cause the same to be removed, or so trodden down as to make the way safe and convenient [1] (and may sell for the benefit of the town, after thirty days' notice in writing to the owners of the same, any trees, brush, or other article of value.[2])

14. No individual not authorized by a surveyor can lawfully enter upon the land without the limits of the worked road, and take and remove earth or interfere with the same by placing rocks, stones, and rubbish upon the same, without leave of the owner of the land bordering upon such highway.[3] The decision of the surveyor acting within the scope of his authority, that a structure in a highway is an obstruction to public travel, is conclusive ; and evidence is not admissible to show that it is not an obstruction in fact, or that the removal will seriously incommode and damage the person who placed it there, or that the surveyor did not act in good faith in deciding that it was an obstruction to public travel.[4]

15. No surveyor or other person shall remove or take down fences, gates, or bars, placed on a highway or town way for the purpose of preventing the spreading of a disease which may be dangerous to the public health.

16. No surveyor of highways shall, without the approbation of the selectmen first had in writing, cause a watercourse occasioned by the wash of a highway or town way to be so conveyed by the side of such way as to incommode any house, store, shop, or other building, or to obstruct any person in the prosecution of his business. Persons aggrieved by a violation of this section may complain to the selectmen or mayor and aldermen, who shall there-

---

[1] Gen. Stats. ch. 44, §§ 4–8.
[2] Stats. 1874, ch. 280.
[3] Hollenbeck v. Rowley, 8 Allen, 473.

[4] Bay State Brick Co. v. Foster, 115 Mass. 431.

upon view the watercourse, and may direct the surveyor to alter the same in such manner as they shall determine.

17. Towns may authorize their surveyors or any other person to enter into contracts for making or repairing the highways or town ways within the same.

18. They may empower their surveyors to collect all such taxes as are not paid in labor or otherwise within the time limited by law, or at such periods as may be agreed upon by the town ; and for that purpose the assessors shall deliver to them warrants of distress, in substance like the warrants prescribed by law for collecting other town taxes ; or they may deliver a warrant for collecting the deficiency in any highway tax to the collector, who shall then proceed to collect the same in like manner as other taxes are by law to be collected, and shall pay over the same to the respective surveyors, who shall account with the selectmen for the expenditure thereof.

19. When there is a deficiency either of labor or money in the amount appropriated for the repair of highways or town ways within the limits of any surveyor, or when said amount is not furnished or paid to him, so that he is unable to make such repairs, he may to an amount not exceeding ten dollars employ persons to make such repairs ; and the persons so employed shall be paid therefor by the town.

20. If a town neglects to vote a sufficient sum of money for the purpose of repairing the highways and town ways, or does not otherwise effectually provide therefor, each of its surveyors, first having obtained the consent of the selectmen for that purpose in writing, may employ persons to repair the highways and town ways in their respective districts, so that the same shall be safe and convenient for travellers at all seasons of the year, and the persons so employed shall be paid therefor by the town.

21. Two-thirds at least of the sums of money granted by each town for repairing highways and town ways, shall be laid out and expended for that purpose before the first day of July next after the same are granted, or at such other time or times as the town at a legal meeting called

for that purpose shall determine. If any part of the money raised is to be expended in labor and materials in the month of March or April of the succeeding year, and after the surveyors of highways for such year are chosen and qualified, it shall be expended by the surveyors to whom the tax was committed, under the direction of the surveyors of the succeeding year having charge of the repairs of the highways and town ways in the district in which the same is to be thus expended.

22. Every surveyor shall exhibit his tax bill to the selectmen on the first Monday of July annually, and also at the expiration of the term for which he is appointed; and at those times shall render an account of all moneys expended by him on highways and town ways. For each neglect he shall forfeit a sum not exceeding fifty dollars.

23. At the expiration of his term the surveyor shall render to the assessors a list of such persons as have neglected or refused to work out or otherwise pay their highway tax, when required by him as provided in section seven; and such deficient sums shall be collected and paid into the treasury like other town taxes.

24. If any money remains unexpended in the hands of a surveyor at the expiration of his office, he shall pay the same to the town treasurer, who, after demand, may recover the same in an action of contract for money had and received, with twenty per cent in addition thereto, to the use of the town.

25. When an owner of land adjoining a highway or town way sustains damage in his property by reason of any raising, lowering, or other act, done for the purpose of repairing such way, he shall have compensation therefor, to be determined by the selectmen or mayor and aldermen; with whom he shall file his petition therefor after the commencement, and within one year from the completion of the work; and who shall finally adjudicate upon the question of damages within thirty days after the filing of the petition therefor, unless the parties agree in writing to extend the time. The benefit, if any, which the complain-

ant may receive by reason of such alteration or repair shall be allowed by way of set-off.[1]

26. If the owner of land receives injury by reason of the turning of a watercourse by a surveyor without authority, his only remedy is under the preceding section.[2]

27. If the petitioner is aggrieved, either by the estimate of his damages or by a refusal or neglect to estimate the same, he may, within one year from the expiration of said thirty days, apply for a jury, and have his damages ascertained in the manner provided where land is taken in laying out highways. Or he may, by agreement with the adverse party, and upon application made within the same time, have them ascertained by a committee to be appointed, in the city of Boston by the superior court, and elsewhere by the county commissioners in their respective jurisdictions.

28. If the life of a person is lost by reason of a defect or want of repair of a highway, town way, causeway, or bridge, or for want of suitable rails on such way or bridge, the county, town, or person, by law obliged to repair the same, shall be liable to a fine of one thousand dollars, to be recovered by indictment to the use of the executor or administrator of the deceased person, for the benefit of his heirs, devisees, or creditors : *provided*, that the county, town, or person, had previous reasonable notice of the defect or want of repair of such way or bridge.[8]

29. Highways, town ways, streets, causeways and bridges shall be kept in repair at the expense of the town, city or place in which they are situated when other provision is not made therefor, so that the same may be reasonably safe and convenient for travellers, with their horses, teams and carriages at all seasons of the year.

30. If a person receives or suffers bodily injury, or damage in his property, through a defect or want of repair, or of sufficient railing in or upon a highway, town way, causeway or bridge which might have been remedied, or which

---

[1] Gen. Stats. ch. 44, §§ 9–19.  [8] Gen. Stats. ch. 44, §§ 20, 21.
[2] Benjamin *v.* Wheeler, 15 Gray, 486.

damage or injury might have been prevented by reasonable care and diligence on the part of the county, town, place or persons by law obliged to repair the same, he may recover in the manner hereinafter provided, of the said county, town, place or persons, the amount of damage sustained thereby, if such county, town, place or persons had reasonable notice of the defect or might have had notice thereof by the exercise of proper care and diligence on their part; but no such damage shall be recovered by a person whose carriage and load thereon exceed the weight of six tons.

31. Any person injured in the manner set forth in the preceding section shall within thirty days thereafter give notice to the county, town, place or persons by law obliged to keep said highway, town way, causeway or bridge in repair, of the time, place and cause of the said injury or damage, and if the said county, town, place or persons do not pay the amount thereof, he may within two years after the date of said injury or damage bring an action of tort against said county, town, place or persons, in the superior court to recover the same : *provided, however*, that no person shall recover in any such action a greater sum for damages than four thousand dollars.

No person shall recover from any town, city, county or place, in any action provided for by chapter two hundred and thirty-four of the acts of the year eighteen hundred and seventy-seven (sections thirty to thirty-four of this chapter inclusive), a greater sum for damages or injury than one-fifth of one per cent of the valuation of such town, city, county or place, as ascertained by the state valuation of estates within the commonwealth last preceding the commencement of the action, nor a greater sum than four thousand dollars.[1]

32. The notice hereinbefore required may be given in the case of a county, to any one of the county commissioners or to the county treasurer ; in the case of a city, to the mayor, the city clerk or treasurer, or to any police officer ; and in the case of a town, to one of the selectmen or to the town treasurer or clerk ; and may also be given by the person injured or by any other person in his behalf: *pro-

[1] Stats. 1878, ch. 259.

*vided, however,* that if from physical or mental incapacity
it be impossible for the person injured to give the notice
within the time hereinbefore provided, he may give notice
within ten days after said incapacity is removed.

33. Such action against any such town, place or persons,
shall be brought in the county wherein the said town or
place is situated or said persons reside : *provided,* that
actions against the city of Boston may be brought in the
county of Middlesex or in the county of Norfolk or in the
county in which the party bringing such action resides ;
and actions against the town of Nantucket, or any town in
Dukes County, may be brought in the county of Bristol.[1]

34. The party injured, in order to recover of the town, must have
been using the way or bridge as a traveller, for legitimate purposes,
in the usual and ordinary mode, including the use of any vehicle or
animal which is suitable for a way prepared for the purpose of supplying the usual and common accommodation for persons having occasion to pass over the same ; therefore a person who is using the highway for play cannot recover damages for injuries caused by a defect
therein ; nor the owner of an animal which has escaped and run into
the highway without a driver ; nor a person who has stopped on a
highway for the purpose of conversation, and leaned against a railing,
which (by reason of its insufficiency) had given way, and caused him
to fall and receive injury ; but one who is walking in the highway
simply for exercise is properly regarded as a traveller.[2]

35. And he must at the time of the accident have been using such
reasonable care as the circumstances required ; and if he knows or
has reason to believe that a road is dangerous, when he enters upon it,
or before he has reached any dangerous place, he cannot, in the exercise of ordinary prudence, proceed and take his chance, and, if injured, hold the town responsible.[3]   And using due care includes using
a proper horse and vehicle, with strong and suitable harness.[4]

36. Under this rule, a town is not liable where a horse, being fright-
ened by an accident, breaks away from his driver, and escapes from
all control ; and afterward, while running at large, meets with an injury through a defect in a highway ;[5] or when a horse, by reason of

[1] Stats. 1877, ch. 234.
[2] Blodgett *v.* Boston, 8 Allen, 238;
Richards *v.* Enfield, 13 Gray, 344;
Gregory *v.* Adams, 14 Gray, 242;
Stickney *v.* Salem, 3 Allen, 374;
Hamilton *v.* Boston, 14 Allen, 475.
[3] Stevens *v.* Boxford, 10 Allen,

25 ; Horton *v.* Ipswich, 12 Cush. 492;
Bigelow *v.* Rutland, 4 Cush. 247;
Wilson *v.* Charlestown, 8 Allen, 138.
[4] Bliss *v.* Wilbraham, 8 Allen, 564;
Murdock *v.* Warwick, 4 Gray, 178,
180.
[5] Davis *v.* Dudley, 4 Allen, 557.

fright, disease, or viciousness, becomes actually uncontrollable, so that his driver cannot stop him, direct his course, or exercise control over him, unless it appears that the injury would have occurred, by reason of the defect in the highway, if the horse had not been so uncontrollable. "But a horse is not to be considered uncontrollable that merely shies or starts, or is momentarily not controlled by the driver." And where one is deficient in any faculty, such as sight or hearing, it would seem that common prudence requires of him greater care in walking upon the streets and avoiding obstructions than of persons not so deficient.[1]

37. It has been held that a traveller may be in the use of due care, even if intoxicated, although that would be an important circumstance to be considered by the jury, upon the question whether due care was used; and the fact that he had previous knowledge of the defect, is not conclusive evidence that he was wanting in due care at the time of the accident.[2]

38. The want of repair or defect in the highway must be the direct and immediate cause of the injury, in order to make the town liable. But it is often a question of much difficulty to determine what is a direct cause.[3]

39. And the party injured cannot recover, unless the defect in the highway was the sole cause of the injury, with this single exception, where the contributing cause was a pure accident, and one which common prudence and sagacity could not have foreseen and provided against.[4]

40. And, in order to render the town liable, the accident must be occasioned by causes which occur entirely within the highway.[5] Nor is an object in the highway, or the condition of the surface of the road which is not otherwise a hindrance or obstacle to travellers, except that it may, by its appearance or shape, be the cause of fright in a horse, and over and by which a traveller might have passed in safety, but for the fear excited in the animal, a defect or want of repair for which a town is liable.[6]

41. But towns are not necessarily chargeable with damage arising from every obstruction even within the limits of a located highway. They are not liable for such obstructions in portions of the highway not a part of the travelled path, and not so connected with it that they

[1] Titus v Northbridge, 97 Mass. 258. Also Horton v. Taunton, ib. 266; Fogg v. Nahant, 98 Mass. 578; Winn v. Lowell, 1 Allen, 177.

[2] Alger v. Lowell, 3 Allen, 406; Whittaker v. West Boylston, 97 Mass. 274.

[3] Jenks v. Wilbraham, 11 Gray, 142; Marble v. Worcester, 4 Gray, 395.

[4] Rowell v. Lowell, 7 Gray, 100; Kidder v. Dunstable, ib. 104; Palmer v. Andover, 2 Cush. 600.

[5] Richards v. Enfield, 13 Gray, 346.

[6] Kingsbury v. Dedham, 13 Allen, 189. See also Barber v. Roxbury, 11 Allen, 318.

will affect the security or convenience for travel of those using the travelled path. Therefore where the injury was sustained by a person using the public road for the purpose of entering upon his private way, although it was occasioned by an obstruction within the limits of the located highway, but without the road for public travel, the town was held not liable.[1] But in order to restrict the liability of towns to defects within the limits of the highway, those limits should be indicated in some way so that the traveller may know when he is without the highway.[2]

42. Nor is a town responsible for a defect or want of repair in a bridge whereby a public highway passes over a railroad, the proprietors of which are bound by law to keep the bridge in repair;[3] but the liability of the town is only limited to the extent to which the construction and operation of the railroad deprives the town of the power to discharge the duty imposed upon it by law.[4]

43. It is difficult to define by any general proposition the extent of the obligation of a town to provide sufficient railing. Mr. Justice Wells says: "They are bound to provide suitable railings against precipices, excavations, steep banks, deep water, &c., within or without the limits of the road, if they are so imminent to the line of public travel as to expose travellers to unusual hazard. Whether or not such a railing is necessary for the reasonable security of the public is a question which depends very much upon the circumstances of the particular locality in reference to which the question arises. But the essential and invariable term, or element, in all cases where a railing is required, is some dangerous object or place outside of the required railing, in or upon which the traveller may come to harm, if not warned or detained therefrom by the railing. The liability of horses to fright from the passage of railway trains near by may render more imperative the necessity and the duty of maintaining a railing, wherever there is occasion for a railing. But whether the absence of a railing is a defect, and the neglect to maintain one a breach of duty which will render a town liable, must be determined by the character of the place or object, between which and the travelled road it is claimed that the barrier should be interposed."[5] A railing suitable for the exigencies of ordinary travel is enough.[6]

But towns are not obliged to put up railings merely to prevent travellers from straying out of the highway where there is no unsafe place immediately contiguous to the way.[7]

[1] Shephardson *v.* Colerain, 13 Met. 55; Smith *v.* Wendell, 7 Cush. 498; Smith *v.* Dedham, 8 Cush. 522.

[2] Hayden *v.* Attleborough, 7 Gray, 338.

[3] Sawyer *v.* Northfield, 7 Cush. 490.

[4] Davis *v.* Leominster, 1 Allen, 184; and cases cited, illustrating the rule.

[5] Adams *v.* Natick, 13 Allen, 429; Morland *v.* Ipswich, 110 Mass. 522.

[6] Lyman *v.* Amherst, 107 Mass. 339.

[7] Sparhawk *v.* Salem, 1 Allen, 30.

44. The injury for which damages are recoverable must be "a physical injury to one's person, or his horse, or other material object which can be denominated property, and does not extend to expenses incurred, or loss, unless they are incident to such physical injury and constitute one item of the damages caused by it." Therefore one cannot recover for trouble, expense, and loss of time in extricating his horses and sleigh from the snow which the town negligently suffered to remain in the road and obstruct his passing over it. Nor can one recover damages caused to him by being prevented by snow from passing over the road with his teams and transporting his logs to a saw-mill, and otherwise working in his wood-lot. Nor can a *husband*, whose wife is injured by a defect in the highway, recover for medical and other expenses incurred by him, or for the loss of her service, such damages being consequential or too remote. But where there is an injury to the person — a bodily injury — which causes a mental suffering, such suffering is a part of the injury for which the party is entitled to damages ; but where he is not injured in his person, but merely has incurred risk and peril which caused fright and mental suffering, he cannot recover damages.[1]

45. "The question what is safe and convenient" (as to a highway) "is a question which in most cases it is the appropriate province of the jury to settle, and considerations relating to the nature and amount of travel, and what it is reasonably practicable to do in constructing and maintaining the way in question, will always have weight with them. Absolute safety beyond the possibility of accident will never be required ; for that would be impracticable. But if the jury find that the defect exists within the reasonable application of the rule given, it is enough." Colt, J.[2]

46. A town is not liable for an injury received by reason of the narrowness and crookedness of a highway duly located.[3]

It is held that an object with which no collision takes place will not make a town liable for an accident resulting from the running of a horse through fright at the sight of the object.[4]

Where the vice of the horse caused or contributed to the running, the plaintiff cannot recover, though the vice was unknown to the plaintiff, and he used reasonable care in obtaining and managing the horse.[5]

47. If, before the entry of an action provided for in the preceding section (section twenty-two of chapter forty-four of General Statutes, now superseded by section thirty

[1] Brailey *v.* Southborough, 6 Cush. 141; Holman *v.* Townsend, 13 Met. 297; Harwood *v.* Lowell, 4 Cush. 310; Canning *v.* Williamstown, 1 Cush. 451.

[2] George *v.* Haverhill, 110 Mass. 510.

[3] Smith *v.* Wakefield, 105 Mass. 473.

[4] Cook *v.* Montague, 115 Mass. 571, and cases cited.

[5] Brooks *v.* Acton, 117 Mass. 204.

of this chapter), the defendant tenders to the plaintiff the amount which he would be entitled to recover, together with all legal costs, and the plaintiff does not accept the same, and does not recover upon the trial more than the sum so tendered, the defendant shall recover his costs.

48. If a town neglects to repair any of the ways or bridges which it is by law obliged to keep in repair, or neglects to make the same safe and convenient when encumbered with snow, such town shall pay such fine as the court in its discretion may order.

49. Except in cases where it is otherwise specially provided, fines imposed on a town for deficiencies in the ways and bridges within the same shall be appropriated to the repairing of such ways and bridges ; and the court imposing such fine shall appoint one or more persons to superintend the collection and application of the same, who shall make a return of their doings therein to the court.

50. If, on the trial of an indictment or action brought to recover damages for an injury received by reason of a deficiency or want of repair in a highway, town way, causeway, or bridge, it appears that the county, town, or person, against whom such suit is brought, has, at any time within six years before such injury, made repairs on such way or bridge, such county, town, or person shall not deny the location thereof.[1]

But a *vote* to make repairs, so long as it remains unexecuted by the actual making of repairs, is not enough.[2]

Repairs made by a duly elected surveyor, within his district, are made by the town.[3]

51. Every town shall, in the manner provided in this chapter, erect and maintain guide-posts on the highways and other ways within the town, at such places as are necessary or convenient for the direction of travellers.

52. The selectmen of each town shall submit to the inhabitants, at every annual meeting, a report of all the

[1] Gen. Stats. ch. 44, §§ 23–26.
[2] Brown *v.* Lawrence, 120 Mass.
1. See Stockwell *v.* Fitchburg, 110 Mass. 305.
[3] Hayden *v.* Attleborough, 7 Gray, 344.

places in which guide-posts are erected and maintained within the town, and of all places at which, in their opinion, they ought to be erected and maintained. For each neglect or refusal to make such report they shall severally forfeit the sum of ten dollars.

53. Upon the report of the selectmen, the town shall determine the several places at which guide-posts shall be erected and maintained, which shall be recorded in the town records. A town which neglects or refuses to determine such places, and to cause a record thereof to be made, shall forfeit the sum of five dollars for every month during which it neglects or refuses so to do; and in such case, upon any trial for not erecting or maintaining guide-posts reported to be necessary or convenient by the selectmen, the town shall be estopped from alleging that such guide-posts were not necessary or convenient.

54. At each of the places determined by the town there shall be erected a substantial post of not less than eight feet in height, near the upper end of which shall be placed a board or boards, and upon each board shall be plainly and legibly painted, or otherwise marked, the name of the next town or place, and such other town or place of note as the selectmen think proper, to which each of such roads leads, together with the distance or number of miles to the same; and also the figure of a hand, with the forefinger thereof pointing towards the towns or places to which said roads lead: *provided*, that the inhabitants of any town may at their annual meeting agree upon some suitable substitute for such guide-posts.

55. Every town which neglects or refuses to erect and maintain such guide-posts, or some suitable substitutes therefor, shall forfeit annually the sum of five dollars for every guide-post which it so neglects or refuses to maintain.

56. A person owning or occupying lands adjoining a highway or road in a town may construct a sidewalk within such highway or road, and along the line of such land, indicating the width of such sidewalk by trees, posts, or curb-stones, set at reasonable distances apart, or by a rail-

ing erected thereto; and where a sidewalk is so constructed, whoever rides or drives a horse or team upon and along the same shall forfeit the sum of one dollar, to be recovered by such owner or occupant in an action of tort. But this section shall not diminish or interfere with the authority of surveyors of highways, or any other authority that can be legally exercised over highways or roads; nor shall it in any manner diminish the liability of any person for unreasonably obstructing highways or roads, nor shall it apply to cities.

57. In cities in which the city council, and in towns in which the inhabitants, have adopted the provisions of this and the following section, the mayor and aldermen or selectmen may establish and grade sidewalks in such streets as in their judgment the public convenience may require, and may assess the abutters on such sidewalks one half the expense of the same, the residue being paid by such city or town. All assessments so made shall be a lien upon the abutting lands in the same manner as taxes are a lien upon real estate.

58. No sidewalk constructed or graded in a city or town shall be dug up or obstructed in any part thereof, without the consent of the mayor and aldermen of the city, or of the selectmen of the town, in which such sidewalk is established.[1]

59. Towns which have adopted or shall adopt the provisions of sections seven and eight of. chapter forty-five of the General Statutes (the two preceding sections) may, at their annual town meetings, establish by-laws to provide for the removal of snow and ice, to such extent as they may deem expedient, from sidewalks ("within the limits of the highways or town ways in such towns").[2]

60. Said by-laws shall determine the time and manner of such removal, and annex penalties, not exceeding ten dollars, for each violation of their provisions by any owner or tenant of the estate abutting upon the sidewalk from which the snow and ice are required to be removed; and

---

[1] Gen. Stats. ch. 45, §§ 1–8.    [2] Stats. 1878, ch. 89.

such penalties shall be recovered, in an action of tort, in the name and to the use of the town.[1]

61. Where buildings or fences have been erected and continued for more than twenty years, fronting upon or against a training-field, burying-place, common landing-place, highway, private way, street, lane, or alley, and from the length of time or otherwise the boundaries thereof are not known or cannot be made certain by the records or by monuments, such fences or buildings shall be deemed and taken to be the true boundaries thereof. When such boundaries can be made certain, no length of time, less than forty years, shall justify the continuance of a fence or building on a town or private way, or on a highway, training-field, burying-place, landing-place, or other land appropriated for the general use or convenience of the inhabitants of the commonwealth, or of a county, town, or parish; but the same may, upon the presentment of a grand jury, be removed as a nuisance.[2]

62. It is sufficient if the fence has been *substantially* in the same place.[3] And where the fence is a Virginia fence, a straight line drawn through its centre is to be taken as the true boundary.[4] If the original boundary can be made certain by ancient monuments, although the same are not now in existence, it must be taken to be the true boundary; but when it cannot be made certain, the fence is conclusively evidence, and not merely *prima facie*, of the true boundary.[5]

63. The question whether a fence, more or less near a highway, is "upon or against the highway," within the meaning of the foregoing statute, is a question of fact for the jury.[6] Fences maintained under a claim of right for forty years within the limits of the highway give to the owner an absolute right to continue them there as against the public.[7]

64. The limitations of time prescribed in the preceding section (section sixty-one) shall take effect from and after the thirty-first day of December, in the year one thousand eight hundred and thirty-nine.

[1] Stats. 1863, ch. 114, §§ 1, 2.
[2] Gen. Stats. ch. 46, § 1.
[3] Hollenbeck *v.* Rowley, 8 Allen, 473.
[4] Holbrook *v.* McBride, 4 Gray, 215.
[5] Wood *v.* Quincy, 11 Cush. 487; Pettingill *v.* Porter, 3 Allen, 349.
[6] Sprague *v.* Waite, 17 Pick. 318.
[7] Cutter *v.* Cambridge, 6 Allen, 20.

65. When a building, fence, or other encumbrance, erected or continued on a town or private way, or on a highway, training-field, burying-place, landing-place, or other land appropriated for the general use or convenience of the inhabitants of the commonwealth, or of a county, town, or parish, is adjudged a nuisance and ordered to be abated, and the materials, upon a sale thereof by auction, shall be insufficient to pay the costs and charges of prosecution and removal, the court may order the deficient sum to be raised and levied from the goods and chattels of the party convicted of erecting or continuing such nuisance.

66. Any person may take down and remove gates, rails, bars, or fence[s], upon or across a highway, unless the same have been there placed for the purpose of preventing the spreading of a disease dangerous to the public health, or have been erected or continued by the license of the county commissioners or of the selectmen of the town; in which case, a person aggrieved by such taking down and removal may apply to the commissioners, or selectmen, respectively, who may order the same to be replaced.

67. If fence[s], gates, rails, or bars are upon or across a town way or private way, the same may be removed by the order of a justice of the peace, unless the same are there placed for the purpose of preventing the spreading of a disease dangerous to the public health, or unless the same are erected or continued by license of the town, or of the person for whose use such private way was laid out; and a person aggrieved by such removal may apply to the commissioners; and if upon examination it appears that the same were erected or continued by license as aforesaid, the commissioners shall order them to be replaced.

68. The mayor and aldermen, selectmen, or any municipal officer of a city or town to whom the care of the streets or roads may be intrusted, may authorize the planting of shade trees therein, wherever it may not interfere with the public travel or with private rights; and shade trees standing and trees planted pursuant to such license shall be deemed and taken to be the private property of the

person so planting them, or upon whose premises they
stand or are planted, and shall not be deemed a nuisance ;
but upon complaint made to the mayor and aldermen, or
selectmen, they may cause such trees to be removed at the
expense of the owner thereof, if the public necessity
seems to them so to require.[1]

Standing, in this section, means standing June 1, 1860, the date
when the statute took effect.[2]

69. Whoever wantonly injures, defaces, tears, or destroys an ornamental or shade tree, or shrub, statue,
fountain, vase, or other plant or fixture of ornament or
utility, in a street, road, square, court, park, public gar-
den, or other enclosure, shall forfeit not less than five, nor
more than one hundred dollars, to be recovered by complaint, one half to the complainant, and the other half to
the use of the person upon whose property, or within whose
premises, the trespass was committed.

70. Whoever negligently or carelessly suffers any horse
or other beast driven by or for him, or any beast belonging
to him and lawfully on the highway, to break down, destroy, or injure any tree not his own, standing for use or
ornament on said highway, or negligently or wilfully by any
other means breaks down, destroys, or injures any such
tree, shall be subject to an action for damages, at the suit
of the owner or tenant of the land in front of which the
tree stands.

71. In a city in which the city council, and in a
town in which the inhabitants, have accepted this section,
the mayor and aldermen or selectmen may set out and
maintain shade trees upon the public squares and highways, at the expense of such city or town, which may
appropriate annually, for that purpose, a sum not exceeding
twenty-five cents for each of its ratable polls in the year
next preceding that in which such appropriation is made.[3]

72. No person who has by law a right to cut down or

---

[1] Gen. Stats. ch. 46, §§ 2–6.       [3] Gen. Stats. ch. 46, §§ 7–9.
[2] White v. Godfrey, 97 Mass. 475.

remove any ornamental or shade tree standing in any highway, town way, or street, shall exercise such right without first giving notice of his intention to one of the selectmen of the town or mayor of the city in which the tree stands; and, if the selectmen of the town or mayor and aldermen of the city desire to retain the tree, they shall give notice thereof to such person within ten days after his notice to them; and in that case, the same course shall be taken and the same rules apply as to the assessment, appeal, and final determination and payment of the damage such person may suffer by the retaining of said tree, as in the case of damage done by an alteration in such highway, town way, or street.

73. If any such person shall cut down, remove, or injure such tree without first giving the notice required in the foregoing section or in violation of any of the provisions thereof, or of the rights of the city or town acquired thereunder to maintain the same, he shall suffer the penalty provided for the injury or destroying of ornamental or shade trees in the seventh section of the forty-sixth chapter of the General Statutes, and the penalty in such case shall accrue to the town or city.

74. This act shall not be in force in any town or city until it shall be accepted by a majority of the legal voters in such town at a meeting legally called therefor, or by the city council.[1]

75. A city or town may make suitable by-laws and regulations to prevent the pasturing of cattle or other animals, either with or without a keeper, upon any or all of the streets or ways in such city or town, and may annex penalties not exceeding twenty dollars for each violation thereof. But no such by-law or regulation shall affect the right of a person to the use of land within the limits of such way adjoining his own premises.

76. A town may, at an annual meeting, establish by-laws to prevent persons from riding or driving horses at a rate faster than a walk over any bridge within the limits

[1] Stats. 1867, ch. 242.

of such town, which shall have cost not less than five hundred dollars; and annex penalties not exceeding one dollar for a breach thereof: but such by-laws shall first be approved by the commissioners for the county in which such town lies.

77. No person shall be liable to any of the penalties in the three (two) preceding sections, unless the commissioners, town, and proprietors, respectively, keep posted up, at each end of such bridges, in some conspicuous place, a board, painted with a white ground, containing in black letters the substance of their said by-laws.[1]

If the by-laws are not posted up, and a person, crossing a bridge, without actual notice of such by-laws, receives an injury while violating them, such violation will be no defence to his action for damages.[2]

78. When the (county) commissioners judge it necessary to establish a ferry, and no person appears to keep the same for the stated profits thereof, the town where such ferry may be shall provide one or more suitable persons to keep and attend the same at such place and in such times of the year as the commissioners order, which persons shall be licensed as aforesaid (that is, by the county commissioners, as provided in chapter forty-seven of General Statutes, and the tolls are established by the same authority); and the expense of maintaining such ferry, beyond the amount received for tolls, shall be paid by the town.

79. If such ferry is established between two towns, they shall maintain the same, either jointly or alternately, as the commissioners shall order.

80. A town neglecting to maintain a ferry, as provided in the two preceding sections, shall forfeit for each month's neglect a sum not exceeding one hundred dollars.[3]

81. In any case of a ferry now established between two towns, or when the county commissioners of any county shall judge it necessary to establish a ferry between two towns, said commissioners, upon the application of ten legal voters of either of such towns, may, after such

[1] Gen. Stats. ch. 45, §§ 10, 12, 14.

[2] Worcester v. Essex & Merri-mack Bridge Corporation, 7 Gray, 457.

[3] Gen. Stats. ch. 47, §§ 6-8.

notice to said towns as said commissioners may order, and hearing thereon, determine and order that they shall maintain said ferry, either jointly or alternately, or that the expense of maintaining said ferry shall be borne by such towns equally or in any proportions that the said commissioners shall judge to be just and equitable. The determination and order of the commissioners, made as aforesaid, shall be final upon the towns interested: *provided, however,* that at any time thereafter and from time to time, as the exigency may require, the county commissioners of such county, upon like application and after like notice and hearing, may make such new determination and order in the manner above provided, as they shall then judge to be just and equitable.

A town neglecting to maintain a ferry, as provided in the foregoing section, shall forfeit for each month's neglect a sum not exceeding one hundred dollars.[1]

82. The mayor and aldermen of cities, and the selectmen of towns, may select and lay out any lots of land within their respective limits, not appropriated to public uses, nor owned by any other city or town, as gravel and clay pits, from which earth and gravel necessary to be used in the construction, repair, or improvement of the streets or ways which such city or town may by law be bound to construct or keep in repair, may be taken, together with such ways as they may deem to be necessary for convenient access thereto. All proceedings in relation to the taking and laying out of such land shall be the same as are now provided by law in the cases of laying out streets and town ways respectively; and the report of such laying out shall specify the extent and depth of excavation to be permitted upon such land, and the time, not exceeding ten years next after such laying out, during which such land or way shall be held and used for the purposes aforesaid.

83. Any person aggrieved in the assessment of his damages by the board of mayor and aldermen, or selectmen, for land taken under this act, may have the matter of his complaint determined by a jury, in the same manner as is now provided by law in cases of highways, which jury shall be applied for within one year after such assessment.

84. Any land taken by virtue of this act shall be held

---

[1] Stats. 1874, ch. 265.

and used by such cities or towns for no other purposes than those herein specified, and shall revert to the owner, his heirs and assigns, upon the expiration of the time limited; and the owner may, during such time, enclose, occupy, and use such land, in any manner not inconsistent with the use of the same by such city or town for the purposes aforesaid.[1]

85. A corporation may, with the assent of the mayor and aldermen or selectmen in writing, dig up and open any street or way for the purpose of placing such pipes as are necessary in constructing its aqueduct, or for repairing or extending the same: *provided*, the same be done in such manner as not to prevent the convenient passing of teams and carriages.[2]

86. Whenever, in the opinion of the mayor and aldermen of a city, or the selectmen of a town, it is necessary to enter upon, use, or take any land for the purpose of securing or protecting any public way or bridge, it shall be lawful for them to enter upon, use, or take the same.

All damages sustained thereby shall be recovered in the manner provided for the assessment and award of damages occasioned by the laying out, altering, or discontinuance of town ways.[3]

87. The selectmen of any town where public convenience requires it, on the application of any person, may authorize such person, on his own land and in such manner as they may order, to construct and maintain within the limits of any highway in such town, or in any place conveniently accessible from such highway, a suitable watering-place for horses and other animals, to be used by the public; and said selectmen, at any time when in their judgment such watering-place is no longer needed, or when public safety and convenience require it, may discontinue the same. Any person maintaining a watering-place in any town, in accordance with the first section of this act (the foregoing paragraph), shall be paid by such town such sum as said

[1] Stats. 1869, ch. 237, §§ 1–3.     [3] Stats. 1868, ch. 264.
[2] Gen. Stats. ch. 65, § 9.

selectmen, in their order authorizing such watering-place, may determine, not exceeding five dollars a year, so long as the same is so maintained.[1]

88. When a party injured in his person or property by a defect in a highway, caused by the operations of a gas company in laying down or repairing its pipes or otherwise obstructing such way, recovers damages therefor of the town wherein such injury is received, such town shall, in addition to the damages so recovered against it, be entitled to recover all the taxable costs of the plaintiff and defendant, in the same action, in a suit brought against said gas company; *provided*, said gas company be liable for said damages; and *provided*, reasonable notice be given by such town to the gas company, so that it might have defended the original action.[2]

Any savings bank in this commonwealth is hereby authorized to receive funds, in trust, on deposit, to an unlimited amount, for any one or all of the hereinafter named purposes: said funds shall be placed upon interest in said bank, and the interest and dividends arising therefrom shall be paid semi-annually to such town, city, or cemetery authorities as may be designated by the donors of said funds or the will of the person bequeathing the same; said interest and dividends to be expended by such town, city, or cemetery authorities, within the precincts of such town, city, or cemetery, in setting out shade-trees in streets and parks, and in improving the same; in purchasing land for parks and improving the same; in maintaining cemeteries or cemetery lots, and in erecting and maintaining drinking-fountains in public places; for any one or all of the before named purposes as may be specified by the donors of said funds or the will of the person bequeathing the same. No part of the principal of said funds shall be withdrawn or expended, and it shall be exempt from attachment or levy on execution.

The funds held in accordance with this act shall be known as the "Shade-tree and Cemetery Fund," and the treasurer of any savings bank in which said funds are deposited shall give a certificate of gift to each donor of such funds, and shall send by mail or deliver in the month of January, every third year after the first deposit, to the mayor of any city, or the chairman of the selectmen of any town, within the limits of which the interests and dividends of said funds are to be expended, a written statement, signed by such treasurer, of the amount of funds on deposit, for the purposes aforesaid, and said

---

[1] Stats. 1870, ch. 119.        [2] Stats. 1860, ch. 121.

statement shall be recorded in full in the office of the clerk for said city or town.

In case any savings bank holding such funds shall surrender its charter or cease to do business, the supreme judicial court is hereby authorized to order said funds transferred and deposited in some other savings bank upon the same trusts as aforesaid; and, if the laws authorizing such banks shall be repealed, said court is hereby authorized to order said funds transferred and deposited in such banking institution as said court may deem proper and for the best interest of said funds, to be by it held upon the trusts aforesaid.[1]

Any executor, administrator, or trustee holding money for any of the foregoing purposes may be authorized by the judge of probate to deposit the same in a savings bank.[2]

[1] Stats. 1875, ch. 174.          [2] Stats. 1877, ch. 162.

# CHAPTER XXVI.

## RAILROADS CROSSING HIGHWAYS, ETC.

1. When a railroad is laid out across a highway or other way, it shall be constructed so as not to obstruct the same; and (unless the county commissioners shall authorize a crossing at the same level as provided in section ninety) (five) it shall be constructed so as to pass either over or under the way, as prescribed in the next section, and conformably to any decree which may be made by the county commissioners under section eighty-eight (three).

2. If the railroad is constructed to pass over the way, a sufficient space shall be left under the railroad conveniently to accommodate the travel on the way. If the railroad is constructed to pass under the way, the railroad corporation shall build such bridges, with their abutments and suitable approaches thereto, as will accommodate the travel upon the way: *provided*, that no bridge for any purpose shall hereafter be constructed over any railroad at a height less than eighteen feet above the track of such railroad, except by the consent in writing of the board of railroad commissioners.

3. A railroad corporation may raise or lower any highway or other way, for the purpose of having its road pass over or under the same; but before proceeding to cross, alter, or excavate, for the purpose of crossing the way, it shall obtain from the county commissioners a decree prescribing what alterations may be made in the way, and the manner and time of making the alterations or structures the commissioners may require at the crossing; and before entering upon, excavating, or altering the way, shall give security, satisfactory to the commissioners, to the city or town in which the crossing is situated, that it will faithfully

comply with the requirements of the decree to the acceptance of the commissioners, and indemnify the city or town from all damages and charges by reason of any failure so to do.

4. A railroad corporation may alter the course of a highway or other way for the purpose of facilitating the crossing of the same by its road, or permitting its road to pass at the side thereof without crossing, upon obtaining a decree of the county commissioners prescribing the manner and time of such alteration. Before granting the decree, the commissioners, after due notice to the city or town in which the way is situated, shall decide that the alteration will not essentially injure the way. The corporation shall pay all damages occasioned to private property by the alteration, as in case of land taken for its road.

5. When a railroad is laid out across a highway or other way, the county commissioners, upon the application of the railroad corporation, or of the mayor and aldermen or selectmen of the city or town in which the crossing is situated, after due notice to all parties interested, and after hearing the parties, may adjudge that public necessity requires the crossing at the same level, and may make a decree to specially authorize and require the corporation so to construct its road, in such manner as shall be prescribed in the decree; and said commissioners may modify the terms of such decree, or revoke the same, at any time before the construction of the railroad at such crossing.

No highway or town way shall hereafter be laid out across a railroad at a level therewith, nor shall any railroad be laid out and constructed across a highway or town way at a level therewith, without the consent in writing of the board of railroad commissioners in addition to the authority of the county commissioners as now required.[1]

6. A railroad corporation whose road is crossed by a highway or other way on a level therewith shall, at its own expense, so guard or protect its rails by plank, timber, or otherwise, as to secure a safe and easy passage across its road; and if, in the opinion of the county commissioners,

1 Stats. 1876, ch. 73.

any subsequent alteration of the highway or other way, or any additional safeguards, are required at the crossing, they may order the corporation to establish the same as provided in section eighty-eight (three).

7. A highway or town way may be laid out across a railroad previously constructed when the county commissioners adjudge that the public convenience and necessity require the same; and in such case, after due notice to the railroad corporation, and hearing all parties interested, they may thus lay out a highway across a railroad, or may authorize a city or town, on petition of the mayor and aldermen or selectmen thereof, to lay out a way across a railroad, in such manner as not to injure or obstruct the railroad, and otherwise in conformity with the provisions of sections eighty-six and eighty-seven (one and two); but not permitting it to cross at a level with the railroad, unless public necessity so requires, in which case they may give special authority for such crossing, as provided in section ninety (five).

8. If, upon application to the county commissioners by the mayor and aldermen or selectmen of any city or town, it appears that a railroad corporation crosses with its road a highway or other way therein, so as to cause an obstruction thereto, contrary to the provisions of section eighty-six (one), or of any decree of the county commissioners made under section eighty-eight (three); or that it refuses or neglects to keep in proper repair any bridge or other structure required or necessary at such crossing, the commissioners, after due notice to the corporation, may pass a decree prescribing what repairs shall be made by the corporation at the crossing, and the time within which they shall be made, and shall order the corporation to pay the costs of the application. They may further order the corporation to give security, as provided in section eighty-eight (three), for the faithful performance of the requirements of the decree and the indemnity of said city or town upon any failure in such performance.

9. Every railroad corporation shall, at its own expense,

construct, and afterwards maintain and keep in repair, all bridges, with their approaches or abutments, which it is authorized or required to construct over or under any turnpike road, canal, highway, or other way; and any city or town may recover of the railroad corporation whose road crosses a highway or town way therein all damages, charges, and expenses incurred by such city or town by reason of the neglect or refusal of the corporation to erect or keep in repair all structures required or necessary at such crossing; but if, after the laying out and making of a railroad, the county commissioners have authorized a turnpike, highway, or other way to be laid out across the railroad, all expenses of and incident to constructing and maintaining the turnpike or way at such crossing shall be borne by the turnpike corporation, or the county, city, town, or other owner of the same; until or unless, in either case, it shall be otherwise determined by an award of a special commission, as provided in the four following sections.

10. If the mayor and aldermen of a city, or the selectmen of a town, wherein a highway or town way which crosses or is crossed by a railroad is situated, or the directors of any railroad corporation whose road crosses or is crossed by such way, are of the opinion that it is necessary for the security or convenience of the public that any alteration should be made in such crossing, or in the approaches thereto, or in the method of such crossing, or in the location of the railroad or in the location of the highway or town way, or in any bridge at such crossing, the county commissioners shall, when, after due notice and hearing of all parties interested, they decide that such alteration is necessary, prescribe the manner and limits within which it shall be made, and forthwith certify their decision in the matter to the parties, and also to the board of railroad commissioners; and, when the county commissioners decide that no alteration is necessary, the party making the application shall pay the costs thereof.

11. If, under the provisions of the preceding section, the county commissioners decide that the location of the rail-

road or of the highway or town way shall be changed, land or other property may be taken therefor, according to the provisions of law; and all damages occasioned by such taking shall be assessed according to the provisions of the laws which now are or hereafter may be in force regulating the taking of land by railroad corporations, or the taking of land for highways and town ways, as the case may be.

12. The party by whom such decision shall be carried into effect shall be determined by the award of a special commission of three disinterested persons, to be appointed as provided in the next section; and the said special commission shall also determine by what party all charges and expenses occasioned by making such alteration, and all future charges for keeping in repair such crossing and the approaches thereto, as well as all costs of the application to the county commissioners, or of the hearing before said special commission, shall be borne; or said special commission may apportion all such charges, expenses, or costs between the railroad corporation and the town, city, or county in which said crossing is situated; and the supreme judicial court shall have jurisdiction in equity to compel compliance with all orders, decrees, and judgments of said special commission.

13. The members of such special commission shall be named within thirty days after the decision that an alteration is necessary, in the following manner: one of them shall be named by the county commissioners, if the way that crosses or is crossed by the railroad is a highway, or by the selectmen or mayor and aldermen if it is a town way; one by the railroad corporation interested; and the third shall be a member of the board of railroad commissioners designated by said board; and if the town, city, county, or railroad corporation does not name a member within thirty days after decision aforesaid, the board of railroad commissioners shall name a member in its behalf. The commission shall meet as soon as may be after the several members are named, and in any case within sixty days after the decision aforesaid.

14. Any award made under the provisions of section ninety-eight shall be filed in the office of the board of railroad commissioners, and the same shall be final, unless some party affected thereby, within thirty days of the rendering of such award, requests in writing the commission established by said section to return said award into the supreme judicial court for the county in which the crossing is situated; and, upon such request, said commission shall so return said award, which shall be subject to revision in the same manner as if said commission had derived its power to act in the premises under the appointment of said court; and said award, when accepted by said court, shall be final.

15. When the party designated for that duty by the award of the special commission has carried into effect the decision of the county commissioners agreeably to said award, such party may recover of any other party, in an action of contract, the proportion awarded to be paid by such other party, with interest; and if the party so designated by the award unreasonably neglects or refuses to carry the decision into effect, any other party affected by such neglect or refusal may proceed to do it; and, in an action of tort against any or all of the others, may recover from each the proportion awarded to be paid by it; and from the party neglecting or refusing, all charges, expenses, and costs occasioned thereby.

16. The original jurisdiction of all questions touching obstructions to turnpikes, highways, or town ways, caused by the construction or operation of railroads, shall be vested in the county commissioners within their respective jurisdictions.

17. The supreme judicial court shall have jurisdiction in equity, and may compel railroad corporations to raise or lower any turnpike, highway, or town way, when the county commissioners have decided, in due and legal form, that such raising or lowering is necessary for the security of the public; and to comply with the orders, decrees, and judgments of county commissioners in all cases touching

obstructions to such ways by railroads. And if it is made to appear to the supreme judicial court, or any justice thereof, in term time or vacation, upon the petition of the mayor and aldermen or selectmen of any place, that a corporation has excavated or altered a highway or town way without obtaining the decree and giving the security required by section eighty-eight (three), or has neglected for fifteen days to give security as required by section ninety-four, the court or justice may, by injunction or other suitable process according to the practice of courts of equity, restrain and prohibit the corporation from entering upon, altering, excavating, or crossing the way until such decree is obtained or the security given.

18. Every railroad corporation shall cause a bell, of at least thirty-five pounds in weight, and a steam-whistle, to be placed on each locomotive engine passing upon its road; and such bell shall be rung or such whistle sounded at the distance of at least eighty rods from the place where the road crosses upon the same level a turnpike, highway, town way, or travelled place, over which a signboard is required to be maintained, as provided in the next two sections; and such bell shall be rung or such whistle sounded, either one or the other, continuously or alternately, until the engine has crossed such turnpike, way, or travelled place.

19. Every railroad corporation shall cause boards, well supported by posts or otherwise, to be placed and constantly maintained across each turnpike, highway, or town way, where it is crossed by the railroad at the same level; said posts and boards shall be of such height as to be easily seen by travellers, without obstructing the travel; and on each side of the boards the following inscription shall be printed in capital letters of at least the size of nine inches each: "Railroad Crossing—Look out for the Engine." When a gate or a flagman is maintained at such crossing, as provided in section one hundred and twenty-six, the corporation may substitute, in place of such posts and boards, warning boards on each side of the crossing,

of such form, size, and description as the board of railroad commissioners shall approve.

20. If the mayor and aldermen or selectmen of a city or town wherein a travelled place is crossed by a railroad at the same level decide that it is necessary for the better security of the public that sign-boards such as are described in the preceding section should be maintained at such travelled place, they may in writing request the corporation owning the railroad to erect and maintain them. If the corporation neglects or refuses so to do, the mayor and aldermen or selectmen may apply to the county commissioners to decide upon the reasonableness of their requests. If the commissioners, after due notice and hearing of the parties, decide that such erection is necessary for the better security of the public, the corporation shall comply with their decision, and pay the costs of the application. If they decide that it is not so necessary, one half of the costs of the application shall be paid by the city or town, and one half by the corporation.

21. If the mayor and aldermen or selectmen of any city or town in which a turnpike, highway, town way, or travelled place is crossed by a railroad at the same level, should be of opinion that it is necessary for the better security of the public that gates should be erected across such turnpike, highway, town way, or travelled place, and that an agent be stationed to open and close such gates when an engine or train passes, or that bars be erected instead of gates, or that a flagman be stationed at the crossing, who shall display a flag whenever an engine or a train passes, such mayor and aldermen or selectmen may in writing request the railroad corporation to erect and maintain gates, and station an agent thereat; or to erect bars; or to station a flagman at the crossing. If the corporation refuses, or neglects to comply with the request, the mayor and aldermen or the selectmen may apply to the county commissioners. Upon such application, or at any time, upon the petition of any party, after due notice and hearing, the commissioners may make such orders for the

17

erection and maintenance of gates or bars, or the stationing of an agent or flagman, or such alteration of arrangements already existing at the crossing, as said commissioners shall decide the better security of human life or the convenience of the public travel require, and may further make such order as to costs as justice may require; and the railroad corporation shall comply with all such orders of the county commissioners, whether made before the railroad is constructed and opened for use, or from time to time afterwards.

22. No railroad corporation, nor its servants or agents, shall wilfully or negligently obstruct, or unnecessarily or unreasonably use or occupy a highway, town way, or street; nor in any case with cars or engines, for more than five minutes at one time; and whenever a highway, town way, or street has been thus used or occupied with cars or engines, no railroad corporation shall again use or occupy the same with the cars or engines of a freight train, until a sufficient time, not less than three minutes, has allowed the passage across the railroad of such travellers as were ready and waiting to cross when the former occupation ceased. For any violation of the provisions of this section, the corporation shall forfeit the sum of one hundred dollars.

23. The selectmen of any town, or the mayor and aldermen of any city, may, upon the petition of any railroad corporation having a passenger station within the limits of such town or city, appoint as many as they may deem proper of the persons in the employ of said corporation police officers, to act as railroad police for the purposes and with the powers hereinafter set forth. A copy of the record of the appointment of any railroad police officer shall be filed by the clerk of the corporation upon whose petition such order is made, with the clerk of each town or city through or into which such railroad extends, and in which it is intended that such police shall act; and the filing of such order shall constitute the persons named therein railroad police within such towns or cities. Such police officers shall hold their offices during the pleasure of the selectmen or mayor and aldermen by

whom they are appointed : *provided*, that when any corporation shall cease to require the services of any of the railroad police appointed upon its petition, it may file a notice to that effect in the several offices in which notice of such appointment was originally filed ; and thereupon the power of said officer shall cease.

24. Whenever a railroad corporation has established and maintained throughout the year for five consecutive years a passenger station at any point upon its road, such station shall not be abandoned, nor shall the accommodation furnished by the stopping of trains thereat be substantially diminished as compared with that furnished at other stations on the same road ; and, in case of any violation of the provisions of this section, it shall be the duty of the attorney-general, at the relation of ten legal voters of the town or city in which said station is located, to proceed in equity by information to enjoin said corporation from further violation thereof.

25. Railroad corporations may re-locate passenger stations and freight depots upon the approval in writing of the board of railroad commissioners, and of the selectmen of the town or the city council of the city in which such stations or depots are situated.

26. No private track shall be constructed across or upon a highway, town way, or travelled place, except with the consent of the mayor and aldermen or selectmen of the city or town, and in a place and manner approved by them. If said mayor and aldermen or selectmen consent, they shall make from time to time such regulations in regard to the motive power to be employed, the rate of speed to be run, and time and manner of using the track over and upon such way or travelled place as in their judgment the public safety and convenience require, and they may order such changes to be made in the track as are rendered necessary by the alteration or repair of such way. If they allow steam power to be used on such track, the provisions of this act relating to the crossing of ways and travelled places by railroad corporations shall apply to

such track, and the person or corporation by whom the same was constructed.

27. The directors (of a railroad corporation organized under statutes of 1874, ch. 372) shall prepare a map of the proposed route on an appropriate scale, with a profile thereof on a vertical scale of ten to one as compared with the horizontal scale ; and with the report of a skilful engineer, based on actual examination and survey, showing the kind and amount of excavation, filling, bridging and masonry required, the proposed grades, the number of highways and other railroads, if any, and of navigable streams and tide-waters, if any, to be crossed, and the manner proposed for crossing the same, which must be conformable to the provisions of section eighty-five, the general profile of the surface of the country through which the road will pass, the feasibility of the route, the manner of constructing the road, and a detailed estimate of the cost of construction.

28. The directors shall submit said map and report of the engineer to the selectmen of any town and the mayor and aldermen of any city named in the articles of association ; such selectmen or mayor and aldermen shall thereupon appoint a place and time for a hearing, of which notice shall be given by publication in one or more newspapers published in the county for two successive weeks, the last publication to be at least two days prior to the hearing, and by posting copies of the notice in at least two public places in the town or city, at least two weeks before such hearing.

29. Whenever the selectmen of any town or the mayor and aldermen of any city named in the articles of association, after such notice, exhibition of the map, and hearing, shall agree with the directors as to the proposed route, or any route of their railroad in said town or city, such agreement shall be sufficient to fix the same ; and said selectmen or mayor and aldermen shall sign and give to the directors a certificate setting forth the route so fixed.

30. Whenever the directors fail to agree with the select-

men of any town or the mayor and aldermen of any city as to the route of their railroad in such town or city, said directors may petition the board of railroad commissioners to fix the route in said town or city, who, after due notice to said selectmen or mayor and aldermen, shall hear the parties, and fix the route in such town or city. Such board shall make a certificate setting forth the route as fixed by them ; and the same shall be certified by the clerk of said board to the directors. The costs of the petition shall be paid by the directors. All variations from the route first proposed shall be made upon the map.

31. The route of a railroad fixed under the two preceding sections may include such spurs and branches and connecting and terminal tracks in any city or town as may be necessary to enable the corporation to conveniently collect and deliver passengers and freight in such city or town ; but no such branch, spur, or connecting or terminal track shall be laid longitudinally within the limits of a public way without the consent of the mayor and aldermen, or the selectmen, and in giving such consent they may impose such conditions as to the location, construction, and use thereof as may be agreed upon between themselves and the directors ; and the corporations owning or operating any such tracks so laid longitudinally in a public way, shall, in respect to the same, be liable to the city or town in which the same are laid, for all loss or damage caused thereto by the construction and use of such tracks, and by the negligence or default of their agents or workmen thereon.

32. When the owner of land through which a railroad, constructed prior to the seventeenth day of April in the year eighteen hundred and forty-one, passes, has not received all damages assessed to him, or has not agreed to maintain suitable fences upon such road, upon the application of the owner, or of the mayor and aldermen or selectmen of the city or town, the county commissioners may require the corporation to make and maintain fences suitable for the benefit and security of the land-owner and of travellers upon the road.

33. Every railroad corporation shall erect and maintain suitable fences, with convenient bars, gates, or openings therein, at such places as may reasonably be required, upon both sides of the entire length of any railroad which it shall have constructed subsequently to the sixteenth day of May in the year eighteen hundred and forty-six, except at the crossings of a turnpike, highway, or other way, or in places where a convenient use of the road would be thereby obstructed; and shall also construct and maintain sufficient barriers at such places as may be necessary, where it is practicable to do so, to prevent the entrance of cattle upon the road. A corporation unreasonably neglecting to comply with the provisions of this section shall, for every such neglect, forfeit a sum not exceeding two hundred dollars for every month during which the neglect continues; and the supreme judicial court, or any justice thereof, either in term time or vacation, may, by injunction or other suitable process in equity, compel the corporation to comply with such provisions; and, upon such neglect, may restrain and prohibit the corporation from crossing any turnpike, highway, or town way, or using any land, until said provisions are complied with.

34. A railroad corporation, having taken land for its road, may vary the direction of the road in the place where such land is situated; but it shall not locate any part thereof without the limits of the route fixed agreeably to sections twenty-five and twenty-six of this act,[1] unless with the consent in writing of the mayor and aldermen or selectmen, if it was fixed under section twenty-five, or of the railroad commissioners, if it was fixed under section twenty-six. The corporation shall, before the expiration of the time required for completing the road, file with the county commissioners the location of the different parts where such variations are made; and the time for completing the road shall not be extended in consequence of such variations.

35. Upon the complaint and application of the selectmen of any town within which any part of any railroad is located, it shall be the

[1] Sections 29 and 30 of this chapter.

duty of the railroad commissioners to make an examination of the condition and operation thereof ; and if twenty or more legal voters in any town shall, by petition in writing, request the selectmen of such town to make the said complaint and application, and the selectmen refuse or decline to comply with the petition, they shall indorse upon the petition the reason of such non-compliance, and return it to the petitioners; and the petitioners may thereupon, within ten days of such refusal and return, present the petition to said commissioners; and said commissioners shall, if upon due inquiry and hearing of the petitioners they think the public good demands the examination, proceed to make it in the same manner as if called upon by the selectmen of any town. Before proceeding to make such examination in accordance with such application or petition, said commissioners shall give to the petitioners and the corporation reasonable notice in writing of the time and place of entering upon the same. If upon such examination it shall appear to said commissioners that the complaint alleged by the applicants or petitioners is well founded, they shall so adjudge, and shall inform the corporation operating such railroad of their adjudication, in the same manner as is provided in section nine.[1]

[1] Stats. 1874, ch. 372.

## CHAPTER XXVII.

### CONSTRUCTION OF ROADS TO SWAMPS, MINES, ETC.

1. ANY town, city, person, company, or body corporate, having the ownership of low lands, lakes, swamps, quarries, mines, or mineral deposits, that on account of adjacent lands belonging to other persons, or occupied as a highway, cannot be approached, worked, drained, or used, in the ordinary manner, without crossing such lands or highway, may be authorized to establish roads, drains, ditches, tunnels, and railway, to such places, in the manner hereinafter provided.

2. The party desiring to make such improvements shall file a petition therefor with the county commissioners within whose jurisdiction the premises are situated, setting forth the names of the persons interested, if known to the petitioner, and also, in detail, the nature of the proposed improvement and the situation of the adjoining lands; which petition shall be accompanied with a bond, satisfactory to said commissioners, for the payment of expenses incurred in the prosecution of the application.

3. The commissioners at their first meeting after the filing of the petition and bond, shall give at least three weeks' public notice of the time and place of meeting to consider the petition, in some newspaper printed in the county; and if there is no such paper, in a newspaper printed in an adjacent county; they shall further give notice to the mayor of any city and the clerk of any town in which the premises are situated.

4. They shall meet at the time and place appointed, and after examination, inspection, and the hearing of evidence, shall determine whether the improvement prayed for is

necessary, and if so, shall proceed to lay out and establish the same in such manner as shall do as little injury as practicable ; and shall assess the amount of damages which in their opinion the proprietor of the adjacent lands will sustain. They shall apportion the damages equitably among all parties to be benefited, having regard to the benefits each will receive ; and such award shall be deemed conclusive upon each of the parties charged with such payment, unless an appeal is taken within the period of one year.[1]

5. But the commissioners have no power to authorize an owner of marshy or wet land to dig a ditch into his neighbor's land, and discharge the water upon the same to his injury, but only to authorize him to dig a ditch across the same, or to some outlet where the water may be discharged without injury.[2]

6. Any party aggrieved by the award may appeal therefrom, and thereupon like proceedings shall be had as are provided in chapter forty-three, for persons aggrieved in the laying out of highways.

7. When it is necessary to repair any improvement thus constructed, a majority of the persons benefited by it may cause such repairs to be made, and compel contributions from each person benefited, on the basis of the award.

8. When the premises mentioned in section (one) are situated entirely in one town or city, the petition may be made to the selectmen or mayor and aldermen thereof, who shall proceed thereon in all respects as above provided for county commissioners upon such petitions, except that they need not give notice to their town or city.

9. The petition under the preceding section shall be filed in the office of the town or city clerk before proceedings are had thereon ; and together with the order or award thereon shall be recorded in said office within two months after the same is made.

10. The selectmen or mayor and aldermen shall each receive for services upon such petitions two dollars a day, and the clerk shall receive for recording petitions

[1] Gen. Stats. ch. 148, §§ 19–22.    [2] Sherman v. Tobey, 3 Allen, 7.

and orders the same fees as for mortgages of personal property.

11. A party aggrieved by any order, award, or refusal of the selectmen or mayor and aldermen herein, may complain to the county commissioners at any meeting held within one year thereafter; and the commissioners may thereupon proceed in all respects as though the petition were originally made to them.[1]

---

[1] Gen. Stats. ch. 148, §§ 23–28.

# CHAPTER XXVIII.

DEDICATION OF WAYS, ASCERTAINING LOCATION, ERECTION OF MONUMENTS, AND WAYS OVER BURYING-GROUNDS.

1. No way opened and dedicated to the public use, which has not become a public way, shall be chargeable upon a city or town as a highway or town way, unless the same is laid out and established by such city or town in the manner prescribed by the statutes of the commonwealth.

2. The mayor and aldermen and selectmen shall, whenever the public safety demands it, direct and cause the entrances of such ways entering on and uniting with an existing public highway, to be closed up; or may by other sufficient means caution the public against entering upon such ways; and if any such way shall not be closed, or sufficient notice given that the same is dangerous, the city or town shall be liable for damages arising from defects therein in the same manner as if it had been duly laid out and established.

3. In cities in which the city council, and in towns in which the inhabitants at a legal meeting, have accepted the provisions of this and the two following sections, if a street or way has been or shall be opened over private land by the owner thereof, and permitted to be used by the public before the same has been accepted and laid out according to law, the owners of the lots abutting thereon shall grade such street or way at their own expense, in such manner as the safety and convenience of the public shall in the opinion of the mayor and aldermen or selectmen require. If the owners of such abutting lots, after reasonable notice from the mayor and aldermen or selectmen, neglect or refuse so to do, or to close the street from public use, the mayor and aldermen or selectmen may

cause the same to be graded, and after due notice to the parties interested shall assess the expense thereof upon the owners in such proportion as shall be judged reasonable. All assessments so made shall be a lien upon the abutting lands in the same manner as taxes are a lien upon real estate.

4. The mayor and aldermen or selectmen may fix and establish the grade of a street or way so opened and used, and cause a plan of such grade to be deposited in the office of the city or town clerk. And all persons making improvements upon the lots abutting thereon, after the grade has been established and recorded, shall conform to the grade. But nothing contained in this and the preceding section shall affect any agreements heretofore made respecting such streets or ways, between the owners of lots and the city or town.

5. The grading of such street or way by the owners of the land, in pursuance of the notice by the mayor and aldermen or selectmen, shall not be construed to be a dedication of the same to the public use, nor shall the establishment and record of the grade, or the grading thereof by the mayor and aldermen or selectmen, constitute an acceptance of the same by the city or town. But no such street or way shall be dug up or obstructed without the consent of the mayor and aldermen or selectmen.[1]

6. The statute which is the basis of and comprises the three preceding sections, has been declared unconstitutional and void by the supreme judicial court.[2]

7. When ten or more freeholders represent to the mayor and aldermen of a city or selectmen of a town, that the exact location of a street, road, or way, over which they have jurisdiction, cannot readily be ascertained, they shall make investigation thereof, and if it appears that the representation is correct, shall, after giving the notice required in laying out a similar road or way, proceed to ascertain the correct location, erect the necessary bounds, and file

[1] Gen. Stats. ch. 43, §§ 82–86.    [2] Morse v. Stocker, 1 Allen, 150.

a certificate thereof, for record, as provided in sections seventy-four and eighty-eight.

8. The county commissioners, mayor and aldermen, and selectmen, shall cause permanent stone bounds not less than three feet long, two feet of which at least shall be inserted in the earth, to be erected at the termini and angles of all roads laid out by them, when practicable ; and when not so, a heap of stones, a living tree, a permanent rock, or the corner of an edifice may be a substitute for such stones ; or said bounds may be permanent stone bounds not less than three feet long, with holes drilled therein, and filled with lead, placed a few inches below the travelled part of the street or way, as the officer whose duty it is to cause the same [to be] erected may determine. And if they neglect to establish such monuments after being notified so to do by an owner of land through which any such way is laid out (since the twenty-fifth of April, eighteen hundred and forty-eight) the county if it be a county road, and the city or town if it be a city or town road, shall pay to the owner of the land the sum of fifty dollars for each month that such neglect continues, to be recovered in an action of tort.[1]

9. A notice to the chairman of the county commissioners is not sufficient under the statute to charge the county with the penalty imposed by that statute for the neglect of the county commissioners to erect bounds at the termination and angles of a county road for one month after being notified so to do by the owner of the land.[2]

10. No highway or town way shall be laid out or constructed in, upon, or through, an enclosure used or appropriated for the burial of the dead, unless authority to that effect is specially granted by law, or the consent of the inhabitants of the town where such enclosure is situated is first obtained.

11. No highway or town way shall be laid out or constructed in, upon, or through, such part of an enclosure belonging to private proprietors, as may be used or appro-

---

[1] Gen. Stats. ch. 43, §§ 87, 88.       [2] Ilsley *et al. v.* Essex County, 7 Gray, 465.

priated to the burial of the dead, unless the consent of such proprietors is first obtained therefor.[1]

12. Towns and cities, by their proper officers, may lay out foot-ways for the use of the public in their respective towns and cities. All proceedings in reference to laying out and establishing such foot-ways, the acceptance thereof, and the assessment and award of damages sustained by any person in his property, shall be in conformity with the provisions of law applicable to the laying out and establishing of town ways.[2]

[1] Gen. Stats. ch. 43, §§ 89, 90.
[2] Stats. 1874, ch. 299. Public foot-ways may be created by dedication. Tyler v. Sturdy, 108 Mass. 196.

# CHAPTER XXIX.

## SEWERS AND DRAINS.

1. IN any city or town in which chapter one hundred and fifteen of the statutes of eighteen hundred and forty-one has been accepted according to the provisions of that act, and in any city in which this and the three following sections of this chapter (sections five, six, and seven below) have been accepted by the city council, and in any town in which the same have been accepted by the legal voters at a meeting called for that purpose, the mayor and aldermen of the city and the selectmen of the town may lay, make, maintain, and repair, all main drains or common sewers; and all the main drains or common sewers shall be the property of such city or town.[1]

This section has been repealed, except as to rights and obligations accrued before March 26, 1869.[2]

2. The mayor and aldermen of any city, and the selectmen of any town, may lay, make, and maintain all such main drains, or common sewers, as they shall adjudge to be necessary for the public convenience or the public health, through the lands of any persons or corporations, and may repair the same from time to time, whenever repair thereof shall be necessary; and all main drains and common sewers so laid, shall be the property of the city or town laying the same.

3. When any lands or real estate shall be taken by virtue of this act, the proceedings in the several cities shall be the same, in all respects, as in the laying out of highways or streets in such cities respectively; and the pro-

[1] Gen. Stats. ch. 48, § 3.      [2] Stats. 1869, ch. 111.

ceedings in the several towns shall be the same in all respects as in the laying out of town ways.

4. All persons or corporations suffering damage in their property, by reason of the laying, making, or maintaining of any main drains or common sewers, shall have the same rights and remedies for ascertaining and recovering the amount of such damage, in the several cities, as in the case of the laying out of highways or streets in such cities respectively, and in the several towns, as in the case of laying out of town ways.[1]

5. Every person who enters his particular drain into such main drain or common sewer, or who, by more remote means, receives benefit thereby for draining his cellar or land, shall pay to the city or town a proportional part of the charge of making and repairing the same (and of the charge, not already assessed, of making and repairing other main drains and common sewers, through which the same discharges),[2] to be ascertained, assessed, and certified by the mayor and aldermen or selectmen, and notice thereof shall be given to the party to be charged, or his tenant or lessee.

6. Assessments so made shall constitute a lien on the real estates assessed for one year after they are laid, and may, together with incidental costs and expenses, be levied by sale thereof, if the assessment is not paid within three months after a written demand for payment, made either upon the person assessed or upon any person occupying the estate; such sale to be conducted in like manner as sales for the non-payment of taxes.

7. A person aggrieved by such assessment may, at any time within three months from receiving notice thereof, apply for a jury. Such application shall be made in like manner, and the proceedings thereon shall be the same as in case of lands taken for laying out of highways : *provided* that, before making his application the party shall give one month's notice in writing to the selectmen or mayor and aldermen of his intention so to apply, and shall therein

---

[1] Stats. 1869, ch. 111, §§ 1–3.      [2] Stats. 1878, ch. 232.

particularly specify his objections to the assessment made by them ; to which specification he shall be confined upon the hearing by the jury.

8. Nothing herein contained shall prevent a city or town from providing, by ordinance or otherwise, that a part of the expense of constructing, maintaining, and repairing, main drains or common sewers, shall be paid by such city or town. And in the city of Boston, not less than one-quarter part of such expense shall be paid by the city, and shall not be charged upon those using the main drains or common sewers.

9. Whoever digs or breaks up the ground in a highway, street, or.lane, in any town, for the laying, altering, or repairing of a drain or common sewer, without the consent of the selectmen in writing, shall forfeit five dollars for each offence to the use of the town.

10. All drains and common sewers in a street or highway shall be substantially made or repaired with brick or stone, or with such other materials, and in such manner, as the selectmen of the town shall permit or direct.

11. When a person, by the consent and under the direction of the selectmen, at his own charge, makes and lays a common sewer or main drain for the benefit of himself and others who think fit to join therein, every person who afterwards enters his particular drain into the same, or by any more remote means receives benefit thereby for the draining of his cellar or land, shall pay to the owners of such common sewer or main drain, a proportional part of the charge of making and repairing the same, to be determined by the selectmen of the town, and certified under their hands ; saving always to the party aggrieved by any such determination the right to a trial by jury, as provided in section six (section seven above).

12. When a common sewer or main drain is stopped or gone to decay, so that it is necessary to open the same in order to repair it or to remove such stoppage, all persons benefited by such repair or removal of obstructions, as well those who do not as those who do cause such repairs to

be made or obstruction to be removed, shall pay to the person incurring the expense their proportional parts thereof, to be determined as provided in the preceding section.

13. Every person so required to pay his proportional part of the expense of making or repairing a drain or common sewer, shall have notice of the sum and of the person to whom the same is to be paid ; and if he does not, within seven days after such notice, pay the same to the person authorized by the selectmen to receive it, he shall be held to pay double the amount certified by the selectmen as aforesaid, with all expenses arising upon such neglect ; and the person so authorized by the selectmen may recover the same in an action of contract in his own name.

14. Whoever has occasion to open a common sewer or main drain in order to clear and repair the same, shall, seven days at least before he begins to open the same, give notice to all parties interested, by advertising in such manner as the selectmen may direct, that such parties may, if they think proper, object thereto and state their objections in person or in writing to the selectmen ; and if the selectmen judge the objections reasonable, the parties making the same shall not be held to pay any part of such expenses ; but if they do not make their objections to the selectmen within three days after such notice, or if the objections are not adjudged reasonable, the selectmen shall, in writing under their hands, give liberty to the persons applying to open such common sewer or main drain, and to clear and repair the same ; and all persons interested therein shall pay their proportions to be determined as provided in section ten.

15. Nothing contained in this chapter shall affect any covenants or agreements among the proprietors of such drains or common sewers.[1]

The previous ten sections apply (so far as the same are applicable) to the laying out of sewers and drains under the act of 1869, ch. 111; which is contained in sections two, three, and four of this chapter.[2]

[1] Gen. Stats. ch. 43, §§ 4–14.     [2] Stats. 1869, ch. 111, § 4.

16. The mayor and aldermen of any city, except the city of Boston, or the inhabitants of any town, in which main drains or common sewers are hereafter laid and constructed under the provisions of chapter one hundred and eleven of the acts of the year eighteen hundred and sixty-nine, may by vote determine, that, instead of paying an assessment under section four of chapter forty-eight of the General Statutes, every person who enters his particular drain into such main drains or common sewers, or uses the same in any way, shall pay for the permanent privilege to his estate such reasonable sum as the mayor and aldermen of said city, or the selectmen of said town shall determine.

17. Any person aggrieved by any determination of the mayor and aldermen, or the selectmen, made under the last provision of the foregoing section, may at any time within six months after the same is made known to him, apply to the county commissioners for a revision thereof. If, after due hearing, the county commissioners reduce the amount to be paid for said privilege, he shall have the benefit of such reduction, and the city or town shall pay the costs of the application and hearing ; otherwise said costs shall be paid by the applicant.

18. All sums due under section one of this act shall constitute a lien upon the real estate using such main drains or common sewers, and benefited thereby for the same length of time, and may be collected in the same manner as taxes upon real estate, or they may be sued for in an action of contract in the name of the city or town.[1]

19. Plans and descriptions of all main drains and common sewers belonging to any city or town, with a true record of the charges of making and repairing the same, and of all assessments therefor, shall be kept in the office of the clerk of such city or town.

20. The city council of any city and the legal voters of any town in a meeting called for that purpose, may adopt a system of sewerage to apply to any part or the whole of the territory of such city or town, and may provide that

[1] Stats. 1878, ch. 184, §§ 1–3.

the assessment authorized by said section four shall be made upon the owners of the estates embraced in such system, by a fixed uniform rate, based upon the estimated average cost of all the sewers therein, according to the number of feet of frontage their estates have on any street or way where a sewer is constructed, or according to the number of feet of area their said estates contain within a fixed depth from such street or way, or both, according to such frontage and area, which rate when adopted shall not be changed.[1]

21. At any time within sixty days after notice is given of a sewer or sidewalk assessment on any real estate, if the owner thereof shall in writing notify the board making the same that he desires to have the amount due on said assessment apportioned, said board shall apportion the same into three equal parts, and certify such apportionment to the assessors of the city or town where such real estate is situate; and said assessors shall add one of said equal parts with the interest due thereon, from the date of the apportionment, to the annual tax of real estate for each of the three years next ensuing. All liens for the collection of such assessments shall continue in force until the expiration of two years from the time the last instalment thereof is committed to the tax collector; and all sewer and sidewalk assessments upon real estate, which remain unpaid after the time stated in the order making the same for payment thereof, shall draw interest from such time until paid.

22. This act shall take effect upon its passage (May 15, 1878), but shall not be in force in any city or town unless adopted by the city council of such city or by the inhabitants of such town.[2]

---

[1] Stats. 1878, ch. 266.        [2] Stats. 1878, ch. 185.

# CHAPTER XXX.

## FENCES AND FENCE VIEWERS.

1. FENCES four feet high and in good repair, consisting of rails, timber, boards, or stone, and brooks, rivers, ponds, creeks, ditches, and hedges, or other things which the fence viewers within whose jurisdiction the same shall lie shall consider equivalent thereto, shall be deemed legal and sufficient fences.

2. The respective occupants of lands enclosed with fences shall, so long as both parties improve the same, keep up and maintain partition fences between their own and the next adjoining enclosures, in equal shares.[1]

3. In Newell v. Hill,[2] Chief Justice Shaw said: " In the first place, it is to be considered that the division fence — that is, the whole of the division fence — is made for their mutual and equal benefit; and therefore, upon the plainest principles of equity, the expense, as well of cost of building as of land to build upon, must be borne by them equally. For although the fence is built, one section by one party and another by the other, this is only an easy and convenient mode of dividing the expense of building. Though thus built in separate sections, each has an interest in the whole and in every section; and, when built, it belongs beneficially to both, as much as if it had been done by contract and the expense divided, or both joined in building the whole. If it is to be, in all respects, for their common benefit and at their common expense, it follows that it is at their equal expense of land as well as cost of building. As every species of fence must take some land, and cannot stand on a mathematical line, and as there is no reason why it should stand more on the land of one than the other, it follows as a necessary consequence that it is to stand equally on the land of both, or one-half on each. It is one of the cases where equality is equity."[2] But this rule as to division fence between adjoining proprietors does not apply as between the public and the owner of land abutting upon a highway, no such mutual duty or obligation existing; and therefore there can be no corresponding right or privilege.[3]

[1] Gen. Stats. ch. 25, §§ 1, 2.
[2] 2 Met. 182.
[3] Holbrook v. McBride, 4 Gray, 215.

4. A reasonable quantity of land can be taken for building such fence upon. And it is to be determined by a just regard to the proper accomplishment of the purpose which both parties have in view, and in which they have a common interest. And great regard should be had to the usage and practice of men of ordinary skill and judgment in the building of fences in their own lands on similar kinds of soil, and for like purposes.[1] And where a ditch is a proper fence, half of it may be cut on the lands of each adjoining owner.

5. If a party refuses or neglects to repair or rebuild a partition fence which he ought to maintain, the aggrieved party may complain to two or more fence viewers of the place, who, after due notice to each party, shall survey the same, and if they determine that the fence is insufficient, they shall signify the same in writing to the delinquent occupant, and direct him to repair or rebuild the same within such time as they judge reasonable, not exceeding fifteen days; and if the fence shall not be repaired or rebuilt accordingly, the complainant may make or repair the same.

6. When a deficient fence built up or repaired by a complainant as provided in the preceding section, is, after due notice to each party, adjudged sufficient by two or more of the fence viewers, and the value thereof, with their fees, ascertained by a certificate under their hands, the complainant may demand, either of the occupant or owner of the land where the fence was deficient, double the sum so ascertained; and in case of neglect or refusal to pay the same so due, for one month after demand, he may recover the same with interest at one per cent a month, in an action of contract.

No action lies to recover upon an award of fence viewers under this and the preceding section, unless they have previously adjudicated that the existing fence was insufficient and illegal, and that the fence which the plaintiff has rebuilt is sufficient.[2]

7. When a controversy arises about the rights of the respective occupants in partition fences and their obligation to maintain the same, either party may apply to two or more fence viewers of the places where the lands lie,

---

[1] Holbrook *v.* McBride, 4 Gray, 215.      [2] Sears *v.* Charlemont, 6 Allen, 437.

who, after due notice to each party, may in writing assign to each his share thereof, and direct the time within which each party shall erect or repair his share, in the manner before provided; which assignment, being recorded in the city or town clerk's office, shall be binding upon the parties and upon the succeeding occupants of the lands; who shall thereafter maintain their respective parts of said fence.[1]

8. A division by fence viewers would ordinarily embrace the whole continuous line of fence between two adjacent proprietors. But a division may be legal, although the assignment to the parties does not include the entire line of the land of the adjacent owner.[2] Under a complaint that *a fence is out of repair*, fence viewers have no authority to assign to each of the owners of adjoining land his respective share of the fence, and to direct the building thereof within a specified time.[3]

9. If a party refuses or neglects to erect and maintain the part of a fence assigned to him by the fence viewers, the same may, in the manner before provided, be erected and maintained by any aggrieved party; and he shall be entitled to double the value thereof ascertained and recovered in the manner aforesaid.

10. When in a controversy between adjoining occupants as to their respective rights in a partition fence, it appears to the fence viewers that either of the occupants had, before any complaint made to them, voluntarily erected the whole fence, or more than his just share of the same, or otherwise become proprietor thereof, the other occupant shall pay the value of so much thereof as may be assigned to him to repair or maintain, to be ascertained and recovered as provided in this chapter.

11. Partition fences shall be kept in good repair throughout the year, unless the occupants of the lands on both sides shall otherwise agree.

12. When lands of different persons which are required to be fenced, are bounded upon or divided from each other by a river, brook, pond, or creek, if the occupant of the

[1] Gen. Stats. ch. 25, §§ 3–5.
[2] Alger v. Pool, 11 Cush. 450.
[3] Sears v. Charlemont, 6 Allen, 437.

land on one side refuses or neglects to join with the occupant of the land on the other side in making a partition fence on the one side or the other, or shall disagree respecting the same, then two or more fence viewers of the place or places wherein such lands lie, on application made to them, shall forthwith view such river, brook, pond, or creek; and if they determine the same not to answer the purpose of a sufficient fence, and that it is impracticable to fence on the true boundary line without unreasonable expense, they shall, after giving notice to the parties to be present, determine how, or on which side thereof, the fence shall be set up and maintained, or whether partly on the one side and partly on the other side, as to them shall appear just, and shall reduce their determination to writing; and if either of the parties refuses or neglects to make and maintain his part of the fence according to the determination of the fence viewers, the same may be made and maintained as before provided, and the delinquent party shall be subject to the same costs and charges to be recovered in like manner.

13. When lands belonging to two persons in severalty have been occupied in common without a partition fence between them, and one of the occupants desires to occupy his part in severalty, and the other occupant refuses or neglects on demand to divide the line where the fence ought to be built, or to build a sufficient fence on his part of the line when divided, the party desiring it may have the same divided and assigned by two or more fence viewers of the same place in the manner provided in this chapter; and the fence viewers may in writing assign a reasonable time, having regard to the season of the year, for making the fence; and if the occupant complained of does not make his part of the fence within the time so assigned, the other party may, after having made up his part of the fence, make up the part of the other, and recover therefor double the expense thereof, together with the fees of the fence viewers, in the manner provided in this chapter.[1]

[1] Gen. Stats. ch. 25, §§ 6–10.

14. Fence viewers, when called to act under the provisions of section ten, chapter twenty-five, of the General Statutes (the foregoing section 13), shall have power to determine whether a partition fence is required between the lands of the respective occupants, and may, when the division line between their lands is in dispute or unknown, designate a line on which the fence shall be built, and may employ a surveyor therefor, if necessary; and such line shall, for the purpose of maintaining a fence, be deemed the division line between such lands until it shall be determined by judicial proceedings, or otherwise, that the true line is in another place, and, until so determined, all provisions of law relating to the erection, maintenance, and protection of fences shall be applicable to the fence erected or to be erected on such line.

15. If, after a fence has been made upon a line thus designated, it shall be determined by judicial proceedings, or otherwise, that the true division line is in another place, each occupant shall remove his part of the fence to, and rebuild the same on such line; and in case of neglect or refusal by either party to remove and rebuild his share thereof, the other may apply to two or more fence viewers, who, upon such application, shall view the premises, and assign a time within which the fence shall be removed and rebuilt, and give the delinquent party notice thereof; and if such party does not remove and rebuild the fence within the time so assigned, the other party may remove and rebuild the same, and recover double the expense therefor, together with the fees of the fence viewers, to be ascertained and recovered in the manner provided in section four, chapter twenty-five, of the General Statutes.[1]

The line designated by the fence viewers for a fence under the provisions of this and the preceding section, has no effect upon the title or right of possession of the land. It is a line established only for the purpose of maintaining a fence.[2]

16. Where a division of fence between the owners of improved lands has been made either by fence viewers or

---

[1] Stats. 1863, ch. 190, §§ 1, 2.      [2] Currier *v.* Esty, 116 Mass. 577.

under an agreement in writing between the parties, recorded in the office of the clerk of the city or town, the several owners of such lands, and their heirs and assigns, shall erect and support said fences agreeably to such division; but if a person lays his lands common, and determines not to improve any part of the same adjoining the fence divided as aforesaid, and gives six months' notice of his determination to all the adjoining occupants of lands, he shall not be required to keep up or support said fence during the time that his lands lie common and unimproved.

17. When one party ceases to improve his land, or lays open his enclosure, he shall not take away any part of the partition fence belonging to him and adjoining to the next enclosure; *provided*, the owner or occupant thereof will allow and pay therefor so much as two or more fence viewers in writing determine to be the reasonable value thereof.

18. When land which has lain unenclosed is afterwards enclosed or used for depasturing, the occupant or owner thereof shall pay for one-half of each partition fence standing upon the line between the same land and the land of the enclosures of any other occupant or owner, the value thereof to be ascertained in writing (in case they do not agree between themselves), by two or more of the fence viewers of the same place wherein such partition fence stands; and if such occupant or owner, after the value has been so ascertained, neglects or refuses, for thirty days after demand made, to pay for one-half of the partition fence, the proprietor of the fence may maintain an action of contract for such value, and the costs of ascertaining the same; but the occupant or owner of unenclosed land on the island of Nantucket, used for depasturing only, shall not be subject to the foregoing provisions of this section.

19. Where the line upon which a partition fence is to be made or divided is the boundary line of one or more cities or towns, or partly in one and partly in another, a fence viewer shall be taken from each place.

20. When a water fence, or fence running into the water, is necessary to be made, the same shall be done in equal shares unless otherwise agreed by the parties ; and in case either party refuses or neglects to make or maintain the share to him belonging, similar proceedings shall be had as in other cases of the like kind respecting other fences before mentioned.

21. Any fence viewer, duly chosen and sworn, who when requested unreasonably neglects to view a fence, or to perform any other duties required of him in this chapter, shall forfeit five dollars, to be recovered by action of tort to the use of the place, or on complaint to the use of the commonwealth, and he shall also be liable for all damages to the party injured.[1]

22. The fees prescribed by law for fence viewers (which are at the rate of two dollars per day for the time he is so employed),[2] shall be paid by all or by such of the parties in dispute, and in such proportions, as shall be determined by a certificate in writing, under the hands of the fence viewers, acting in each case. And if any person or persons, so required to pay the whole or any portion of said fees, shall neglect to pay the fence viewers within thirty days after the certificate has been delivered, the fence viewers may recover double the amount of the fees due from such delinquent party.

23. Fence viewers shall hereafter be chosen by ballot.[8]

[1] Gen. Stats. ch. 25, §§ 11-16.  [8] Stats. 1862, ch. 93, §§ 1, 3.
[2] Gen. Stats. ch. 25, § 17.

# CHAPTER XXXI.

## POUNDS AND IMPOUNDING CATTLE. FIELD DRIVERS.

1. EACH city and town shall, at its own expense and in such places therein as the city council of the city or the inhabitants of the town direct, maintain one or more sufficient pounds. A city or town that for three months neglects to provide or maintain a sufficient pound shall forfeit fifty dollars.

2. Whoever wilfully injures a city or town pound shall be punished by fine not exceeding fifty dollars, or by imprisonment in the common jail not exceeding ninety days.

3. Each city and town shall annually appoint a suitable keeper of each pound therein.[1]

4. Every field driver, within his city or town, shall take up, at any time, swine, sheep, horses, asses, mules, goats, or neat cattle, going at large in the public highways or town ways or on common and unimproved lands, and not under the care of a keeper; and for any such cattle or beasts so going at large on the Lord's day, the field driver or any other inhabitant of the city or town may, in an action of tort, recover for each beast the same fees which the field driver is entitled to receive for like beasts when distrained and impounded.[2]

5. The duty of the field driver, under the last section, is confined to the taking up of cattle going at large, and impounding them. And he is not required to state the cause of such acts, has no claim for any damage, and can demand only his fees, which are provided by statute. No notice is required by the statute to be given at the time of impounding by the field driver, as it seems to be taken for granted that the pound keeper will be bound to take notice of the public office, power, and duty of the field driver in the performance of his duties under the statute.[3]

[1] Gen. Stats. ch. 25, §§ 18, 20.
[2] Gen. Stats. ch. 25, § 21.
[3] Wild v. Skinner, 23 Pick. 251; Pickard v. Howe, 12 Met. 198.

6. A turnpike road is a highway within the meaning of the statute restraining cattle from going at large.[1]

7. And the owner of land adjoining a highway, and who owns to the centre thereof, has a right to depasture his land in the highway; but he cannot, in virtue of this right, be exempted from the duty of preventing his cattle from going at large thereon without the care of a keeper, but is bound by the same law which is applicable to others;[2] viz., that cattle must be "actually under the efficient care of a keeper" while upon the highways, or they will be "going at large," and may be impounded by a field driver.[3]

8. When beasts are so taken up and distrained by a field driver, they shall be forthwith impounded in the city or town pound, and the keeper shall furnish them with suitable food and water while they are detained in his custody.[4]

9. When beasts are taken up and distrained by a field driver, in pursuance of the provisions of chapter twenty-five of the General Statutes, he may impound them in any suitable place on his own premises; and for the purposes of said chapter he shall be considered a pound keeper, and such place on his own premises shall be considered a town pound, in relation to beasts therein impounded.

This shall apply only to such towns as shall adopt the same by a vote of the majority of the legal voters present and voting at a town meeting duly held for the purpose.[5]

10. To "forthwith impound," is to impound without unnecessary delay. The act of impounding by the field driver does not require that he should open or close a gate. The pound is under the care and in the custody of a keeper elected for the purpose.[6]

11. A pound keeper may lawfully impound beasts which have been distrained damage feasant in a yard furnished and used by the town as a town pound, if the town have furnished and used no other place as a pound, although the inhabitants of the town have passed no vote concerning the same, and taken no action at any town meeting for the purpose of establishing it as a pound.[7]

12. The field driver shall be entitled to fifty cents per head for horses, asses, mules, and neat cattle, and ten cents

---

[1] Pickard v. Howe, 12 Met. 198.
[2] Parker v. Jones, 1 Allen, 270.
[3] Bruce v. White, 4 Gray, 345.
[4] Gen. Stats. ch. 25, § 22.

[5] Stats. 1869, ch. 366, §§ 1, 2.
[6] Byron v. Crippen, 4 Gray, 312.
[7] Anthony v. Anthony, 6 Allen, 408.

per head for sheep, goats, and swine, so taken up by him, and the pound keeper shall be entitled to four cents per head for the animals so impounded; but if more than ten sheep are taken up at the same time, the fees for all above that number shall be only one-half of the above fees.[1]

13. The foregoing section is so far amended, as to make the fees of the field drivers fifty cents per head for driving swine to the pound.[2]

14. The pound keeper shall not deliver to the owner any beasts so impounded, until the owner pays him his fees, the expense of keeping the beasts, and the fees of the field driver, which latter, when received, he shall pay to the field driver.

15. When a person is injured in his land by sheep, swine, horses, asses, mules, goats, or neat cattle, he may recover his damages in an action of tort against the owner of the beasts, or by distraining the beasts doing the damage, and proceeding therewith as hereinafter directed; but if the beasts were lawfully on the adjoining lands, and escape therefrom in consequence of the neglect of the person who suffered the damage to maintain his part of the division fence, the owner of the beasts shall not be liable for such damage.[3]

16. The restriction, in the foregoing section, upon the right to maintain an action clearly applies, and applies only, to cases where there has been a division of fence. It is when the party neglects to maintain "his part of the division fence;" but it cannot with propriety be said that any particular part of the fence is to be kept in repair by one rather than the other until a division has taken place.

17. In the same case,[4] Dewey, J. further said: "Upon general principles, it is no more the duty of the individual who has a field adjacent to that his neighbor proposes to depasture with his cattle, to take the incipient steps to cause a partition of the fence between their adjacent lands, than of him who owns the cattle, and intends to use his lands for depasturing them. Both parties are entitled to the privileges given by statute, authorizing proceedings for dividing their fences, and assigning to each his proper portion thereof; and if either wishes to avail himself of its provisions for his protection, he must move in the matter if his neighbor does not. By taking the proper

---

[1] Gen. Stats. ch. 25, § 23.
[2] Stats. 1863, ch. 178.
[3] Gen. Stats. ch. 25, §§ 24, 25.
[4] Thayer v. Arnold, 4 Met. 589.

steps, and causing a partition to be made of the fences, and duly maintaining and keeping in repair the part assigned to him, he can easily avoid all liability to an action, if his cattle escape into the adjacent lot through defect of the fence assigned to the owner of such lot. If he neglects to procure a division of the fence, it is not for him to complain that the owner of the adjacent lot has been alike inactive in the matter; but the result must be, that both parties must be presumed to elect to occupy and improve their lands under the rules of the common law, and subject to the common-law responsibilities; which is, that at common law no man is bound to fence against an adjoining close, unless by force of prescription; but that every man must, at his peril, keep his cattle on his own close, and prevent their escape therefrom. We take the rule therefore to be, that the obligation to make and maintain a partition fence is equally operative upon both adjacent owners; each party is equally bound to move in the matter; and, until such division, there can be no deficiency or neglect alleged as to the fence of either party, separately and individually. If either, therefore, puts cattle on his own land, and they enter upon the land of the adjacent proprietors, there being no partition of the fence separating the lots, he will be liable to an action of trespass therefor."

18. If beasts doing damage are distrained, and driven to the distrainer's yard till the pound keeper can be called, and then delivered to the latter in the highway, it is the duty of the distrainer to state his demand, and to give notices, as required in Gen. Stats. ch. 25, §§ 27, 29, 30 (sections 20, 22, and 24 below); and, if he omits to do so, he will be liable as a trespasser *ab initio*.[1]

19. The beasts so distrained for doing damage shall be impounded in the city or town pound, or in some suitable place, under the immediate care and inspection of the person who distrained them, and he shall furnish them with suitable food and water while they remain impounded. (See section nine above.)

20. If the beasts are impounded in the city or town pound, the distrainer shall leave with the pound keeper a memorandum in writing under his hand stating the cause of impounding, and the sum that he demands from the owner for the damage done by the beasts, and also for the daily charges of feeding them; and if they are impounded in any other place, he shall give a like memorandum to the owner of the beasts if demanded by him.[2]

[1] Merrick *v.* Work, 10 Allen, 544;   [2] Gen. Stats. ch. 25, §§ 26, 27.
Sherman *v.* Braman, 13 Met. 407.

21. The owner of the land where the damage is committed is not required to employ a field driver to take up and impound the cattle, but he may do it himself.[1]

22. The pound keeper, when the beasts are in his custody, shall not deliver them to the owner until the owner pays him his fees, the sum so demanded by the distrainer for the damages and charges aforesaid, the expense of advertising the beasts if they are advertised, and all other legal costs and expenses.[2]

23. A pound keeper, who receives and impounds beasts for going at large, and refuses to deliver them to the owner on demand, is justified in his refusal until his fees and those of the field drivers are paid. And is not liable therefor in an action of replevin.[3]

24. When beasts are impounded, the person impounding them shall within twenty-four hours thereafter give notice thereof in writing to the owner or person having the care of them, if known and living within six miles from the place of impounding, which notice shall be delivered to the party or left at his place of abode, and shall contain a description of the beasts and a statement of the time, place, and cause of impounding.[4]

25. Such notice *must* be given within twenty-four hours after the beasts are taken up and impounded; and the notice is valid, although the hour of the day on which they were thus taken up does not appear on the face of it. It is sufficient if it is left at the dwelling-house of the party; and a personal service of it upon the owner of the beasts is not required.[5]

26. An oral notice is not sufficient; and the owners of the beasts impounded have a right to insist on the precise notice required by law. Upon it their rights and remedies might materially depend; and unless by their actions the persons impounding the beasts are induced to omit it, the failure to give such notice is a fatal defect in their proceedings, and deprives them of their justification.

Neither is the notice rendered unnecessary where the owners of the beasts impounded have actual knowledge of it.[6]

27. But a written notice, posted up and published in a newspaper by a field driver who has impounded beasts going at large in a public

---

[1] Wild *v.* Skinner, 23 Pick. 253.

[2] Gen. Stats. ch. 25, § 28.

[3] Folger *v.* Hinckley, 5 Cush. 263.

[4] Gen. Stats. ch. 25, § 29.

[5] Pickard *v.* Howe, 12 Met. 198.

[6] Coffin *v.* Field, 7 Cush. 355; Sanderson *v.* Lawrence, 2 Gray, 178.

highway, which states that the beasts were "going at large, and without a keeper," sets forth a sufficient cause of impounding under the statute.

28. In the same case,[1] Merrick, J. said: "There are but two causes for which animals can lawfully be taken up by a field driver and impounded in the town pound. He may take them up, in the first place, when they are at large without a keeper in highways or town ways, or on common and unimproved land; or, in the second place, as the agent of a private proprietor other than the owner, when they are unlawfully upon his enclosed or improved land, doing or having done damage there. In either of these cases the animals may be impounded, and then the notices required by law are to be given, containing a description of the animals, and a statement of the time, place, and cause of impounding. It is not essential to the validity of the notices to be given that they should be framed in the very words of the statute; but any form of expression which evinces in a clear and intelligible manner the cause for which the animals were taken up and impounded is sufficient."

29. If there is no person entitled to notice according to the provisions of the preceding section, the person impounding the beasts shall within forty-eight hours thereafter cause to be posted in some public place in the city or town, and in a public place in each of any two adjoining cities or towns, if within four miles from the place where they were taken, a written notice containing a description of the beasts, and a statement of the time, place, and cause of impounding them; and in such case, if the value of the beasts exceeds thirty dollars, and if no person appears to claim them within seven days after the day of impounding, a like notice shall be published three weeks successively in some public newspaper if there is any published within twenty miles from the place of impounding, the first publication to be within fifteen days after the day of impounding.

30. If the owner or keeper of the beasts is dissatisfied with the claim of the person impounding them, he may have the amount for which he is liable ascertained and determined by two disinterested and discreet persons, to be appointed and sworn for that purpose by a justice of the peace or by the city or town clerk; and the sum so deter-

[1] Cleverly v. Fowle, 3 Allen, 39.

mined by them shall be received instead of the sum demanded by the person who impounded the beasts, and they shall thereupon be delivered to the owner or keeper thereof.

31. If the sum for which the beasts are impounded and detained is not paid within fourteen days after notice of the impounding has been given as before directed, or after the last publication of such notice in a newspaper, the person who impounded them shall apply to a justice of the peace, or to the city or town clerk, and obtain a warrant to two disinterested and discreet persons, to be appointed and sworn by the justice or clerk, and the persons so appointed shall ascertain and determine the sum due from the owner or keeper of the beasts for the damages, costs, and expenses for which they are impounded and detained, including a reasonable compensation for their own services.

32. If the sum so found to be due is not forthwith paid, the person who impounded the beasts shall cause them to be sold by auction, in the city or town where they are impounded, first advertising the sale by posting up a notice thereof twenty-four hours beforehand at some public place in the same city or town.

33. The proceeds of such sale, after paying all said damages, costs, expenses, and charges for advertising and selling the beasts, shall be deposited in the treasury of the city or town, for the use of the owner of the beasts, in case he substantiates his claim thereto within two years from the sale.

34. If beasts lawfully distrained or impounded escape or are rescued, the pound keeper, field driver, or other person who distrained them, may at any time within seven days thereafter retake the beasts and hold and dispose thereof as if no such escape or rescue had taken place.

35. Whoever rescues beasts lawfully distrained or impounded for any cause whatever, shall be liable in an action of tort brought by any person injured to pay all damages which such person sustains thereby, and the fees and charges incurred before the rescue ; and he shall also

forfeit a sum not less than five nor more than twenty dollars, to be recovered by complaint.

36. The defendant in an action brought for rescuing beasts distrained or impounded shall not be allowed to allege or give in evidence the insufficiency of the fences, or any other fact or circumstance to show that the distress or impounding was illegal; but if there is such ground of objection to the proceeding of which he is entitled to avail himself, he may have the advantage thereof in an action of replevin.

37. If the owner of a ram or he-goat suffers it to go at large out of his enclosure between the first day of July and the twenty-fifth day of December, he shall forfeit five dollars for each offence, if prosecuted within thirty days next after such ram or he-goat is found going at large, to be recovered on complaint in the county in which such owner lives.[1]

[1] Gen. Stats. ch. 25, §§ 30–38.

# CHAPTER XXXII.

## PUBLIC SCHOOLS.

1. In every town there shall be kept, for at least six months in each year, at the expense of said town, by a teacher or teachers of competent ability and good morals, a sufficient number of schools for the instruction of all the children who may legally attend public school therein, in orthography, reading, writing, English grammar, geography, arithmetic, the history of the United States, drawing, and good behavior. Agriculture, algebra, vocal music, drawing, physiology, and hygiene shall be taught by lectures or otherwise, in all the public schools in which the school committee deem it expedient.[1]

Any town may, and every town having more than ten thousand inhabitants shall, annually make provision for giving free instruction in industrial or mechanical drawing to persons over fifteen years of age, either in day or evening schools, under the direction of the school committee.[2]

2. Every town may, and every town containing five hundred families or householders shall, besides the schools prescribed in the preceding section, maintain a school to be kept by a master of competent ability and good morals, who, in addition to the branches of learning before mentioned, shall give instruction in general history, bookkeeping, surveying, geometry, natural philosophy, chemistry, botany, the civil polity of this commonwealth and of the United States, and the Latin language. Such last mentioned school shall be kept for the benefit of all the inhabitants of the town, ten months at least, exclusive of vacations, in each year, and at such convenient place, or

[1] Gen. Stats. ch. 38, § 1; Stats. 1862, ch. 7; Stats. 1870, ch. 248.     [2] Stats. 1870, ch. 248.

alternately at such places, in the town, as the legal voters at their annual meeting determine. And in every town containing four thousand inhabitants, the teacher or teachers of the schools required by this section shall, in addition to the branches of instruction before required, be competent to give instruction in the Greek and French languages, astronomy, geology, rhetoric, logic, intellectual and moral science, and political economy.[1]

In order to ascertain that any town is subject to the requirement of the foregoing section, "the number of families or householders thereof shall be determined by the latest public census which shall have been taken, by the authority either of this commonwealth or of the United States."[2]

3. Two adjacent towns, having each less than five hundred families or householders, may form one high school district, for establishing such a school as is contemplated in the preceding section, when a majority of the legal voters of each town, in meetings called for that purpose, so determine.

4. The school committees of the two towns so united shall elect one person from each of their respective boards, and the two so elected shall form the committee for the management and control of such school, with all the powers conferred upon school committees and prudential committees.

5. The committee thus formed shall determine the location of the school-house authorized to be built by the towns forming the district, or if the towns do not determine to erect a house, shall authorize the location of such school alternately in the two towns.

6. In the erection of a school-house for the permanent location of such school, in the support and maintenance of the school, and in all incidental expenses attending the same, the proportions to be paid by each town, unless otherwise agreed upon, shall be according to its proportion of the county tax.[3]

[1] Gen. Stats. ch. 38, § 2.
[2] Stats. 1868, ch. 226.
[3] Gen. Stats. ch. 38, §§ 3–5.

Two or more towns may unite in establishing union schools for the accommodation of such contiguous portions of each as shall be mutually agreed upon, when a majority of the legal voters in each town, in meetings called for that purpose, so determine. In providing for the management and control of said school; in determining the location of said school-houses, or of the schools; in apportioning the expenses of erecting such school-houses, and of the maintenance of said school, with all expenditures incident to the same, — all proceedings shall be governed by the provisions of the three preceding sections.[1]

7. Any town may establish and maintain, in addition to the schools required by law to be maintained therein, schools for the education of persons over twelve [2] years of age; may determine the term or terms of time in each year, and the hours of the day or evening, during which said school shall be kept; and appropriate such sums of money as may be necessary for the support thereof.

8. When a school is so established, the school committee shall have the same superintendence over it as they have over other schools; and shall determine what branches of learning may be taught therein.

9. In every public school having an average of fifty scholars, the school district or town to which such school belongs shall employ one or more female assistants, unless such district or town, at a meeting called for the purpose, votes to dispense with such assistant.

10. It shall be the duty of the president, professors, and tutors of the university at Cambridge and of the several colleges, of all preceptors and teachers of academies, and of all other instructors of youth, to exert their best endeavors to impress on the minds of children and youth committed to their care and instruction, the principles of piety and justice, and a sacred regard to truth; love of their country, humanity, and universal benevolence; sobriety, industry, and frugality; chastity, moderation, and temperance; and those other virtues which are the ornament of human society and the basis upon which a republican constitution is founded; and it shall be the duty of such instructors to endeavor to lead their pupils, as

[1] Stats. 1868, ch. 278.      [2] Stats. 1869, ch. 305.

their ages and capacities will admit, into a clear understanding of the tendency of the above-mentioned virtues to preserve and perfect a republican constitution and secure the blessings of liberty, as well as to promote their future happiness, and also to point out to them the evil tendency of the opposite vices.

11. It shall be the duty of the resident ministers of the gospel, the selectmen, and the school committees, to exert their influence and use their best endeavors that the youth of their towns shall regularly attend the schools established for their instruction.

12. The several towns shall, at their annual meetings, or at a regular meeting called for the purpose, raise such sums of money for the support of schools as they judge necessary; which sums shall be assessed and collected in like manner as other town taxes.[1]

13. Any town in this commonwealth may raise, by taxation or otherwise, and appropriate money to be expended by the school committee, in their discretion, in providing for the conveyance of pupils to and from the public schools.[2]

14. Nothing contained in this chapter shall affect the right of any corporation established in a town to manage any estate or funds given or obtained for the purpose of supporting schools therein, or in any wise affect such estate or funds.

15. A town which refuses or neglects to raise money for the support of schools, as required by this chapter, shall forfeit a sum equal to twice the highest sum ever before voted for the support of schools therein. A town which refuses or neglects to choose a school committee to superintend said schools, or to choose prudential committees in the several districts, when it is the duty of the town to choose such prudential committee, shall forfeit a sum not less than five hundred nor more than one thousand dollars, to be paid into the treasury of the county.

16. Three-fourths of any forfeiture paid into the treas-

[1] Gen. Stats. ch. 38, §§ 6-12.    [2] Stats. 1869, ch. 132.

ury of the county, under the preceding section, shall be paid by the treasurer to the school committee, if any, otherwise to the selectmen of the town from which it is recovered, who shall apportion and appropriate the same to the support of the schools of such town, in the same manner as if it had been regularly raised by the town for that purpose.

17. Every town shall, at the annual meeting, choose, by written ballots, a board of school committee, which shall have the general charge and superintendence of all the public schools in town. Said board shall consist of any number of persons divisible by three, which said town has decided to elect, one-third thereof to be elected annually, and continue in office three years. If a town fails or neglects to choose such committee, an election at a subsequent meeting shall be valid.[1] No person shall be deemed to be ineligible to serve upon a school committee by reason of sex.[2]

The charge and superintendence which they are to take of the schools is general; they can delegate subordinate matters.[3] But the power of fixing times of vacation and granting holidays for schools resides only in the committee.[4]

18. If any person elected a member of the school committee, after being duly notified of his election in the manner in which town officers are required to be notified, refuses or neglects to accept said office, or if any member of the board declines further service, or, from change of residence or otherwise, becomes unable to attend to the duties of the board, the remaining members shall, in writing, give notice of the fact to the selectmen of the town, or to the mayor and aldermen of the city, and the two boards shall thereupon, after giving public notice of at least one week, proceed to fill such vacancy; and a majority of the ballots of persons entitled to vote shall be necessary to an election.

19. If all the persons elected as members of the school

---

[1] Gen. Stats. ch. 38, §§ 13–16.
[2] Stats. 1874, ch. 389.
[3] Huse v. Lowell, 10 Allen, 149.
[4] Ninth School District in Weymouth v. Loud, 12 Gray, 61.

committee, after such notice of their election, refuse or neglect to accept the office, or, having accepted, afterwards decline further service, or become unable to attend to the duties of the board, the selectmen or the mayor and aldermen shall, after giving like public notice, proceed by ballot to elect a new board, and the votes of a majority of the entire board of selectmen, or of the mayor and aldermen, shall be necessary to an election.

20. The term of service of every member elected in pursuance of the provisions of the two preceding sections, shall end with the municipal or official year in which he is chosen, and if the vacancy which he was elected to fill was for a longer period, it shall, at the first annual election after the occurrence of the vacancy, be filled in the manner prescribed for original elections of the school committee.

21. All the members of the school committee shall continue in office for the purpose of superintending the winter terms of the several schools, and of making and transmitting the certificate, returns, and report of the committee, notwithstanding the election of any successor at the annual meeting; but for all other duties, the term of office shall commence immediately after election.[1]

22. Any town may, at the annual meeting, vote to increase or diminish the number of its school committee. Such increase shall be made by adding one or more to each class to hold office according to the tenure of the class to which they are severally chosen. Such diminution shall be made by choosing, annually, such number as will in three years effect it, and a vote to diminish shall remain in force until the diminution under it is accomplished.

23. The school committee shall appoint a secretary and keep a permanent record book, in which all its votes, orders, and proceedings shall by him be recorded.

24. The school committee, unless the town at its annual meeting determines that the duty may be performed by the prudential committee, shall select and contract with the teachers of the public schools; shall require full and

[1] Gen. Stats. ch. 38, §§ 17-20.

satisfactory evidence of the good moral character of all instructors who may be employed ; and shall ascertain, by personal examination, their qualifications for teaching and capacity for the government of schools.[1]

25. The power conferred on school committees " to select and contract with the teachers for the town and district schools," includes the power to fix the compensation to be paid them, and to bind the town to pay the same.[2]  And the town authorities have no power to interfere with such duties of the committee ; they can only vote to limit the school to the time prescribed by statute, and resolve, if they choose, not to continue it beyond such time.[3]

26. The authority and duty of the school committee of a town are not confined to ascertaining by examination the literary qualifications of teachers selected by the prudential committee, and their capacity for the government of schools; but they are the sole judges of their qualification in all respects to teach and govern the school for which they are selected.[4]

27. Every instructor of a town or district school shall, before he opens such school, obtain from the school committee a certificate in duplicate of his qualifications, one of which shall be deposited with the selectmen before any payment is made to such instructor on account of his services ; and upon so filing such certificate, the teacher of any public school shall be entitled to receive, on demand, his wages due at the expiration of any quarter, or term longer or shorter than a quarter, or upon the close of any single term of service, subject to the condition specified in section thirteen of chapter forty.

28. The school committee may dismiss from employment any teacher whenever they think proper, and such teacher shall receive no compensation for services rendered after such dismissal.[5]

And a teacher so dismissed can recover only that portion of the salary due at the time of such dismissal, even if under an annual salary payable at stated periods of time.[6]

[1] Gen. Stats. ch. 38, §§ 21–23.

[2] Batchelder *v.* Salem, 4 Cush. 599.

[3] Charlestown *v.* Gardner, 98 Mass. 587 ; Batchelder *v.* Salem, *supra.*

[4] School Dist. No. 10 in Uxbridge *v.* Mowry *et al.*, 9 Allen, 94.

[5] Gen. Stats. ch. 38, §§ 24, 25.

[6] Knowles *v.* Boston, 12 Gray, 339.

29. The school committee, in each city or town where there is no superintendent of schools, or some one or more of them, for the purpose of organizing and making a careful examination of the schools, and of ascertaining that the scholars are properly supplied with books, shall visit all the public schools in the town on some day during the first week after the opening of such schools, and also on some day during the two weeks preceding the close of the same ; and shall also for the same purposes visit, without giving previous notice thereof to the instructors, all the public schools in town once in each month, and they shall, at such examinations, inquire into the regulation and discipline of the schools, and the habits and proficiency of the scholars therein.[1]

30. The school committee shall require the daily reading of some portion of the Bible, without written note or oral comment, in the public schools, but they shall require no scholar to read from any particular version, whose parent or guardian shall declare that he has conscientious scruples against allowing him to read therefrom, nor shall they ever direct any school books calculated to favor the tenets of any particular sect of Christians to be purchased or used in any of the public schools.[2]

31. The school committee shall direct what books shall be used in the public schools, and shall prescribe, as far as is practicable, a course of studies and exercises to be pursued in said schools.

In any town or city in this commonwealth, a change may be made in the school books used in the public schools by a vote of two-thirds of the whole school committee thereof, at a meeting of said committee, notice of such intended change having been given at a previous meeting of said committee.

32. If any change is made, as provided for in the preceding section, each pupil then belonging to the public schools and requiring the substituted book shall be furnished with the same by the school committee, at the expense of said town or city,[3] on giving up a copy of the superseded book in condition fit to be used.[4]

---

[1] Gen. Stats. ch. 38, § 26, and Stats. 1876, ch. 186.
[2] Stats. 1862, ch. 57.
[3] Stats. 1876, ch. 47.
[4] Stats. 1877, ch. 24.

33. The school committee shall procure, at the expense of the city or town, a sufficient supply of text-books for the public schools, and give notice of the place where they may be obtained. Said books shall be furnished to the pupils at such prices as merely to reimburse the expense of the same. The school committee may also procure, at the expense of the city or town, such apparatus, books of reference, and other means of illustration as they deem necessary for the schools under their supervision, in accordance with appropriations therefor previously made.

Any town, by legal vote, may authorize the school committee to purchase text-books and stationery [1] for use in the public schools, said text-books to be the property of the city or town, and to be loaned to pupils under such regulations as the school committee may provide. [2]

34. If any scholar is not furnished by his parent, master, or guardian with the requisite books, he shall be supplied therewith by the school committee, at the expense of the town.

35. The school committee shall give notice in writing to the assessors of the town of the names of the scholars supplied with books under the provisions of the preceding section, of the books so furnished, the prices thereof, and the names of the parents, masters, or guardians who ought to have supplied the same. The assessors shall add the price of the books to the next annual tax of such parents, masters, or guardians ; and the amount so added shall be levied, collected, and paid into the town treasury, in the same manner as the town taxes.

36. If the assessors are of opinion that any parent, master, or guardian is unable to pay the whole expense of the books so supplied on his account, they shall omit to add the price of such books, or shall add only a part thereof, to his annual tax, according to their opinion of his ability to pay.

37. In any town containing five hundred families, in which a school is kept for the benefit of all the inhabi-

[1] Stats. 1878, ch. 23.          [2] Stats. 1873, ch. 106.

tants, as before provided, the school committee shall perform the like duties in relation to such school, the house where it is kept, and the supply of all things necessary therefor, as the prudential committee may perform in a school district.

38. The members of the school committee shall be paid in cities one dollar, and in towns two [1] dollars and a half, each, a day, for the time they are actually employed in discharging the duties of their office, together with such additional compensation as the town or city may allow.

39. Any town annually, by legal vote, and any city by an ordinance of the city council, may require the school committee annually to appoint a superintendent of public schools, who, under the direction and control of said committee, shall have the care and supervision of the schools, with such salary as the city government or town may determine ; and in every city in which such ordinance is in force, and in every town in which such superintendent is appointed, the school committee shall receive no compensation, unless otherwise provided by such city government or town. [2]

The compensation of said superintendent shall in no case be less than one dollar and fifty cents for each day of actual service. [3] And by statutes 1870, ch. 118, a school committee required to appoint a superintendent shall have authority to determine his salary.

Any two or more towns may, by a vote of each, form a district for the purpose of employing a superintendent of public schools therein, who shall perform in each town the duties prescribed by law.

Such superintendent shall be annually appointed by a joint committee composed of the chairman and secretary of the school committee of each of the towns in said district, who shall determine the relative amount of service to be performed by him in each town, fix his salary, and apportion the amount thereof to be paid by the several towns, and certify the same to the treasurer of each town. Said joint committee shall, for the purposes last named, be held to be the agents of each town composing the district aforesaid. [4]

40. Every town not divided into school districts shall provide and maintain a sufficient number of school-houses,

[1] Stats. 1873, ch. 157.　　　　　[3] Stats. 1860, ch. 101.
[2] Gen. Stats. ch. 38, §§ 29–35.　　[4] Stats. 1870, ch. 183.

properly furnished and conveniently located, for the accommodation of all the children therein entitled to attend the public schools ; and the school committee, unless the town otherwise direct, shall keep them in good order, procuring a suitable place for the schools, where there is no school-house, and providing fuel and all other things necessary for the comfort of the scholars therein, at the expense of the town.

A town which for one year refuses or neglects to comply with the requisitions of this section, shall forfeit a sum not less than five hundred nor more than one thousand dollars, under the same provisions as those made in sections fifteen and sixteen of this chapter.[1]

41. Any town, at a meeting legally called for the purpose, may determine the location of its school-houses, and adopt all necessary measures to purchase or procure the land for the accommodation thereof.[2]

42. When land has been designated by a city council, town, school district, or those acting under its authority, or determined upon by the mayor and aldermen of a city, or by the selectmen of a town, as a suitable place for the erection of a school-house and the necessary buildings, or for enlarging a school-house or school-house lot, the mayor and aldermen, or the selectmen, may proceed to select, at their discretion, and to lay out a school-house lot or an enlargement thereof, and to appraise the damages to the owner of such land in the manner provided for laying out town ways and appraising damages sustained thereby ; and upon such selection and laying out of such lot, or any enlargement thereof, being accepted and adopted by the city council or the town, the land shall be taken, held, and used for the purpose aforesaid. But no lot so taken or enlarged shall exceed in the whole eighty square rods, exclusive of the land occupied by the school buildings.[3]

43. Where the owner feels aggrieved by the laying out or enlargement of such lot, or by the award of damages, he may, upon application therefor in writing to the county

---

[1] Stats. 1871, ch. 145.

[2] Gen. Stats. ch. 38, §§ 36, 37.

[3] Stats. 1874, ch. 342.

commissioners, within one year thereafter, have the matter of his complaint tried by a jury, and the jury may change the location of such lot or enlargement, and assess damages therefor. The proceedings shall in all respects be conducted in the manner provided in cases of damages by laying out highways. If the damages are increased, or the location changed, by the jury, the damages and all charges shall be paid by the town ; otherwise, the charges arising on such application shall be paid by such applicant. The land so taken shall be held and used for no other purpose than that contemplated by this chapter, and shall revert to the owner, his heirs or assigns, upon the discontinuance there, for one year, of such school as is required by law to be kept by the town.

44. The school committee of a town in which the school-district system has been abolished, or does not exist, shall have the general charge and superintendence of the school-houses in said town, so far as relates to the use to which the same may be appropriated.

45. Except as may be otherwise provided in their respective charters, or acts in amendment thereof, the provisions of this chapter, so far as applicable, shall apply to cities. And the mayor and aldermen in the several cities are authorized to execute the powers given in section thirty-eight of this chapter to the selectmen and town.

46. Upon the abolition or discontinuance of any district, its corporate powers and liabilities shall continue and remain so far as may be necessary for the enforcement of its rights and duties ; and the property which it possessed at the time shall be subject to all legal process against it.[1]

The school-district system in Massachusetts as well as union districts and contiguous school districts in adjoining towns has been abolished. It is supposed the duties of town officers attending the abolition, such as taking possession of the property of the districts, appraising the same, &c., have been performed, and therefore it is thought to be unnecessary to insert them here. By the leading act abolishing the school-district system it was provided that the corporate powers and liabilities of any school district abolished by this act

[1] Gen. Stats. ch. 39, § 6.

shall continue and remain for the purposes expressed in the foregoing section.[1] But it has since been provided by law that towns in which the school-district system was abolished as above, may at a meeting called for the purpose, within two years from the passage of the act (April 22, 1870), by a vote of two-thirds of the legal voters present and voting thereon, re-establish such school districts. School districts re-established under this provision shall possess corporate rights and powers, and be subject to liabilities the same as before they were abolished. When any town votes to re-establish its school districts under this provision, all school-district property appraised and taken under the provisions of the law abolishing school districts, which is still in the possession of the town and used for public-school purposes, may forthwith be re-appraised under the direction of the town and restored to said districts. And at the next annual assessment thereafter, a tax shall be levied and paid into the treasury of the towns, upon each district, equal to the amount of the appraised value of its property thus restored, or the public-school property may be divided among the several districts and adjusted in any other manner agreed upon by the town at a legal meeting: *provided*, nothing in this act shall be construed to require an appraisal of school property in towns where the school-district property has not been taken, appraised, and the value thereof remitted to the several districts as provided by law.[2] Any town in which the school-district system now (March 15, 1873) exists, may abolish the same, by vote, at a town meeting called for the purpose; and such town shall thereafter be subject to the provisions of chapters one hundred and ten and four hundred and twenty-three of the acts of eighteen hundred and sixty-nine.[3]

47. Sewing shall be taught, in any city or town, in all the public schools in which the school committee of such city or town deem it expedient.

The action of the school committee of any city or town in causing sewing to be taught in the public schools thereof, is ratified, confirmed, and made valid to the same extent as if this act had passed prior to such teaching.[4]

48. The city council of any city, and any town, may establish and maintain one or more industrial schools and raise and appropriate the money necessary to render them efficient. Such schools shall be under the superintendence of the board of school committee of the city or town wherein they are established, and such board shall employ

---

[1] Stats. 1869, ch. 110, and ch. 423.  
[2] Stats. 1870, ch. 196.  
[3] Stats. 1873, ch. 95.  
[4] Stats. 1876, ch. 3.

the teachers, prescribe the arts, trades, and occupations to be taught in such schools, and shall have the general control and management thereof: *provided*, that in no case shall the expense of any such school exceed the appropriation specifically made therefor ; and *provided*, that nothing in this act contained shall authorize the school committee of any city or town to compel any scholar to study any trade, art, or occupation without the consent of the parent or guardian of such scholar, and that attendance upon any such school shall not take the place of the attendance upon public schools required by law.[1]

49. The city council of any city, and the inhabitants of any town, may establish and maintain one or more schools for the purpose of training young men or boys in nautical duties, with the powers and subject to the provisions of law contained in chapter eighty-six of the laws of the year eighteen hundred and seventy-two, except that the school committee of such city or town may excuse boys attending such nautical schools from attendance on other schools. Such schools may be maintained upon shore, or upon ships or other vessels, at the option of the said school committee.[2]

[1] Stats. 1872, ch. 86.    [2] Stats. 1878, ch. 159.

# CHAPTER XXXIII.

## SCHOOL FUNDS.

1. THE present school fund of this commonwealth, together with such additions as may be made thereto, shall constitute a permanent fund, to be invested by the treasurer with the approbation of the governor and council, and called the "Massachusetts School Fund;" the principal of which shall not be diminished, and the income of which, including the interest on notes and bonds taken for sales of Maine lands and belonging to said fund, shall be appropriated as hereinafter provided.[1]

2. The secretary of the board of education and the treasurer and receiver-general shall be commissioners whose duty shall be to invest and manage the Massachusetts school fund, and report annually to the legislature the condition and income thereof. All new investments of said fund, or any part of the same, shall be made with the approval of the governor and council.[2]

3. One-half of the annual income of the Massachusetts school fund shall be apportioned and distributed for the support of public schools without a specific appropriation, and in the manner following, to wit: Each town complying with all laws in force relating to the distribution of said income, and whose valuation of real and personal estate, as shown by the last returns thereof, does not exceed one million dollars, shall annually receive two hundred dollars; each town complying as aforesaid, whose valuation is more than one million, and does not exceed three million dollars, shall receive one hundred and fifty dollars; and each town complying as aforesaid, whose valuation is more than three millions, and does not exceed

---

[1] Gen. Stats. ch. 36, § 1.          [2] Stats. 1866, ch. 53.

five million dollars, shall receive one hundred dollars. The remainder of said moiety, after the division above provided, shall be distributed to all the towns and cities of the commonwealth whose valuation does not exceed ten million dollars, in proportion to the number of persons belonging to each, between five and fifteen years of age.

All money appropriated for other educational purposes, unless otherwise provided in the act appropriating the same, shall be paid from the other half of said income. If the income in any year exceeds such appropriations, the surplus shall be added to the principal of said fund.[1]

4. The income of the school fund appropriated to the support of public schools, which may have accrued upon the thirty-first day of December,[2] in each year, shall be apportioned by the secretary and treasurer, and on the twenty-fifth day of January thereafter be paid over by the treasurer to the treasurers of the several towns and cities for the use of the public schools, according to the number of persons therein between the ages of five and fifteen years, ascertained and certified as provided in sections three and four of chapter forty. But no such apportionment shall be made to a town or city which has not complied with the provisions of sections five and six of said chapter, or which has not raised by taxation for the support of schools during the school year embraced in the last annual returns, including only wages and board of teachers, fuel for the schools, and care of fires and school-rooms, a sum not less than one dollar and fifty cents for each person, between the ages of five and fifteen years, belonging to said town or city on the first day of May of said school year.[3]

5. No apportionment and distribution of the annual income of the school fund, as provided by the second and third sections of chapter thirty-six of the General Statutes, shall be made to any town or city which has not complied with the requisitions of the first and second sections of chapter thirty-eight, and the fifth and sixth sections of chapter forty of the General Statutes, and of any amendments to either of said sections; (and the laws of the commonwealth relating to truancy;[4]) or which has not raised

[1] Stats. 1874, ch. 348.
[2] Stats. 1867, ch. 98.
[3] Gen. Stats. ch. 38, § 3.
[4] Stats. 1878, ch. 234, § 1. *Provided*, however, that nothing in this chapter 234, Stats. 1878, shall affect the apportionment and distribution of the annual income of the school fund prior to the year eighteen hundred and eighty.

by taxation for the support of schools, during the school year embraced in the last annual returns, including only wages and board of teachers, fuel for the schools, and care of fires and school-rooms, a sum not less than three dollars for each person between the ages of five and fifteen years, belonging to said town or city on the first day of May of said school year.[1]

6. Any town which shall maintain the school required to be maintained by the second section of chapter thirty-eight of the General Statutes, not less than thirty-six weeks, exclusive of vacations in each year, shall not be liable to the forfeiture provided in the foregoing section for non-compliance with the requisitions of the aforesaid second section.[2]

7. In the distribution of the moiety of the income of the school fund, for the support of the public schools of the state, every city and town complying with all laws in force relating to the distribution of the same shall annually receive one hundred dollars; and the residue of said moiety shall annually be apportioned among the several cities and towns, in proportion to the number of children in each between the ages of five and fifteen years.[3]

8. The income of the school fund received by the several cities and towns shall be applied by the school committees thereof to the support of the public schools therein, but said committees may, if they see fit, appropriate therefrom any sum, not exceeding twenty-five per cent of the same, to the purchase of books of reference, maps, and apparatus for the use of said schools.[4]

[1] Stats. 1865, ch. 142, § 1.
[2] Stats. 1866, ch. 208.
[3] Stats. 1869, ch. 168.
[4] Gen. Stats. ch. 36, § 4.

# CHAPTER XXXIV.

## SCHOOL REGISTERS AND RETURNS.

1. THE clerks of the several cities and towns, upon receiving from the secretary of the board of education the school registers and blank forms of inquiry for school returns, shall deliver them to the school committee of such cities and towns.

2. If a school committee fails to receive such blank forms of return on or before the last day of March, they shall forthwith notify the secretary of the board of education, who shall transmit such forms as soon as may be.[1]

3. The school committees shall annually, in the month of May, ascertain, or cause to be ascertained, the names and ages of all persons belonging to their respective towns and cities on the first day of May, between the ages of five and fifteen years, and make a record thereof.

4. The school committee shall annually, on or before the last day of the following April, certify under oath the numbers so ascertained and recorded, and also the sum raised by such city or town for the support of schools during the preceding school year, including only wages and board of teachers, fuel for the schools, and care of the fires and school-rooms, and they shall transmit such certificate to the secretary of the board of education. The form of such certificate shall be as follows, to wit : —

We, the school committee of          , do certify that on the first day of May, in the year          , there were belonging to said town the number of          persons between the ages of five and fifteen; and we further certify that said town raised the sum of dollars for the support of public schools for the preceding school year, including only the wages and board of teachers, fuel for the schools, and care of fires and school-rooms; and that said town main-

[1] Gen. Stats. ch. 40, §§ 1, 2.

tained, during said year, each of the schools required to be kept by
the first section of the thirty-eighth chapter of the General Statutes
for a period not less than six months; and we further certify that
said town maintained during said year     school for the benefit
of all the inhabitants of the town as required by section two of chapter thirty-eight of the General Statutes for     months and
days

$\left.\begin{array}{r}\\ \\ \end{array}\right\}$ *School Committee.*

     *ss.* On this     day of     personally appeared the
above named school committee of     and made oath that the
above certificate by them subscribed is true.
          Before me,     *Justice of the Peace.*[1]

5. In the returns made by the school committee to the
secretary of the board of education, twenty days or forty
half-days of actual session shall be counted as one month.[2]

6. The school committee shall cause the school registers
to be faithfully kept in all the public schools, and shall
annually, on or before the last day of April, return the
blank forms of inquiry, duly filled up, to the secretary of
the board of education; and shall also specify in said returns the purposes to which the money received by their
town or city from the income of the school fund has been
appropriated.

7. The school committee shall annually make a detailed
report of the condition of the several public schools, which
report shall contain such statements and suggestions in
relation to the schools as the committee deem necessary
or proper to promote the interests thereof. The committee
shall cause said report to be printed for the use of the
inhabitants, in octavo, pamphlet form, of the size of the
annual reports of the board of education, and transmit
two copies thereof to the secretary of said board, on or
before the last day of April, and deposit one copy in the
office of the clerk of the city or town.

"A town may appropriate money to indemnify its school committee for expenses incurred in defending an action for an alleged
libel contained in a report made by them in good faith and in which
judgment has been rendered in their favor."[3]

---

[1] Stats. 1874, ch. 303, §§ 1, 2.     [3] Fuller *v.* Groton, 11 Gray, 340.
[2] Stats. 1865, ch. 142, § 3.

"A school committee of a city caused to be printed an address by them to the people of the city regarding an occurrence in the public schools, and referred to such address in their subsequently printed annual report as a part thereof. *Held,* that they were authorized to charge the expense of printing the address upon the city, under this section." [1]

8. When a school committee fails, within the prescribed time, to make either the returns or report required of them by law, the secretary of the board of education shall forthwith notify such committee, or the clerk of the city or town, of such failure; and the committee or clerk shall immediately cause the same to be transmitted to the secretary.

9. If a report or return is found to be informal or incorrect, the secretary shall forthwith return the same, with a statement of all deficiencies therein, to the committee for its further action.

10. The returns or reports of a city or town so returned by the secretary for correction, or which have not reached his office within the time prescribed by law, shall be received by him if returned during the month of May; but in all such cases ten per cent shall be deducted from the income of the school fund which such city or town would have been otherwise entitled to. If such returns or reports fail to reach his office before the first day of June, then the whole of such city or town's share of the income shall be retained by the treasurer of the commonwealth, and the amount so retained, as well as the ten per cent when deducted, shall be added to the principal of the school fund. And such city or town shall in addition thereto forfeit not less than one hundred nor more than two hundred dollars: *provided, however,* if said returns and reports were duly mailed in season to reach said office within the time required by law, then the city or town from which said returns or reports are due shall be exempt from the forfeiture otherwise incurred.

11. The clerk of each city and town shall deliver one copy of the reports of the board of education and its

1 Wilson *v.* Cambridge, 101 Mass. 142.

secretary to the secretary of the school committee of the city or town, to be by him preserved for the use of the committee, and transmitted to his successor in office ; and two additional copies of said reports, for the use of said committee ; and shall also deliver one copy of said reports to the clerk of each school district, to be by him deposited in the school-district library, or, if there is no such library, carefully kept for the use of the prudential committee, teachers, and inhabitants of the district, during his continuance in office, and then transmitted to his successor ; and in case the city or town shall not be districted, said reports shall be delivered to the school committee, and so deposited by them as to be accessible to the several teachers and to the citizens ; and such reports shall be deemed to be the property of the town or city, and not of any officer, teacher, or citizen thereof.

12. When the school committee of a city or town is not less than thirteen in number, the chairman and secretary thereof may, in behalf of the committee, sign the annual school returns and the certificate required by sections four and five.

13. A city or town which has forfeited any part of its portion of the income of the school fund through the failure of the school committee to perform their duties in regard to the school report and school returns, may withhold the compensation of the committee.

14. The several school teachers shall faithfully keep the registers furnished to them, and make due return thereof to the school committee, or such person as they may designate ; and no teacher shall be entitled to receive payment for services until the register, properly filled up and completed, shall be so returned.[1]

And the school committee have no authority to waive this keeping of the register.[2]

[1] Gen. Stats. ch. 40, §§ 5–13.        [2] Jewell v. Abington, 2 Allen, 592.

# CHAPTER XXXV.

## ATTENDANCE OF CHILDREN IN THE SCHOOLS.

1. EVERY person having under his control a child between the ages of eight and fourteen years shall annually cause such child to attend some public day school in the city or town in which he resides, at least twenty weeks; which time shall be divided into two terms each of ten consecutive weeks so far as the arrangement of school terms will allow; and for every neglect of such duty the party offending shall forfeit to the use of the public schools of such city or town a sum not exceeding twenty dollars; but if the party so neglecting was not able, by reason of poverty, to send such child to school, or such child has attended a private day school, approved by the school committee of such city or town for a like period of time; or is regularly attending a public or private day school, known as a half-time school, also approved by them; or that such child has been otherwise furnished with the means of education for a like period of time, or has already acquired the branches of learning taught in the public schools; or if his physical or mental condition is such as to render such attendance inexpedient or impracticable, the penalty before mentioned shall not be incurred: *provided*, that no objection shall be made by the school committee to any such school on account of the religious teaching in said school.

(For the purposes designated in this section,) school committees shall approve private schools in their respective localities only when satisfactory evidence is afforded them that the teaching in such schools corresponds in thoroughness and efficiency to the teaching in the public schools, and that the progress made by the pupils in studies required by law is equal to the progress made during the same time in the public schools; and such teaching shall be in the English language.

2. The truant officers and the school committee of the several cities and towns shall vigilantly inquire into all cases of neglect of the duty prescribed in the preceding section, and ascertain the reasons, if any, therefor; and such truant officers, or any of them, shall, when so directed by the school committee, prosecute, in the name of the city or town, any person liable to the penalty provided for in the preceding section.

Justices of police of district courts, trial justices, trial justices of juvenile offenders, and judges of probate shall have jurisdiction within their respective counties of the offences described in this act.[1]

3. All children within the commonwealth may attend the public schools in the place in which they have their legal residence, subject to the regulations prescribed by law.

4. The school committee shall determine the number and qualifications of the scholars to be admitted into the school kept for the use of the whole town.

5. Children living remote from any public school in the town in which they reside may be allowed to attend the public schools in an adjoining town, under such regulations and on such terms as the school committees of the said towns agree upon and prescribe; and the school committee of the town in which such children reside shall pay out of the appropriations of money raised in said town for the support of schools the sum agreed upon.

6. Minors under guardianship, their father having deceased, may attend the public schools of the city or town of which their guardian is an inhabitant.

7. With the consent of school committees first obtained, children[2] may attend school in cities and towns other than those in which their parents or guardians reside; but whenever a child resides in a city or

---

[1] Stats. 1878, ch. 171; Stats. 1873, ch. 279; Stats. 1874, ch. 233.   [2] Stats. 1873, ch. 292, § 4.

town different from that of the residence of the parent or guardian, for the sole purpose of attending school there, the parent or guardian of such child shall be liable to pay to such city or town, for tuition, a sum equal to the average expense per scholar for such school for the period the child shall have so attended.

8. The school committee shall not allow any child to be admitted to or connected with the public schools, who has not been duly vaccinated.

9. No person shall be excluded from a public school on account of the race, color, or religious opinions of the applicant or scholar.[1]

The school committee of a town may lawfully pass an order that the schools thereof shall be opened each morning with reading from the Bible and prayer, and that during the prayer each scholar shall bow the head, unless his parents request that he should be excused from doing so, and may lawfully exclude from the school a scholar who refuses to comply with such order, and whose parents refuse to request that he shall be excused from doing so.[2]

10. Every member of the school committee under whose directions a child is excluded from a public school, and every teacher of such school from which a child is excluded, shall, on application by the parent or guardian of such child, state in writing the grounds and reason of the exclusion.

11. A child unlawfully excluded from any public school shall recover damages therefor in an action of tort, to be brought in the name of such child by his guardian or next friend against the city or town by which such school is supported.

12. The plaintiff in such action may, by filing interrogatories for discovery, examine any member of the school committee, or any other officer of the defendant city or town, as if he were a party to the suit.[3]

[1] Gen. Stats. ch. 41, §§ 2–9.     [3] Gen. Stats. ch. 41, §§ 10–12.
[2] Spiller *v.* Woburn, 12 Allen, 127.

# CHAPTER XXXVI.

## EMPLOYMENT OF CHILDREN AND REGULATIONS RESPECTING THEM.

1. No child under the age of ten years shall be employed (except during the vacations of the public schools [1]) in any manufacturing, mechanical, or mercantile establishment in this commonwealth, and any parent or guardian who permits such employment shall, for such offence, forfeit a sum of not less than twenty nor more than fifty dollars, for the use of the public schools of the city or town.

2. No child under the age of fourteen years shall be so employed, unless during the year next preceding such employment he has attended some public or private day school, under teachers approved by the school committee of the place where such school is kept, at least twenty weeks, which time may be divided into two terms, each of ten consecutive weeks, so far as the arrangements of school terms will allow ; nor shall such employment continue, unless such child shall attend school as herein provided, in each and every year ; and no child shall be so employed who does not present a certificate, made by or under the direction of said school committee, of his compliance with the requirements of this act : *provided, however,* that a regular attendance during the continuance of such employment in any school known as a half-time day school, or an attendance in any public or private day school, twenty weeks, as above stated, may be accepted by said school committee as a substitute for the attendance herein required.

For the purposes designated in this section, school committees shall approve private schools in their respective localities only when

[1] Stats. 1878, ch. 257, § 5.

satisfactory evidence is afforded them that the teaching in such schools corresponds in thoroughness and efficiency to the teaching in the public schools, and that the progress made by the pupils in studies required by law is equal to the progress made during the same time in the public schools; and such teaching shall be in the English language.[1]

3. Every owner, superintendent, or overseer in any establishment above named, who employs or permits to be employed any child in violation of the second section of this act, and every parent or guardian who permits such employment, shall for such offence forfeit a sum of not less than twenty nor more than fifty dollars for the use of the public schools of such city or town.

4. The truant officers shall, at least once in every school term, and as often as the school committee require, visit the establishments described by this act in their several cities and towns, and inquire into the situation of the children employed therein, ascertain whether the provisions of this act are duly observed, and report all violations to the school committee.[2]

5. Every owner, superintendent, or overseer of any manufacturing, mechanical, or mercantile establishment in this commonwealth shall require and keep on file a certificate of the age and place of birth of every minor child under the age of sixteen years in his employ, or in the employ of such establishment, so long as such minor shall be so employed; which certificate shall also state, in the case of a minor under the age of fourteen years, the amount of his or her school attendance during the year next preceding such employment. Said certificate shall be made by or under the direction of the school committee of the place where such attendance has been had, or where such establishment is located.

6. In case no such certificate shall have been required by such owner, superintendent, or overseer, then such employment shall be deemed to have been a violation of the second section of chapter fifty-two of the acts of the year eighteen hundred and seventy-six (section two above).

[1] Stats. 1878, ch. 171.  [2] Stats. 1876, ch. 52.

7. The truant officers may demand the names of the minor children under the age of sixteen years employed in the establishments above named in their several cities and towns, and may require that the certificates of age and school attendance prescribed in this act[1] shall be produced for their inspection; and if the name and certificate as aforesaid be not produced in any case, it shall be *prima facie* evidence that the employment of such child is illegal.

8. On and after the first day of May, eighteen hundred and eighty, no child under fourteen years of age shall be employed in any manufacturing, mechanical, or mercantile establishment, while the public schools in the city or town where such child lives are in session, unless such child can read and write. Every owner, superintendent, or overseer in any establishment above named, who employs or permits to be employed any child in violation of this section, and every parent or guardian who permits such employment, shall for every such offence forfeit a sum of not less than twenty nor more than fifty dollars for the use of the public schools of such city or town.[2]

---

[1] Sections 5 to 8 of this chapter.     [2] Stats. 1878, ch. 257, §§ 1–4.

# CHAPTER XXXVII.

## TRUANT CHILDREN, ABSENTEES FROM SCHOOL, AND NEGLECTED CHILDREN.

1. EACH city and town shall make all needful provisions and arrangements concerning habitual truants and children between the ages of seven and fifteen years who may be found wandering about in the streets or public places of such city or town, having no lawful occupation or business, not attending school, and growing up in ignorance ; and shall also make such by-laws as shall be most conducive to the welfare of such children, and to the good order of such city or town ; and shall provide suitable places for the confinement, discipline, and instruction of such children : *provided*, that said by-laws shall be approved by the superior court, or a justice thereof, or by the judge of (the) probate (court) of the county.

2. The school committee of the several cities and towns shall appoint and fix the compensation of two or more suitable persons, to be designated as truant officers, who shall, under the direction of said committee, inquire into all cases arising under such by-laws, and shall alone be authorized, in case of violation thereof, to make complaint and carry into execution the judgment thereon,

And may serve all legal processes issued by the courts in pursuance of this act (sections one to seven inclusive), but shall not be entitled to or receive any fees therefor.[1]

3. Any minor convicted under such by-law of being an habitual truant, or of wandering about in the streets and public places of any city or town, having no lawful employment or business, not attending school, and growing up in ignorance, shall be committed to any institution of instruction or suitable situation provided for the purpose

[1] Stats. 1874, ch. 233.

under the authority of section one [1] of this act, or by law, for such time, not exceeding two years, as the justice or court having jurisdiction may determine. Any minor so committed may, upon proof of amendment, or for other sufficient cause shown upon a hearing of the case, be discharged by such justice or court.

4. Justices of police or district courts, trial justices, trial justices of juvenile offenders, and judges of probate (courts) shall have jurisdiction, within their respective counties, of the offences described in this act.

5. When three or more cities or towns in any county shall so require, the county commissioners shall establish at convenient places therein, other than the jail or house of correction, at the expense of the county, truant schools, for the confinement, discipline, and instruction of minor children convicted under the provisions of this act,[2] and shall make suitable provisions for the government and control of said schools, and for the appointment of proper teachers and officers thereof.

6. Any city or town may assign any such truant school as the place of confinement, discipline, and instruction for persons convicted under the provisions of this act;[2] and shall pay such sum for the support of those committed thereto as the county commissioners shall determine, not exceeding the rate of two dollars per week for each person.

7. Any city or town may, with the assent of the board of state charities, assign the state primary school at Monson as the place of confinement, discipline, and instruction for persons convicted under the provisions of this act, instead of the truant schools heretofore mentioned; and shall pay for the support of such persons committed thereto such sum as the inspectors of said school shall determine, not exceeding two dollars per week for each person. Any minor, so committed, may, upon satisfactory proof of amendment, or for other sufficient cause, be discharged by the board of state charities.[3]

[1] Section 1 of this chapter.

[2] Sections 1 to 7, inclusive, of this chapter.

[3] Stats. 1873, ch. 262.

8. Any person who shall employ or exhibit, or who shall sell, apprentice, or give away for the purpose of employing or exhibiting, any child under the age of fifteen years, in or for the vocation, occupation, service, or purpose of dancing, playing on musical instruments, singing, walking on a wire or rope, or riding or performing as a gymnast, contortionist, or acrobat in any circus or theatrical exhibition, or in any public place whatsoever, or who shall cause, procure, or encourage any such child to engage therein, shall be punished by a fine not exceeding two hundred dollars, or by imprisonment in the county jail not exceeding six months : *provided*, *however*, that nothing in this act (this section) shall be construed to prevent the education of children in vocal and instrumental music, or their employment as musicians in any church, chapel, or school or school exhibition, or prevent their taking part in any concert or musical exhibition on the special written permission of the mayor and aldermen of any city or the board of selectmen of any town.[1]

9. Each of the several cities and towns in this commonwealth is hereby authorized and empowered to make all needful provisions and arrangements concerning children under sixteen years of age, who, by reason of the neglect, crime, drunkenness, or other vices of parents, or from orphanage, are suffered to be growing up without salutary parental control and education, or in circumstances exposing them to lead idle and dissolute lives ; and may also make all such by-laws and ordinances respecting such children as shall be deemed most conducive to their welfare and the good order of such city or town : *provided*, that said by-laws and ordinances shall be approved (by the superior court, or in vacation by a justice thereof[2]), and shall not be repugnant to the laws of the commonwealth.

It shall be the duty of every town of five thousand inhabitants or more to take action under this section concerning the care and education of neglected children.[3]

[1] Stats. 1877, ch. 172.
[2] Stats. 1867, ch. 2.
[3] Stats. 1878, ch. 217.

10. The mayor and aldermen of cities and the selectmen of towns availing themselves of the provisions of this act shall severally appoint suitable persons to make complaints in case of violations of such ordinances or by-laws as may be adopted, who alone shall be authorized to make complaints under the authority of this act.[1]

The officers and duly appointed agents of the Massachusetts Children's Protective Society may also make complaints.[2]

11. When it shall be proved to any judge of the superior court, or judge or justice of a municipal or police court, or to any trial justice, that any child under sixteen years of age, by reason of orphanage, or of the neglect, crime, drunkenness, or other vice of parents, is growing up without education or salutary control, and in circumstances exposing said child to an idle and dissolute life, any judge or justice aforesaid shall have power to order said child to such institution of instruction or other place that may be assigned for the purpose, as provided in this act,[1] by the authorities of the city or town in which such child may reside, for such term of time as said judge or justice may deem expedient, not extending beyond the age of twenty-one years for males, or eighteen years for females, to be there kept, educated, and cared for according to law.

12. Whenever it shall be satisfactorily proved that the parents of any child committed under the provisions of this act,[1] shall have reformed and are leading orderly and industrious lives, and are in a condition to exercise salutary parental control over their children, and to provide them with proper education and employment; or whenever, said parents being dead, any person may offer to make suitable provision for the care, nurture, and education of such child as will conduce to the public welfare, and will give satisfactory security for the performance of the same, then the directors, trustees, overseers, or other board having charge of the institution to which such child may be committed, may discharge said child to the parents or to the party making provision for the care of the child as aforesaid.[3]

[1] Sections 9 to 12 of this chapter, inclusive.  [2] Stats. 1878, ch. 217.  [3] Stats. 1866, ch. 283.

Whenever the town, city, or state authorities charged with the custody of destitute children shall delegate to the directors or managers of any charitable institution incorporated by law the custody of an infant of less than four years old, the said directors or managers shall be held to comply with all the provisions of law, and be subject to all the restrictions concerning such infant as may be required by law of the authorities so delegating the trust.[1]

[1] Stats. 1870, ch. 92.

# CHAPTER XXXVIII.

## JURORS.

1. ALL persons who are qualified to vote in the choice of representatives in the general court shall be liable to be drawn and serve as jurors, except as is hereinafter provided.

2. The following persons shall be exempt from serving as jurors, to wit : —

The governor, lieutenant-governor, members of the council, secretary of the commonwealth, members and officers of the senate and house of representatives during the session of the general court, judges and justices of any court (except justices of the peace), county and special commissioners, clerks of courts, registers of probate and insolvency, registers of deeds, sheriffs and their deputies, coroners, constables, marshals of the United States and their deputies, and all other officers of the United States, counsellors and attorneys-at-law, settled ministers of the gospel, officers of colleges, preceptors and teachers of incorporated academies, practising physicians and surgeons regularly licensed, cashiers of incorporated banks, constant ferrymen, persons who are more than sixty-five years old, members of the volunteer militia, members of the ancient and honorable artillery company, and enginemen and members of the fire department of the city of Boston ; and enginemen and members of the fire department of other places may be exempt by the vote of the city council of the city or the inhabitants of the town.[1]

The superintendents, officers, and assistants employed in or about either of the state hospitals, state almshouses, jails, lunatic hospitals,

---

[1] Gen. Stats. ch. 132, §§ 1, 2.

houses of correction, houses of industry, reform schools, or the state prison, keepers of light-houses, conductors and engine-drivers of rail-road trains, and teachers in public schools, shall be exempt from service as jurors.[1]

No officer or soldier shall be liable to jury duty while in the active militia service; and any officer or soldier who shall have served continuously and faithfully for nine years in the volunteer militia shall be exempt for life thereafter from the performance of jury duty.[2]

3. No person shall be liable to be drawn and serve as a juror in any court oftener than once in three years, except as provided in the two following sections, but he shall not be so exempt unless he actually attends and serves as a juror in pursuance of the draft.

4. The inhabitants of the counties of Nantucket and Dukes County shall be liable to be drawn and serve as jurors once in every two years.

5. No person shall be exempt from serving on a jury in any other court, in consequence of his having served before a justice of the peace or police court. No person shall be compelled to serve as a juror before any justice of the peace or police court more than twenty-four days in any one year, nor more than fourteen days at any one time, except to finish a case commenced within that time.[3]

" Any court " in the foregoing includes courts of the United States.[4]

6. The selectmen of each town shall once in every year prepare a list of such inhabitants of the town not absolutely exempt, as they think well qualified to serve as jurors, being persons of good moral character, of sound judgment, and free from all legal exceptions; which list shall include not less than one for every one hundred inhabitants of the town, and not more than one for every sixty inhabitants, computing by the then last census, except that in the county of Dukes County it may include one for every thirty inhabitants.

7. The list when so prepared shall be posted up by the selectmen in public places in the town, ten days at least

---

[1] Stats. 1864, ch. 215.
[2] Stats. 1878, ch. 265, § 149.
[3] Gen. Stats. ch. 132, §§ 3–5.
[4] Swan's case, 16 Mass. 220.

before it is submitted for revision and acceptance, and shall then be laid before the town ; and the town may alter it by adding the names of any persons liable to serve, or striking any names therefrom.

8. The selectmen shall cause the names borne on the list to be written each on a separate paper or ballot, and shall roll up or fold the ballots so as to resemble each other as much as possible, and so that the name written thereon shall not be visible on the outside ; and they shall place the ballots in a box to be kept by the town clerk for that purpose.

9. If any person whose name is so placed in the jury box is convicted of any scandalous crime, or is guilty of any gross immorality, his name shall be withdrawn therefrom by the selectmen, and he shall not be returned to serve as a juror.

10. The clerks of the supreme judicial and superior courts, in due season before each term (except the terms of the superior court in the county of Suffolk for criminal business commencing at other times than in January, April, July, and October), and at such other times as the respective courts may order, shall issue writs of *venire facias* for jurors, and shall therein require the attendance of the jurors on such day of the term as the court may order. The jurors returned for the superior court for criminal business in the county of Suffolk shall serve three terms.

11. The clerks in issuing the *venires* shall require from each town and city a number of jurors as nearly as may be in proportion to their respective number of inhabitants, so as to equalize as far as possible the duty of serving as jurors.

12. The *venires* shall be delivered to the sheriff of the county, and by him transmitted to a constable in each of the towns and cities to which they are respectively issued, and they shall be served by the constable, without delay, on the selectmen and town clerk.

13. Nothing contained in the preceding sections shall prevent any court from issuing *venires* for additional jurors

in term time whenever it is necessary for the convenient despatch of their business; in which·case the *venires* shall be served and returned, and the jurors required to attend on such days, as the court shall direct.

14. When a suit is pending in the superior court for the county of Dukes County, wherein the inhabitants of any town in said county are disqualified from acting as jurors, any justice of the court, in term time or in vacation, may order the clerk of the court to issue writs of *venire facias* for a sufficient number of jurors to try such cause, from any town whose inhabitants are not so disqualified; and the clerk shall issue a *venire facias* accordingly.

15. All jurors, whether required to serve on a grand or traverse jury, by force of the laws relating to highways or mills, or on any other occasion (except inquests and proceedings relating to the commitment of insane persons), shall be selected by drawing ballots from the jury box, and the persons whose names are borne on the ballots so drawn shall be returned to serve as jurors.

16. When jurors are to be so drawn, the town clerk and selectmen shall attend at the clerk's office or some other public place appointed for the purpose, and if the clerk is absent, the selectmen may proceed without him. The ballots in the jury box shall be shaken and mixed together, and one of the selectmen without seeing the names written thereon shall openly draw therefrom a number of ballots equal to the number of jurors required. If a person so drawn is exempt by law, or is unable by reason of sickness or absence from home to attend as a juror, or if he has served as a juror in any court within three years then next preceding, his name shall be returned into the box and another drawn in his stead.

17. When a person is drawn and returned to serve as a juror in any court, the selectmen shall indorse on the ballot the date of the draft and return it into the box, and whenever there is a revision and renewal of the ballots in the box, the selectmen shall transfer to the new ballots the date of all the drafts made within three years then next preceding.

18. Any town may at a legal meeting order that all drafts for jurors therein shall be made in open town meeting, in which case the draft shall be made by the selectmen in the manner prescribed in the two preceding sections, except that it shall be done in a town meeting. In such town when a *venire* is served upon the selectmen they shall cause a town meeting to be notified and warned for that purpose in the manner ordered by the town or otherwise prescribed by law.[1]

19. The meeting for drawing jurors, whether the draft is made in town meeting or before the selectmen and town clerk only, shall be held not less than seven nor more than twenty-one days before the day when the jurors are required to attend.

20. The constable shall, four days at least before the time when the jurors are required to attend, summon each person who is drawn, by reading to him the *venire* with the indorsement thereon of his having been drawn, or by leaving at his place of abode a written notification of his having been drawn, and of the time and place of the sitting of the court at which he is to attend, and shall make a return of the *venire* with his doings thereon to the clerk, before the opening of the court from which it was issued.[2]

It is not necessary that notice to jurors, who are drawn to assess damages caused by the laying out of a highway or railroad, should be served by a constable; such notice may be served by the officer to whom the warrant for summoning a jury is directed.[3]

21. Grand jurors shall be drawn, summoned, and returned in the same manner as jurors for trials; and when drawn at the same time with jurors for trials, the persons whose names are first drawn, to the number required, shall be returned as grand jurors, and those afterwards drawn shall be jurors for trials.

22. In case of deficiency of grand jurors in any court, writs of *venire facias* may be issued to the constables of such cities or towns as the court may direct, to return

[1] Gen. Stats. ch. 132, §§ 6–18.
[2] Gen. Stats. ch. 132, §§ 19, 20.
[3] Wyman *v.* Lexington, &c. R. R., 13 Met. 316.

forthwith such further number of grand jurors as may be required.[1]

23. If a person duly drawn and summoned to attend as a juror in any court neglects to attend without sufficient excuse, he shall pay a fine not exceeding forty dollars, which shall be imposed by the court to which the juror was summoned, and shall be paid into the county treasury.

24. When, by neglect of any of the duties required in this chapter to be performed by any of the officers or persons herein mentioned, the jurors to be returned from any place are not duly drawn and summoned to attend the court, every person guilty of such neglect shall pay a fine not exceeding twenty dollars, to be imposed by the same court to the use of the county in which the offence is committed.

25. If such neglect occurs with regard to jurors required to serve on any other occasion than in the supreme judicial court, the superior court, or before any justice of the peace or police court, the sheriff or other officer before whom the jurors were required to appear shall make known the fact to the superior court next to be held in the same county, and the court, after due examination and a hearing of the parties who are charged, shall impose the fine.

26. If any city or town clerk, selectmen, mayor, or alderman is guilty of fraud, either by practising on the jury box previously to a draft, or in drawing a juror, or in returning into the box the name of any juror which had been lawfully drawn out and drawing or substituting another in his stead, or in any other way in the drawing of jurors, he shall be punished by a fine not exceeding five hundred dollars.[2]

27. Nothing contained in the foregoing shall affect the power and duty of coroners or magistrates to summon and empanel jurors when authorized by other provisions of law.[3]

[1] Gen. Stats. ch. 171, §§ 3, 4.
[2] Gen. Stats. ch. 132, §§ 36–39.
[3] Gen. Stats. ch. 132, § 40.

# CHAPTER XXXIX.

## CENSUS.

1. A CENSUS of the inhabitants of each city and town in the commonwealth, on the first day of May, shall be taken in the year eighteen hundred and sixty-five, and in every tenth year thereafter, and shall contain a special enumeration of the legal voters residing in each town, and in each ward of the several cities.

2. In taking the census, the following particulars shall be ascertained and enumerated, in separate columns of the schedule, to wit : —

1. Dwelling-houses numbered in the order of visitation.
2. Families numbered in the order of visitation.
3. Name of each person in the family or dwelling.
4. Age of each person one year old and upward.
5. Sex of each person.
6. Color of each person ; whether white, black, mulatto, or Indian.
7. Place of birth ; naming state, territory, or country.
8. Condition ; whether single, married, or widowed.
9. Profession, trade, or occupation of every person over fifteen years of age.
10. Persons over twenty years of age who cannot read and write.
11. Whether deaf and dumb, blind, insane, idiotic, pauper, or convict.
12. Ratable polls.
13. Legal voters.
14. Naturalized voters.

3. The census shall be taken in cities by agents appointed by the mayor and aldermen, and in towns by the

selectmen, or by agents appointed by them.[1]  Such selectmen or agents shall be sworn, shall make out in words, at
length, a return of the aggregates and results of said
census, and shall sign and make oath to the truth thereof;
and a certificate of the oath, by the magistrate administer-
ing it, shall be annexed thereto.  They shall, on or before
the twentieth day of August of the same year, deliver the
return to the sheriff of the county, who shall transmit it to
the office of the secretary of the commonwealth on or before the last day of said August; or the selectmen or
agents may themselves transmit the return to the office of
the secretary on or before the day last named.

·4. The secretary shall, on or before the first day of May
in each year in which the census is to be taken, transmit
to the clerks of the several cities and towns printed forms
for the returns required by this act, with such instructions
as he may deem necessary, and a notice that the returns
must be made into his office on or before the last day of
August of the same year.

5. The secretary shall prepare an abstract from the
census, showing the number of legal voters in each town,
and in each ward of the several cities, arranged by counties, and shall submit the same to the general court, within
the first ten days of the annual session following the taking of such census.

6. If any selectman or agent wilfully refuses to perform
any duty required of him by this act, he shall forfeit a sum
not exceeding five hundred dollars; and if he is guilty of
wilful deceit and falsehood in the discharge of his duty, he
shall forfeit a sum not exceeding two thousand dollars, or
be imprisoned not exceeding one year.  A sheriff who
shall wilfully refuse or neglect to perform the duty required by this act shall forfeit a sum not exceeding one
thousand dollars.[2]

---

[1] Stats. 1874, ch. 386, provides
that the census shall be taken by
such of the assessors of the several
towns as the bureau of statistics of
labor shall appoint, and the returns
thereof shall be returned into the
office of the secretary of the commonwealth; and so much of section 3
above as is inconsistent with said
chapter 386 is repealed.

[2] Stats. 1865, ch. 69.

# CHAPTER XL.

## WEIGHTS AND MEASURES.

1. THE weights, measures, and balances received from the United States, and now in the treasury of the common-wealth, to wit, one half-bushel, one wine gallon, one wine quart, one wine pint, one wine half-pint, one yard measure; a set of avoirdupois weights, consisting of fifty, twenty-five, twenty, ten, five, four, three, two, and one pounds, and from eight ounces down to one drachm; one set of troy weights, from five thousand pennyweights down to half a grain, and from one pound down to the ten-thousandth part of an ounce; and three sets of balances: also the measures caused to be made by the treasurer and now in the treasury, to wit, one of eight quarts, one of four quarts, one of two quarts, and one of one quart, dry measure, shall be, remain, and be used as the sole authorized public standards of weights and measures.

It is now lawful to use the weights and measures of the metric system.[1]

2. Such weights, measures, and balances as may be procured from time to time to replace those before mentioned shall be preserved in the same form and of the same dimensions, the denominations of the weights and measures being marked and stamped thereon respectively, and they shall be sealed with the seal which is kept for that purpose by the treasurer.

3. The treasurer shall keep the authorized public standard weights, measures, and balances, in the treasury, in his care and custody. He shall furnish duplicates thereof to a deputy appointed by him, who shall be sworn and give

---

[1] Stats. 1877, ch. 40.

bond for the faithful discharge of the duties of his office.
The duplicates shall be kept by the deputy, and used by
him for sealing weights, measures, and balances, in like
manner as the standards kept in the treasury may be used
by the treasurer.

4. The treasurer shall furnish to each town hereafter
incorporated, at a cost not exceeding one hundred and
fifty dollars, a complete set of standard weights, measures,
and balances, such as have been furnished to other towns,
made to conform as near as practicable to the models
caused to be made by the treasurer as town standards.
The expense of transportation shall be defrayed by the
town.

But no town shall be supplied the second time at the expense of
the commonwealth, in case the weights, measures, or balances should
be lost or destroyed.[1]

5. The several county, city, and town treasurers shall,
at the expense of their respective counties, cities, and
towns, provide therein places for the safe and suitable
keeping and preservation of the weights, measures, and
balances furnished by the commonwealth, which shall be
used only as standards. They shall have the care and
oversight thereof; shall see that they are kept in good
order and repair; and if any portion of them are lost,
destroyed, or irreparably damaged, shall, at the expense
of the county, city, or town, replace the same by similar
weights, measures, or balances.

6. Each treasurer who neglects to provide a suitable
place for keeping such weights, measures, and balances,
or to keep them in good order and repair, or who suffers
any of them, through his neglect, to be lost, damaged, or
destroyed, shall forfeit two hundred dollars, to be recovered
by indictment.

7. Each treasurer shall, once at least in every ten years,
have the standards in his custody tried, adjusted, and sealed
by the treasurer of the commonwealth or his deputy; the

[1] Stats. 1877, ch. 150.

expense whereof shall be paid by the respective counties, cities, and towns. Every treasurer who neglects to have the standards under his charge so sealed shall forfeit a sum not exceeding fifty dollars.

8. When a city or town votes to have more than one sealer of weights and measures, the treasurer shall, at the expense thereof, procure and preserve the necessary additional seals, weights, and measures, before specified; so that each sealer may have a complete set of the same.

9. Every sealer of weights and measures shall receive of the treasurer a set of the standards and seal, and shall give him a receipt therefor, expressing the condition in which the same are; and he shall be accountable to the city or town for the due preservation of the same in the like condition, until he redelivers them to the treasurer.

10. The treasurer of the commonwealth and his deputy, the county treasurers, and the city and town sealers, shall each keep a seal for their several uses. The seals of the treasurer and of his deputy shall be the letters *C. M.*, those of county treasurers shall be the initial and final letters of their respective counties, followed by the letters *Co.*; those of city and town sealers, the name of their respective cities or towns, or such intelligible abbreviation thereof as the mayor and aldermen or selectmen may prescribe.

11. Every sealer of weights and measures shall annually, in May, advertise in some newspaper, or post up notifications in different parts of the city or town, for every inhabitant who uses weights and measures for the purpose of buying and selling, and for public weighers who have the same, to bring in their measures, weights, balances, scales, and beams, to be adjusted and sealed; and he shall forthwith adjust and seal all weights and measures brought to him for that purpose (see section twenty-seven below).

12. The sealers of each city and town shall go annually to every hay scale or platform balance which cannot be readily removed, and try, adjust, and seal the same.

No sealer, except for the purposes of this section, shall carry his standards of weights, measures, or scales, from one place to another, for the purpose of adjusting others (see section twenty-seven below).

13. For every neglect of any duty prescribed in the three preceding sections, the sealer shall forfeit a sum not exceeding twenty dollars.

14. Each sealer of weights and measures, including the deputy of the treasurer and county treasurers, shall receive a fee of three cents for every weight, measure, scale, beam, or balance, by him sealed, except platform balances. For sealing each platform balance weighing five thousand pounds and upwards, the sealer shall receive one dollar; and for each platform balance weighing less, fifty cents. Every sealer shall also have a reasonable compensation for all repairs, alterations, and adjustments, which it is necessary for him to make (see section twenty-seven below).

15. The vibrating steelyards which have been heretofore allowed and used in this State may continue to be used: *provided*, that each beam and the poises thereof shall be annually tried, proved, and sealed, by a sealer of weights and measures, like other beams and weights.

16. Whoever sells by any other weights, measures, scales, beams, or balances, than those which have been sealed as before provided, shall forfeit a sum not exceeding twenty dollars for each offence; and when by the custom of trade they are provided by the buyer, if he purchases by any other weights, measures, scales, beams, or balances, he shall be subject to a like penalty, to be recovered by an action of tort to the use of the complainant. (But see section thirty-four.)

Where a sale is made in violation of this statute, no action can be maintained for the price of the goods sold.[1]

17. When commodities are sold by the hundred weight, it shall be understood to mean the net weight of all packages from one to one hundred pounds avoirdupois; and

[1] Sawyer *v.* Smith, 109 Mass. 220.

all contracts concerning goods sold by weight shall be understood and construed accordingly.

18. Every public weigher of goods or commodities shall weigh the same according to the provisions of the preceding section, and make his certificate accordingly; and for each refusal or neglect he shall forfeit a sum not exceeding ten dollars. Every weigher of goods appointed by a city or town, and every weigher for hire or reward, shall be deemed and taken to be a public weigher within the provisions of this section.

19. In every city and town in which section twenty-three of chapter thirty of the Revised Statutes has been adopted according to the provisions thereof, or in which the provisions of this section shall be accepted by the city council of the city, or by the inhabitants of the town, at a legal meeting, every measure by which salt or grain is sold, in addition to being conformable in capacity and diameter to the public standards, shall have a bar of iron across the middle thereof at the top, to be approved by a sealer of weights and measures, and a bar or standard of iron from the centre of the first-mentioned bar to the centre of the bottom of the measure, to be approved in like manner; and every such measure shall be filled by shovelling such salt or grain into the same, and the striking thereof shall always be lengthwise of the first described bar. And whoever sells or exposes to sale any salt or grain in any other measure, or fills or strikes such measure in any other manner than is provided in this section, shall forfeit fifty cents for every bushel of salt or grain so measured, filled, or stricken: *provided*, that salt may be measured from vessels in such measures as are used by the government of the United States, and that nothing contained in this section shall prevent the measuring of salt in tubs, or any proportional parts of hogsheads, without bars, as may be determined by any city or town.[1]

20. The respective sealers of weights and measures in the several cities and towns are authorized and required

[1] Gen. Stats. ch. 51, §§ 1-19.

to go to the houses, stores, and shops of all such persons within their respective cities and towns, using weights and measures for the purpose of buying and selling, as shall neglect to bring in their weights, measures, milk-cans, balances, scales, and beams to be adjusted and sealed, and there, at the said houses, stores, and shops, having entered the same with the assent of the occupant thereof, to adjust and seal the same, or send the same to his office to be adjusted and sealed, and shall be entitled to receive therefor the fees provided by law, together with all the expense of removing the same (see section twenty-seven below).

21. If any such person shall refuse to have his measures, milk-cans, weights, balances, scales, or beams so tried, adjusted, and sealed, the same not having been tried, adjusted, and sealed within one year preceding such refusal, he shall forfeit ten dollars for each offence, one-half to the use of the city or town, and one-half to the use of the sealer of weights and measures.

22. If any person shall alter any weight, measure, milk-can, scale, balance, or beam, after the same shall have been adjusted and sealed, so that the same thereby shall not conform to the public standard, and shall fraudulently make use of the same, he shall forfeit, for each offence, the sum of fifty dollars, one-half to the use of the city or town, and one-half to the use of the complainant. And any sealer when he shall have reasonable cause to believe that any weight, measure, milk-can, scale, balance, or beam has been altered since the same was last adjusted and sealed, is authorized and required to enter the premises in which any such weight, measure, milk-can, scale, balance, or beam is kept or used, and examine the same.

23. The city council of any city may by ordinance, and any town may by by-law, provide that the sealer of weights and measures for their respective city or town be paid by a salary, and that he account for and pay into the treasury of the city or town the fees received by him by virtue of his office.

24. The mayor and aldermen of any city are authorized to remove the sealer of weights and measures at any time they may see fit.

25. No milk-can shall be sealed by any sealer, which does not contain one or more quarts without any fractional part of a quart.

26. This act (six preceding sections) shall not take effect in any city or town until it shall have been accepted by the city council of such city, or by the inhabitants of such town, at a legal meeting.[1]

27. The sealers of weights and measures in the several cities and towns shall annually give public notice by advertisement, or by posting notice in one or more public places in their respective cities and towns, to all inhabitants or persons having a usual place of business therein, who use scales, weights, measures, or milk-cans for the purpose of selling any goods, wares, merchandise, or other commodities, or for public weighing, to bring in their scales, weights, measures, and milk-cans to be adjusted and sealed, and such sealers shall attend in one or more convenient place or places, and shall adjust, seal, and record all scales, weights, measures, and milk-cans so brought in.

In those cities or towns where a salary is paid to sealers of weights and measures, no fees shall be charged for such services. In other cities and towns, the said sealers shall receive the compensation set forth in section fourteen of chapter fifty-one of the General Statutes.

At any time after said notice,[2] the said sealers of weights and measures shall go to the houses, stores, and shops of persons mentioned in the foregoing section who have neglected to comply with the notice given thereunder, and having entered the same, with the assent of the occupants thereof, shall adjust and seal their scales, weights, measures, and milk-cans, and shall be entitled to receive for said service the compensation set forth in said section fourteen.

The said sealers of weights and measures shall go once a year, and oftener if necessary, to every hay and coal scale, dormant or other platform balance, within their respective cities and towns, that cannot be easily or conveniently removed, and test the accuracy of and adjust and seal the same, and shall receive therefor the compensation set forth in said section fourteen.

All persons using any scales, weights, measures, or milk-cans for the purpose of buying or selling any commodity, may have the same tested and sealed by the sealers of weights and measures, at

---

[1] Stats. 1863, ch. 179, §§ 1–7.    [2] Stats. 1877, ch. 151, § 2.

the office of any of said sealers, whenever such persons desire to have it done.

Whenever a complaint is made to a sealer of weights and measures by any person, that he has reasonable cause to believe, or whenever a sealer of weights and measures shall himself have reasonable cause to believe, that any scale, weight, measure, or milk-can used in the sale of any commodity within the city or town is incorrect, the said sealer shall go the place where such scale, weight, measure, or milk-can is, and test and mark the same according to the result of the test applied thereto ; and if the same be incorrect and cannot be adjusted, the said sealer shall attach a notice thereto, certifying the fact, and forbidding the use thereof until the same has been made to conform to the authorized standard. Any person using any scales, weights, measures, or milk-cans after a sealer of weights and measures has demanded permission to test the same, and has been refused such permission, shall be liable to a penalty of not less than ten nor more than one hundred dollars.

All scales, weights, measures, and milk-cans that cannot be made to conform to the standard, shall be stamped "condemned" or "C. D." by the sealer of weights and measures ; and no person shall thereafter use the same for weighing or measuring any commodity sold or exchanged, under the penalties provided in the case of the use of false weights and measures.

If any person shall knowingly use any false weight, measure, milk-can, scale, balance, or beam, or shall alter any weight, measure, milk-can, scale, balance, or beam after the same shall have been adjusted and sealed, so that the same thereby shall not conform to the public standard, and shall fraudulently make use of the same, he shall forfeit for each offence the sum of fifty dollars, one-half to the use of the city or town, and one-half to the use of the complainant. And any sealer, when he shall have reasonable cause to believe that any weight, measure, milk-can, scale, balance, or beam has been altered since the same was last adjusted and sealed, is authorized and required to enter the premises in which such weight, measure, milk-can, scale, balance, or beam is kept or used, and examine the same.

The city council of any city may by ordinance, and any town may by by-law, provide that the sealers of weights and measures for their respective city or town be paid by a salary, and that they account for and pay into the treasury of the city or town the fees received by them by virtue of their office.[1]

28. Instead of appointing more than one sealer of weights and measures, the mayor and aldermen of any city and the selectmen of any town, where it may be

[1] Stats. 1876, ch. 123.

necessary for the proper discharge of the duties of such office, shall appoint annually one or more deputy-sealers, who shall act under the direction of the sealer; and the mayor and aldermen of cities and the selectmen of towns are authorized to remove the sealer or deputy-sealers of weights and measures in such city or town whenever they may deem it expedient.

29. In case any sealer of weights and measures cannot seal any scales, weights, and measures with the stamp as now provided by law, he may mark them with a stencil or other suitable means, so as to show they have been inspected; but he shall in no case seal or mark as correct any weights, scales, or measures which do not conform to the standards; if such scales, weights, or measures can be readily adjusted by such means as he has at hand, he may adjust and seal them; but if they cannot be readily adjusted, he shall affix to such scales, weights, or measures a notice forbidding their use until he is satisfied that they have been so adjusted as to conform to the standards; and whoever removes said notice without the consent of the officer affixing said notice shall, for each offence, forfeit a sum not exceeding fifty dollars, one-half to the use of the city or town, and one-half to the use of the complainant.

30. Whenever visiting the place of business of any person for the purpose of testing any scales, weights, and measures, the sealer or his deputy is hereby authorized to use for that purpose such scales, weights, or measures as he can conveniently carry with him; and each city and town shall furnish, for the purposes of this act, the sealer of weights and measures with one or more duplicate sets of scales, weights, and measures, which shall at all times be kept to conform to the standards furnished by the commonwealth; and all such scales, weights, and measures so sealed shall be deemed legally sealed, the same as if tested and sealed with the standard scales, weights, and measures.

31. Any sealer or deputy-sealer of weights and meas-

ures is authorized to seize without a warrant such scales, weights, or measures as may be necessary to be used as evidence in cases of violation of this or any act relating to the sealing of weights and measures ; such scales, weights, or measures to be returned to the owners or be forfeited, as the court may direct.

32. All provisions of law requiring the sealing of milk-cans, and acts and parts of acts inconsistent herewith, are hereby repealed : *provided, however*, this repeal shall not affect any suit or legal proceedings now pending, or any liabilities or penalties already incurred.[1]

33. All apparatus for linear measurements used by any land surveyor shall be tested and proved once in each year by the sealer of weights and measures in the town where such surveyor resides, or where he has his business office ; and all chains, tapes, or other implements used for linear measurements, that cannot be made to conform to the standard, shall be marked " condemned " or " C. D." by the sealer of weights and measures, and no surveyor shall thereafter use the same for measuring land, under the penalty of twenty dollars for each offence. The selectmen of any town may, if in their judgment they shall deem it expedient so to do, appoint any suitable and competent person, other than the sealer of weights and measures, to test and prove such measuring implements used by land surveyors. In all cases, the standards used for such tests shall be based upon and shall correspond to the standards furnished by the state to sealers of weights and measures. The fee for such testing and proof of such article of apparatus shall be twenty-five cents, to be paid by the person presenting the apparatus for test.[2]

34. Whenever a sale is made of goods, wares, or merchandise of any kind, and the same are weighed or measured for the purpose of such sale upon scales, measures, weights, beams, or balances not sealed according to law, or are weighed or measured by a person not a sworn weigher or

---

[1] Stats. 1877, ch. 151.        [2] Stats. 1871, ch. 330.

measurer, or by a person not a sworn weigher or measurer within the city or town where such sale is made, the seller may nevertheless recover the fair market value of such goods, wares, or merchandise : *provided*, said sale is made in good faith, and the purchaser is not injured thereby.[1]

[1] Stats. 1875, ch. 153.

## CHAPTER XLI.

### INSPECTION AND SALE OF ARTICLES.

1. THE mayor and aldermen and selectmen of each city and town where beef cattle are sold for the purpose of market or barrelling, shall appoint one or more persons, conveniently situated in such city or town, and not dealers in cattle, to be weighers of beef; who shall be sworn.

2. The fees for weighing shall be as follows: For weighing any number of cattle not exceeding five, twenty cents each; for all above five and not exceeding ten, fifteen cents each; for all above ten and not exceeding twenty, ten cents each; for all above twenty, five cents each after the first twenty; and twelve and a half cents for each certificate, which shall contain the several weights of all the cattle offered for weight by one person, unless otherwise regulated by the seller thereof; which shall be paid by the seller.

3. In all contracts for the sale and delivery of wheat, corn, rye, oats, barley, buckwheat, cracked corn, ground corn or corn meal, ground rye or rye meal, and any other meal except oatmeal, the same shall be bargained for and sold by the bushel.[1]

This statute prohibits the selling of these articles by the bag, and consequently the seller cannot receive the price unless sold by the bushel.[2]

4. The provisions relating to certain sales do not apply to sales made out of the commonwealth, although the articles sold are in the commonwealth at the time of sale.[3]

5. A bushel of wheat shall be sixty pounds; a bushel of corn or rye, fifty-six pounds; a bushel of oats, thirty-two pounds; a bushel of barley or buckwheat, forty-eight pounds; and a bushel of cracked corn, corn meal, rye

[1] Gen. Stats. ch. 49, §§ 3, 4, 63.    [3] Hardy v. Potter, 10 Gray, 89.
[2] Eaton v. Kegan, 114 Mass. 434.

meal, or any other meal except oatmeal, fifty pounds avoirdupois.

6. The mayor and aldermen of cities and selectmen of towns shall annually appoint one or more measurers of grain; and when but one is appointed by them, they may authorize him to appoint deputy-measurers. Each of such measurers and deputies shall, when called upon by either of the parties to a contract for the sale of any quantity exceeding one bushel of either of the articles mentioned in the preceding section, ascertain the weight thereof, and give a certificate of the number of bushels as ascertained by weight according to the rule therein prescribed.

7. Whoever sells or delivers any quantity exceeding one bushel of either of the articles aforesaid, without the same having been weighed by one of the public measurers appointed under the preceding section, shall forfeit the sum of two dollars for every measured bushel so delivered not containing the number of pounds herein before required, to be recovered by the purchaser in an action of tort.

8. The fees of such measurers shall be prescribed by the mayor and aldermen or the selectmen of the several places in which they are appointed, and shall be paid one-half by the seller and one-half by the purchaser.

9. If a measurer or deputy-measurer uses, or has in his possession with intent to use, for the purposes herein provided, any false weights, scales, balance, or other instrument for weighing, or colludes with the purchaser or seller with intent to defraud the other party, or makes and utters a false and fraudulent certificate under this chapter, he may be removed from office by the mayor and aldermen or selectmen, and shall also, on conviction thereof, be punished by a fine not exceeding five hundred dollars and by imprisonment not exceeding six months in the house of correction.[1]

10. In cities in which the city council and in towns in which the inhabitants shall adopt this and the three following sections, the mayor and aldermen and selectmen

[1] Gen. Stats. ch. 49, §§ 64–68.

may from time to time appoint, for a term not exceeding one year, some person or persons to have the superintendence of the hay scales belonging to their place, who shall weigh hay offered for sale therein, and any other article offered to be weighed.

11. The persons so appointed shall conform to all such rules and regulations as shall be established by the city council or selectmen respectively, concerning the hay scales, and the compensation or fees for weighing hay and other articles.

12. The mayor and aldermen or selectmen may remove any weigher of hay, and fill any vacancy that may occur from death or otherwise.[1]

13. Pressed hay offered for sale without being so branded shall be forfeited, one-half to the person or persons prosecuting therefor, and the other half to the use of the city or town where the same is so offered for sale, and may be seized and libelled.[2]

14. The mayor and aldermen and selectmen of each city and town in which bale or bundle hay is sold may, on the petition of ten or more legal voters of such city or town, annually appoint one or more persons as inspectors of bale or bundle hay, who shall be sworn; and may remove any inspector so appointed, and fill any vacancy that may occur from death or otherwise.

15. Each inspector shall inspect and weigh all bale or bundle hay within the limits of the city, town, or ward, for which he may be appointed, when requested so to do by the owner or vendor.

16. Bales or bundles of hay so inspected which are found to be sweet, of good quality, and free from damage or improper mixture, shall be branded or marked *No.* 1. Bales or bundles found to be sweet, and free from damage or improper mixture, but consisting of hay of a secondary quality, shall be branded or marked *No.* 2.

---

[1] Gen. Stats. ch. 49, §§ 72–74.
[2] This is section 77 of ch. 49, Gen. Stats. Section 76 provides for branding hay, but section 76 was repealed, Stats. 1878, ch. 146.

Bales or bundles found to be wet, or in any way damaged, or which shall contain straw or other substances not valuable as hay, shall be branded or marked *bad*. Each bale or bundle so inspected shall be branded or marked with the first letter of the christian name and the whole of the surname of the inspector, and the name of the place for which he is inspector, together with the month and year when inspected, and also the net weight of the bundle.

17. Each inspector shall furnish himself with proper scales, weights, seals, and other suitable instruments, for the purposes aforesaid.

18. The fees for inspecting, weighing, and marking hay, as provided for in this chapter, shall be fixed by the respective officers having the power of appointment, and shall be paid by the employer of the inspector.

19. Whoever sells bale or bundle hay in a place where an inspector is appointed, which has not been inspected and weighed as herein provided, shall forfeit for each bale or bundle so sold two dollars; but no inspection need be made where the vendor and vendee agree to waive an inspection.[1]

20. The provisions relating to the inspection, weighing, branding, and sale of pressed or bundled hay shall also apply to pressed or bundled straw.[2]

21. In every maritime place from which staves are usually exported, there shall be annually chosen two or more suitable persons to be viewers and cullers of staves and hoops, who shall be sworn.

22. White oak butt staves shall be at least five feet in length, five inches wide, and one inch and a quarter thick on the heart or thinnest edge and every part thereof; white oak pipe staves shall be at least four feet and eight inches in length, four inches broad in the narrowest part, and not less than three-quarters of an inch thick on the heart or thinnest edge; white oak and red oak hogshead staves shall be at least forty-two inches long, and not less than half an inch thick on the heart or thinnest edge;

---

[1] Gen. Stats. ch. 49, §§ 77–83.        [2] Stats. 1861, ch. 67.

white oak and red oak barrel staves for foreign market shall be thirty-two inches long, and for home use thirty inches long, and shall average half an inch thick on the heart or thinnest edge ; white oak and red oak hogshead and barrel staves shall be at least four inches in breadth, and none less than three inches in breadth in the narrowest part, and those of the breadth last mentioned shall be clear of sap ; and all staves shall be well and proportionably split.[1]

23. Hogshead hoops that are exposed to sale or exported shall be from ten to fourteen feet in length, of white oak or walnut, of good and sufficient substance, and well shaved, and shall not be less than one inch broad at the least end ; each bundle shall consist of twenty-five hoops, and all hoops of ten, twelve, and fourteen feet respectively shall be made up in distinct bundles by themselves.  If hoops of less dimensions than those prescribed by law are packed, or if a bundle contains less than twenty-five hoops, the bundle shall be forfeited, and may be seized by the culler of hoops and libelled for the benefit of the place where it is offered for sale.[2]

24. Cullers shall be allowed for their time and services, fifty cents a thousand for hoops, twenty-eight cents a thousand for barrel staves, thirty-three cents a thousand for hogshead staves, forty cents a thousand for pipe staves, and forty-four cents a thousand for butt staves, as well refuse as merchantable ; the merchantable to be paid for by the buyer, the refuse by the seller.

25. If a culler connives at or is guilty of fraud in culling staves or hoops, he shall forfeit fifty dollars for each offence ; and if he refuses to perform service when requested shall forfeit five dollars.[3]

26. Each city and town in which lime is manufactured, or into which it is imported, may annually choose one or more inspectors of lime, who shall be sworn, and shall inspect all lime manufactured in such place at the time when it is filled at the kiln, and all lime imported or sold therein.

[1] Gen. Stats. ch. 49, §§ 84–85.    [3] Gen. Stats. ch. 49, §§ 86–88.
[2] Stats. 1878, ch. 116.

27. Every cask of lime so inspected shall be branded with the word *inspected*, with the first letter of the christian name and the whole of the surname of the inspector, and with the name of the place where it is manufactured.

28. The inspectors shall receive, for the inspection and branding of each cask of such manufactured lime, four cents, to be paid by the manufacturer or owner; and for the inspection of each cask of lime so imported or sold, the same sum, to be paid by the purchaser.

29. No stone lime manufactured within this state shall be sold or exposed to sale, or shipped on board of a vessel, in casks, unless it is well burnt and pure, in good and sufficient new casks, containing either fifty or one hundred gallons each, made of well-seasoned heads and staves, with ten good and sufficient hoops on each cask, well driven and sufficiently secured with nails or pins.[1]

30. When an inspection is demanded of lime manufactured in and imported from the state of Maine, the inspector shall require that such lime be in casks manufactured from sound and well seasoned lumber, with staves and headings well fixed on the inside, with at least eight good and strong hoops on each; all of which hoops shall be of oak, ash, beech, birch, maple, cherry, or elm wood, well driven and secured with nails; the staves of said casks to be made of sawed or rift timber, not less than thirty inches in length, and half an inch thick on the thinnest edge; each of the heads to be not less than three-fourths of an inch thick, and well crozed in; each hoop to be not less than one inch wide in the narrowest part, and each cask to be not less than twenty-six inches in length between the heads, sixteen inches in width between the chimes, and eighteen inches in the clear on the inside at the bilge, and made in a workmanlike manner; and the same rules, regulations, restrictions, and liabilities shall apply to lime imported from the state of Maine as are provided respecting lime manufactured in this state.[2]

---

[1] Gen. Stats. ch. 49, §§ 118–121.    [2] Stats. 1878, ch. 71.

31. Whoever sells, exposes to sale, ships, or receives on board of a vessel, in casks, any lime manufactured within this state, or the state of Maine, other than such as is contained in casks made according to the provisions of the preceding sections, and having the aforesaid marks or brands respectively, shall forfeit one dollar and fifty cents for each cask sold, offered for sale, shipped, or received on board of a vessel : *provided*, that nothing contained in this chapter shall be construed to restrain any person from retailing lime by the bushel, or other quantities not in casks.

32. If a cask of lime is sold, or exposed to sale, or put on board of a vessel, contrary to the provisions of this chapter, the same shall be forfeited, and an inspector may seize and libel the same.

33. If, after a cask containing lime has been branded as aforesaid, any person shifts the contents of such cask and puts therein other lime with intent to sell the same, he shall forfeit one dollar and fifty cents for each cask of lime so shifted.[1]

34. The mayor and aldermen or selectmen of any place, when thereto requested by two or more citizens thereof, shall annually in April appoint one or more persons as measurers of upper leather, who shall be sworn.[2]

35. Each measurer who is appointed a measurer of upper leather for one place in a county may, upon application made to him, measure and seal leather in any other place of the same county, when there is no measurer in such other place ; and he shall, upon the like application, measure and seal leather in any place of an adjoining county, when there is no measurer appointed in such adjoining county.[3]

36. Each measurer shall furnish himself with proper racks or measures, and suitable seals ; shall, when requested, go to any place within the city or town for which he is appointed measurer, and there ascertain the number of square feet in each side of upper leather made of the

---

[1] Gen. Stats. ch. 49, §§ 123–125.    [3] Stats. 1866, ch. 236, § 2.
[2] Gen. Stats. ch. 49, § 112.

hides of neat cattle, buffalo, or other animal, usually heretofore sold by measure, except such as shall have been
previously measured and sealed by a measurer of some
place in this state, or by some person lawfully appointed
for that purpose in another of the United States; and
shall seal the same, impressing thereon his name and
the name of the place for which he is a measurer, at
full length, and the measure thereof in square feet, as low
as a quarter.[1]  " No such upper leather, except what has
been previously measured and sealed by one of the measurers of this state, or by some measurer lawfully appointed
for that purpose in some other of the United States, shall
be sold for any purpose whatsoever, until it has been
measured and sealed ; and whoever sells such upper leather
not measured and sealed as aforesaid, shall forfeit one
dollar for each side of leather so sold ; and such forfeiture
may, in addition to the methods now provided, be recovered by an action at law in favor of any person injured by
the sale of such leather not so measured and sealed." [2]

37. Every measurer shall be paid for measuring and
sealing each side of upper leather the sum of one cent,
which shall be paid by the person who requests him to
measure and seal the same.

38. Whoever counterfeits, wilfully alters, or defaces
such marks on any side of upper leather so measured, shall
for each offence forfeit the sum of twenty-five dollars.[3]

39. The buyer and manufacturer of leather may, by
agreement, waive inspection, measurement, and sealing of
leather as provided in this act (section thirty-five and part
of thirty-six above).[4]

40. The mayor and aldermen and selectmen of a city
or town may establish such regulations, with suitable
penalties, respecting the appointment of a surveyor, and
the survey and admeasurement of marble of every description (soapstone and free stone),[5] foreign or American, that

---

[1] Gen. Stats. ch. 49, § 113.
[2] Stats. 1866, ch. 236, § 3.
[3] Gen. Stats. ch. 49, §§ 114, 115.
[4] Stats. 1866, ch. 236, § 1.
[5] Stats. 1862, ch. 70.

is imported or brought into such place for sale, as they from time to time deem expedient.[1]

41. The mayor and aldermen of cities shall, and the selectmen of towns may, annually appoint one or more persons to be inspectors of milk for their respective places, who shall, before entering upon the duties of their offices, be sworn. Each inspector shall give notice of his appointment by publishing the same two weeks in a newspaper published in his city or town ; or, if no newspaper is published therein, by posting up such notice in two or more public places in such city or town.

42. The inspectors shall keep an office and books for the purpose of recording the names and places of business of all persons engaged in the sale of milk within their limits. They may enter any place where milk is stored or kept for sale, and all carriages used in the conveyance of milk ; and whenever they have reason to believe any milk found therein is adulterated, they shall take specimens thereof and cause the same to be analyzed, or otherwise satisfactorily tested, the result of which they shall record and preserve as evidence ; and a certificate of such result, sworn to by the analyzer, shall be admissible in evidence in all prosecutions under this act. The inspectors shall receive such compensation as the mayor and aldermen or selectmen shall determine. All measures, cans, or other vessels used in the sale, or buying at wholesale, of milk, shall be annually sealed by the sealer of weights and measures, by wine measure ; and all cans so used shall be marked by the sealer with figures showing the quantity which they hold. (All acts and parts of acts which require the sealing of cans in which milk is transported or sold are hereby repealed.)

43. Whoever neglects to cause his name and place of business to be recorded in the inspector's books, and his name legibly placed upon all carriages used by him in the conveyance of milk, before engaging in the sale thereof, shall forfeit twenty dollars for the first offence, and for a second and each subsequent offence, fifty dollars. And

---

[1] Gen. Stats. ch. 49, § 145.          [2] Stats. 1867, ch. 204.

whoever offers for sale milk produced from cows fed upon the refuse of distilleries, or any substance deleterious to the quality of the milk, or whoever knowingly offers for sale milk produced from sick or diseased cows, shall forfeit twenty-five dollars for the first, and fifty dollars for every subsequent, offence. Whoever sells, or keeps, or offers for sale, adulterated milk, or milk to which water or any foreign substance has been added, shall for the first offence be punished by a fine of twenty dollars, and for a second offence by a fine of fifty dollars; and for any subsequent violation he shall be imprisoned in the house of correction not less than thirty, nor more than ninety days; and whoever, in the employment of another, knowingly violates any provision of this section, shall be held equally guilty with the principal, and suffer the same penalty.

Any person who shall sell, or shall offer for sale, any milk, knowing that the cream or any part thereof has been removed therefrom, or who shall with such knowledge deliver any such milk to any person to be made into butter or cheese, without giving notice at the time to the person to whom such milk is sold, offered for sale, or delivered, that such cream has been removed, shall be punished by a fine of not less than twenty dollars nor more than one hundred dollars.[1]

44. It shall be the duty of the inspector to cause the name and place of business of all persons convicted under the preceding section, to be published in two newspapers printed in the town or county where the offence may have been committed.[2]

45. Whoever sells or exchanges, or has in his possession with intent to sell or exchange, or offers for sale or exchange, adulterated milk, or milk to which water or any foreign substance has been added, shall, for each offence, be punished by a fine of not less than twenty no more than one hundred dollars.

46. Whoever adulterates, by water or otherwise, milk to

---

[1] Stats. 1870, ch. 311.      [2] Stats. 1864, ch. 122.

be delivered for manufacture into butter or cheese, shall be liable to the penalties provided in the preceding section.

47. It shall be the duty of every inspector of milk to institute complaint, on the information of any person who shall lay before him satisfactory evidence on which to sustain the same.

48. Each inspector of milk in this commonwealth is hereby required to cause the provisions of this act to be published in his town, at least three times, by publication in some newspaper printed in said town, or some newspaper in the county in which the town is situated.[1]

49. Cord wood exposed for sale shall be either four, three, or two feet long, including half the kerf; and the wood, being well and close laid together, shall measure in quantity equal to a cord of eight feet in length, four in width, and four in height.

50. If any fire wood or bark exposed to sale in a market, or upon a cart or other vehicle, is offered for sale before the same has been measured by a public measurer of wood and bark, and a ticket thereof signed by him delivered to the driver, certifying the quantity which the load contains, the name of the driver, and the place in which he resides, the driver and owner shall, for each load thereof, severally forfeit the sum of five dollars.[2]

This section does not apply to a sale of bark on the owner's land in the country.[3]

51. The measurers of wood and bark in any place shall be entitled to such fees for their services as the mayor and aldermen or selectmen shall establish ; and the fees shall in each case be paid to the measurer by the driver, and shall be repaid by the purchaser.

52. Cord wood brought by water into a place for sale, and landed, shall be measured by a public measurer ; and for that purpose the wood shall be corded and piled by itself in ranges, making up in height what shall be wanting

[1] Stats. 1869, ch. 150.
[2] Gen. Stats. ch. 49, §§ 181, 182.
[3] Huntington *v.* Knox, 7 Cush. 371.

in length, and being so measured, a ticket shall be given to the purchaser, who shall pay the stated fees for such service. But cities and towns may establish ordinances and regulations, with suitable penalties, for the inspection, survey, admeasurement, and sale of wood, coal, and bark for fuel, brought into such places for sale, and may also provide for the appointment of such surveyors, inspectors, and other officers, and establish their fees of office.

53. Each wharfinger, carter, or driver, who conveys any firewood or bark from a wharf or landing-place, shall be furnished by the owner or seller with a ticket certifying the quantity which the load contains and the name of the driver; and if firewood or bark is thus conveyed without such ticket accompanying the same, or if a driver refuses to produce and show such ticket on demand to any sworn measurer, or to give his consent to have the same measured, or if such ticket certifies a greater quantity of wood or bark than the load contains, in the opinion of the measurer after measuring the same, the driver and owner shall for each load thereof forfeit the sum of five dollars. But nothing contained in this chapter shall be construed to extend to a person who transports, carts, or causes to be transported or carted, from a wharf or landing-place to his own dwelling-house or store, cord wood or bark which he has purchased on a wharf or landing-place, or has landed thereon upon his own account.

54. The city council of a city may establish ordinances and regulations, with suitable penalties, for the inspection, survey, admeasurement, and sale of bark for fuel or manufacturing purposes brought into said city for sale, whether the same is exposed for sale in ranges or upon a cart or other vehicle; and said city may provide for the appointment of such surveyors, inspectors, and other officers, as may be necessary to carry into effect said ordinances, and may establish their fees: *provided*, that no penalty for any one violation shall exceed the sum of five dollars.[1]

55. All anthracite, bituminous, or mineral coal shall

[1] Gen. Stats. ch. 49, §§ 183–186.

hereafter be sold by weight, and, except when sold by the cargo, two thousand pounds avoirdupois shall be the standard for the ton by which the same shall be weighed and sold.

56. The mayor and aldermen or selectmen of every place where such coal is sold shall appoint suitable persons, one or more of whom shall not be engaged in the business of selling coal, to be weighers of coal, who shall be sworn, and be removable at the pleasure of the board appointing them, and all coal shall be weighed by such sworn weighers.

57. On or before the delivery of any such coal to a purchaser, the seller shall cause the same to be weighed by a sworn weigher of the place in which the same is sold or delivered, who shall keep a record thereof for the use of both parties, and a certificate of the weight thereof, signed by such weigher, when so requested, shall be delivered to the purchaser or his agent at the time of the delivery of the coal.

58. When the purchaser of coal, in quantities of five hundred pounds or more, shall so request before the delivery thereof, the seller shall cause the same to be weighed by a sworn weigher, not the seller nor in his employ, and not engaged in the business of selling coal, and a certificate of the weight thereof shall be delivered, signed by such weigher, to the purchaser or his agent, at the time of the delivery of the coal. The fees for such weighing to be paid by the purchaser.

59. Any fraud or deceit in the weight of coal, on the part of the seller or those employed by him to sell, weigh, or deliver the same, shall be punishable by a fine of not less than twenty-five dollars, and not more than seventy-five dollars for each offence.

60. Whoever violates any of the provisions of the first, second, third, and fourth sections of this act (sections fifty-five to fifty-eight inclusive), shall be punished by a fine of not less than twenty-five dollars, and not more than seventy-five dollars for each offence.[1]

[1] Stats. 1870, ch. 205.

61. In the sale of charcoal, the baskets, tubs, or vessels used in measuring the same, except as hereinafter provided, shall be of a cylindrical form and of the following dimensions in the inside thereof, to wit: nineteen inches in diameter in every part and eighteen inches and one-tenth of an inch in depth, measured from the highest part of the bottom thereof; each of which shall be deemed to be of the capacity of two bushels, and shall be filled level full; and every such vessel shall be sealed by a sealer of the place in which the person using the same shall usually reside or do business.

62. Charcoal may be measured in boxes, bins, or cans, of the following capacities, to wit: of five, ten, twenty, thirty, forty, or fifty bushels, such boxes, bins, or cans being first lawfully sealed as aforesaid; and five thousand one hundred and thirty-two cubic inches shall be deemed equal to two bushels, or the level basket, tub, or vessel described in the preceding section.

63. Every vendor of charcoal, who has in his possession any basket, tub, box, bin, vessel, or measure of less dimensions than those required by the two preceding sections, or not sealed as therein provided, with intent to use the same or permit the same to be used for measuring charcoal, sold or agreed to be sold, shall forfeit ten dollars for every such measure in his possession. And every person who measures, in any such basket, vessel, or measure, any charcoal sold or offered for sale, unless by special agreement of the buyer and seller, shall forfeit a sum not exceeding one dollar for every two bushels so measured or pretended to be measured, and such basket, vessel, or measure shall be destroyed.

64. The mayor and aldermen or selectmen of every place shall appoint one or more suitable persons to seize all baskets, vessels, or measures used or intended to be used for measuring charcoal, and not conforming to the foregoing provisions; and to arrest without warrant any person having in his possession such baskets, vessels, or measures, and take him and them before the proper tribunal for pros-

ecution; and upon his being convicted or found guilty, such tribunal shall order said baskets, vessels, and measures to be destroyed.[1]

65. Surveyors of lumber in cities and towns, when requested so to do by either the purchaser or seller, shall survey oak and other hard wood commonly used in shipbuilding, mahogany, ash, and other ornamental wood, and all other lumber brought for sale into, or manufactured in, this state. But no surveyor shall survey lumber in which he has a pecuniary interest.

66. Of pine boards and planks, except southern pine, there shall be six sorts. The first sort shall be denominated number one, and include boards not less than one inch thick, square edged, free from rot, shakes, and nearly free from knots and sap, except such boards and planks as are not less than fifteen inches wide and not more than one-eighth waste, which shall be received as number one. The second sort shall be denominated number two, and include boards not less than one inch thick, and of which not less than seven-eighths is suitable for planing and first-class finish : *provided*, that such boards as are clear but deficient in thickness as aforesaid shall be received as number two. The third sort shall be denominated number three, and include boards not less than seven-eighths of an inch thick, and of which not less than three-fourths is suitable for planing and second-class finish. The fourth sort shall be denominated number four, and include boards not less than seven-eighths of an inch thick, nearly free from rot and nearly square edged, free from loose and large branch knots, and suitable for covering buildings; all Norway pine boards and planks shall be included in the fourth, fifth, and sixth sorts. The fifth sort shall be denominated number five, and include all boards and planks of every description not being within the other four denominations, except when one-third is worthless, which boards and planks shall be denominated refuse.

67. Of pine joists and dimension timber there shall be

[1] Gen. Stats. ch. 49, §§ 191–194.

three sorts. The first sort shall be denominated number one, and include all joists and dimension timber that are sound and nearly square edged. The second sort shall be denominated number two, and include all other descriptions, except when one-third is worthless, which joists and dimension timber shall be denominated refuse.

68. Of spruce, hemlock, juniper, and southern pine boards, planks, sawed timber, and joists, there shall be three sorts. The first sort shall be denominated number one, and include all boards, planks, sawed timber, and joists, that are sound and nearly square edged. The second sort shall be denominated number two, and include all other descriptions, except when one-third is worthless, which boards, planks, sawed timber, and joists shall be denominated refuse.

69. Of ash, maple, and other hard wood and ornamental boards, planks, and joists, there shall be three sorts. The first sort shall be denominated number one, and include all boards, planks, and joists that are free from rot, shakes, and bad knots. The second sort shall be denominated number two, and include all other descriptions, except when one-third is worthless, which boards, planks, and joists shall be denominated refuse.

70. Of hewn timber, except mahogany and cedar, there shall be three sorts. The first sort shall be denominated number one, and include all timber that is sound and nearly square edged. The second sort shall be denominated number two, and include timber of all other descriptions, except [when] one-third is worthless, which timber shall be denominated refuse.

71. Of oak, juniper, and spruce knees, there shall be two sorts. The first sort shall be denominated number one, and include all sound knees of the following dimensions : arm or root one foot six inches long, body of knee three feet long, working thickness four inches ; arm or root two feet and six inches long, body of knee three feet long, working thickness five inches ; arm or root two feet and nine inches long, body of knee three feet and six

inches long, working thickness six inches ; arm or root three feet and three inches long, body of knee four feet and six inches long, working thickness seven inches ; arm or root three feet and six inches long, body of knee four feet and three inches long, working thickness eight inches ; arm or root three feet and nine inches long, body of knee four feet and six inches long, working thickness nine inches ; arm or root four feet long, body of knee five feet long, working thickness ten inches and upwards. The second sort shall be denominated refuse, and shall include all other descriptions of less dimensions than those specified in the first denomination ; all knees shall have the working thickness marked thereon, and on the first sort, the number " *one* " shall be marked.

72. Of mahogany and cedar there shall be but one sort, and it shall be the duty of the surveyors who are especially appointed to survey mahogany and cedar, to number all the mahogany and cedar logs or sticks contained in each lot or cargo in regular numerical order, and to mark the number of each log or stick upon the same in legible characters. And the said surveyor shall, to the best of his ability, ascertain the whole number of feet, board measure, in each and every log or stick, and what quantity thereof is merchantable, and what is refuse. And said surveyor shall thereupon issue a certificate or survey bill of said survey, in which shall be stated the number of each log or stick, and the whole number of feet contained in the same, and specifying the number of feet which is merchantable and refuse, respectively.

73. Hewn timber, and round timber, used for masts and ship-building, shall be surveyed and sold as ton timber, at the rate of forty cubic feet to the ton ; oak and other timber and planks commonly used in ship-building shall have the true contents marked thereon in cubic feet or board measure, and in the first and second sorts, the numbers " *one*" and " *two* " shall be marked thereon respectively. In the survey of white and Norway pine boards, planks, joists, sawed timber, and dimensions, the contents of the

same shall be truly marked thereon in legible numbers, and on the first, second, third, fourth, and fifth sort of white and Norway pine boards, planks, and dimensions, the numbers shall be marked respectively. All boards, planks, joists, sawed timber, and dimension lumber shall be received and sold according to the contents thereof, as fixed and marked under the aforesaid regulations. In the admeasurement of round timber, one-fourth of the girth shall be taken for the side of the square.

74. The fees for surveying and marking shall be paid by the purchaser, as follows: for white, southern, and Norway pine, spruce, hemlock, juniper, and white wood boards, planks, joists, sawed timber, and dimension, (thirty) [1] cents for every thousand feet board measure; for southern pine flooring-boards, thirty-four cents for every thousand feet board measure; for all kinds of pine, spruce, hemlock, and juniper timber, twelve cents for every ton; for oak and other hard wood, twenty-four cents for every ton; for knees commonly used in ship-building, three cents for each knee; for ash, maple, and other hard wood and ornamental boards, planks, and joists, forty cents for every thousand feet board measure; for Cuba, Saint Domingo, and other branch or hard mahogany, one dollar for every thousand feet board measure; and for mahogany from the bay of Honduras, and for cedar, seventy-five cents for every thousand feet board measure.

75. If a surveyor is guilty of or connives at any fraud or deceit in the surveying, numbering, or marking the contents of any kind of wood or lumber required by this chapter to be surveyed; or if a surveyor, when requested by the owner of lumber to survey the same, refuses, without good reason, to perform the duty, he shall forfeit for each offence a sum not less than ten nor more than fifty dollars.

76. Whoever sells or purchases any lumber or wood herein named, brought into this state for sale, which has not been surveyed, numbered, and marked according to

[1] Stats. 1865, ch. 115, § 1.

the provisions hereof, shall forfeit a sum equal to double the amount of fees for surveying the same.

This does not apply to a sale made out of the state, though the lumber is in the state.[1]

77. Whoever presumes to perform any of the duties of surveyor of lumber, without authority, shall forfeit not less than fifty nor more than two hundred dollars.[2]

78. The mayor and aldermen of cities and the select-men of towns may annually appoint one or more persons to be inspectors of provisions and animals intended for slaughter, who shall be sworn to faithfully discharge the duties of their office, and who shall receive such compensation as the city council of cities or the selectmen of towns shall determine.

79. Said inspectors shall have power to inspect all animals intended for slaughter, and all meats, fish, vegetables, produce, fruits, and provisions of all kinds found in said cities or towns, or exposed for sale or kept with intent to sell therein; and may for this purpose enter into all buildings or enclosures where said animals, meats, fish, vegetables, produce, fruits, or provisions are kept, stored, or exposed for slaughter or sale. When such animals, meat, fish, vegetables, produce, fruit, or provisions are found on such inspection to be tainted, diseased, corrupted, decayed, or unwholesome from any cause, said inspectors shall seize the same, and cause them or it to destroyed or disposed of otherwise than for food : *provided, however*, that if the owner of the property seized shall, at the time of the seizure, notify said inspector in writing of his desire to appeal to the board of health, said inspector shall cause said animals, meat, fish, vegetables, produce, fruit, or provisions to be inspected by said board of health, or by a committee thereof consisting of not less than two members, and if said board or committee shall find the same to be tainted, diseased, corrupted, or unwholesome, they shall order the same to be destroyed or disposed of otherwise than for food; if said board or

committee shall not so find, they shall order said animals, meat, fish, vegetables, produce, fruit, or provisions to be forthwith returned to the owner thereof. All moneys received by said inspector or board of health, for property disposed of as aforesaid, shall, after deducting all expenses incurred by reason of such seizure, be paid to the owner thereof.

80. Said inspectors shall have the power to inspect all veal found in said cities or towns, or offered or exposed for sale or kept with intent to sell therein, and if said veal is, in the judgment of the inspector, that of a calf killed under four weeks old, he shall seize the same and cause it to be destroyed or disposed of as provided in the preceding section, subject, however, to the same provisions concerning appeal and the disposal of moneys that are therein contained.

81. When complaint is made on oath to any police, municipal, or district court or magistrate authorized to issue warrants in criminal cases, that the complainant believes that any diseased animals, or any tainted, diseased, corrupted, decayed, or unwholesome meat, fish, vegetables, produce, fruit, or provisions of any kind, or veal of any calf killed under four weeks old, is kept or concealed in any particular house or place with the intent to kill, sell, or offer the same for sale for food, the court or magistrate, if satisfied there is reasonable cause for such belief, shall issue a warrant to search for such animals or articles, and all such warrants shall be directed and executed as provided in the third section of chapter one hundred and seventy of the General Statutes. If, upon hearing, said court or magistrate shall determine that said animals or articles, or any of them, were kept or concealed for the purposes aforesaid, the same shall be destroyed or disposed of by the inspector, or by any officer designated by the court or magistrate, according to the provisions of the second section of this act (section seventy-nine) ; if the court or magistrate shall not so determine, said animals or articles shall be returned to the owner.

82. Whoever knowingly sells, or offers or exposes for sale, or has in his possession with intent to sell for food any diseased animal, or any tainted, diseased, corrupted, decayed, or unwholesome meat, fish, vegetables, produce, fruit, or provisions of any kind whatever, shall be punished by imprisonment in jail not exceeding sixty days, or by fine not exceeding one hundred dollars.

83. The place where property condemned under this act (sections seventy-eight to eighty-four inclusive) shall be found, and the name of every person in whose possession it may be found and condemned, or who shall be convicted of an offence under section five (eighty-two) of this act, shall be published in two newspapers published in the county.

84. The foregoing sections of this act (sections seventy-eight to eighty-three inclusive) shall not be in force in any city or town unless this act shall be adopted by the city council of such city or by the inhabitants of such town.[1]

[1] Stats. 1876, ch. 180.

# CHAPTER XLII.

## CERTAIN LICENSES GRANTED BY SELECTMEN.

1. Licenses to innholders and victuallers in towns are granted **by** the county commissioners.

The clerk of the county commissioners shall seasonably, before the time for granting licenses in each year, transmit to the selectmen of every town within the jurisdiction of such commissioners, a list of the persons in such town who were licensed as innholders or victuallers the preceding year.

2. No such license shall be granted or renewed to any person by the county commissioners unless he produces a certificate from the selectmen of the town for which he applies to be licensed, in substance as follows, to wit : —

We, the subscribers, a majority of the selectmen of the town of ＿, do hereby certify that ＿ has applied to us to be recommended as (here expressing the employment and a particular description of the place for which the license is applied for) in said town, and that, after mature consideration had thereon at a meeting held for that purpose, at which we were each of us present, we are of opinion that the public good requires that the petition of said ＿ be granted, he being to the best of our knowledge and belief a person of good moral character.

3. Whoever produces such certificate shall be heard, and his application decided upon, either on a motion made orally by himself, or his counsel, or upon a petition in writing, as he elects.

4. If the selectmen of any town unreasonably neglect or refuse to make and deliver such a certificate, either for the original granting or the renewal of a license, the person aggrieved thereby may apply for a license to the commissioners, first giving twenty-four hours' notice to a majority of said selectmen of his intended application, so that if they see fit they may appear and object thereto ;

and if on such application it appears that the selectmen did unreasonably neglect or refuse to give such certificate, and that the public good requires that the license be granted, the commissioners may grant the same.[1]

5. No innholder, tavern-keeper, retailer, confectioner, or keeper of any shop or house for the sale of drink or food, or any livery-stable keeper for horse or carriage hire, shall give credit to any student in an incorporated academy or other educational institution within this state.

6. No person shall be approved or licensed for either of the employments aforesaid, if it appears that he has given credit contrary to the provisions of the preceding section.[2]

7. Every innholder shall at all times be furnished with suitable provisions for the supply of food for strangers and travellers, and shall also have upon his premises suitable rooms, with beds and bedding, for lodging strangers and travellers. He shall also be furnished with stable-room, hay, and provender for the horses and cattle of his guests, whenever the authorities issuing the license shall so require.

8. Every common victualler shall be at all times furnished with suitable provisions for the supply of food for strangers and travellers.

9. No innholder's license shall be granted or issued to any person unless at the time of making application for the same he shall have upon his premises the necessary implements and facilities for cooking, preparing, and serving food for the purposes specified in section one (seven) of this act, and with the rooms, beds, and bedding specified in said section; nor unless he shall have the stable-room and provender for horses and cattle required by said section.

10. No common victualler's license shall be granted or issued to any person, unless, at the time of making application for the same, he shall have upon his premises the necessary implements and facilities for cooking, preparing, and serving food for strangers and travellers.

[1] Gen. Stats. ch. 88, §§ 4–7.    [2] Gen. Stats. ch. 88, §§ 18, 19.

11. If an innholder, when requested, refuses to receive and make suitable provisions for a stranger or traveller, and also for his horses and cattle, when he may under the provisions of this act be legally required so to do, he shall upon conviction be punished by a fine not exceeding fifty dollars ; and any person so convicted shall, in addition to said penalty, forfeit his license. '

12. If a common victualler, when requested, upon any other than the Lord's day, refuses to supply food to a stranger or traveller, he shall upon conviction be punished by a fine not exceeding fifty dollars ; and any person so convicted shall, in addition to said penalty, forfeit his license.

13. Whenever in the opinion of the mayor and aldermen of any city or the selectmen of any town, any person holding a license as an innholder or a common victualler ceases to be engaged in the business he is licensed to pursue, or fails to maintain upon his premises the implements and facilities required by this act, they shall immediately revoke the same.

14. No innholder's or victualler's license shall be issued until it has been signed by the mayor and a majority of the aldermen of the city, or by a majority of the selectmen of the town, in which it is granted. Any mayor, alderman, or selectman may refuse to sign any license granted to a person who in his opinion has not complied with the provisions of this act, and any such officer who shall sign any license granted contrary to the provisions of this act shall upon conviction be punished with a fine not exceeding fifty dollars.

15. All licenses issued under the provisions of this act (eight preceding sections) shall expire on the first day of April of each year. Licenses may be granted during the preceding month of March, to take effect upon said first day of April, and after that day may be granted at any time for the remainder of the year, when the officers authorized to issue the same deem it expedient.[1]

[1] Stats. 1878, ch. 241, §§ 1-9.

16. Whoever, without a license therefor, establishes or keeps an intelligence office for the purpose of obtaining or giving information concerning places of employment for domestics, servants, or other laborers, except seamen, or for the purpose of procuring or giving information concerning such persons for or to employers (or for the purpose of procuring or giving information concerning employment in business),[1] shall pay a fine of ten dollars for each day such office is so kept.

17. The mayor and aldermen or selectmen of any city or town may, for the purposes mentioned in the preceding section, grant licenses to suitable persons for the term of one year, and may revoke the same at pleasure. They shall receive one dollar for each license so granted.[2]

18. The mayor and aldermen or selectmen of any city or town which has adopted by-laws therefor, may license suitable persons to be dealers in and keepers of shops for the purchase, sale, or barter of junk, old metals, or second-hand articles, within their respective cities and towns.

19. The license shall designate the place where the business is to be carried on, and contain such conditions and restrictions as may be prescribed by such by-laws, and shall continue in force for one year unless sooner revoked.

20. Whoever not so licensed keeps a shop or is a dealer in such city or town, or being licensed keeps such shop, or is such dealer, in any other place or manner than that designated in his license, or after notice to him that his license has been revoked, shall pay a fine of twenty dollars for each offence.[3]

21. Every city and town may provide, by ordinance or by-law, that every keeper of a shop for the purchase, sale, or barter of junk. old metals, or second-hand articles, within their respective limits, shall keep a book, in which shall be written, at the time of every purchase of any such article, a description of the article or articles purchased, the name, age, and residence of the person from whom, and

[1] Stats. 1872, ch. 237.
[2] Gen. Stats. ch. 88, §§ 23, 24.
[3] Gen. Stats. ch. 88, §§ 25-27.

the day and hour when, such purchase was made; that such book shall at all times be open to the inspection of the mayor and aldermen of the city or the selectmen of the town in which such shop is located, and to any person by them respectively authorized to make such inspection; that every keeper of such shop shall put in some suitable and conspicuous place on his shop, a sign, having his name and occupation legibly inscribed thereon in large letters; that such shops and all articles of merchandise therein may be examined by the mayor and aldermen of any city, or the selectmen of any town, or by any person by them respectively authorized to make such examination, at all times; and that no keeper of such shop shall, directly or indirectly, either purchase, or receive by way of barter or exchange, any of the articles aforesaid, of any minor or apprentice, knowing or having reason to believe him to be such; and that no article purchased or received shall be sold until a period of at least one week from the date of its purchase or receipt shall have elapsed. Every city and town may also prescribe in like manner the hours in which such shops shall be closed, and that no keeper thereof shall make purchase of any of the articles aforesaid during such hours.

22. Every rule, regulation, and restriction which shall be made by any city or town in accordance with the provisions of this act (preceding section), in regard to the keeping of, and traffic in, the articles aforesaid, shall be incorporated in every license granted in such city or town for dealing in the said articles.

23. Any person who shall violate either of the rules, regulations, or restrictions contained in his license, as aforesaid, shall forfeit a sum not exceeding twenty dollars for each offence.[1]

24. The mayor and aldermen or selectmen of any city or town, which has adopted by-laws therefor, may license suitable persons to carry on the business of pawnbrokers within their respective cities and towns.

[1] Stats. 1862, ch. 205.

25. The license shall designate the place where the business is to be carried on, contain such conditions and restrictions as may be prescribed by such by-laws, and continue in force one year unless sooner revoked.

Licenses granted to keepers of intelligence offices, dealers in junk, old metals, and second-hand articles, pawnbrokers and keepers of billiard-saloons and bowling-alleys, under chapter eighty-eight of the General Statutes, shall be signed by the clerk of the city or town in which they are granted, and every such license shall be recorded by such clerk in a book kept for that purpose before being delivered to the licensee; such license shall set forth the name of the person licensed, the nature of the business, and the building or place in such city or town in which it is to be carried on, and shall continue in force until the first day of May next ensuing, unless sooner revoked, as provided in said chapter. The clerk issuing any such license shall be entitled to receive for the use of the city or town for each license the sum of two dollars.

Such licenses may be granted at any time during the month of April, to take effect on the first day of May then next ensuing, and after the first day of May they may be granted for the remainder of the year ending on the first day of the following May.

No license issued as aforesaid shall be valid to protect the licensee in any building or place other than that designated in the license, unless consent to removal be granted by the mayor and aldermen or selectmen.

Whenever any such license shall be revoked the clerk of such city or town shall note such revocation upon the face of the record of such license, and shall give written notice of such revocation to the holder of the license, said notice to be delivered to him in person or left at the place of business designated in the license.

So much of chapter eighty-eight of the General Statutes as is inconsistent herewith is hereby repealed.[1]

26. Whoever not being licensed carries on such business or is concerned therein within such city or town, or being licensed carries on such business or is concerned therein in any other place or manner than that designated in his license, or after notice to him that his license is revoked, shall pay a fine not exceeding fifty dollars for each offence.[2]

27. Whoever occupies or uses a building in any maritime place for a livery stable, except in such part thereof

---

[1] Stats. 1876, ch. 147.  [2] Gen. Stats. ch. 88, §§ 28–30.

as the mayor and aldermen or selectmen shall direct, shall forfeit a sum not exceeding fifty dollars for every month he so occupies or uses such building, and in like proportion for a longer or shorter time.

28. Whoever erects, occupies, or uses a building for a stable for more than four horses, in any city or town, except in such part thereof as the mayor and aldermen or selectmen direct, shall forfeit a sum not exceeding fifty dollars for every month he so occupies or uses such building, and in like proportion for a longer or shorter time. And the supreme judicial court, or any one of the justices thereof, either in term time or vacation, may issue an injunction to prevent such erection, occupancy, or use, without such direction.[1]

29. No furnace for melting iron or making glass, and no stationary steam-engine designed for use in any mill for planing or sawing boards or turning wood, or in which any other fuel than coal is used to create steam, shall be erected or put up to be used in any city or town by which the provisions relating thereto of chapter one hundred ninety-seven of the statutes of eighteen hundred and forty-five or chapter ninety-six of the statutes of eighteen hundred and forty-six respectively have been adopted, or by which this and the seven following sections shall have been adopted, at a legal meeting of the city council of the city or the inhabitants of the town called for that purpose, unless the mayor and aldermen or selectmen thereof have granted a license therefor, prescribing the place where the building in which such steam-engine or furnace is to be used shall be erected, the materials and construction thereof, with such regulations as to the height of flues and protection against fire as they deem necessary for the safety of the neighborhood. Such license may be granted on a written application, and shall be recorded in the records of the city or town.

30. Upon application for such license the mayor and aldermen or selectmen shall assign a time and place for the

[1] Gen. Stats. ch. 88, §§ 31, 32.

consideration of the same, and cause at least fourteen days' public notice thereof to be given, at the expense of the applicant, in such manner as they may direct, in order that all persons interested may be heard thereon.

31. In any city or town by which chapter one hundred and ninety-seven of the statutes of eighteen hundred and forty-five has been adopted, or by which sections thirty-three to forty inclusive shall have been adopted at a legal meeting of the city council of the city or inhabitants of the town called for that purpose, the mayor and aldermen or selectmen, after due notice in writing to the owner of such steam-engine or furnace, except for making glass, erected or in use therein before the time of such adoption, and a hearing of the matter, may adjudge the same to be dangerous or a nuisance to the neighborhood, and make and record an order prescribing such rules, restrictions, and alterations, as to the building in which the same is constructed or used, the construction and height of its smoke flues, with such other regulations as they deem necessary for the safety of the neighborhood ; and the city or town clerk shall deliver a copy of such order to a constable, who shall serve on the owner an attested copy thereof and make return of his doings thereon to said clerk within three days from the delivery thereof to him.

32. The owner of a steam-engine or furnace who is aggrieved by such order, may apply to the superior court, or a justice thereof in vacation, for a jury ; and the court or justice shall issue a warrant for a jury to be empanelled by the sheriff in like manner as is provided in chapter forty-three in regard to the laying out of highways. Such application shall be made within three days after the order is served upon the owner, and the jury shall be empanelled within fourteen days from the issuing of the warrant.

33. The court or justice, on granting the application for a jury, may issue an injunction restraining the further use of such engine or furnace until the final determination of the application.

34. The jury may find a verdict either affirming or annulling the order in full, or making alterations therein; which verdict shall be returned by the sheriff to the next term of the court for acceptance as in the case of highways, and when accepted shall take effect as an original order.

35.  If the order is affirmed, costs shall be recovered by the city or town against the applicant; if it is annulled, damages and costs shall be recovered by the complainant against the city or town; and if it is altered, the court may render such judgment as to costs, as to justice shall appertain.          •

36. Any steam-engine or furnace erected or used contrary to the provisions of the seven preceding sections shall be deemed a common nuisance.  And the mayor and aldermen or selectmen shall have like authority to remove the same as is given to boards of health to remove nuisances by sections eight, nine, and ten of chapter twenty-six (of Gen. Stats.).

37. The mayor and aldermen or selectmen of any city or town, or any person by them authorized, may, after notice to the parties interested, examine any steam-engine or steam-boiler therein; and for that purpose may enter any house, shop, or building; and if upon such examination it appears probable that the use of such engine or boiler is unsafe, they may issue a temporary order to suspend such use, and if after giving the parties interested, so far as known, an opportunity to be heard, they adjudge such engine or boiler unsafe, or defective, or unfit to be used, they may pass a permanent order prohibiting the use thereof until it is rendered safe.  If, after notice to the owner or person having charge thereof, such engine or boiler is used contrary to either of such orders, it shall be deemed a common nuisance, without any other proof thereof than its use.

38. The mayor and aldermen and selectmen shall have the same authority to abate and remove any steam-engine or steam-boiler erected or used contrary to the provisions

of the preceding section, as boards of health have to remove nuisances, by sections eight, nine, and ten of chapter twenty-six (of Gen. Stats.).

39. No person shall manufacture, set up, use, or cause to be used, any steam-boiler, unless it is provided with a fusible safety plug made of lead or some other equally fusible material, and of a diameter of not less than one-half an inch; which plug shall be placed in the roof of the fire-box, when a fire-box is used, and in all cases, in a part of the boiler fully exposed to the action of the fire, and as near the top of the water line as any part of the fire-surface of the boiler; and for this purpose Ashcroft's " protected safety fusible plug " may be used.

40. Whoever without just and proper cause removes from any boiler the safety plug thereof, or substitutes therefor any material more capable of resisting the action of the fire than the plug so removed. shall be punished by a fine not exceeding one thousand dollars.

41. Whoever manufactures, sets up, knowingly uses, or causes to be used, for six consecutive days, a steam-boiler unprovided with a safety fusible plug as named in section forty-three (section thirty-nine above), shall be punished by fine not exceeding one thousand dollars.[1]

42. No stationary engine, propelled by steam or other motive-power, shall be hereafter erected or put up for use in any city or town, within five hundred feet of any dwelling-house or public building, unless a licence therefor shall have been first granted in the manner provided in chapter eighty-eight of the General Statutes (preceding sections), in respect to licenses of steam-engines, furnaces, and boilers; and such license shall be applied for, granted, and recorded in manner as therein provided.

43. Any stationary engine hereafter erected, without such license, shall be deemed a common nuisance, and the mayor and aldermen, or selectmen, shall have like authority to remove the same, as is given to them by section forty of said chapter (section thirty-six above).

[1] Gen. Stats. ch 88, §§ 33–45.

44. This act (two preceding sections) shall not be in force in any city or town until it has been adopted at a legal meeting of the city council of the city, or of the inhabitants of the town, called for that purpose.[1]

The assessors of each city and town shall, in each year, at the time of making the returns required by the first section of chapter two hundred and eighty-three of the acts of the year eighteen hundred and sixty-five, return to the tax commissioner a statement showing the whole number of steam-boilers located in their respective cities and towns on the first day of May then next preceding; by whom and when built, and the aggregate estimated amount of horse-power which such boilers are capable of furnishing. Such return shall also state the number of accidents causing permanent injuries to persons which have arisen from the use of such boilers during the year, with the causes thereof, as far as may be ascertained by the assessors.

The tax commissioner shall in due season forward to the assessors, blanks suitable for making the returns required by the first section, and shall include in his annual report to the legislature a tabular statement of statistics derived from such returns.[2]

45. Whoever sells, gives away, or offers for sale, or has in his possession with intent to sell, any of the fireworks called rockets, crackers, squibs, or serpents, without license from the mayor and aldermen or selectmen of the city or town, shall for every such offence forfeit a sum not exceeding ten dollars.

46. Whoever sets fire to, or has in his possession with intent to set fire to, any rocket, cracker, squib, or serpent, or throws any lighted rocket, cracker, squib, or serpent, within any city or town, without the license of the mayor and aldermen or selectmen, shall for every offence forfeit a sum not exceeding ten dollars.

47. The city council of a city and the inhabitants of a town may order that no gunpowder shall be kept in any place within the limits thereof, unless it is well secured in tight casks or canisters; that no gunpowder, above the quantity of fifty pounds, shall be kept or deposited in any shop, store, or other building, or in a ship or vessel, which is within the distance of twenty-five rods from any other building or wharf; that no gunpowder, above the quantity

---

[1] Stats. 1862, ch. 74.      [2] Stats. 1873, ch. 321.

of twenty-five pounds, shall be kept or deposited in any shop, store, or other building, within ten rods of any other building ; and that no gunpowder, above the quantity of one pound, shall be kept or deposited in any shop, store, or other building, within ten rods of another building, unless it is well secured in copper, tin, or brass canisters, holding not exceeding five pounds each, and closely covered with copper, brass, or tin covers.   They may make a like order in regard to gun-cotton, or other substances prepared like it for explosion, and, if considered necessary for public safety, may restrict the quantity to be so kept to one-fifth of the weight of gunpowder allowed by this section.

48. Upon complaint made to a justice of the peace or police court by the mayor or either of the aldermen, selectmen, or firewards of any place, that he has probable cause to suspect, and does suspect, that gunpowder, gun-cotton, or other substance prepared like it for explosion, is deposited and kept within the limits thereof contrary to law, such justice or court may issue a warrant, directed to either of the constables of such place, ordering him to enter any shop, store, or other building, or vessel, specified in the warrant, and there make diligent search for such gunpowder, gun-cotton, or other substance, suspected to have been so deposited or kept, and to make return of his doings to said justice or court forthwith.

49. Whoever commits an offence against any order made under section forty-eight (forty-seven above), shall forfeit a sum not exceeding twenty dollars ; but the four preceding sections shall not extend to any manufactory of gunpowder, gun-cotton, or other substance aforesaid, nor in any case prevent the transportation thereof through any city or town, or from one to another part thereof.

50. The city council of any city and the inhabitants of any town may adopt such rules and regulations as they deem reasonable in relation to the storage and sale, within the limits thereof, of camphene or any similar explosive or inflammable fluid, and may affix penalties for breaches thereof, not exceeding twenty dollars for any one offence.[1]

[1] Gen. Stats. ch. 88, §§ 46–51.

51. The mayor and aldermen or selectmen of any city or town may license theatrical exhibitions, public shows, public amusements, and exhibitions of every description to which admission is obtained upon payment of money or the delivery of any valuable thing, or by a ticket or voucher obtained for money or any valuable thing, upon such terms and conditions as they deem reasonable ; and they may revoke or suspend the same at their pleasure.[1]

No license shall be granted by the selectmen of any town for any exhibition mentioned in this section at which children under the age of fifteen years are employed as acrobats, contortionists, or in any feats of gymnastics or equestrianism.[2]

No person shall move a building in any public street or way in any town without written permission from the selectmen of such town, to be granted upon such terms and conditions as in their opinion the public safety may require; and these provisions may be enforced by injunction, to be issued on petition by the superior court in term time, or by a single justice thereof in vacation.[3]

No dwelling-house, shop, warehouse, barn, stable, or any other structure of more than eight feet in length or breadth, and seven feet in height, shall be erected and set up within such limits of any town of this commonwealth, as said town may from time to time determine, but of stone, brick, or other incombustible material, and covered with slate, tin, tile, or other incombustible material, unless in particular cases where the public good permits or necessity requires, to be so judged and signified in writing, by license, under the hands of the selectmen of said town, or a major part of them : *provided*, this shall not apply to any detached house, shop, stable, barn or structure which is located more than a hundred feet from any other house, barn, shop, stable, or warehouse, nor to wooden structures erected upon wharves of wood.

Any such building or structure hereafter erected without license duly granted by the selectmen, and recorded in the records of the town where the same is erected, shall be deemed and taken to be a common nuisance, without any other proof thereof than proof of its use. And the selectmen of any town shall have the same power to abate and remove any building or structure mentioned in this act, erected contrary to the provisions of this act, as boards of health have to remove nuisances by sections eight, nine and ten of chapter twenty-six of the General Statutes.

This act shall not be in force in any town unless the inhabitants thereof shall adopt the same at a legal meeting of said inhabitants called for that purpose.[4]

[1] Gen. Stats. ch. 88, § 74.
[2] Stats. 1874, ch. 279.
[3] Stats. 1870, ch. 314.
[4] Stats. 1870, ch. 375.

52. The mayor and aldermen or selectmen of any city or town may grant a license to any person to keep a billiard table or bowling alley for hire, gain, or reward, upon such terms and conditions as they deem proper, to be used for amusement merely, but not for the purpose of gaming for money or other property. Such license may be revoked at the pleasure of the authority granting it.[1]

53. Any marshal or his deputy, sheriff or his deputy, constable, police officer, or watchman, may at any time enter into a billiard room, bowling alley, or other room connected therewith, for the purpose of enforcing any law of the state ; and whoever obstructs or hinders the entrance of such officer shall be punished by fine of not less than five nor more than twenty dollars.[2]

The provisions of this section are extended to all buildings or other places named in any license granted to common victuallers by the county commissioners, or by the mayor and aldermen or selectmen of any city or town.[3]

54. The selectmen of any town may license any person to run a steamboat for the conveyance of passengers on lakes, ponds, and waters within this commonwealth, and not within the maritime jurisdiction of the United States.

No person shall run a steamboat for the conveyance of passengers as aforesaid, without having previously obtained a license therefor from the selectmen of the town or towns within whose limits such steamboat shall land or receive passengers.

Such licenses shall be granted for a term not exceeding one year, and shall be recorded by the clerk of the town by which they are granted, who shall receive a fee of one dollar for every such license and record. Every such license shall set forth the name of the vessel and of the master and owner, the number of passengers such vessel shall be permitted to carry at any one time, and shall be posted in a conspicuous place thereon, and the number of passengers specified in such license shall in no case be exceeded.

Whoever violates any of the provisions of this section shall be punished by fine not exceeding fifty dollars for each offence.[4]

[1] Gen. Stats. ch. 88, § 69.
[2] Gen. Stats. ch. 88, § 72.
[3] Stats. 1862, ch. 222.
[4] Stats. 1876, ch. 100.

# CHAPTER XLIII.

## SALES BY AUCTIONEERS, HAWKERS, AND PEDLERS.

1. THE mayor and aldermen and selectmen of any city or town, by writing under their hands, may license one or more suitable inhabitants of their respective cities and towns, to be auctioneers within the same for the term of one year, and may receive to the use of the city or town for each license the sum of two dollars. They shall record every license in a book to be kept by them for that purpose.

2. If on application made to them in writing they unreasonably refuse or neglect to license the applicant, he may, after giving them fourteen days' notice and bonds to pay all costs, apply to the county commissioners, who, upon hearing the parties, may grant a license.

3. Each auctioneer shall, if required, give bonds, in a reasonable penalty with sufficient sureties to the treasurer of the city or town where he is licensed, with condition that he shall in all things conform to the laws relating to auctions.

4. Every auctioneer shall keep a fair and particular account of all goods and chattels sold by him, and of the persons from whom received, and to whom sold.

5. An auctioneer who receives for sale by auction any goods from a minor, knowing him to be such, or sells by auction any of his own goods before sunrise or after sunset, shall forfeit to the use of the town a sum not exceeding two hundred dollars for each offence.

6. An auctioneer may sell at public auction in any place within his county; and when employed by others may sell real or personal estate upon the premises where the same is situated in any place within the state. If an auctioneer sells by auction in any place where he is not authorized to sell, he shall forfeit fifty dollars.

7. If a person sells or offers for sale by auction any goods or chattels in any city or town except as is provided in this chapter, the same shall be forfeited to the use of the city or town, and may be seized by the mayor and aldermen or selectmen, and libelled according to the provisions of chapter one hundred and fifty-three.

8. The tenant or occupant of any house or store, having the actual possession and control of the same, who knowingly permits a person to sell real or personal estate by public auction in such house or store, or in any apartment or yard appurtenant to the same, contrary to the provisions of this chapter, shall forfeit a sum not exceeding five hundred dollars.

9. If a person, not licensed and qualified as an auctioneer, sells or attempts to sell any real or personal estate by public auction, he shall for each offence forfeit a sum not exceeding five hundred dollars.[1]

"Special trust and confidence is placed in an auctioneer which he cannot delegate. Yet this does not require that he should make all the sales in person. He may employ all necessary and proper clerks and servants. And in the course of a protracted sale, he may, undoubtedly, without a violation of law, relieve himself by employing others to use the hammer and make the outcry. But this should be done under his immediate direction and supervision. We do not mean, however, by this, that he must be actually present during the whole time of the sale. An occasional absence would not subject his servant or substitute to the penalties of the statute. If the auctioneer really conducted the auction and made the sale, he might, within his authority, call to his aid such assistance as might be needed to transact the business in a convenient and proper manner; but he clearly could not appoint deputies to make sales at different places and times in his absence. But the provisions of the section do not in its terms or its spirit prohibit other persons (than auctioneers) from appointing the time and place of a sale, advertising, giving notice to interested parties and making adjournments. It must be strictly construed, as it is a penal statute, and applies only to the act of sale."[2]

10. Nothing in the preceding sections shall extend to sales made by sheriffs, deputy-sheriffs, coroners, constables, collectors of taxes, executors, administrators, guar-

[1] Gen. Stats. ch. 50, §§ 1–9.
[2] Commonwealth v. Harnden, 19

Pick. 482; Hosmer v. Sargent, 8 Allen, 99.

dians, assignees of insolvent debtors, or any other person required by law to sell real or personal estate.

11. Every auctioneer or other person who is guilty of fraud or deceit in relation to any sale by auction, shall for each offence forfeit a sum not exceeding one thousand dollars.

12. Licenses may be granted upon such conditions respecting the places of selling goods and chattels within a city or town as the mayor and aldermen or selectmen may deem expedient; and if an auctioneer makes a sale by auction at a place not authorized by his license, he shall be liable to like penalties as if he had sold without a license.[1]

13. Any person may go about from town to town, or from place to place, or from dwelling-house to dwelling-house in the same town, exposing to sale and selling fruits and provisions, live animals, brooms, agricultural implements, (and tools used in making boots and shoes,[2]) fuel, newspapers, books, pamphlets, agricultural products of the United States, and the products of his own labor or the labor of his family.[3]

Nothing in the thirteenth section of the fiftieth chapter of the General Statutes (this section) shall be so construed as to include therein any articles of the growth or production of foreign countries.[4]

14. The city council of any city, and the inhabitants of any town, may authorize the mayor and aldermen or selectmen thereof to restrain the sale by minors of any goods, wares, or merchandise, the sale of which is permitted in the preceding section, and while such authority remains in force the mayor and aldermen and selectmen may make rules restraining such sales by minors, or may grant licenses to minors to make such sales upon such terms and conditions as they shall prescribe; but such restraints and licenses shall not remain in force beyond their term of office. Whoever is guilty of a violation of the rules and regulations so made, or sells any such

[1] Gen. Stats. ch. 50, §§ 10–12.
[2] Stats. 1878, ch. 216, § 2.
[3] Gen. Stats. ch. 50, § 13.
[4] Stats. 1862, ch. 178.

articles without a license when the same has been required, shall forfeit a sum not exceeding ten dollars for each offence.

15. The sale of jewelry, wines, spirituous liquors, playing cards, indigo, and feathers, in the manner specified in section thirteen, is prohibited.[1]

A hawker and pedler may sell jewelry as lawfully as any other person, unless he sells it in the capacity or character of hawker and pedler. And as this involves the question of what constitutes the character of a hawker or pedler, it may be of interest to consider it as has been construed by the supreme court. The leading primary idea of a hawker and pedler is that of an itinerant or travelling trader, who carries goods about in order to sell them, and who actually sells them to purchasers, in contradistinction to a trader who has goods for sale and sells them in a fixed place of business. Superadded to this, by a hawker is generally understood one who not only carries goods for sale, but seeks for purchasers either by outcry, or by attracting notice and attention to them as goods for sale by an actual exhibition or exposure of them, by placards or labels, or by a conventional signal, like the sound of a horn for the sale of fish.[2]

16. The secretary of the commonwealth may grant a license to go about exposing to sale and selling any goods, wares, or merchandise, not prohibited in the preceding section, to any applicant who files in his office a certificate signed by the mayor of a city or by a majority of the selectmen of a town, stating that to the best knowledge and belief of such mayor or selectmen, the applicant therein named is a citizen of the United States, or has declared his intention to become a citizen of the United States, and of good repute for morals and integrity. The mayor or selectmen before granting such certificate shall require the applicant to make oath that he is the person named therein, that he is a citizen of the United States, or has declared his intention to become a citizen of the United States; which oath shall be certified by a justice of the peace, and accompany the certificate. Every license so

[1] Gen. Stats. ch. 50, §§ 14, 15.     14 Gray, 29; Commonwealth *v.* Ober,

[2] Commonwealth *v.* Bruckheimer,     12 Cush. 493.

granted shall bear date the day it is issued, and shall continue in force one year and no longer.[1]

17. The secretary shall cause to be inserted in every license the names of such cities and towns as the applicant selects, with the sum to be paid to the respective treasurers thereof annexed, and shall receive from the applicant one dollar for each city or town so inserted. Every person so licensed may sell as aforesaid any goods, wares, and merchandise, not prohibited in section fifteen, in any city or town mentioned in his license, upon first paying the sum so required to the treasurer of such city or town, who shall certify on the face of the license the sum so received.

18. Every person licensed under the two preceding sections shall pay to the treasurer of each city or town mentioned in his license, the sums following: for every town containing not more than one thousand inhabitants, according to the United States census next preceding the date of his license, three dollars; for every town containing more than one thousand and not more than two thousand inhabitants, six dollars; for every town containing more than two thousand and not more than three thousand inhabitants, eight dollars; for every town containing more than three thousand and not more than four thousand inhabitants, ten dollars; and for every city and town containing more than four thousand inhabitants, ten dollars, and one dollar for every thousand inhabitants over four thousand contained therein; but the sum so to be paid to a treasurer shall in no case exceed twenty-five dollars.

19. Any person resident, paying taxes upon his stock in trade, and qualified to vote, in a city or town, may there expose to sale and sell goods, wares, or merchandise, upon obtaining a license pursuant to the provisions of sections sixteen and seventeen, and shall not be required to pay to the treasurer of such city or town any sum therefor.

20. The secretary, upon the conditions required in section sixteen, may grant special state licenses, upon pay-

[1] Gen. Stats. ch. 50, § 16; Stats. 1870, ch. 331, § 1.

ment, by the applicant, of (fifty dollars and no more [1])
for each license; and the person so licensed may expose
to sale any goods, wares, or merchandise, not prohibited,
in any city or town. (And the secretary of the commonwealth is hereby authorized to grant a special license to
any disabled soldier or sailor belonging to this commonwealth, according to the provisions of this section of
the fiftieth chapter of the General Statutes, without the
payment of any sum therefor, upon satisfactory evidence
of the identity of such soldier or sailor, and that he is
wholly or partially disabled by reason of wounds received
in the service of the United States, or by sickness or disability contracted therein, and has received an honorable
discharge from such service.[2]) He may also grant as
aforesaid, upon payment by the applicant of one dollar for
each county mentioned therein, special county licenses;
and the person so licensed may expose to sale, within such
counties, any tin, britannia, glass, (earthen, iron, plated,[3])
or wooden wares, of the manufactures of the United
States, or any other goods, wares, or merchandise, manufactured by himself or his employer, and not prohibited in
section fifteen, upon tendering to the treasurer of each
county mentioned in said license, respectively, the sums
following: for Suffolk, Essex, Middlesex, and Worcester,
each four dollars; for Norfolk, Berkshire, Hampden, Bristol, and Plymouth, each three dollars; for Franklin,
Hampshire, and Barnstable, each two dollars; for Nantucket, one dollar; for the county of Duke's County, one
dollar. And the county treasurers, respectively, upon the
receipt of any sum, as aforesaid, shall certify the amount
so received on the face of the license.

21. The secretary shall keep a record of all licenses
granted, with the number of each, the name and residence
of the persons licensed, the counties, cities, and towns,
mentioned therein, of all special state licenses, and of all
transfers of licenses. The treasurers of the counties,

---

[1] Stats. 1864, ch. 151, § 2.
[2] Stats. 1866, ch. 197.
[3] Stats. 1870, ch. 331.

cities, and towns shall severally keep records of all licenses upon which the sums provided in this chapter have been paid, with the number of each, the name and residence of the persons licensed, and the sums received thereon, and all such records shall be open for public inspection.

22. All sums paid to the secretary under this chapter shall be for the use of the state; and all sums paid to the treasurer of a county, city, or town, shall be for the use of such county, city, or town.

23. A license granted under the provisions of section sixteen or nineteen may be transferred by the secretary, upon application therefor and upon evidence furnished by the applicant like that required for granting a license. The person to whom it is transferred shall thereafter be liable in all respects as if he were the person originally licensed. No person shall sell under such license except the person named therein or in such transfer.

24. Every person licensed to peddle as herein before provided shall post his name, residence, and the number of his license, in a conspicuous manner upon his parcels or vehicle, and when such license is demanded of him by any mayor, alderman, selectman, town or city treasurer or clerk, constable, police officer, or justice of the peace, shall forthwith exhibit it, and if he neglects or refuses so to do, shall be subject to the same penalty as if he had no license. So much of this chapter as relates to hawkers and pedlers, or a synopsis thereof, shall be printed on every license.

25. No license to go about offering for sale or selling as aforesaid shall operate to defeat or bar a prosecution against the person licensed, if it is proved that he exposed to sale any article except such as are permitted in section thirteen in any county, city, or town, where he was not licensed to sell, or in which he had not paid the sum mentioned in his license; but no person so licensed shall be required to make payment to the treasurer of any county, city, or town, before he is prepared to trade therein. The license of any person convicted of a violation of any provision of this or the ten preceding sections shall be void.

26. Whoever counterfeits or forges a license, or has a counterfeited or forged license in his possession, with intent to utter or use the same as true, knowing it to be false or counterfeit, or attempts to sell under a license which has expired, or is forfeited, or which was not granted or has not been transferred to him, shall forfeit a sum not (less than fifty dollars nor [1]) exceeding one thousand dollars.

27. Whoever goes from town to town, or from place to place, or from dwelling-house to dwelling-house, carrying for sale or exposing to sale any goods, wares, or merchandise (named in section fifteen, or carries for sale or exposes for sale any other goods, wares, or merchandise [1]), or takes a residence in any town for that purpose for a less term than one year, except as herein before provided, shall forfeit a sum not (less than fifty dollars nor [1]) exceeding two hundred dollars for each offence.

28. No hawker, pedler, or other itinerant trader, holding an auctioneer's license, shall sell or expose for sale by public auction any goods, wares, or merchandise, in any other city or town than that from whose authorities such license was obtained; nor in any place in such city or town, except such as shall be expressly described or set forth in said license.[2]

29. It shall be the duty of constables and police officers, within their respective towns and cities, to arrest and prosecute any person whom they may have reason to believe guilty of violating the provisions of said fiftieth chapter, relating to hawkers and pedlers; and one-half of any forfeiture which may be incurred and recovered under the twenty-seventh section (twenty-seven above) of said chapter shall be paid to the complainant.[3]

[1] Stats. 1870, ch. 331.
[2] Gen. Stats. ch. 50, §§ 17–28.
[3] Stats. 1864, ch. 151, § 3.

## CHAPTER XLIV.

### MASTERS, APPRENTICES, AND SERVANTS.

1. CHILDREN under the age of fourteen years may be bound as apprentices or servants until that age; and minors above the age of fourteen years may be bound as apprentices or servants, females to the age of eighteen years or to the time of their marriage within that age, and males to the age of twenty-one years.

2. Children under the age of fourteen years may be bound by their father, or in case of his death or incompetency, by their mother or legal guardian. If illegitimate, they may be bound by their mother during the lifetime of the putative father as well as after his decease. If they have no parent competent to act, and no guardian, they may with the approbation of the selectmen of the town where they reside, bind themselves. The power of a mother to bind her children shall cease upon her subsequent marriage, and shall not be exercised by herself or husband during the continuance of such marriage.

3. Minors above the age of fourteen years may be bound in the same manner, but when bound by their parent or guardian, the minor's consent shall be expressed in the indenture and testified by his signing the same.

4. A minor child who is, or either of whose parents is, chargeable to a town as having a lawful settlement therein, or supported there at the expense of the state, may be bound as an apprentice or servant by the overseers of the poor.[1]

In this case the overseers are public officers and not agents of the town, so that their admissions or acts cannot be regarded as the acts of the town.[2]

[1] Gen. Stats. ch. 111, §§ 1–4.
[2] New Bedford *v.* Taunton, 9 Allen, 207.

5. Such children, whether under or above the age of fourteen years, may be so bound, females to the age of eighteen years or to the time of their marriage within that age, and males to the age of twenty-one years; and provision shall be made in the contract for teaching them to read, write, and cipher, and for such other instruction, benefit, and allowance, either within or at the end of the term, as the overseers may deem reasonable.[1]

They cannot be bound for a less time, and if the provision for teaching is omitted the contract is void. It is better to insert the provision literally.[2]

6. No minor shall be so bound unless by an indenture of two parts sealed and delivered by both parties; and when made with the approbation of the selectmen, they shall certify such approbation in writing upon each part of the indenture.

7. One part of the indenture shall be kept by the parent or guardian executing it, for the use of the minor; and when made with the approbation of the selectmen or by the overseers of the poor, shall be deposited with the town clerk, and safely kept in his office for the use of the minor.[3]

8. No minor shall be bound as an apprentice or servant, unless his parent or guardian, or some responsible person in his behalf, shall give a written bond in the sum of two hundred dollars to the master, with condition that the minor shall serve him for the full term of such apprenticeship or service, and that the master shall be held harmless from any loss or damage from the breach of such condition: *provided*, that minor children who have no parents able to give such bond, may be so bound by giving a bond in such sum as may be agreed upon by and between the master and the parents, or guardian of such minor. And the master shall also give bond to the minor in a like sum, with

---

[1] Gen. Stats. ch. 111, § 5.
[2] Reidell *v.* Congdon, 16 Pick. 44; Butler *v.* Hubbard, 5 Pick. 250.

[3] Gen. Stats. ch. 111, §§ 6, 7.

condition that he shall comply with the conditions of the indenture, and shall not be guilty of any misconduct towards the apprentice or servant, and shall hold the apprentice or servant harmless from any loss or damage by reason of any failure on his part to comply with the terms of the indenture or contract: *provided*, that whenever minors are bound by state, town, or municipal authorities or authorized agents, the bond required to be given to the master may be waived by the parties. The bond given by the master shall be kept for the use of the minor, by the parent or guardian, and when there is no parent or guardian, it shall be deposited with the town clerk where the master resides, and safely kept in his office for the use of the minor.[1]

9. All considerations of money or other things paid or allowed by the master upon a contract of service or apprenticeship made in pursuance of this chapter, shall be paid or secured to the sole use of the minor bound thereby.

10. Parents, guardians, selectmen, and overseers, shall inquire into the treatment of all children bound by them respectively or with their approbation, and of all bound by or with the approbation of the predecessors in office of any of them, and defend them from all cruelty, neglect, and breach of contract, on the part of masters.

11. Complaints by parents, guardians, selectmen, or overseers, for misconduct or neglect of the master, and by the master, for gross misbehavior, or refusal to do his duty, or wilful neglect thereof, on the part of the apprentice or servant, may be filed in the superior court in the county where the master resides, setting forth the facts and circumstances of the case. The court shall order notice to the adverse party, and if the complaint is by the master, to all persons who have covenanted in behalf of the apprentice or servant, and to the selectmen who approved of the indenture, or their successors in office, and shall hear and determine the case with or without a jury, as the allegations of the parties may require.

12. The court may render a judgment or decree, that the

[1] Stats. 1865, ch. 270.

minor be discharged from his apprenticeship or service, or the master from his contract, and the minor thus discharged may be bound out anew.

13. Costs may be awarded to the prevailing party and execution issued therefor; but no costs shall be awarded against selectmen or overseers, unless it appears that the complaint was made without just and reasonable cause. Costs in favor of the master may be recovered of the parent or guardian who executed the indenture, or if there is no parent or guardian liable therefor, such costs may be recovered in an action against the minor when he arrives at full age.

14. Every master shall be liable to an action on the indenture for the breach of any covenant on his part therein contained. All damages recovered in such action, after deducting the necessary charges in prosecuting the same, shall be the property of the minor, and may be applied and appropriated to his use by the person who recovers the same, and the residue shall be paid to the minor, if a male, at the age of twenty-one years, and if a female, at the age of eighteen years, or at the time of her marriage within that age.

15. Such action may be brought by the parent or his executors or administrators, the guardian, or any one who succeeds him in that trust, or the overseers or their successors in office; or it may be brought in the name of the minor by his guardian or next friend, as the case requires; or by himself after the expiration of the term of apprenticeship or service.

16. If the action is brought by the overseers, it shall not abate by the death of any of them, or by their being succeeded in office; but shall proceed in the names of the original plaintiffs, or the survivor of them, or the executors or administrators of the survivor; and the money recovered therein shall be deposited in the city or town treasury to be applied and disposed of as provided in section thirteen (fourteen above).

17. No such action shall be maintained, unless com-

menced during the term of apprenticeship or service, or within two years after the expiration thereof.

18. If judgment in such action is rendered for the plaintiff, the court may, upon motion of the plaintiff, discharge the minor from his apprenticeship or service, if not already done as before provided, and the minor may be bound out anew.

19. No indenture of apprenticeship or service made in pursuance of this chapter shall bind the minor after the death of his master, but the apprenticeship or service shall be thenceforth discharged, and the minor may be bound out anew.

20. All the foregoing provisions shall apply as well to mistresses as to masters.

21. Nothing contained in this chapter shall affect the father's right at common law to assign or contract for the services of his children during their minority.[1]

[1] Gen. Stats. ch. 111, §§ 8-17, 21-23.

# CHAPTER XLV.

## FIRES AND FIRE DEPARTMENTS.

1. The selectmen of any town may annually, in March or April, appoint such number of suitable persons to be firewards, as they deem necessary; and each person so appointed shall forthwith have notice thereof, and within seven days after such notice shall enter his acceptance or refusal of the office with the town clerk. Whoever, after such notice, neglects so to enter his acceptance or refusal shall, unless excused by said selectmen, forfeit ten dollars.[1]

2. When a fire occurs in any wood-lands, the firewards, or any two of them, of a town in which the same is burning, or of any town comprising wood-lands endangered thereby, being present at a place in immediate danger of being burned over by such fire, may direct such back-fires to be set and maintained, and such other precautions to be taken to prevent the spread of the same, as they may deem necessary.[2]

3. When a fire breaks out in any place, the firewards shall immediately repair thereto, and shall carry a suitable staff or badge of their office.

4. The firewards, or any three of them, present at a place in immediate danger from a fire, and where no firewards are appointed, the selectmen or mayor and aldermen present, or in their absence two or more of the civil officers present, or in their absence two or more of the chief military officers of the place present, may direct any house or building to be pulled down or demolished when they

[1] Stats. 1871, ch. 21.          [2] Stats. 1874, ch. 228.

judge the same to be necessary in order to prevent the spreading of the fire.[1]

By chapter two hundred and one of the statutes of eighteen hundred and seventy-three, the engineer of a fire department in command at a fire shall, to the exclusion of all other persons, have the power conferred upon firewards by the preceding section; but only in those towns in which said chapter is accepted by the legal voters.

5. One fireward has no more authority than any other person to direct the destruction of a house to prevent the spreading of a conflagration, although it may be impossible for the other firewards or the other officers named in the statute to get to the place when the occasion for action upon the subject arises.[2]

6. If such pulling down or demolishing of a house or building is the means of stopping the fire, or if the fire stops before it comes to the same, the owner shall be entitled to recover a reasonable compensation from the city or town; but when such building is that in which the fire first broke out, the owner shall receive no compensation.[3]

7. In Ruggles v. Inhabitants of Nantucket, Bigelow, J. said: "The plain intent of the statute is, that no house or building shall be demolished, unless it shall be judged necessary by three firewards, or by the other officers authorized to act in their absence, or where no firewards have been appointed. It is the united judgment of the officers to whom the power is given, acting upon the immediate exigency, and determining the necessity which is contemplated by the statute. Its language is capable of no other reasonable interpretation. It is a joint authority expressly given to the officers designated, acting together, and cannot be exercised by a minority or by any one of them. It is not sufficient, therefore, that a general conclusion or judgment was arrived at by three firewards, or the other officers mentioned, that it was necessary to destroy some buildings in order to put a stop to the further extension of a fire. They must go further. They must determine upon the particular house or building which they shall adjudge necessary to be destroyed for the purpose. This cannot be left to the individual judgment of any of the firewards."[4]

The provision of this section does not apply to a building which is pulled down by such order, after it is so far burnt that it is impossible to save it from destruction by fire.[5]

---

[1] Gen. Stats. ch. 24, §§ 3, 4.
[2] Parson v. Pettingell, 11 Allen, 507.
[3] Gen. Stats. ch. 24, § 5.
[4] 11 Cush. 433.
[5] Taylor v. Plymouth, 8 Met. 462.

8. Such firewards or other officers may, during the continuance of a fire, require assistance for extinguishing the same, and removing furniture, goods, or merchandise from a building on fire or in danger thereof; and may appoint guards to secure the same. They may also require assistance for pulling down or demolishing any house or building when they judge it necessary; and may suppress all tumults and disorders at such fire.

9. They may direct the stations and operations of the enginemen with their engines, and of all other persons for the purpose of extinguishing the fire; and whoever refuses or neglects to obey such orders shall forfeit for each offence a sum not exceeding ten dollars.

10. Whoever purloins, embezzles, conveys away, or conceals any furniture, goods or chattels, merchandise or effects, of persons whose houses or buildings are on fire or endangered thereby, and does not within two days restore or give notice thereof to the owner if known, or if unknown, to one of the firewards, mayor and aldermen, or selectmen, of the place, shall be deemed guilty of larceny.

11. The mayor and aldermen or selectmen of places provided with fire engines may appoint suitable persons for enginemen; who shall continue in office during the pleasure of the authority appointing them.

12. Such engines shall be manned as follows: each common engine, or suction engine when used as a common engine only, with not exceeding thirty men; each suction engine, when used as such, with not exceeding forty-five men; but this provision shall not affect the present right of any place to have a greater number of enginemen appointed than is herein prescribed.

13. The mayor and aldermen or selectmen may select from the enginemen any number for each engine, who shall, under the direction of the firewards, attend fires with axes, fire-hooks, fire-sails, and ladders, and do such further duty as the mayor and aldermen or selectmen shall from time to time prescribe; and they shall be entitled to all exemptions and privileges of other enginemen.

14. Each company of enginemen so appointed shall meet annually in May, and choose a foreman or director, and a clerk, and establish such rules and regulations not repugnant to the laws of the commonwealth, respecting their duty as enginemen, as shall be approved by the mayor and aldermen or selectmen; and they shall annex penalties thereto, not exceeding ten dollars, which may be recovered by the clerk in an action of tort.

15. Such companies shall meet together once a month, and oftener if necessary, for the purpose of examining the engine and its appendages, and seeing that they are in good repair and ready for use. They shall, by night and day, under the direction of the firewards, use their best endeavors to extinguish any fire that may happen in their city or town or the vicinity thereof.

16. When the proprietors of an engine apply to the mayor and aldermen or selectmen of a city or town in which the engine is owned, setting forth that they desire that the same should be employed for the benefit of such place, the mayor and aldermen or selectmen may appoint enginemen in the same manner, with the same privileges, and subject to the same regulations, as if the engine belonged to the place; and if the proprietors do not agree as to where the engine shall be kept, the mayor and aldermen or selectmen shall determine the same.

17. If the mayor and aldermen or selectmen upon such application refuse or delay for the space of fourteen days so to appoint enginemen, the proprietors may apply therefor in writing to the county commissioners, giving notice in writing to such mayor and aldermen or selectmen seven days at least before the sitting of the commissioners, that they may appear and show cause, if any they have, why such enginemen should not be appointed; and if sufficient cause is not shown by them, the commissioners may appoint the number of enginemen prescribed in section ten.

18. Enginemen appointed under the two preceding sections shall, if such can be obtained, be persons living at or near the place where the engine is kept, and they shall

enjoy all the privileges and exemptions of other engine-men.

19. If an engineman is negligent in his duties, the mayor and aldermen or selectmen shall discharge him and appoint another in his stead.

20. Persons appointed enginemen or members of the fire department in any place, and who have done duty as such for one year preceding the first day of May in any year, shall be entitled to receive from the treasurers of their respective towns a sum equal to the poll tax for state, county, and town taxes (exclusive of highway taxes), paid by them, or by their parents, masters, or guardians, and such further compensation as the town determines.

21. The chief engineer or the officer who holds the first office in any fire department, and the foreman or director of each company in any place where no fire department is established by law, shall annually on or before the first day of May make out and certify to the assessors of their respective places a list of all persons in their department or companies who through the year preceding have performed all the duties therein required by law. The assessors shall within ten days thereafter examine such lists and certify to the treasurers of their respective places the amount to be paid to each person named therein. Such treasurers shall after deducting all taxes due from the persons so named pay the same to them, or if minors to their parents, masters, or guardians ; and upon refusal of the treasurer to pay any sums so certified and returned, the persons entitled may severally recover the same from such places in an action of contract.

22. If such chief engineer or other officer wilfully refuses to make such certificate, he shall forfeit for each person whose name ought to have been so certified, a sum not exceeding five dollars, to be recovered in an action of tort to his use, or on complaint to the use of the commonwealth ; and if such engineer or other officer makes a false certificate in such case, he shall forfeit a sum not ex-

ceeding fifty nor less than twenty dollars, to be recovered in an action of tort to the use of the city or town, or on complaint to the use of the commonwealth.

23. The provisions of the three preceding sections shall be in force only in those cities and towns which have adopted or may adopt the same at the annual meeting of the town or by the city council of the city. When such adoption shall be revoked by the town at an annual meeting, or by the city council of a city, said provisions shall cease to be in force therein.

24. Whoever wantonly or maliciously injures a fire engine or the apparatus belonging thereto, shall be punished by fine not exceeding five hundred dollars, or by imprisonment not exceeding two years, and be further ordered to recognize with sufficient surety or sureties for his good behavior during such term as the court shall order.

25. The selectmen of any town may establish a fire department therein in the manner hereinafter provided, and such department and every other fire department, unless different provisions are specially made therefor, shall be organized in the manner, and the members thereof may exercise the powers and shall be subject to the liabilities, hereinafter mentioned.

26. The selectmen of such town shall annually in April appoint for such department as many engineers not exceeding twelve as they may think expedient, for the term of one year from the first day of May following and until others are appointed in their stead; and the selectmen shall fill all vacancies.

27. They shall immediately after such appointment issue a notice to each of said engineers to meet at a time and place designated in the notice; at which meeting the engineers shall choose a chief engineer, a clerk, and such other officers as they may deem necessary for their complete organization.

28. The engineers in relation to the extinguishment of fires shall exercise the powers which firewards may by law have and exercise, and in relation to the nomination

and appointment of enginemen shall exercise the powers and perform the duties of selectmen. They may appoint such number of men to the engines, hose, hook, ladder, and sail carriages, and to constitute fire companies for securing property endangered by fire, as they may think expedient; but the number of men appointed shall not exceed to each suction fire engine, fifty; to each common engine, thirty-five; to each hose-carriage, five; to each hook and ladder and sail carriage, twenty-five; and to each fire company, twenty-five.[1]

29. (But) selectmen, engineers of fire departments, and the board of engineers of fire-districts, in towns having one or more steam fire engines, or in which water for extinguishing fires is supplied from hydrants (or reservoirs [2]), may appoint such number of men to hose-carriages as they deem expedient, not to exceed twenty men to each hose-carriage.[3]

30. The engine, hose, hook and ladder, and sail carriage men, and fire companies, may organize themselves into distinct companies, elect the necessary officers, and establish such rules, regulations, and by-laws, as may be approved by the board of engineers; and may annex penalties to the breach of the same, not exceeding ten dollars in any case; and the same may be recovered by the clerk in an action of tort to the use of the company.

31. The engineers and all persons appointed by them shall be subject to the same duties and liabilities and entitled to the same privileges and exemptions as enginemen appointed by selectmen.

32. The board of engineers shall have the care and superintendence of the public engines, hose, fire-hooks, ladder-carriages, and ladders, in their respective towns, together with the buildings, fixtures, and appendages, belonging thereto, and all pumps, reservoirs for water, and apparatus, owned by the town and used for extinguishing fires; and shall cause the same to be kept

---

[1] Gen. Stats. ch. 24, §§ 6–26.      [3] Stats. 1869, ch. 92.
[2] Stats. 1870, ch. 28.

in repair, and when worn out to be replaced ; and, from time to time, shall make such alterations therein and additions thereto as they shall deem necessary ; but such alterations, additions, or repairs, shall not in any one year exceed the sum of one hundred dollars, unless the town has authorized a larger appropriation.

33. They may at any meeting establish such rules and regulations as they judge proper to prohibit or regulate the carrying of fire, firebrands, lighted matches, or other ignited materials, openly in the streets or thoroughfares of such town, or such parts thereof as they may designate, or to prohibit owners or occupants of buildings within their town, or such part thereof as they may designate, from erecting or maintaining any defective chimney, hearth, oven, stove, or stove-pipe, fire-frame, or other fixture, deposit of ashes, or any mixture or other material which may produce spontaneous combustion, or whatever else may give just cause of alarm or be the means of kindling or spreading fire.

34. They may make and ordain rules and regulations not repugnant to the constitution and laws of the state, for their own government and the conduct of citizens at fires, and annex penalties for the breach thereof not exceeding twenty dollars for one offence ; which may be recovered by the chief engineer in an action of tort and appropriated by the engineers to the improvement of the fire apparatus of the town : but such rules and regulations shall not be binding until approved by the inhabitants of the town at a meeting held for the purpose, and published as the town shall direct.

· 35. No act hereafter passed establishing a fire department in any town, shall take effect until it is accepted and approved by the inhabitants of such town at a meeting held for the purpose.

36. Fire departments may be established in villages or districts containing not less than one thousand inhabitants, the officers of which shall have charge of and be responsible for the engines and other apparatus for the

extinguishment of fire therein, in the same manner as fire-wards and enginemen of towns.

37. Before a district is constituted and organized, a petition shall be presented to the town at a legal meeting, stating the limits of the proposed district and requesting the town to raise taxes for the establishment and mainte-nance of a sufficient fire department for the reasonable protection from fire of the inhabitants and property within said limits. If the town refuses or neglects so to do, the inhabitants of the proposed district may proceed to con-stitute and organize the same and to establish a fire de-partment therein as hereinafter provided.

38. The selectmen upon the application in writing of not less than seven freeholders, inhabitants of such pro-posed district, setting forth the limits thereof, and requiring them to notify a meeting of the inhabitants thereof duly qualified to vote in town affairs, for the purpose of con-sidering the expediency of organizing such district and establishing a fire department, shall forthwith give notice to such inhabitants, in the manner of notifying town meet-ings, to assemble at some suitable place within the district for said purpose, the substance of which shall be expressed in the notification. If the selectmen refuse or neglect to notify such meeting, any justice of the peace in the county may notify the same.

39. If at any such meeting the voters present deter-mine to organize such district, they shall choose a clerk, who shall be sworn to keep a true record of the proceed-ings of all meetings and to perform all the duties of clerk so long as he holds the office. He may be removed by the district, or may resign, and in case of a vacancy an-other may be chosen.

40. The district at such meeting may vote to establish a fire department to consist of a chief engineer, and as many assistant engineers, enginemen, hosemen, and hook and ladder men, as they may deem necessary, not exceed-ing for each suction engine, seventy-five, for each common engine, thirty-five, for each one hundred and fifty feet of

leading hose kept for use within the district, five and not exceeding twenty-five hook and ladder men; each of said officers and members shall be furnished with a certificate under the hands of the chief engineer and clerk, declaring his station in the department.

41. The chief engineer and assistant engineers shall be chosen (annually [1]) by the district and shall be sworn.

42. Meetings of the district shall be called by the clerk when requested in writing by the chief engineer, or two assistant engineers, or seven voters of the district; and he shall give notice of the same by posting written notifications in at least six public places in the district not less than seven days prior to the meeting, or by publishing the same in a newspaper, if one is printed in the town where the district is situated, which notifications shall briefly state the purposes of the meeting. At each of the meetings a moderator shall be chosen, who shall have the powers of the moderator of a town meeting. After the choice of a clerk, he shall preside at subsequent meetings with like powers until a moderator is chosen.

43. The board of engineers may from time to time make and publish rules and regulations for their own government, and that of other members of the department, and of persons present at fires, and for regulating or prohibiting the carrying of fire or ignited substances in or through the streets or ways of the district, and prescribe penalties for the violation thereof, not exceeding twenty dollars for each offence. The board may appoint enginemen, hosemen, hook and ladder men, remove them, and fill vacancies in the companies.

44. Engineers shall have and exercise the same powers and authority relative to the extinguishment of fires, and the demolishing of buildings for that purpose within the district, as firewards of towns; and the inhabitants of districts shall be liable for acts done by such engineers, or by their orders, in the same manner as towns are liable for acts done by firewards.

[1] Stats. 1871, ch. 25.

45. Engineers and other members of the fire department of such district shall have the immunities and privileges of firewards and enginemen of towns, and shall receive such compensation as the district determines.[1]

46. Fire districts duly organized under the provisions of the twenty-fourth chapter of the General Statutes may, at meetings called for the purpose, raise money for the purchase of engines and other articles necessary for the extinguishment of fires, for the purchase of land and erection and repairs of necessary buildings, and other incidental expenses of the fire department. They shall choose a prudential committee, which shall expend the same for the purposes prescribed by votes of the district.

47. Such districts shall also choose a treasurer, who shall give bond in such sum as the prudential committee require, with sureties to their satisfaction, for the faithful discharge of the duties of his office. The treasurer so chosen and qualified shall receive and take charge of all sums of money belonging to the district, and pay over and account for the same according to the order of such district or the prudential committee.

48. When the office of treasurer is vacant by reason of death, removal, or other cause, or when the treasurer is prevented from performing the duties of his office, the prudential committee may by writing under their hands appoint a treasurer *pro tempore*, who shall give a bond in like manner as provided in the (preceding) section of this act, and hold his office until another is chosen.[2]

49. The clerk shall certify to the assessors of the town all sums of money voted to be raised by the district, which shall be assessed and collected by the officers of the town in the same manner that the town taxes are assessed and collected, and be paid over to the treasurer, who shall hold the same subject to the order of the (treasurer of the district[2]). The assessors, treasurer, and collector of any town in which such district is organized shall have the powers and perform the duties in reference to the assess-

[1] Gen. Stats. ch. 24, §§ 27–42.   [2] Stats. 1874, ch. 151.   See ch. 15, § 97.

ment and collection of the money voted by the fire district, as they have and exercise in reference to the assessment, collection, and abatement of town taxes, (and[1]) the sums so voted shall be assessed upon the (polls and[1]) property, real and personal, within the district.

50. No by-law, rule, or regulation, adopted by the district, and having a penalty attached to it, shall be in force until it is approved by the superior court for the county in which such fire district is.

51. Penalties under the provisions of the twelve preceding sections may be recovered by action of tort in the name of the chief engineer, and appropriated to pay the expenses of the fire department of the district, or on complaint or indictment to the use of the commonwealth. If the chief engineer shall die, resign, or remove, during the pendency of such suit, it shall not abate, but his successor shall be admitted to prosecute it. No inhabitant of the district shall be disqualified to act as judge, magistrate, juror, or officer, in a suit brought for such penalties.

52. Such district, at a meeting called for that purpose, may alter the limits thereof so as to include any adjacent territory and its inhabitants, if (a majority of[2]) the voters of said territory have petitioned therefor, setting forth the limits of the territory to be annexed; or exclude any person, or the estate of any person, who has thus petitioned, if the town within which the district is situated has assented thereto.

53. Fire districts heretofore legally organized shall continue and be subject to the provisions of this chapter in relation to fire districts.[3]

54. (And) fire districts duly organized under the provisions of the twenty-fourth chapter of the General Statutes, may, at meetings legally called for that purpose in the manner provided in the thirty-ninth section of said chapter, raise money for the erection and maintenance of street lamps within their respective limits.[4]

[1] Stats. 1876, ch. 114.
[2] Stats. 1875, ch. 122.
[3] Gen. Stats. ch. 24, §§ 44–48.
[4] Stats. 1864, ch. 159.

55. No association, society, or club, organized as firemen, shall be allowed in any city or town, except by the written permission of the mayor and aldermen or selectmen.

56. Whoever joins, belongs to, or assembles with, such association, society, or club, existing without such permission, shall be punished by fine not less than five nor more than one hundred dollars, or by imprisonment in the house of correction for a term not exceeding three months.

57. The provisions of the two preceding sections shall be in force in those cities and towns only which have adopted or may adopt the same.[1]

58. The selectmen of towns, containing fire districts, shall at least ten days before the annual fire district election, make correct alphabetical lists of all the persons qualified to vote in such election, for the several officers to be elected, shall cause such lists to be posted up in two or more public places in said district, and shall perform the same duties in reference to the correction of said lists as they are now required by law to perform in reference to the correction of check lists for town elections.

59. In fire districts composed of portions of two or more towns, the duties which the preceding section requires the selectmen to perform, shall be performed by the prudential committee of said district.

60. The provisions of sections nine, twelve, and thirteen of chapter seven of the General Statutes shall be so construed as to apply to fire districts.

61. The polls at fire district elections shall be kept open not less than two hours and not more than six hours.[2]

62. Any city or town which has established, or may hereafter establish, a fire department under the provisions of chapter twenty-four of the General Statutes, or acts in addition thereto or amendment thereof, may by vote of the city council in such city, or of the inhabitants of such town, at a meeting called for the purpose, appoint the term of office for the engineers, enginemen, and other mem-

---

[1] Gen. Stats. ch. 24, §§ 49–51.    [2] Stats. 1871, ch. 124.

bers of the fire department, to begin at any future day, and to end in one year from the day so appointed, and so on from year to year.

63. Whenever a year is thus appointed other than the year beginning on the first day of May, which is prescribed in said chapter twenty-four, all dates or other provisions of said chapter that have reference to the month of May, shall be so far altered as to have like reference to the first month of the year thus appointed.

64. For the purpose of changing, in accordance with a vote passed as provided in section one (sixty-one above), the system existing at any time, any city or town may, by another vote which may be passed at the same time, abridge or protract the current term of office of the engineers, enginemen, and other members of the fire department : *provided*, that no term shall be made shorter than six months nor longer than eighteen months ; and *provided*, *further*, that the incumbents of such offices shall in all cases hold office until others are appointed in their stead.[1]

65. Cities and towns may, by ordinances and by-laws not repugnant to the laws of the commonwealth, prescribe rules and regulations for the inspection, materials, construction, alteration, and safe use of buildings and structures within their respective limits not owned or occupied by the United States or the commonwealth, and excepting bridges, quays, and wharves, for the purpose of securing the prevention of fire and the preservation of life ; and may prescribe penalties, not exceeding one hundred dollars for each and every violation of any provision of such ordinances or by-laws.

66. Such ordinances and by-laws may be made operative upon and within the whole territory of any city or town, or upon and within any prescribed and defined district or districts of such territory.

67. The supreme judicial court, or any justice thereof, in term time or vacation, may, by injunction or other suitable

[1] Stats. 1877, ch. 38.

process in equity, restrain any person or corporation from constructing, altering, maintaining, or using any building or structure contrary to or in violation of any lawful ordinance or by-law made under or by virtue of this act, and may order and enforce the removal, or abatement as a nuisance, of any building or structure constructed, altered, maintained, or used in violation of such ordinance or by-law.

68. This act (this and three preceding sections) shall not be in force in any city or town unless the city council or the inhabitants of the town shall, by legal vote, decide to adopt the same ; and it shall not apply to the city of Boston.[1]

69. The mayor and aldermen of each city, and the selectmen of each town in this commonwealth, shall annually in the month of January return to the insurance commissioner a statement showing the number of fires which have occurred in their respective cities and towns during the preceding year. Such return shall also state the names of the owners or occupants of the premises damaged or destroyed, the cause or origin of the fire, if known, the amount of loss or damage and the insurance thereon.

70. The insurance commissioner shall in due season prepare and forward to the officials named, blanks suitable for making the returns required by the first section of this act (preceding section), and shall include in his annual report to the legislature a condensed statement of statistics derived from such returns.[2]

71. Whoever wilfully and maliciously obstructs or retards the passage of any engine or other apparatus of any fire department, while going to a fire through any street, lane, alley, or other way, shall be punished by imprisonment in the house of correction not exceeding three months, or by fine not exceeding fifty dollars.[3]

72. The fees of the magistrate and the expenses of any inquisition hereafter held under the provisions of chapter

[1] Stats. 1872, ch. 243.      [3] Stats. 1874, ch. 37.
[2] Stats. 1878, ch. 104.

three hundred and three of the acts of the year eighteen hundred and sixty-seven, shall be returned to the mayor and aldermen or selectmen of the city or town where the property was destroyed, and being audited and certified by them shall be paid by such city or town, (and shall be the same as are provided by statute for similar services and expenses at coroners' inquests [1]).

73. Section one of chapter three hundred and three of the acts of eighteen hundred and sixty-seven, as amended by chapter two hundred and eighty-three of the acts of eighteen hundred and seventy-three, is further amended by striking therefrom the limitation of time within which complaints may be subscribed and sworn to.[2]

74. When the selectmen of any town consider it necessary, for the protection of persons and property in such town, against fire, to take water from any or all the pipes or conductors of any aqueduct company running through such town, said selectmen may order the engineers of the fire department in said town to request said aqueduct company to put conductors into such pipes or conductors of said company, for the purpose of attaching hydrants or conducting water into reservoirs, and in such places as said engineers shall think necessary to secure the safety of such persons and property against fire.

This section is in addition to the provision of the General Statutes, which seems to be still in force; as follows: —

A city or town in which such aqueduct is situated may put conductors into the pipes for the purpose of drawing therefrom, free of expense, as much water as is necessary when a building is on fire therein: *provided*, that the conductors are so secured that water shall not be drawn therefrom unless for the purpose of extinguishing fires.

75. If said aqueduct company shall refuse or neglect to make such connections for two weeks from the time of said notice, then said engineers may proceed to make such connections as provided in the preceding section.

Said engineers shall have the right to use all necessary

---

[1] Stats. 1877, ch. 85.    [2] Stats. 1874, ch. 267.

means for making such connections, and shall use reasonable care for the protection of the pipes and works of such aqueduct company.

The cost of such connections, in all cases, shall be paid by the town whose selectmen shall make such order.[1]

[1] Stats. 1867, ch. 158.

# CHAPTER XLVI.

## DUTIES OF SELECTMEN AS TO OFFENCES AGAINST THE PUBLIC PEACE.

1. IF any persons, to the number of twelve or more, being armed with clubs or other dangerous weapons, or if any persons, to the number of thirty or more, whether armed or not, are unlawfully, riotously, or tumultuously assembled in any city or town, it shall be the duty of the mayor and of each of the aldermen of such city, and of each of the selectmen of such town, and of every justice of the peace living in any such city or town, and also of the sheriff of the county and his deputies, to go among the persons so assembled, or as near to them as may be with safety, and in the name of the commonwealth to command all the persons so assembled immediately and peaceably to disperse; and if such persons do not thereupon immediately and peaceably disperse, it shall be the duty of each of said magistrates and officers to command the assistance of all persons there present, in seizing, arresting, and securing such persons in custody, so that they may be proceeded with for their offence, according to law.

2. If any person present, being commanded by any of the magistrates or officers mentioned in the preceding section to aid or assist in seizing and securing such rioters or persons so unlawfully assembled, or in suppressing such riot or unlawful assembly, refuses or neglects to obey such command, or, when required by such magistrate or officer to depart from the place, refuses or neglects so to do, he shall be deemed one of the rioters, or persons unlawfully assembled, and may be prosecuted and punished accordingly.

3. If any mayor, alderman, selectman, justice of the

peace, sheriff, or deputy-sheriff, having notice of any such riotous or tumultuous and unlawful assembly, in the city or town in which he lives, neglects or refuses immediately to proceed to the place of such assembly, or as near thereto as he can with safety, or omits or neglects to exercise the authority with which he is invested by this chapter for suppressing such assembly, and for arresting and securing the offenders, he shall be punished by fine not exceeding three hundred dollars.

4. If any persons who are so riotously or unlawfully assembled, and who have been commanded to disperse, as before provided, refuse or neglect to disperse without unnecessary delay, any two of the magistrates or officers before mentioned may require the aid of a sufficient number of persons, in arms or otherwise as may be necessary, and shall proceed in such manner as in their judgment is expedient, forthwith to disperse and suppress such assembly, and seize and secure the persons composing the same, so that they may be proceeded with according to law.

5. When any armed force called out in the manner provided by chapter thirteen, to suppress a tumult or riot, or to disperse any body of men acting together by force and with intent to commit a felony, or to offer violence to persons or property, or with intent by force or violence to resist or oppose the execution of the laws of this state, arrives at the place of such unlawful, riotous, or tumultuous assembly, they shall obey such orders for suppressing the riot or tumult, and for dispersing and arresting all persons who are committing any of said offences, as they have received from the governor, or any judge of a court of record, or the sheriff of the county, and also such orders as they there receive from any two of the magistrates or officers before mentioned.

6. If, by reason of the efforts made by any two or more of said magistrates or officers, or by their direction, to disperse such assembly, or to seize and secure the persons composing the same, who have refused to disperse, though the number remaining may be less than twelve, any such

person, or other person then present, is killed or wounded, the magistrates and officers, and all persons acting by their order, or under their directions, and all persons acting under the two preceding sections, shall be held guiltless and fully justified in law ; and if any of said magistrates or officers, or any person acting under or by the direction of any of the officers before mentioned, is killed or wounded, all persons so assembled, and all other persons who, when commanded or required, refused to aid and assist said magistrates or officers, shall be held answerable therefor.

7. If any of the persons so unlawfully assembled demolishes, pulls down, or destroys, or begins to demolish, pull down, or destroy, any dwelling-house, or other building, or ship or vessel, he shall be punished by imprisonment in the state prison not exceeding five years, or by fine not exceeding one thousand dollars and imprisonment in the jail not exceeding two years, and shall also be answerable to any person injured, to the full amount of the damage, in an action of tort.

8. When property of the value of fifty dollars or more is destroyed, or property is injured to that amount, by any persons to the number of twelve or more, riotously, routously, or tumultuously assembled, the city or town within which the property was situated shall be liable to indemnify the owner thereof, to the amount of three-fourths of the value of the property destroyed, or of the amount of such injury thereto, to be recovered in an action of tort : *provided*, that the owner of such property uses all reasonable diligence to prevent its destruction or injury, and to procure the conviction of the offenders.

9. A city or town which pays any sum under the provisions of the preceding section may recover the same against any or all of the persons who destroyed or injured such property.[1]

[1] Gen. Stats. ch. 164, §§ 1–9.

# CHAPTER XLVII.

## DUTIES OF TOWN OFFICERS AS TO THE SUPPRESSION OF COMMON NUISANCES.

1. IN any city or town which has adopted chapter four hundred and sixty-nine of the statutes of eighteen hundred and fifty-five, or which shall adopt this and the four following sections, at a legal meeting of the city council or inhabitants of the town, if the mayor and aldermen or selectmen, after due notice in writing to the owner of any burnt, dilapidated, or dangerous building, and a hearing of the matter, adjudge the same to be a nuisance to the neighborhood, or dangerous, they may make and record an order prescribing such disposition, alteration, or regulation thereof as they deem necessary ; and thereupon the city or town clerk shall deliver a copy of the order to a constable, who shall forthwith serve an attested copy thereof upon such owner, and make return of his doings thereon to said clerk.

2. Any owner aggrieved by such order may within three days of the service thereof upon him apply for a jury to the superior court, if sitting in the county, or to any justice thereof in vacation. The court or justice shall issue a warrant for a jury, to be empanelled by the sheriff within fourteen days from the date of the warrant in the manner provided in chapter forty-three relating to highways.

3. The jury may affirm, annul, or alter such order; and the sheriff shall return the verdict to the next term of the court for acceptance, and, being accepted, it shall take effect as an original order.

4. If the order is affirmed, costs shall be taxed against the applicant ; if it is annulled, the applicant shall recover

damages and costs against the city or town; if it is altered in part, the court may render such judgment as to costs as justice shall require.

5. The mayor and aldermen or selectmen of any city or town shall have the same power and authority to abate and remove any such nuisance, as are given to the board of health in sections eight, nine, and ten, of chapter twenty-six (of General Statutes [1]).

6. The mayor and aldermen or selectmen of any place, upon complaint made to them under oath, that the complainant has reason to believe, and does believe, that any booth, shed, or other temporary erection, situated within one mile of any muster-field, cattle-show ground, or other place of public gathering, is used and occupied for the sale of spirituous or fermented liquors, or for the purpose of gaming, may, if they consider the complaint well founded, order the owner or occupant thereof to vacate and close the same forthwith. If the owner or occupant refuses or neglects so to do, the mayor and aldermen or selectmen may forthwith abate such booth, shed, or erection, as a nuisance, and pull down or otherwise destroy the same, in any manner they choose, or through the agency of any force, civil or military.[2]

7. Whoever in any city or town containing more than four thousand inhabitants erects, occupies, or uses any building for carrying on therein the business of slaughtering cattle, sheep, or other animals, or for melting or rendering establishments, or for other noxious or offensive trades and occupations, or permits or allows said trades or occupations to be carried on upon premises owned or occupied by him or them, without first obtaining the written consent and permission of the mayor and aldermen, or selectmen of such city or town, shall forfeit a sum not exceeding two hundred dollars for every month he or they so occupy or use such building or premises, and in like proportion for a longer or shorter time: *provided*, that the terms of this section shall not apply to any building or

---

[1] See chapter on Board of Health.     [2] Gen. Stats. ch. 87, §§ 1-5, 10.

premises now occupied or used for the trades or occupations before described ; but no person or persons or corporation now occupying or using any building or premises for the trades or occupations aforesaid, shall enlarge or extend the same without first obtaining the written consent and permission of the mayor and aldermen or selectmen of the city or town in which such building or premises are situated in the manner provided in this section.

8. Whenever in any city or town containing more than four thousand inhabitants any building or premises are occupied or used by any person or persons or corporation for carrying on the business of slaughtering cattle, sheep, or other animals, or for melting or rendering establishments, or for other noxious or offensive trades, the state board of health may, if in their judgment the public health or the public comfort and convenience shall require, order any person or persons or corporation carrying on said trades or occupations, to desist and cease from further carrying on said trades or occupations in such building or premises, and any person or persons or corporation continuing to occupy or use such building or premises for carrying on said trades or occupations after being ordered to desist and cease therefrom by said board, shall forfeit a sum not exceeding two hundred dollars for every month he or they continue to occupy and use such building or premises for carrying on said trades or occupations after being ordered to desist and cease therefrom by said board as aforesaid, and in like proportion for a longer or shorter time : *provided*, that on any application to said board to exercise the powers in this section conferred upon them, a time and place for hearing the parties shall be assigned by said board, and due notice thereof given to the party against whom the application is made, and the order herein before provided shall only be issued after such notice and hearing.

9. The supreme judicial court, or any one of the justices thereof, in term time or vacation, shall have power to issue an injunction to prevent the erection, occupancy, use, enlargement, or extension of any building or premises occu-

pied or used for the trades or occupations aforesaid, without the written consent and permission provided in section one (seven) of this act being first obtained; and also in like manner to enforce the orders of the state board of health issued under section two (eight) of this act.[1]

[1] Stats. 1871, ch. 167, §§ 1–3.

# CHAPTER XLVIII.

## DUTIES OF SELECTMEN AS TO DISEASED CATTLE.

1. THE selectmen of towns and the mayor and aldermen of cities, in case of the existence in this commonwealth of the disease called pleuro-pneumonia, or any other contagious disease among cattle, shall cause the cattle in their respective towns and cities, which are infected, or which have been exposed to infection, to be secured or collected in some suitable place or places within such city or town, and kept isolated ; and, when taken from the possession of their owners, to be maintained, one-fifth of the expense thereof to be paid by the town or city wherein the animal is kept, and four-fifths at the expense of the commonwealth ; such isolation to continue so long as the existence of such disease, or other circumstances, renders the same necessary.

2. Said selectmen and mayor and aldermen, when any such animal is adjudged by a veterinary surgeon or physician, by them selected, to be infected with pleuro-pneumonia, or any other contagious disease, may, in their discretion, order such diseased animal to be forthwith killed and buried at the expense of such town or city.

3. Said selectmen and mayor and aldermen shall cause all cattle which they shall so order to be killed, to be appraised by three competent and disinterested men, under oath, at the value thereof at the time of the appraisal, and the amount of the appraisal shall be paid as provided in the first section.

4. Said selectmen and mayor and aldermen, within their respective towns and cities, are hereby authorized to prohibit the departure of cattle from any enclosure, or to exclude cattle therefrom.

5. Said selectmen and mayor and aldermen may make regulations in writing to regulate or prohibit the passage from, to, or through their respective cities or towns, or from place to place within the same, of any neat cattle, and may arrest and detain, at the cost of the owners thereof, all cattle found passing in violation of such regulations, and may take all other necessary measures for the enforcement of such prohibition, and also for preventing the spread of any such disease among the cattle in their respective towns and cities, and the immediate vicinity thereof.

6. The regulations made by selectmen and mayors and aldermen, in pursuance of the foregoing section, shall be recorded upon the records of their towns and cities respectively, and shall be published in such towns and cities in such manner as may be provided in such regulations.

7. Said selectmen and mayor and aldermen are authorized to cause all cattle infected with such disease, or which have been exposed thereto, to be forthwith branded upon the rump with the letter P, so as to distinguish the animal from other cattle; and no animal so branded shall be sold or disposed of except with the knowledge and consent of such selectmen and mayor and aldermen. Any person, without such knowledge and consent, selling or disposing of an animal so branded, or selling or disposing of an animal known to be affected with such disease, or known to have been exposed thereto within one year previous to such sale or disposal, shall be punished by a fine not exceeding five hundred dollars, or by imprisonment not exceeding one year.

8. Any person disobeying the orders of the selectmen or mayor and aldermen, made in conformity with the fourth section, or driving or transporting any neat cattle contrary to the regulations made, recorded, and published as aforesaid, shall be punished by fine not exceeding five hundred dollars, or by imprisonment not exceeding one year.

9. Whoever knows or has reason to suspect the exist-

ence of any such disease among the cattle in his possession, or under his care, shall forthwith give notice to the selectmen of the town or mayor and aldermen of the city where such cattle may be kept, and for failure so to do shall be punished by fine not exceeding five hundred dollars, or by imprisonment not exceeding one year.

10. Any town or city whose officers shall neglect or refuse to carry into effect the provisions of sections one, two, three, four, five, six, and seven, shall forfeit a sum not exceeding five hundred dollars for each day's neglect.

11. All appraisals made under the provisions of this act shall be in writing and signed by the appraisers, and the same shall be certified to the governor and council and to the treasurer of the several cities and towns wherein the cattle appraised were kept by the selectmen and mayors and aldermen respectively.

12. The selectmen of towns and mayor and aldermen of cities are hereby authorized, when in their judgment it shall be necessary to carry into effect the purposes of this act, to take and hold possession, for a term not exceeding one year, within their respective towns and cities, of any land, without buildings other than barns thereon, upon which it may be necessary to enclose and isolate any cattle, and they shall cause the damages sustained by the owner in consequence of such taking and holding to be appraised by the assessors of the town or city wherein the lands so taken are situated ; and they shall further cause a description of such land, setting forth the boundaries thereof, and the area as nearly as may be estimated, together with said appraisal by the assessors, to be entered on the records of the town or city. The amount of said appraisal shall be paid as provided in the first section, in such sums and at such times as the selectmen or mayor and aldermen respectively may order. If the owner of any land so taken shall be dissatisfied with the appraisal of said assessors, he may by action of contract recover of the town or city wherein the lands lie a fair compensation for the damages sustained by him ; but no costs shall be taxed, unless the damages

27

recovered in such action, exclusive of interest, exceed the appraisal of the assessors. And the commonwealth shall reimburse any town or city four-fifths of any sum recovered of such town or city in any such action.[1]

13. The selectmen of towns, the mayor and aldermen of cities, and the cattle commissioners of this common-wealth, shall have and may exercise the powers and shall be subject to the duties for the prevention of the diseases known as farcy and glanders among horses, asses, and mules, and for the prevention of contagious and infectious diseases among domestic animals, that are now conferred or imposed upon them by the laws relating to the prevention of contagious diseases among cattle.

14. The penalties imposed by chapter two hundred and nineteen of the acts of the year one thousand eight hundred and sixty, entitled "An Act concerning contagious diseases among cattle," (this chapter,) are hereby made applicable to any violation of law relating to the diseases in horses, asses, and mules, known as farcy and glanders, or relating to contagious or infectious diseases in domestic animals.[2]

[1] Stats. 1860, ch. 219.    [2] Stats. 1878, ch. 24, §§ 1, 2.

# CHAPTER XLIX.

## REGISTRY AND RETURNS OF BIRTHS, MARRIAGES, AND DEATHS.

1. THE clerk of each city and town shall receive or obtain, and record and index, the following facts concerning the births, marriages, and deaths, therein, separately numbering and recording the same in the order in which he receives them, designating in separate columns ;

In the record of births, the date of the birth, the place of birth, the name of the child, (if it have any,) the sex and color of the child, the names and the places of birth of the parents, the occupation of the father, the residence of the parents, and the date of the record ;

In the record of marriages, the date of the marriage, the place of marriage, the name, residence, and official station of the person by whom married, the names and the places of birth of the parties, the residence of each, the age and color of each, the condition of each, (whether single or widowed,) the occupation, the names of the parents, and the date of the record ;

In the record of deaths, the date of the death, the name of the deceased, the sex, the color, the condition, (whether single, widowed, or married,) the age, the residence, the occupation, the place of death, the place of birth, the names and places of birth of the parents, the disease or cause of death, the place of burial, and the date of the record.

2. Parents shall give notice to the clerk of their city or town of the births and deaths of their children ; every householder shall give like notice of every birth and death happening in his house ; the eldest person next of kin shall give such notice of the death of his kindred ; the keeper of a workhouse, house of correction, prison, hospital, or alms-

house, except the state almshouses at Tewksbury, Bridgewater, and Monson, and the master or other commanding officer of any ship shall give like notice of every birth and death happening among the persons under his charge. Whoever neglects to give such notice for the space of six months after a birth or death, shall forfeit a sum not exceeding five dollars.

3. Any physician having attended a person during his last illness, shall, when requested within fifteen days after the decease of such person, forthwith furnish for registration a certificate of the duration of the last sickness, the disease of which the person died, and the date of his decease, as nearly as he can state the same. If any physician refuses or neglects to make such certificate, he shall forfeit and pay the sum of ten dollars to the use of the town in which he resides.

4. Every sexton, undertaker, or other person having charge of a burial-ground, or the superintendent of burials having charge of the obsequies or funeral rites preliminary to the interment of a human body, shall forthwith obtain and return to the clerk of the city or town in which the deceased resided or the death occurred, the facts required by this chapter to be recorded by said officer concerning the deceased, and the person making such return shall receive from his city or town the fee of (twenty-five [1]) cents therefor.

The clerk, upon recording such facts, shall forthwith give to the person making such return, a certificate that such return has been made, which certificate such person shall deliver to the person having charge of the interment, if other than himself, before the burial when practicable, otherwise within seven days thereafter. When a burial takes place and no certificate is delivered as aforesaid, the sexton. undertaker, or other person having charge of the interment, shall forthwith give notice thereof to the clerk under penalty of twenty dollars.

5. The clerk of each city and town shall annually on or

[1] Stats. 1873, ch. 202.

before the first day of February, transmit to the secretary of the commonwealth certified copies of the records of the births, marriages, and deaths, which have occurred therein during the year ending on the last day of the preceding December.

6. The record of the town clerk relative to any birth, marriage, or death, shall be *prima facie* evidence, in legal proceedings, of the facts recorded. The certificate signed by the town clerk for the time being shall be admissible as evidence of any such record.

7. The clerk shall receive from his city or town for obtaining, recording, indexing, and returning to the secretary of the commonwealth, the facts in relation to a birth, twenty cents ; a marriage, ten cents ; a death, twenty cents for each of the first twenty entries, and ten cents for each subsequent entry, as the same shall be certified by the secretary of the commonwealth ; but a city or town containing more than ten thousand inhabitants may limit the aggregate compensation allowed to their clerk. He shall forfeit a sum not less than twenty nor more than one hundred dollars for each refusal or neglect to perform any duty required of him by this chapter.

See section fourteen of this chapter for fees of clerk ; and so much of this section as is inconsistent with section fourteen of this chapter is repealed.

8. The superintendents of the state almshouses at Tewksbury, Bridgewater, and Monson, shall obtain, record, and make return of, the facts in relation to the births and deaths which occur in their respective institutions, in like manner as is required of town clerks. The clerks of said towns shall, in relation to the births and deaths of persons in said almshouses, be exempt from the duties otherwise required of them by this chapter.

9. The secretary shall at the expense of the commonwealth prepare and furnish to the clerks of the several cities and towns, and to the superintendents of the state almshouses, blank books of suitable quality and size to be

used as books of record under this chapter, blank books for indexes thereto, and blank forms for returns, on paper of uniform size ; and shall accompany the same with such instructions and explanations as may be necessary and useful.    City and town clerks shall make such distribution of blank forms of returns furnished by the secretary as he shall direct.

10. The secretary shall cause the returns received by him for each year to be bound together in one or more volumes with indexes thereto.   He shall prepare from the returns such tabular results as will render them of practical utility, make report thereof annually to the legislature, and do all other acts necessary to carry into effect the provisions of this chapter.

11. Any city or town containing more than ten thousand inhabitants, may choose a person other than the clerk to be registrar, who shall be sworn, and to whom all the provisions of this chapter concerning clerks shall apply.   The returns and notices required to be made and given to clerks shall be made and given to such registrar under like penalties.

As to fees of registrar, see section fourteen of this chapter.

12. The secretary of this commonwealth shall prosecute, by an action of tort, in the name of the commonwealth, for the recovery of any penalty or forfeiture imposed by this [chapter] [*act*].

13. Any city or town may make rules and regulations to enforce the provisions of this chapter, or to secure a more perfect registration of births, marriages, and deaths, therein.[1]

14. The clerk of each city and town, except in such cities and towns as choose a registrar, under the eleventh section of the twenty-first chapter of the General Statutes, in which cases the provisions of this act shall apply to the registrar, for receiving or obtaining, recording, indexing, and returning the facts relating to marriages, births, and

[1] Gen. Stats. ch. 21, §§ 1–13.

deaths occurring therein, shall be entitled to receive therefrom the sums following; viz., for each marriage, fifteen cents; for each birth, thirty cents; for each death returned to him by the persons specified in sections two, three, and four of chapter twenty-one of the General Statutes, twenty cents for each of the first twenty entries, and ten cents for each subsequent entry; for each death not so returned, but by him obtained and recorded, thirty-five [1] cents. [2]

15. No human body shall be buried, or removed from any city or town, until a proper certificate has been given by the clerk or local registrar of statistics to the undertaker or sexton, or person performing the burial, or removing the body. This certificate shall state that the facts required by chapter twenty-one of the General Statutes (foregoing portion of this chapter) have been returned and recorded; and no clerk or local registrar shall give such certificate or burial permit until the certificate of the cause of death has been obtained from the physician, if any, in attendance at the last sickness of the deceased, and placed in the hands of said clerk or local registrar: *provided*, that in those cities and towns where local boards of health have been established, the certificate of the cause of death shall be approved by such board before a permit to bury is given by the registrar or clerk. Upon application, the chairman of the local board of health or any physician employed by any city or town for such purpose, shall sign the certificate of the cause of death to the best of his knowledge and belief, if there has been no physician in attendance. He shall also sign such certificate, upon application, in case of death by dangerous contagious disease, or in any other event when the certificate of the attending physician cannot for good and sufficient reasons be early enough obtained. In case of death by violence, the medical examiner attending shall furnish the requisite medical certificate. Any person violating the provisions of this section shall be punished by a fine not exceeding twenty-five dollars.

[1] Stats. 1873, ch. 341.          [2] Stats. 1866, ch. 138, § 1.

16. This act (this and the preceding section) shall take effect on the first day of May in the year eighteen hundred and seventy-eight; and all acts and parts of acts inconsistent herewith are hereby repealed.[1]

[1] Stats. 1878, ch. 174.

# CHAPTER L.

## BOARD OF HEALTH.

1. A TOWN respecting which no provision is made by special law for choosing a board of health, may, at its annual meeting or at a meeting legally warned for the purpose, choose a board of health, to consist of not less than three nor more than nine persons ; or may choose a health officer. If no board or officer is chosen the selectmen shall be the board of health. (The election shall be by written ballot.[1])

2. Except where different provision is made by law,. the city council of a city may appoint a board of health ; may constitute either branch of such council, or a joint or separate committee of their body, a board of health, either for general or special purposes, and may prescribe the manner in which the powers and duties of the board shall be exercised and carried into effect. In default of the appointment of a board with full powers, the city council shall have the powers and perform the duties prescribed to boards of health in towns.

3. Every board of health may appoint a physician to the board, who shall hold his office during its pleasure.

4. The board shall establish the salary or other compensation of such physician, and shall regulate all fees and charges of persons employed by it in the execution of the health laws and of its own regulations.[2]

5. Boards of health in the several cities and towns in this commonwealth, may appoint an agent or agents to act for them, respectively, in cases of emergency, or when such board cannot be conveniently assembled ; and such

---

[1] Stats. 1878, ch. 26.　　　[2] Gen. Stats. ch. 26, §§ 1–4.

agent so appointed shall have and exercise all the authority which the board of health appointing him had; but he shall, within two days, report his action in each case to the board of health for their approval, and shall be directly responsible to and under the control and direction of the board of health from which he received such appointment.[1]

6. The board shall make such regulations as it judges necessary for the public health and safety, respecting nuisances, sources of filth, and causes of sickness, within its town, or on board of vessels within its harbor; and respecting articles which are capable of containing or conveying infection or contagion, or of creating sickness, brought into or conveyed from its town, or into or from any vessel. Whoever violates any such regulation shall forfeit a sum not exceeding one hundred dollars.

7. Notice shall be given by the board of all regulations made by it, by publishing the same in some newspaper of its town, or where there is no such newspaper by posting them up in some public place in the town. Such notice shall be deemed legal notice to all persons.

8. The board shall examine into all nuisances, sources of filth, and causes of sickness, within its town, or in any vessel within the harbor of such town, that may in its opinion be injurious to the health of the inhabitants, and the same shall destroy, remove, or prevent, as the case may require.

9. The board or the health officer shall order the owner or occupant at his own expense to remove any nuisance, source of filth, or cause of sickness, found on private property, within twenty-four hours or such other time as it deems reasonable after notice served as provided in the following section; and if the owner or occupant neglects so to do, he shall forfeit a sum not exceeding twenty dollars for every day during which he knowingly permits such nuisance or cause of sickness to remain after the time prescribed for the removal thereof.[2]

[1] Stats. 1866, ch. 271.          [2] Gen. Stats. ch. 26, §§ 5–8.

Such order for the removal of a nuisance is valid without previous notice to the parties interested, and opportunity for them to appear and be heard.

But it is necessary that the order should be so explicit as to sufficiently inform the party of the nature and locality of the nuisance to be removed. And it need not prescribe a mode for the removal, as the owner or occupant of the property on which the nuisance is found is not restricted by such prescription if made.[1]

10. Any person aggrieved by the neglect or refusal of any board of health in any city or town to pass all proper orders abating a nuisance or nuisances in said city or town, may appeal to the board of county commissioners in the same county for a redress of such grievances, and the said commissioners shall have full power to hear and determine the matter of such appeal, and may make such decree and exercise and perform all the powers in such case as a board of health may exercise and perform in a town, as specified in chapter twenty-six of the General Statutes.

11. The party so appealing shall, within twenty-four hours after such neglect or refusal by any board of health, give written notice to the opposite party of his intention so to appeal, and within seven days after such neglect or refusal, shall present a petition to some member of the said board of commissioners, setting forth the grievances complained of, and the action of the board of health thereon, and shall thereupon enter into such recognizance before said board of commissioners, in such sum and with such surety or sureties as they shall order.

12. The said commissioners, when acting under the provisions of this act, shall tax three dollars per day for time, and five cents a mile for travel to and from the place of meeting, to be paid into the county treasury; and such costs shall be in the first instance paid by the appellant, and said commissioners may award that such costs and any other costs of the proceeding shall be paid by either party, as in their judgment justice shall require.

[1] Salem v. Eastern R. R., 98 Mass. 431.

13. This act shall not affect any suit or proceeding now pending, nor shall it affect the jurisdiction of any court.[1]

14. Such order shall be made in writing, and served by any person competent to serve a notice in a civil suit, personally on the owner, occupant, or his authorized agent; or a copy of the order may be left at the last and usual place of abode of the owner, occupant, or agent, if he is known and within the state. But if the premises are unoccupied and the residence of the owner or agent is unknown or without the state, the notice may be served by posting the same on the premises and advertising in one or more public newspapers in such manner and for such length of time as the board or health officer may direct.

15. If the owner or occupant fails to comply with such order, the board may cause the nuisance, source of filth, or cause of sickness, to be removed, and all expenses incurred thereby shall be paid by the owner, occupant, or other person who caused or permitted the same, if he has had actual notice from the board of health of the existence thereof.[2]

16. Upon the failure of the owner or occupant of the property on which the nuisance is found to remove the same, the board is not restricted to the mode prescribed in the order, but may adopt any which is suitable, even if, in so doing, it is necessary to subvert soil adjoining that on which the nuisance exists.

17. And in an action by the authorities against a party alleged to have caused a nuisance, to recover money expended by the board of health for removing it, if such party had no opportunity to be heard before the board, none of the findings or adjudications of the board preliminary to the incurring of such expenses are conclusive upon him, and all the facts on which the recovery is sought are open to be controverted, and must be established by the proofs.[3]

18. The board, when satisfied upon due examination that any cellar, room, tenement, or building, in its town, occupied as a dwelling-place, has become, by reason of the

---

[1] Stats. 1866, ch. 211, §§ 1–4.
[2] Gen. Stats. ch. 26, §§ 9, 10.
[3] Salem v. Eastern R. R., 98 Mass. 431.

number of occupants, or want of cleanliness, or other cause, unfit for such purpose and a cause of nuisance or sickness to the occupants or the public, may issue a notice in writing to such occupants, or any of them, requiring the premises to be put into a proper condition as to cleanliness, or if they see fit requiring the occupants to remove or quit the premises within such time as the board may deem reasonable. If the persons so notified, or any of them, neglect or refuse to comply with the terms of the notice, the board may cause the premises to be properly cleansed at the expense of the owners, or may remove the occupants forcibly and close up the premises, and the same shall not be again occupied as a dwelling-place without the consent in writing of the board. If the owner thereafter occupies or knowingly permits the same to be occupied without such permission in writing, he shall forfeit a sum not less than ten nor more than fifty dollars.

19. When a person is convicted on an indictment for a common nuisance injurious to the public health, the court in their discretion may order it to be removed or destroyed at the expense of the defendant, under the direction of the board of health; and the form of the warrant to the sheriff or other officer may be varied accordingly.

20. The superior court, or a justice thereof in term time or vacation, may, either before or pending a prosecution for a common nuisance affecting the public health, issue an injunction to stay or prevent the same until the matter shall be decided by a jury or otherwise; may enforce such injunction according to the course of proceedings in chancery; and may dissolve the same when the court or one of the justices shall think proper.[1]

21. When the board thinks it necessary for the preservation of the lives or health of the inhabitants, to enter any land, building, premises, or vessel, within its town, for the purpose of examining into and destroying, removing, or preventing, any nuisance, source of filth, or cause of sickness, and said board or any agent thereof sent for

[1] Gen. Stats. ch. 26, §§ 11–13.

that purpose shall be refused such entry, any member of the board, or such agent, may make complaint under oath to any justice of any court of record, or to two justices of the peace of the county, stating the facts of the case so far as he has knowledge thereof, and said justice or justices may thereupon issue a warrant directed to the sheriff or any of his deputies, or to any constable of such town, commanding him to take sufficient aid, and at any reasonable time repair to the place where such nuisance, source of filth, or cause of sickness, complained of may be, and the same to destroy, remove, or prevent, under the directions of said board.[1]

22. The board may grant permits for the removal of any nuisance, infected articles, or sick person, within the limits of its town, when it thinks it safe and proper so to do.

23. When any person coming from abroad or residing in any town in this state is infected, or lately has been infected, with the plague or other sickness dangerous to the public health, except as is otherwise provided in this chapter, the board shall make effectual provision in the manner which it judges best for the safety of the inhabitants, by removing such person to a separate house or otherwise, and by providing nurses and other assistance and necessaries, which shall be at the charge of the person himself, his parents, or master, if able, otherwise at the charge of the town to which he belongs; and if he is not an inhabitant of any town, at the charge of the commonwealth.

24. If the infected person cannot be removed without danger to his health, the board shall make provision for him as directed in the preceding section in the house in which he may be; and may cause the persons in the neighborhood to be removed, and take such other measures as it judges necessary for the safety of the inhabitants.

25. The board of health of any town near to or bordering upon either of the neighboring states, may appoint,

[1] Stats. 1873, ch. 2, § 1.

by writing, suitable persons to attend at places by which travellers may pass from infected places in other states; who may examine such travellers as it suspects of bringing any infection dangerous to the public health, and if need be may restrain them from travelling until licensed thereto by the board of health of the town to which such person may come. A traveller coming from such infected place who shall without such license travel within this state, (except to return by the most direct way to the state from whence he came,) after he has been cautioned to depart by the persons so appointed, shall forfeit a sum not exceeding one hundred dollars.

26. Two justices of the peace may if need be make out a warrant directed to the sheriff of the county, or his deputy, or to any constable, requiring them under the direction of the board to remove any person infected with contagious sickness, or to impress and take up convenient houses, lodgings, nurses, attendants, and other necessaries, for the accommodation, safety, and relief, of the sick.

27. When, upon the application of the board, it appears to a justice of the peace that there is just cause to suspect that any baggage, clothing, or goods, found within the town, are infected with the plague or other disease which may be dangerous to the public health, the justice shall, by warrant directed to the sheriff or his deputy, or to any constable, require him to impress so many men as said justice may judge necessary to secure such baggage, clothing, or other goods, and to post said men as a guard over the house or place where said articles are lodged; who shall take effectual care to prevent persons from removing or coming near the same, until due inquiry is made into the circumstances.

28. The justice may by the same warrant, if it appears to him necessary, require the officers, under the direction of the board, to impress and take up convenient houses or stores for the safe-keeping of such articles; and the board may cause them to be removed thereto, or otherwise de-

tained, until, in the opinion of the board, they are freed from infection.

29. The officers, in the execution of the warrant, shall if need be break open any house, shop, or other place, mentioned in the warrant, where such articles are; and may require such aid as is necessary to effect the execution of the warrant. Whoever neglects or refuses to assist in the execution of the warrant, after being commanded to assist by either of said officers, shall forfeit a sum not exceeding ten dollars.

30. The charges of securing such articles, and transporting and purifying the same, shall be paid by the owners, at such rates and prices as may be determined by the board.

31. When a sheriff or other officer impresses or takes up any houses, stores, lodging, or other necessaries, or impresses men, as provided in this chapter, the several parties interested shall be entitled to a just compensation therefor, to be paid by the town in which such persons or property are so impressed.

32. When a person confined in a common jail, house of correction, or workhouse, has a disease which, in the opinion of the physician of the board or of such other physician as it may consult, is dangerous to the safety and health of other prisoners or of the inhabitants of the town, the board shall by its order in writing direct the removal of such person to some hospital or other place of safety, there to be provided for and securely kept so as to prevent his escape until its further order. If such person recovers from the disease he shall be returned to said prison or other place of confinement.

33. If the person so removed is committed by order of court or under judicial process, the order for his removal, or a copy thereof attested by the presiding member of the board, shall be returned by him, with the doings thereon, into the office of the clerk of the court from which the process of commitment was issued. No prisoner so removed shall thereby commit an escape.

34. Parents and guardians shall cause their children and wards to be vaccinated before they attain the age of two years, and revaccinated whenever the selectmen or mayor and aldermen shall after five years from the last vaccination require it. For every year's neglect the party offending shall forfeit the sum of five dollars.

35. The selectmen and mayor and aldermen shall require and enforce the vaccination of all the inhabitants, and, whenever in their opinion the public health requires it, the revaccination of all the inhabitants who do not prove to their satisfaction that they have been successfully vaccinated or revaccinated within five years. All persons over twenty-one years of age, not under guardianship, who neglect to comply with any such requirement, shall forfeit the sum of five dollars.

36. Towns shall furnish the means of vaccination to such of their inhabitants as are unable to pay for the same.

37. Incorporated manufacturing companies; superintendents of almshouses, state reform, and industrial schools, lunatic hospitals, and other places where the poor and sick are received; masters of houses of correction, jailers, keepers of prisons, the warden of the state prison, and superintendents or officers of all other institutions supported or aided by the state; shall at the expense of their respective establishments or institutions cause all inmates thereof to be vaccinated immediately upon their entrance thereto, unless they produce sufficient evidence of previous successful vaccination within five years.

38. Each town may make further provision for the vaccination of its inhabitants, under the direction of the board or a committee chosen for the purpose.

39. A town may establish a quarantine ground in a suitable place either within or without its own limits; but if such place is without its limits, the assent of the town within whose limits it may be established shall be first obtained.

40. Two or more towns may at their joint expense estab-

lish a quarantine ground for their common use in any suitable place either within or without their own limits ; but if such place is without their limits, they shall first obtain the assent of the town within whose limits it may be.

41. The board of health in each seaport town may from time to time establish the quarantine to be performed by vessels arriving within its harbor ; and may make such quarantine regulations as it judges necessary for the health and safety of the inhabitants.

42. Such regulations shall extend to all persons, goods, and effects, arriving in such vessels, and to all persons who may visit or go on board of the same.

43. Whoever violates any such regulation after notice thereof has been given in the manner before provided in this chapter, shall forfeit a sum not less than five nor more than five hundred dollars.

44. The board in each seaport town may at all times cause a vessel arriving in such port, when such vessel or the cargo thereof is in its opinion foul or infected so as to endanger the public health, to be removed to the quarantine ground and thoroughly purified at the expense of the owners, consignees, or persons in possession of the same ; and may cause all persons arriving in or going on board of such vessel, or handling the cargo, to be removed to any hospital under the care of the board, there to remain under their orders.

45. If a master, seaman, or passenger, belonging to a vessel on board of which any infection then is or has lately been, or suspected to have been, or which has been at or has come from a port where any infectious distemper prevails that may endanger the public health, refuses to make answer on oath to such questions as may be asked him relating to such infection or distemper by the board of health of the town to which such vessel may come, (which oath any member of the board may administer,) such as master, seaman, or passenger, shall forfeit a sum not exceeding two hundred dollars ; and if not able to pay said sum he shall suffer six months' imprisonment.

46. All expenses incurred on account of any person, vessel, or goods, under quarantine regulations, shall be paid by such person or the owner of such vessel or goods respectively.

But this does not include the expenses of a seaman at a hospital, to which he had been transferred by order of the board of health of a town, and which is under their care.[1]

47. Any town may establish within its limits, and be constantly provided with, one or more hospitals for the reception of persons having a disease dangerous to the public health.

Any town may erect, establish, and maintain a hospital for the reception of persons who, by misfortune or poverty, may require relief during temporary sickness. And the selectmen of any town shall have power to make such ordinances, rules, and regulations as they may deem expedient, for the appointment of trustees and all other officers, agents, and servants necessary for managing such hospital.[2]

48. Such hospitals shall be subject to the orders and regulations of the board, or of a committee of the town appointed for that purpose.

49. No such hospital shall be established within one hundred rods of an inhabited dwelling-house situated in an adjoining town, without the consent of such town.

50. When a hospital is so established, the physician, nurses, attendants, the persons sick therein, and all persons approaching or coming within the limits of the same, and all furniture and other articles used or brought there, shall be subject to such regulations as may be made by the board of health or the committee appointed for that purpose.

51. When a disease dangerous to the public health breaks out in any town, the board shall immediately provide such hospital or place of reception for the sick and infected as is judged best for their accommodation and the safety of the inhabitants; which shall be subject to the regulations of the board; and the board may cause any sick and in-

---

[1] Provincetown v. Smith, 120 Mass. 96.　　[2] Stats. 1873, ch. 192.

fected person to be removed thereto, unless the condition of such person will not admit of his removal without danger to his health, in which case the house or place where he remains shall be considered as a hospital, and all persons residing in or in any way concerned within the same shall be subject to the regulations of the board as before provided.

52. When such disease is found to exist in a town, the selectmen and board of health shall use all possible care to prevent the spreading of the infection, and to give public notice of infected places to travellers, by displaying red flags at proper distances, and by all other means which in their judgment shall be most effectual for the common safety. (And whoever obstructs the selectmen, board of health, or their agent, in using such means to prevent the spreading of the infection, or wilfully removes, obliterates, defaces, or handles the red flags, or other signals so displayed, shall forfeit for such offence a sum not less than ten or more than one hundred dollars.[1])

53. If a physician or other person in any of the hospitals or places of reception before mentioned, or who attends, approaches, or is concerned with, the same, violates any of the regulations lawfully made in relation thereto, either with respect to himself, or his or any other person's property, he shall for each offence forfeit a sum not less than ten nor more than one hundred dollars.

54. When a householder knows that a person within his family is taken sick of small-pox or any other disease dangerous to the public health, he shall immediately give notice thereof to the selectmen or board of health of the town in which he dwells. If he refuses or neglects to give such notice, he shall forfeit a sum not exceeding one hundred dollars.

55. When a physician knows that any person whom he is called to visit is infected with small-pox or any other disease dangerous to the public health, he shall immediately give notice thereof to the selectmen or board of health of

[1] Stats. 1873, ch. 2, § 2.

the town; and if he refuses or neglects to give such notice, he shall forfeit for each offence a sum not less than fifty nor more than one hundred dollars.

56. Expenses incurred by a town in the removal of nuisances or for the preservation of the public health, and which are recoverable of a private person or corporation by virtue of any provisions of law, may be sued for and recovered in an action of contract.

57. Fines and forfeitures incurred under general laws, the special laws applicable to a town, or the by-laws and regulations of a town relating to health, shall inure to the use of such town.[1]

58. (The provisions of foregoing sections twenty-three, twenty-four, fifty-one, fifty-two, and fifty-three, shall not apply to small-pox.)

59. The board shall from time to time assign certain places for the exercising of any trade or employment which is a nuisance or hurtful to the inhabitants, or dangerous to the public health, or the exercise of which is attended by noisome and injurious odors, or is otherwise injurious to their estates, and may prohibit the exercise of the same in places not so assigned; the board may also forbid the exercise of such trade or employment within the limits of the town or in any particular locality thereof. All such assignments shall be entered in the records; and may be revoked when the board shall think proper.[2]

60. If the selectmen acting as a board of health bring a bill in equity to restrain the exercise of an offensive trade or employment which they have prohibited, under the foregoing section the supreme court have power to allow an amendment thereof, by substituting the inhabitants of the town as plaintiffs, after the term of office of the selectmen has ceased.[3]

61. When it appears on trial before the superior court for the county, upon a complaint made by any person, that any place or building so assigned has become a nuisance, by reason of offensive smells or exhalations proceeding

---

[1] Gen. Stats. ch. 26, §§ 15–50.
[2] Gen. Stats. ch. 26, § 52.
[3] Winthrop v. Farrar, 11 Allen, 398.

from the same, or is otherwise hurtful or dangerous to the neighborhood or to travellers, the court may revoke such assignment and prohibit the further use of such place or building for the exercise of either of the aforesaid trades or employments, and may cause such nuisance to be removed or prevented.

62. A person injured either in his comfort or the enjoyment of his estate by such nuisance, may have an action of tort for the damage sustained thereby.

63. Orders of prohibition under section fifty-two (fifty-nine above) shall be served upon the occupant or person having charge of the premises where such trade or employment is exercised. If the party upon whom such order is served, for twenty-four hours after such service refuses or neglects to obey the same, the board shall take all necessary measures to prevent such exercise; and the person so refusing or neglecting shall forfeit a sum not less than fifty nor more than five hundred dollars.[1]

64. But an order by the selectmen of a town, acting as a board of health, forbidding the exercise of an offensive trade or employment therein, need not be served by an officer.[2]

65. Any person aggrieved by such order may appeal therefrom, and shall within three days from the service thereof upon him apply to the superior court, if in session in the county where such order is made, or in vacation to any justice of said court, for a jury; and such court or justice shall issue a warrant for a jury, to be impanelled at a time and place expressed in the warrant, in the manner provided in regard to the laying out of highways.[3]

66. Whenever any person by mistake of law or fact or by accident fails to appeal from any order of any board of health and to apply to the superior court or any justice thereof for a jury within the three days limited therefor by section fifty-six of chapter twenty-six of the General Statutes (preceding section), such person may at any time thereafter appeal from such order and apply for a jury

---

[1] Gen. Stats. ch. 26, §§ 53–55.     [3] Gen. Stats. ch. 26, § 56.
[2] Winthrop v. Farrar, 11 Allen, 398.

with the same effect as if done within the said three days : *provided*, that such person so appealing and applying shall make it appear to the court or justice that such failure was caused by mistake or accident ; and *provided*, *also*, that such appeal and application shall be made within thirty days after service of such order upon such applicant.[1]

67. During the pendency of the appeal such trade or employment shall not be exercised contrary to the order ; and upon any violation of the same the appeal shall forthwith be dismissed.

68. The verdict of the jury, which may either alter the order, or affirm or annul it in full, shall be returned to the court for acceptance as in case of highways ; and said verdict when accepted shall have the authority and effect of an original order from which no appeal had been taken.

69. If the order is affirmed by the verdict, the town shall recover costs against the appellant ; if it is annulled, the appellant shall recover damages and costs against the town ; and if it is altered, the court may render such judgment as to costs as in their discretion may seem just.[2]

70. The boards of health of towns and the mayor and aldermen of cities shall, on or before the first day of July next (1872), and each year thereafter, license a suitable number of undertakers to take charge of the obsequies or funeral rites preliminary to the interment of a human body, if, in the judgment of such boards, a sufficient number are not already licensed in their respective places. Any undertaker, having such charge, shall forthwith obtain and return, to the clerk of the city or town in which the deceased resided or the death occurred, the facts required, by chapter twenty-one of the General Statutes (chapter forty-nine of this work), to be recorded by said officer concerning the deceased ; the clerk shall thereupon give to the undertaker a certificate as provided for in section four of said chapter, which certificate the undertaker shall deliver to the person having charge of the interment in accordance with the provisions of said fourth section.

---

[1] Stats. 1865, ch. 263.  [2] Gen. Stats. ch. 26, §§ 57–59.

Any undertaker violating any of the provisions of this act shall be punished by a fine of twenty dollars for each violation of the duties herein prescribed, to be imposed by any court of competent jurisdiction.

71. Nothing herein contained shall exempt any sexton or other person named in the fourth section of the twenty-first chapter of the General Statutes (chapter forty-nine section four of this work) from the provisions and penalties prescribed in said section in cases where an undertaker appointed as provided in this act is not employed in charge of the obsequies.[1]

72. The mayor and aldermen of any city or the selectmen of any town may license any person to establish or keep within their respective cities and towns a lying-in hospital, hospital ward, or other place for the reception, care, and treatment of women in labor: *provided*, that the board of health in such city or town shall first certify to the mayor and aldermen or selectmen that the person applying for such license is in their judgment a suitable person and that from the inspection and examination of such hospital, hospital ward, or other place aforesaid by said board of health, the same is suitable and properly arranged and provided for such business.

73. Such licenses shall continue in force for the term of two years, subject, however, to revocation by the mayor and aldermen or selectmen of the city or town.

74. Every hospital, hospital ward, or other place established or kept by virtue of a license granted as hereinbefore provided, shall be subject to visitation and inspection by the board of health, the chief of police, the mayor of the city or selectmen of the town, at any time, and any such hospital, hospital ward, or other place which receives in a year more than six women as patients in labor, shall also be subject to visitation and inspection by the state board of health.

75. Whoever establishes or keeps, or is concerned in establishing or keeping any hospital, hospital ward, or

[1] Stats. 1872, ch. 275, §§ 1, 2.

other place for the purposes aforesaid, or whoever is engaged in any such business, without such license, shall for the first offence forfeit a sum not exceeding five hundred dollars, one half of which forfeiture shall be paid to the complainant and the other half to the city or town, and for any subsequent offence shall be punished by imprisonment in the jail or house of correction for a term not exceeding two years.[1]

76. Whoever engages in the business of taking nursing infants or infants under three years of age to board, or of entertaining or boarding more than two such infants in the same house at the same time, shall within two days after the reception of each such infant beyond the first two, give written notice to the board of health of the city or town where such infant is so to be entertained or boarded, specifying the name and age of the child and the name and place of residence of the party so undertaking its care ; and such board of health shall have the right to enter and inspect said house and premises while said business is being carried on, and to direct and enforce such sanitary measures respecting such children and premises as it may deem proper.

77. Any person violating any of the provisions of this act, or refusing admission to such board of health for the purpose mentioned in the preceding section, shall, on conviction thereof, be punished by a fine of not less than fifty, nor more than five hundred dollars.[2]

78. In any case arising under the provisions of the twenty-sixth chapter of the General Statutes and the acts in addition thereto, in which the board of health shall have acted, said board of health shall retain charge of the same to the exclusion of the overseers of the poor of any city or town.

79. All reasonable expenses which have been heretofore, or may hereafter be incurred by the board of health of any city or town, in making the provision required by law for any person infected with the small-pox or any other

---

[1] Stats. 1876, ch. 157.     [2] Stats. 1876, ch. 158.

disease dangerous to the public health, shall be paid by
the person himself, his parents, or master, if able; otherwise by the town in which he has a legal settlement, and
if he has no settlement in any town, by the commonwealth,
in which case the bills therefor shall be approved by the
board of state charities.[1]

[1] Stats. 1874, ch. 121.

# CHAPTER LI.

## THE PROMOTION OF ANATOMICAL SCIENCE.

1. THE overseers of the poor of a town, the mayor and aldermen of a city, and the inspectors and superintendent of a state almshouse, may to any physician or surgeon, upon his request, give permission to take the bodies of such persons dying in such town, city, or almshouse, as are required to be buried at the public expense, to be by him used within the state for the advancement of anatomical science; preference being given to medical schools established by law, for their use in the instruction of students.

2. Every physician or surgeon, before receiving any such dead body, shall give to the board of officers surrendering the same to him, a sufficient bond that each body shall be used only for the promotion of anatomical science within this state, and so as in no event to outrage the public feeling; and that, after having been so used, the remains thereof shall be decently buried.

3. Persons having charge of a poorhouse, workhouse, or house of industry, in which a person required to be buried at the public expense dies, shall forthwith give notice of such death to the overseers of the poor of the town or to the mayor and aldermen of the city in which such death occurs; and except in case of necessity the body of such person shall not be buried until such notice is given, and permission therefor granted by such overseers or mayor and aldermen; nor without their permission shall the body be surrendered for dissection or mutilation.

4. If the deceased person during his last sickness, of his own accord requested to be buried, or if, within twenty-four hours after his death, any person claiming to be and satis-

fying the proper authorities that he is a friend or of kindred to the deceased, asks to have the body buried, or if such deceased person was a stranger or traveller who suddenly died, the body shall not be so surrendered, but shall be buried.[1]

[1] Gen. Stats. ch. 27, §§ 1–4.

# CHAPTER LII.

## CEMETERIES AND BURIALS.

1. EACH town and city shall provide one or more suitable places for the interment of persons dying within its limits.

2. Except in the case of the erection or use of a tomb on private land for the exclusive use of the family of the owner, no land, other than that already so used or appropriated, shall be used for the purpose of burial, unless by permission of the town or of the mayor and aldermen of the city in which the same is situated.

3. Boards of health may make all regulations which they judge necessary concerning burial grounds and interments within their respective limits ; may prohibit the use of tombs by undertakers, (as places of deposit for bodies committed to them for burial,) for the purpose of speculation, and may establish penalties not exceeding one hundred dollars for any breach of such regulations.

4. Notice of such regulations shall be given by publishing the same in some newspaper of the town, or city, or, if there is no such newspaper, by posting a copy in some public place therein ; which shall be deemed legal notice to all persons.[1]

5. And they may make regulations prohibiting all persons, except the superintendent of the cemetery, or a duly appointed undertaker, or other person specially authorized, from removing the dead body of any person from any house or place within the city or town, to the place of burial, and may require from each undertaker a bond with a reasonable penalty, and with condition to collect and account for the burial fees. And the fact that such a regulation may be made with reference to a particular person, will not affect its validity. And if such person, having been so appointed as undertaker, fails to give

---

[1] Gen. Stats. ch. 28, §§ 4–7.

the required bond, the board of health may revoke his appointment at pleasure, without previous notice to him.[1]

6. The word "interments" properly includes and describes the removal of the bodies of deceased persons for the purpose of burial. That this necessary duty shall be performed, especially when undertaken for hire by suitable and trustworthy persons, and that the moving of dead bodies through public streets shall be conducted with decency and safety, are obviously matters proper for municipal regulation, and which, as well as the mode of burial, may concern the public health to no slight extent.[1]

7. Before a tomb, burial ground, or cemetery, is closed by order of the board of health, for a time longer than one month, all persons interested shall have an opportunity to be heard, and personal notice of the time and place of hearing shall be given to at least one owner of the tomb, and to three at least, if so many there are, of the proprietors of such burial ground or cemetery, and notice shall also be published two successive weeks at least preceding such hearing, in two newspapers, if so many there are, published in the county.

8. The owner of a tomb aggrieved by the order of the board of health closing any tomb, burial ground, or cemetery, may appeal therefrom, and at any time within six months from the date of the order enter his appeal in the superior court; and the appellant shall give the board of health fourteen days' notice of his appeal previous to the entry thereof. But the order of the board shall remain in force until a decision shall be had on the appeal.

9. Appeals shall be tried in regular course before a jury, and if the jury find that the tomb, burial ground, or cemetery, so closed, was not a nuisance, nor injurious to the public health at the time of the order, the court shall rescind the same so far as it affects such tomb, burial ground, or cemetery, and execution for costs of the appeal shall issue in favor of the appellant against the town or city in which the same was situated. But if the order is sustained, execution shall issue for double costs against the appellant in favor of the board of health for the use of the town or city.

[1] Commonwealth *v.* Goodrich, 13 Allen, 546.

10. For every interment in violation of section five (section two above) in a town or city in which the notice prescribed in section seven (section four above) has been given, the owner of the land so used shall forfeit not less than twenty nor more than one hundred dollars.

11. Whoever wrongfully destroys, impairs, injures, or removes, a tomb, gravestone, building, fence, railing, or other thing, lawfully erected in or around a place of burial or cemetery, or a tree, shrub, or plant, situate within its limits; or wrongfully injures a walk or path therein, or places rubbish or offensive matter within a place of burial or cemetery, or commits any nuisance therein, or in any way desecrates or disfigures the same, shall forfeit for every such offence not less than five nor more than one hundred dollars. Upon the trial of a prosecution for the recovery of such penalty, use and occupation for the purposes of burial shall be deemed sufficient evidence of title.[1]

12. As to the question what constitutes a public burial ground, in Commonwealth *v.* Viall,[2] it is held that an ancient burial ground, which for sixty years has been separated by a fence from the adjoining land, and used occasionally for burials until the present time, may be described as a public burial ground in an indictment for destroying trees in a place of burial, under the foregoing section, although it can only be reached by a way, which has always been used for the purpose, over an adjoining private estate, of which it was originally a part, and the owners of which built and have maintained the fence for their own convenience, and have depastured the burial ground, cut the trees upon it, and cultivated part of it at their pleasure, under a claim of right, and no one else has exercised or claimed any control over the same until the town in which it lies assumed the charge thereof within three years.

And the court further say, that cutting trees upon a public burial ground for purposes of private profit, without consent of the public authorities having charge of it, is a violation of the foregoing section, although the person who cuts them is the owner of the fee of the land, and honestly believes that his acts are lawful.

13. Any person holding, occupying, or interested in any lot in the public burying grounds in any city or town in this commonwealth, may deposit with the treasurer of any such city or town any sum of money, not exceeding five hundred dollars, which sum thus depos-

---

[1] Gen. Stats. ch. 28, §§ 8–12.  [2] 2 Allen, 512.

ited shall be entered upon the books of the treasury, and held in accordance with the provisions of the ordinances or by-laws of such city or town, in relation to the interment of the dead.

The purpose for which such deposit may be made, shall be to provide for the care, keeping, and preservation of the fences, trees, shrubbery, monuments, tombs, and other appendages of the lot of such person.

Any city or town may receive money for the purpose aforesaid, and allow interest for the same at a rate not exceeding six per centum per annum; and may establish any by-laws or ordinances not repugnant to the laws of this commonwealth, as may be necessary for the purposes of this act [1] (this section).

14. When there is a necessity for a new burial ground in any town, or for the enlargement of any burial ground already existing in and belonging to a town, and the owner or any person interested in the land needed for either purpose refuses to sell the same, or demands therefor a price deemed by the selectmen of said town unreasonable, or is unable for any reason to convey the land, said selectmen may, with the approbation of the town, make application therefor by written petition to the commissioners of the county wherein the land is situated.

15. The commissioners shall appoint a time and place for a hearing, and shall cause notice thereof, together with a copy of said petition, to be served personally upon the land owner or owners, or left at his or their place or places of abode fourteen days at least before the time appointed for the hearing. If the land be held in trust or by a corporation, or the ownership be uncertain, the commissioners shall also require notice by public advertisement or otherwise, as justice to all persons interested shall seem to them to require.

16. The commissioners shall hear the parties at the time and place appointed, or at an adjournment thereof; and as soon as may be after the hearing shall consider and adjudicate upon the necessity of such taking, and upon the quantity, boundaries, damages, and value of the land adjudged necessary to be taken, and shall forthwith file a description of such land with a plan thereof in the registry

[1] Stats. 1870, ch. 225.

of deeds of the county and district wherein such land lies, and thereupon such land shall be taken and held in fee by the town as a burial ground or as part of the burial ground of such town.

17. Each commissioner shall be paid by the town three dollars per day for each day spent in acting under the petition, and five cents a mile for travel to and from the place of hearing.

18. When the owner or owners of the land, or any person in interest, is aggrieved by the award of damages, he or they may, upon application therefor within one year, have the matter of the complaint determined by a jury, as in the case of assessment of damages for highways, and all proceedings shall be conducted as in such case is provided. If the sum allowed for damages, including the value of the land, is increased by the jury, the sum so allowed by the jury, and all charges, shall be paid by the town ; otherwise the charges arising upon such application for a jury shall be paid by the applicant. The applicant for a jury shall enter into a recognizance in such sum and with such surety as the commissioners shall order for the payment of such charges.

19. Towns may grant and vote such sums as they may judge necessary for inclosing any cemetery or burial ground provided by them according to law, or to construct paths and avenues and to embellish the grounds in the same, and they may establish all necessary rules in relation to such cemeteries or burial grounds as are not repugnant to the laws of the commonwealth. Towns may lay out any such cemetery or burial ground into lots or subdivisions for burial places as they may think proper, but they shall set apart a suitable portion as a public burial place for the use of the inhabitants, free of charge therefor. Towns may sell and convey to any persons, whether residents of the town or otherwise, the exclusive right of burial and of erecting tombs and cenotaphs upon any lot, and of ornamenting the same, upon such terms, conditions, and regulations as they shall prescribe, and the pro-

29

ceeds of such sales in any cemetery or burial ground shall be paid into the town treasury, be kept separate and apart from other funds, and be appropriated to reimburse the town for the cost of land or for the improvement and embellishment of such cemetery or burial ground.[1]

20. Cemetery corporations may take and hold funds upon trust to apply the income thereof to the improvement or embellishment of the cemetery, or to the care, preservation, or embellishment of any lot, or its appurtenances.[2]

[1] Stats. 1877, ch. 69.        [2] Stats. 1874, ch. 190.

# CHAPTER LIII.

## STREET RAILWAYS.

1. THE board of aldermen of any city, or the selectmen of any town, in which any corporation is authorized to construct a street railway, may, upon the petition of such corporation, locate the tracks thereof within their respective jurisdictions, pursuant to the provisions of its charter : *provided*, that before proceeding to locate such tracks, they shall give notice to all parties interested, by publication in such newspapers, or otherwise, as they may determine, at least fourteen days before their meeting, of the time and place at which they will consider such location. After a hearing of all parties interested, they shall pass an order refusing the location, or granting the same, or any portion thereof, under such restrictions as they deem the interests of the public may require, and the location thus granted shall be deemed and taken to be the true location of the tracks of the corporation, if its acceptance thereof in writing is filed with said mayor and aldermen or selectmen within thirty days after receiving notice thereof.[1]

2. The location and position of the tracks of any corporation may be altered upon application of any party interested, by the same authority, and in the same manner, as is provided in the preceding section, for the original location. The expense of such alteration, which shall be made by the corporation within such time after such alteration shall have been ordered, as the board of aldermen or selectmen may determine, shall be borne by such party as the board of aldermen or selectmen may determine.

[1] Stats. 1874, ch. 29, § 6, makes the same provision as to locating roads of corporations organized under the general laws.

3. The board of aldermen of any city, or the selectmen of any town, may, at any time after the expiration of one year from the times of the opening for use of any street railway in such city or town, if in their judgment the interests of the public require, after notice published as provided in the preceding sections and a hearing, order that the location of any of the tracks in any street or highway shall be revoked, and the railway corporation shall thereupon remove the same, in conformity with such order, and put the street in as good condition as it was in immediately before being occupied by said tracks.

4. If any corporation neglects to execute any order and make the repairs as prescribed in the preceding section, after thirty days' notice thereof, then the board of aldermen or selectmen may cause the same to be executed and made at the expense of the corporation, to be recovered in an action of tort.

5. The board of aldermen of any city, or the selectmen of any town, in which a street railway is operated, may, from time to time, establish by an order such rules and regulations as to the rate of speed, mode and use of the tracks, and removal of snow and ice from the same, as in their judgment the interest and convenience of the public may require.

6. If any corporation, its servants or agents, wilfully or negligently violates any rule or regulation established in the manner provided in the preceding section, such corporation shall be liable to a penalty of not more than five hundred dollars for each offence.

7. Cities and towns may take up any of the streets or highways traversed by street railways, for any purpose for which they are now authorized to take up the same, or may alter or discontinue the same, as now authorized by law, without being liable in damages therefor to any railway corporation or the owners of its stock.

8. Every corporation, its lessees or assigns, shall keep in repair such portions of any paved streets, roads, and bridges as are occupied by its tracks; and when such

tracks occupy streets or roads that are not paved, it shall, in addition to the portion occupied by its tracks, keep in repair eighteen inches on each side thereof, to the satisfaction of the superintendent of streets, the street commissioner, or the surveyors of highways, and shall be liable for any loss or injury that any person may sustain by reason of any carelessness, neglect, or misconduct of its agents and servants, in the construction, management, and use of its tracks.

9. In case any recovery is had against any city or town, steam railroad, turnpike or bridge corporation respectively, by reason of any defect or want of repair caused or permitted by a corporation of that part of any street, highway, or bridge occupied by its tracks, or by reason of any defect in any part of any street, highway, or bridge occupied by its tracks, caused by a corporation, its lessees or assigns or their agents or employés, said corporation, its lessees or assigns, shall be liable to said city, town, or corporation respectively, for any sums recovered against either of them, together with all costs and reasonable expenditures incurred in the defence of any suit or suits in which recovery is had by reason of such defect or want of repair: *provided*, the corporation, its lessees or assigns, had reasonable notice of such suit or suits, and an opportunity to assume the defence thereof; and *provided*, *further*, that such defect or want of repair was not caused by said city or town, its agents or servants, exercising the powers reserved to cities and towns in section twenty-one of this act (preceding section), or by said other corporations, their agents or servants.

10. Every corporation, its lessees or assigns, shall erect and maintain upon every bridge or draw of a bridge over which its track is located and used, suitable guards or railings sufficient to prevent the cars of said corporation from running off said bridge or draw; such guards or railings to be erected and maintained to the satisfaction of the board of aldermen of the city, or the selectmen of the town, in which such draw or bridge or any portion thereof may be situated.

11. If any corporation, its lessees or assigns, for sixty days neglects to comply with any order of a board of aldermen of a city, or the selectmen of a town, duly served upon it under the provisions of the preceding section, it shall for each month during which such neglect shall continue, in excess of such sixty days, forfeit the sum of two hundred dollars, to be recovered to the use of said city or town.

12. If a corporation voluntarily discontinues the use of any part of its tracks for a period of six months, the streets or highways occupied by the same shall, upon the order of the board of aldermen of the city, or the selectmen of the town, forthwith, at the expense of said company, be cleared of said tracks, and put in as good condition for the public travel as they were in immediately before being so occupied.

13. The board of aldermen of any city, or the selectmen of any town, may order any corporation to discontinue, temporarily, the use of any tracks within the limits of such city or town, whenever they adjudge that the safety or convenience of the inhabitants require such discontinuance.

14. All corporations shall construct and maintain their tracks of a uniform gauge of four feet eight and one-half inches.

15. The board of aldermen of any city, or the selectmen of any town, may establish such regulations for giving notice or warning of the approach of street cars by the driver or conductor, as shall in their opinion best secure the unobstructed use of the tracks and the free passage of the cars.

16. Whoever wilfully and maliciously obstructs any corporation, its lessees or assigns, in the legal use of any railway tracks, or delays the passing of the cars or railway carriages thereon, such person, and all who shall be aiding and abetting therein, shall be punished by a fine not exceeding five hundred dollars, or may be imprisoned in the common jail for a period not exceeding three months.

17. If any corporation, its agents or servants, wilfully or negligently obstructs any street or highway, or hinders the passing of carriages over the same, or wilfully detains the cars of any other company having the lawful right to pass thereon, such corporation shall be punished by a fine not exceeding five hundred dollars; and the agent or servant so offending shall be punished by a fine not exceeding ten dollars for each offence, or by imprisonment in the common jail for a period not exceeding three months.[1]

18. Every corporation shall furnish reasonable accommodations for the conveyance of passengers, and for every wilful neglect to provide the same shall be punished by a fine of not less than five nor more than twenty dollars for each offence, and the directors thereof may establish the rates of fare on all passengers and property conveyed or transported in its cars, subject, however, to the limitations named in its charter, or hereinafter set forth.

19. The board of aldermen of any city, the selectmen of any town, or fifty legal voters of any city or town in which any street railway is located, may apply to the board of railroad commissioners, who shall, after due notice and hearing of the parties interested, revise and regulate the fares as determined by the corporations; but such fare shall not, without the consent of the corporation, be so reduced as to yield, with all other profits derived from operating its road, an income of less than ten per centum upon the actual cost of the construction of its road and the purchase of property for its necessary use, to be determined by said commissioners. The report of the commissioners shall be final and conclusive for at least one year. The expense of said application and hearing shall be borne by such party as the said board may determine.

20. Nothing contained in the two preceding sections shall be held to authorize any corporation or said commissioners to raise the rate of fare, or the price of tickets, above what has been heretofore established as such rate or price for any locality, by agreement made as a condi-

[1] Stats. 1871, ch. 381, §§ 14–30.

tion of location or otherwise between a corporation or its directors, and the mayor and aldermen of any city or the selectmen of any town, except by a mutual arrangement with the mayor and aldermen or selectmen with whom such agreement was made.[1]

21. Corporations may use such motive power on their respective tracks or roads as the board of aldermen of cities, or the selectmen of towns, through which they are located, may from time to time permit.

22. Every corporation shall be responsible in damages to any person whose buildings or other property is injured by fire communicated by its locomotive engines, and shall have an insurable interest in the property, upon its route, for which it may be so held responsible, and may procure insurance thereon in its own behalf.[2]

23. The board of aldermen of any city and the selectmen of any town may, from time to time, upon petition, authorize and empower any street railway corporation, its lessees and assigns, whose charter has been duly accepted, and whose tracks have been located and constructed, to extend the location of its tracks within the territorial limits of such city or town, whenever it can be done without entering upon or using the tracks of any other street railway corporation, under such restrictions as they deem the interests of the public may require. And the location thus authorized shall be deemed and taken to be the true location of the tracks of the corporation, if its acceptance thereof, in writing, is filed in the office of the clerk of such city or town within thirty days after receiving notice thereof. Before acting upon the petition, notice of the time and place of hearing shall be given to all parties interested, by publication at least fourteen days prior thereto, in such newspapers or otherwise as the board of aldermen or selectmen may determine.

Whenever the board of aldermen of any city, or the selectmen of any town, after due notice and hearing, shall decide that public necessity and convenience so require, they may authorize and empower

[1] Stats. 1871, ch. 381, §§ 33–35.   [2] Stats. 1871, ch. 381, §§ 44, 45.

any street railway corporation, its lessees and assigns, whose tracks have been duly located in such city or town and who own and operate not less than two consecutive miles of track, to enter upon and use with its horses and cars, within defined limits, the tracks of any other street railway corporation therein, which it may meet or cross, subject to the provisions of law relating to such entry and use.

The board of aldermen or selectmen may, from time to time, make such regulations as to the manner and extent of use of tracks and the number and routes of cars of any and all companies running over the same within their city or town, as the interests of public travel shall require.

Where the track, operated by a corporation, seeking to enter upon and use, or sought to be entered upon and used by another under the provisions of this section, is in two or more cities or towns, and the selectmen or boards of aldermen of such cities or towns are unable to agree as to the public necessity for such entrance and use, the board of railroad commissioners shall, upon the petition of either corporation, and after due hearing, decide whether such entry and use is required on grounds of public convenience and necessity, and determine the extent of use of tracks, and the number and routes of cars; and the decision of said board shall be final.[1]

[1] Stats. 1874, ch. 29, §§ 11–14.

# CHAPTER LIV.

## TELEGRAPH COMPANIES.

1. (EVERY company incorporated for the transmission of intelligence by electricity) may under the provisions of the following section construct lines of electric telegraph upon and along the highways and public roads, and across any waters within the state, by the erection of the posts, piers, abutments, and other fixtures (except bridges), necessary to sustain the wires of its lines; but shall not incommode the public use of highways or public roads, nor endanger or interrupt the navigation of any waters.

2. The mayor and aldermen or selectmen of any place through which the lines of a company are to pass, shall give the company a writing specifying where the posts may be located, the kind of posts, and the height at which and the places where the wires may run. After the erection of the lines, having first given the company or its agents opportunity to be heard, they may direct any alteration in the location or erection of the posts, piers, or abutments, and in the height of the wires. Such specifications and decisions shall be recorded in the records of the city or town.[1]

The foregoing sections apply to companies incorporated under the laws of this state. The determination of the selectmen as to where the posts may stand, is conclusive upon the rightfulness of their erection within the limits of a highway.[2]

3. An owner of land near to or adjoining a highway or road along which lines are constructed by the company, who considers himself injured thereby, may within three months after such construction apply to the mayor and aldermen or selectmen to assess and appraise his damage. Before entering upon the service they shall severally be

---

[1] Gen. Stats. ch. 64, §§ 2, 3.    [2] Commonwealth v. Boston, 97 Mass. 555.

sworn faithfully and impartially to perform the duties required of them by this chapter. They shall on view make a just appraisal in writing of the loss or damage, if any, to the applicant, sign duplicates thereof, and on demand deliver one copy to the applicant and the other to the company or its agent. If damages are assessed, the company shall pay the same with the costs of the appraisers. If the appraisers award that the applicant has suffered no damage, he shall pay the costs of the appraisers.

Any person aggrieved by the assessment of his damages may have the matter determined by a jury as in case of highways.

4. The mayor and aldermen and selectmen shall each receive for services performed under this chapter (the foregoing sections) two dollars.a day.[1]

[1] Gen. Stats. ch. 64, §§ 4, 5, 6.

# CHAPTER LV.

## STORAGE, SALE, AND INSPECTION OF PETROLEUM OIL AND ITS PRODUCTS.

1. THE mayor and aldermen of every city, and the selectmen of every town of more than fifteen hundred inhabitants, and of every town of less than fifteen hundred inhabitants, upon the written application of five or more citizens of such town therefor, shall appoint, annually, one or more suitable persons, not interested in the sale of crude petroleum, or in the sale or manufacture of petroleum, earth rock oil, or in any of their products, to be inspector or inspectors thereof in said city or town, and fix their compensation, to be paid by persons requiring their services under the provisions of this statute, and who before entering upon the duties of their office shall be duly sworn. Any inspector guilty of fraud, deceit, or culpable negligence in the performance of his duties, shall be punished by fine not exceeding one hundred dollars, or imprisonment in the county jail or house of correction not exceeding one month, or by both, in the discretion of the court.

2. No person shall mix for sale, naphtha and illuminating oils, or shall sell or offer for sale such mixture, or shall sell or offer for sale, except for purposes of re-manufacture, illuminating oils made from coal or petroleum, which will evaporate a gas under one hundred degrees Fahrenheit or ignite at a temperature of less than one hundred and ten degrees Fahrenheit, to be ascertained by the application of Tagliabue's or some other approved instrument, and any person so doing shall for each offence be punished by fine or imprisonment, as provided in the first section hereof; and shall also be liable therefor, to any person suffering damage from the explosion or ignition of such oil thus unlawfully

sold or kept, or offered for sale ; and such oil thus unlawfully sold or kept, or offered for sale, and the casks or
packages containing the same, shall be forfeited and sold,
one half of the proceeds of such sale to go to the commonwealth and the other half to the informer.

3. For all the purposes of this act, all illuminating oils
made from coal or petroleum having an igniting point of
less than one hundred and ten degrees Fahrenheit, to be
determined in the manner provided in the second section
of this act, shall be deemed to be mixed with naphtha and
shall be branded unsafe for illuminating purposes.

4. Any person who shall sell, or keep, or offer for sale,
naphtha under any assumed name, shall for each offence,
upon conviction thereof, be liable to the same penalties
provided, and shall be subject to the same liabilities set
forth in the first two sections of this act.

5. Crude petroleum, or any of its products, may be
stored, kept, manufactured, or refined in detached and
properly ventilated buildings specially adapted for the purpose, and surrounded by an embankment constructed so as
to effectually prevent the overflow of said petroleum or any
of its products beyond the premises on which the same
may be kept, manufactured, or refined : said buildings to
be occupied in no part as a dwelling ; and if less than fifty
feet from any other building must be separated therefrom
by a stone or brick wall at least ten feet high and twelve
inches thick ; and any person keeping such articles in any
other kind of building, except as is hereinafter provided in
the sixth section hereof, shall be punished by fine or imprisonment, in the manner provided in the first two sections
hereof.

6. No person shall manufacture, refine, mix, store, or
keep for sale, any oil or fluid composed wholly or in part
of any of the products of petroleum, in any city or town,
except as provided in the fifth section of this act, without
a license first having been obtained from the mayor and
aldermen of said city or the selectmen of said town, and
in said license there shall be expressed the manner, and the

portion of any locality or building in which said articles may be mixed, stored, or kept; and whoever mixes, stores, or keeps said articles in any one locality, except as aforesaid, without having first obtained a license as herein required, or having obtained such license, mixes, stores, or keeps said articles in a different manner, or in any other portion of said locality or building than is expressed in said license, shall forfeit and pay a sum not exceeding five hundred dollars, to be recovered in any appropriate form of action, to be instituted in the name of the mayor of said city, or of the selectmen of said town; and the license granted in accordance with the provisions of this act shall continue to be in force from the time of granting the same until the first day of April next succeeding, unless sooner revoked; and said license shall be revocable at all times by the authorities granting the same.

7. Upon complaint made to the justice of any municipal or police court, or to a justice of the peace, by the mayor or by an alderman of any city, or by a selectman of any town, or by an inspector appointed under the provisions of this act, or any engineer of a fire department, fireward, chief of police, or city marshal, that he has probable cause to suspect, and does suspect, that any of the articles enumerated in this act are offered for sale, or are deposited and kept within the limits of said city or town, contrary to the provisions of this act, said justice or court may issue a warrant directed to any such inspector, engineer, or fireward, or to any sheriff, deputy-sheriff, constable, or police officer, ordering him to enter any shop, warehouse, manufactory, or any other building specified in the warrant, to make diligent search for such article or articles suspected to be so offered for sale, deposited, or kept, and to make return of his doings to said justice or court forthwith.

8. None of the articles enumerated in this act shall be allowed to remain in any street, lane, alley, or travelled way, or upon any wharf, or in any yard, or on the grounds of any railroad corporation in any city for a longer time than twenty-four hours, and in any town for a longer time than

forty-eight hours, without a special permit from the mayor and aldermen of said city, or the selectmen of said town, or from some person by them duly authorized; and any and all persons so keeping such articles for a longer time, shall be punished by a fine of not more than fifty dollars for each and every such offence.

9. The city council of any city, and the inhabitants of any town, may adopt such ordinances, by-laws, and regulations, not inconsistent with the provisions of this act, as they may deem reasonable in relation to the manufacture, mixing, storing, keeping, or selling within the corporate limits of said city or town, any of the articles herein enumerated, and may affix penalties for breaches thereof not exceeding fifty dollars for each offence, reasonable notice of which shall be given to all concerned.

10. No person shall sell, or keep for sale, or in storage, any crude or refined petroleum, naphtha, kerosene, earth rock, machinery or illuminating oil, in any city or town, without having the same inspected and approved by an authorized inspector. And any person violating the provisions of this section shall be fined and imprisoned in the manner provided in the section of this act (first of this chapter) in relation to inspectors.[1]

The following provisions are in force, except so far as they are inconsistent with the foregoing: —

11. The mayor and aldermen of any city, or the selectmen of any town, where oils are manufactured from coal or petroleum, and the mayor and aldermen of any city and the selectmen of any town where oils are sold but not made, and where five or more inhabitants petition for the same, shall appoint annually one or more suitable persons, not interested in the sale or manufacture of said oils, as inspectors thereof, and fix their compensation, to be paid by the parties requiring the services of said inspectors.

12. Every inspector, before entering upon the duties of his office, shall be duly sworn, and when called upon by any manufacturer, refiner, vendor, purchaser, or by any

[1] Stats. 1869, ch. 152, §§ 1-9, 11.

officer mentioned in the sixth section of this act (section thirteen below), to test such oils, shall do so with all reasonable despatch, by applying the fire-test, as indicated and determined by G. Tagliabue's pyrometer, or some other instrument equally accurate. Any inspector guilty of fraud, deceit, or culpable negligence in inspecting such oils, shall be punished by fine not exceeding one hundred dollars, or imprisonment in the county jail or house of correction not exceeding one month, or both, in the discretion of the court.

13. The selectmen of the towns, and the mayors, aldermen, and police of the cities in which inspectors are appointed in conformity with the first section of this act, or any one of said officers, within their respective towns and cities, and the members of the state police, or any of them, shall cause all persons violating any of the provisions of this act to be prosecuted therefor.[1]

[1] Stats. 1867, ch. 286, §§.1, 2, 6.

# CHAPTER LVI.

## CONCERNING DOGS. PROTECTION OF SHEEP, ETC.

1. Every owner or keeper of a dog shall annually, on or before the thirtieth day of April, cause it to be registered, numbered, described, and licensed for one year from the first day of the ensuing May, in the office of the clerk of the city or town wherein said dog is kept, and shall cause it to wear around its neck a collar distinctly marked with its owner's name and its registered number, and shall pay for such license, for a male dog two dollars, and for a female dog five dollars.

2. Any person becoming the owner or keeper of a dog not duly licensed, on or after the first day of May, shall cause said dog to be registered, numbered, described, and licensed until the first day of the ensuing May, in the manner and subject to the terms and duties prescribed in this act.

Any person becoming the owner or keeper of a dog after the first day of May, not duly licensed, shall cause said dog to be registered, numbered, described, and licensed until the first day of the ensuing May, in the manner and subject to the terms and duties prescribed in section one of this chapter: *provided*, that no dog shall be required to be licensed until it is three months old.

Any owner of a dog may, at any time, have it licensed until the first day of the ensuing May, upon paying the sum provided in section one of this chapter; and such license shall exempt him from the penalty of section five of this chapter, unless such complaint is made prior to issuing the license.[1]

3. The clerks of cities or towns shall issue said licenses, and receive the money therefor, and pay the same into the treasuries of their respective counties, except in the county of Suffolk, on or before the first day of December of each

---

[1] Stats. 1872, ch. 330.

year, retaining to their own use twenty cents for each license, and shall return therewith a sworn statement of the amount of moneys thus received and paid over by them. They shall also keep a record of all licenses issued by them, with the names of the keepers or owners of dogs licensed, and the names, registered numbers, and descriptions of all such dogs.

4. It shall be the duty of each county treasurer, and of each city or town treasurer, except in the county of Suffolk, to keep an accurate and separate account of all moneys received and expended by him under the provisions of this act.

5. Any person keeping a dog contrary to the provisions of this act, shall forfeit fifteen dollars, to be recovered by complaint or indictment; and of said fine or forfeiture, five dollars shall be paid to the complainant, and ten dollars shall be paid to the treasurer of the county in which the dog is kept; except that in the county of Suffolk the ten dollars shall be paid to the treasurer of the city or town wherein said dog is kept. A license from the clerk of any city or town shall be valid in any part of the commonwealth and may be transferred with the dog licensed: *provided,* said license be recorded by the clerk of the city or town where such dog is kept.

6. The assessors of the cities and towns shall annually take a list of all dogs owned or kept in their respective cities or towns, on the first day of May, with the owners' or keepers' names, and return the same to the city or town clerk, on or before the first day of July. Any owner or keeper of a dog who shall refuse to give just and true answers, or shall answer falsely to the assessors relative to the ownership thereof, shall be punished by a fine of not less than ten dollars, to be paid, except in the county of Suffolk, into the county treasury.

7. Mayors of cities and the chairman of selectmen of towns shall annually, within ten days from the first day of July, issue a warrant to one or more police officers, or constables, directing them to proceed forthwith either to kill

or cause to be killed all dogs within their respective cities or towns, not licensed and collared according to the provisions of this act, and to enter complaint against the owners or keepers thereof, and any person may, and every police officer and constable shall, kill or cause to be killed all such dogs whenever or wherever found.   Such officers, other than those employed under regular pay, shall receive one dollar for each dog so destroyed, from the treasurers of their respective counties, except that in the county of Suffolk they shall receive it from the treasurers of their respective cities or towns.   All bills for such services shall be approved by the mayor, or chairman of the selectmen, of the city or town in which said dogs are destroyed, and shall be paid from moneys received under the provisions of this act.

8. Each police officer or constable to whom the warrant named in the preceding section shall have been issued shall return the same, on or before the first day of the October following. to the mayor or chairman of selectmen issuing the same, and shall state in said return the number of dogs killed, and the names of the owners or keepers thereof, and whether all unlicensed dogs in his city or town have been killed, and the names of persons against whom complaints have been made under the provisions of this act, and whether complaints have been entered against all the persons who have failed to comply with the provisions of this act.

9. The mayors of cities and the chairman of selectmen of towns shall annually, within ten days from the first day of October, transmit a certificate, regularly subscribed and sworn to, of the fact of the issue of the warrant named in section seven, and whether the same has been duly executed and returned, agreeably to the provisions of this act, to the district attorneys of their respective districts, whose duty it shall be to prosecute all such city, town, or county officers as fail to comply with the provisions of this act.

10. Whoever suffers loss by the worrying, maiming, or

killing of his sheep, lambs, fowls, or other domestic animals by dogs, may inform the mayor of the city or the chairman of the selectmen of the town wherein the damage was done, who shall proceed to the premises where the damage was done and determine whether the same was inflicted by dogs, and if so, appraise the amount thereof and return a certificate of said amount, except in the county of Suffolk, to the county commissioners, on or before the first day of December : *provided, however*, that if, in the opinion of said mayor or chairman of selectmen, the amount of said damage shall exceed the sum of twenty dollars, he shall appoint two disinterested persons, who, with the said mayor or chairman of selectmen, shall appraise the amount of such damage and return a certificate of the same, except in the county of Suffolk, to the county commissioners, on or before the first day of December.  The county commissioners shall, during the month of December, examine all such bills, and, when any doubt exists, may summon the appraisers and all parties interested, and make such examination as they may think proper, and shall issue an order upon the treasurer of the county in which the damage was done, for all or any part thereof, as justice and equity may require.

The treasurer shall annually, on the first Wednesday of January, pay all such orders in full, if the gross amount received by him and not previously paid out under the provisions of this act is sufficient therefor ; otherwise he shall divide such amount *pro rata* among such orders, in full discharge thereof.

The appraisers shall receive from the county, or in the county of Suffolk from the city or town treasurer, out of the moneys received under the provisions of this act, the sum of one dollar each for every examination made by them as prescribed in this section ; and the mayor or the chairman of selectmen acting in the case, shall receive twenty cents per mile one way for his necessary travel in the case.

The owner of sheep, lambs, or other domestic animals

worried, maimed, or killed by dogs, shall have his election whether to proceed under the provisions of this section or under the provisions of sections sixty-one, sixty-two, and sixty-three of chapter eighty-eight of the General Statutes; but, having signified his election by proceeding in either mode, he shall not have the other remedy. In the absence or sickness of the mayor of the city, or chairman of the selectmen of the town, in which the damage is done, it shall be the duty of any one of the aldermen of said city, or of the selectmen of said town, who may be duly informed of damage supposed to have been done by dogs, to discharge forthwith the duties imposed by this section upon the mayor or chairman of selectmen.

11. Any city, town, or county officer refusing or wilfully neglecting to perform the duties herein imposed upon him, shall be punished by a fine not exceeding one hundred dollars, to be paid, except in the county of Suffolk, into the county treasury. Any person aggrieved by such refusal or neglect on the part of any city, town, or county officer, may report the same forthwith to the district attorney of his district.

12. The treasurer of any county may, and, when ordered by the county commissioners, shall, bring an action of tort against the owner or keeper of any dog concerned in doing damage to sheep, lambs, or other domestic animals in said county, which damage the county commissioners have ordered to be paid, to recover the full amount thereof to the use of said county. All fines and penalties provided in this act may be recovered on complaint or indictment before any court of competent jurisdiction in the county where the offence is committed.

13. In the county of Suffolk, all moneys received for licenses or recovered as fines or penalties under the provisions of this act, which, if received or recovered in any other county, would be paid into the county treasury, shall be paid into the treasury of the city or town in which said licenses are issued or said fines or penalties recovered. All claims for damage done by dogs in said county shall

be determined by appraisers as specified in section ten of this act, and, when approved by the board of aldermen or selectmen of the city or town where the damage was done, shall be paid in full on the first Wednesday of January of each year by the treasurer of said city or town, if the gross amount received by him and not previously paid out under the provisions of this act is sufficient therefor; otherwise such amount shall be divided *pro rata* among such claimants in full discharge thereof.

After such claims have been approved by the board of aldermen or selectmen, the treasurer of said city or town may, and, when ordered by the board of aldermen or selectmen, shall, bring an action of tort to recover, against the owner or keeper of any dog concerned in doing the damage, the full amount thereof.

14. Any person owning or keeping a licensed dog, who may have received a notice, in accordance with section sixty-one of chapter eighty-eight of the General Statutes, that said dog is mischievous or dangerous, and who does not kill it or keep it thereafter from ever going at large, shall, on complaint or indictment, forfeit ten dollars, if it be proved that said dog be mischievous or dangerous.

15. The warrants required to be issued by the seventh section of this act may be in the following form, viz. : —

COMMONWEALTH OF MASSACHUSETTS.

[Seal.]

M        ss.   To          , constable of the town (or city) of

In the name of the Commonwealth of Massachusetts, you are hereby required to proceed forthwith to kill or cause to be killed all dogs within the said town not duly licensed and collared according to the provisions of the act of the year eighteen hundred and sixty-seven, entitled "An Act concerning Dogs, and for the protection of Sheep and other Domestic Animals," and you are further required to make and enter complaint against the owner or keeper of any such dog.

Hereof fail not, and make due return of this warrant with your doings therein, stating the number of dogs killed and the names of the owners or keepers thereof, and whether all unlicensed dogs in said town (or city) have been killed, and the names of persons against whom complaints have been made under the provisions of said act, and whether complaints have been made and entered against all the persons who have failed to comply with the provisions of said act, on or before the first day of October next.

Given under my hand and seal at        aforesaid, the     **day** of        in the year eighteen hundred and

(Mayor of) or Chairman of the

Selectmen of [1]

16. Moneys received by the treasurer of any county, under the provisions of chapter one hundred and thirty of the acts of the year eighteen hundred and sixty-seven, and not expended in the payment of damages done by dogs in accordance with the provisions of said act, shall be paid back to the treasurers of the several cities and towns of said county, in the month of January of each year, in proportion to the amount paid by said city or town to said county treasurer; and the moneys so refunded shall be expended for the support of public libraries or schools, in addition to the amount annually appropriated by said city or town for those purposes. In the county of Suffolk, moneys received by any treasurer of a city or town, under the provisions of said act, and not expended in accordance with the provisions of the same, shall be appropriated by the school committee of said city or town for the support of the public schools therein established.[2]

17. The mayor and aldermen of any city or the selectmen of any town may order that any dog or dogs within the limits of such city or town respectively, shall be muzzled or restrained from running at large during such time as shall be prescribed by such order. After passing such order and the publication of the same by posting a certified copy thereof in two or more public places in such city or town, or in case a daily newspaper shall be published in such city or town, by publication thereof once in such newspaper, said mayor and aldermen or selectmen may issue their warrant to one or more of the police officers or constables of such city or town, who shall, after twenty-four hours from the publication of such notice, kill any or all dogs found unmuzzled or running at large contrary to such order.

Said police officers or constables shall be compensated for service under this act, as provided in section seven of this chapter, and any such city or town officer refusing or wilfully neglecting to perform the duties herein imposed upon him shall be punished as provided in section eleven of this chapter.

[1] Stats. 1867, ch. 130.        [2] Stats. 1869, ch. 250, § 1.

The mayor and aldermen of any city or the selectmen of any town may cause special service of any order passed by them respectively, as provided for in this section, to be made upon any person, requiring that any dog owned or kept by such person shall be muzzled or restrained from running at large, by causing a certified copy of such order to be delivered to him. Any person, who after receiving such certified copy shall refuse or neglect, for the period of twelve hours after receiving such notice, to muzzle or restrain such dog as required by such order, shall pay a fine not exceeding twenty-five dollars; said fine to be recovered as provided in section twelve.

Every license issued to the owner of any dog in this commonwealth shall have printed thereon a description of the symptoms of the disease in dogs known as hydrophobia, said description to be supplied by the secretary of the state board of health to the clerks of the several cities and towns of the commonwealth upon application therefor.[1]

[1] Stats. 1877, ch. 167.

# CHAPTER LVII.

## HERRING FISHERIES.

1. **The** mayor and aldermen of any city, and the selectmen of any town, in this commonwealth, are hereby empowered to authorize, in writing, any three or more persons, and their associates, to organize a corporation, with a capital stock of not less than one thousand, and not more than five thousand dollars, for the purpose of opening outlets, canals, or ditches, for the introduction and propagation of herrings and alewives, in the ponds, creeks, and rivers within the limits of such town or city, as aforesaid; and said corporation, when organized, shall have all the powers and privileges, and be subject to all the duties, liabilities, and restrictions, set forth in the sixty-first chapter of the General Statutes, and in all general laws which now are or may hereafter be in force relating to corporations.

2. Said corporations may purchase and hold real estate necessary for the purpose of opening outlets, canals, sluiceways, or ditches, for the passage of herring and alewives to and from said ponds and other waters.

3. Towns and cities, in their corporate capacity, may open ditches, sluiceways, or canals, into any ponds within their limits, for the introduction and propagation of herrings and alewives, and for the creation of fishery for the same; and the land for opening such ditches, sluiceways, or canals, within such town or city, may be taken under the provisions of the statutes which now regulate and limit the taking of land for highways and other purposes.

4. Any fishery so created by any town or city shall be deemed to be the property of such town or city, and such town or city may make any proper regulations concerning the same, and may lease such fishery for a period not ex-

ceeding five years, upon such terms as may be agreed upon between such town or city and the lessees of the same. And any town may lease for a like period, and upon like terms, any fishery now owned by such town, or any public fishery which has heretofore been regulated and controlled by such town.

5. No person without the permission of such town or city, or of the lessees of such fishery, in any fishery created by such town or city, or in any fishery created by any corporation, without the permission of said corporation, shall take, kill, or haul on shore any herrings or alewives, in any fishery so created by any town, city, or corporation, for the introduction and propagation of herrings or alewives.

6. Whoever violates any of the provisions of the preceding section, shall forfeit and pay a sum not less than five nor more than fifty dollars for each offence, to be recovered by prosecution before any court competent to try the same.

7. All prosecutions under the preceding section shall be instituted within thirty days from the time the offence was committed.

8. Nothing contained in this act shall be held to impair the rights of any person under any law heretofore passed, or to deprive any person of any right under any contract now existing, or to authorize any town, city, or corporation to enter upon or build any canals or sluiceways into any pond which is the private property of any individual or corporation.[1]

[1] Stats. 1866, ch. 187, §§ 1-8.

# CHAPTER LVIII.

## SHELL FISH.

1. THE mayor and aldermen or selectmen of any city or town in which there are oyster beds may give permits in writing to any person to take oysters from their beds at such times, in such quantities, and for such uses, as they shall express in their permits; and every inhabitant of such city or town may, without such permit, take oysters from the beds therein for the use of his family, from the first day of September to the first day of June annually.

2. Whoever takes any other shell fish from their beds, or destroys them, or wilfully obstructs their growth therein, in any city or town, except as is hereinafter provided, shall forfeit for every bushel of such other shell fish (including the shells) one dollar. But the mayor and aldermen or selectmen of each of said places may at all times give permits in writing to any person to take such other shell fish from their beds therein, at such times, in such quantities, and for such uses, as they shall express in their permit; and every inhabitant of each of said places may, without such permit, take such other shell fish from the beds therein, for the use of his family.

3. Nothing contained in the two[1] preceding sections shall be construed to deprive native Indians of the privilege of digging shell fish for their own consumption, or to prevent any fisherman (an inhabitant of this state[2]) from taking any quantity of shell fish which he may want for bait, not exceeding at any one time seven bushels including their shells.

4. The mayor and aldermen or selectmen of any city or town may, by writing under their hands, grant a license

<hr>

[1] Stats. 1872, ch. 46.  [2] Stats. 1867, ch. 70.

for a term not exceeding twenty years to any inhabitant thereof, to plant, grow, and dig oysters, at all times of the year, upon and in any flats and creeks therein, at any place where there is no natural oyster bed; not, however, impairing the private rights of any person, nor materially obstructing the navigable waters of any creek or bay.

5. Such license shall describe by metes and bounds the flats and creeks so appropriated, and shall be recorded by the city or town clerk before it shall have any force; and the person licensed shall pay to the mayor and aldermen or selectmen, for their use, two dollars, and to the clerk fifty cents.[1]

[1] Gen. Stats. ch. 83, §§ 12-17.

## CHAPTER LIX.

### POWER OF TOWNS TO PURCHASE WATER RIGHTS.

1. ANY city or town in this commonwealth may, for the purpose of supplying pure water to its inhabitants, purchase of any aqueduct company, or of any municipal or other corporation, now existing, or that may hereafter be organized under any special charter or general law of this commonwealth, the right to take water from any of its sources of supply or from pipes leading therefrom; or may purchase its whole water-rights, estates, properties, franchises, and privileges, and by such latter purchase become entitled to all the rights and privileges and subject to all the duties and liabilities appertaining and belonging to said company or corporation (or may make any contract for a supply of water with any such company or corporation [1]) : *provided, however*, that no city shall exercise such authority to purchase (or contract [1]) without the consent of two-thirds of each branch of its city council, sanctioned and ratified by a majority of the voters of said city, present and voting thereon at a legal meeting duly called in their several ward-rooms for that purpose, and at which the check-list shall be used ; and *provided, further*, that no town shall exercise such authority to purchase (or contract [1]) without the consent of two-thirds of its selectmen, sanctioned and ratified by a majority of the voters of said town, present and voting thereon at a legal meeting duly called for that purpose, and at which the check-list shall be used.

2. Any city or town which shall make such purchase, may issue bonds in payment thereof, at a rate of interest not exceeding seven per cent, payable semiannually, and

[1] Stats. 1873, ch. 255.

redeemable at some time not exceeding twenty years from the date thereof. ·

3. Any city or town which shall make such purchase and issue bonds as aforesaid, may, for the purpose of purchasing materials, laying pipes, and doing other work necessary in order to supply its inhabitants with pure water for domestic uses, or for extinguishment of fires, issue additional bonds similar to those heretofore specified (and any city or town which may make any such contract as aforesaid may, for the purpose named in this section, issue similar bonds [1]) : *provided*, the whole amount issued under this and the preceding section does not exceed ten per cent of its valuation.

4. In case the water should be brought through another city or town, pipes may be laid through such streets and highways of said city or town as shall be designated by the mayor and aldermen, or selectmen thereof; and the party exercising the privilege of laying pipes under such permission, shall be liable in an action of contract or tort, for all damages to any party damnified thereby.

5. All purchase-money received by any city or town under or by authority of the provisions of this act, shall be applied to the payment of its water-debt; or, if no such debt exists, then into the general treasury of such city or town. [2]

6. The city council of any city and the inhabitants of any town, in which water is supplied or distributed at the public expense, may prescribe rules and regulations for the inspection, materials, construction, alteration, or use of all water-pipes and of water-fixtures of every kind, through which water so supplied or distributed is used by any person or corporation within said city or town, and may impose penalties not exceeding twenty dollars for each and every violation of any provision of any ordinance or by-law passed by authority of this act, to be recovered before any municipal, district, or police court, or any trial justice having jurisdiction in the place where the penalty is in-

[1] Stats. 1873, ch. 255.      [2] Stats. 1870, ch. 93.

curred ; and may prohibit the use of water by any person or corporation neglecting or refusing to comply with any provision of any ordinance or by-law so passed : and any ordinance or by-law so passed may be made operative upon and within the whole territory of such city or town, or upon and within any prescribed or defined district or districts of said territory.

7. The powers conferred by this act upon the city council of any city or the inhabitants of any town, except the power to impose penalties, may be exercised by them through any water board or other board or commission which they may designate ; but the powers so delegated to any such board or commission may at any time be revoked by the authority delegating them.[1]

Any town may regulate by suitable ordinances or by-laws, to be made in the manner now provided by law, with penalties not exceeding fifty dollars for each violation thereof, the use of reservoirs and land and drive ways appurtenant thereto, forming a part of its system of water supply within its limits.[2]

[1] Stats. 1875, ch. 105.          [2] Stats. 1876, ch. 139.

# CHAPTER LX.

## DUTIES OF TOWN OFFICERS UNDER MILITIA LAW.

1. EVERY able-bodied male citizen, resident within this state, of the age of eighteen years, and under the age of forty-five years, excepting persons exempted by sections two, three, and five, and idiots, lunatics, common drunkards, vagabonds, paupers, and persons convicted of any infamous crime, shall be enrolled in the militia. Persons so convicted after enrolment shall forthwith be disenrolled; and, in all cases of doubt respecting the age of a person enrolled, the burden of proof shall be upon him.

2. In addition to the persons exempted from enrolment in the militia by the laws of the United States, the persons hereinafter mentioned shall also be absolutely exempted from enrolment, viz.: —

Justices and clerks of courts of record;

Registers of probate and insolvency;

Registers of deeds, and sheriffs;

Officers who have held or may hold commissions in the regular or volunteer army or navy of the United States;

Officers who have held, for a period of five years, commissions in the militia of this or any other state of the United States, or who have been superseded and discharged, or who held commissions in any organization of the Massachusetts volunteer militia at the time of its disbandment;

Ministers of the gospel;

Practising physicians;

Superintendents, officers, and assistants, employed in or about either of the state hospitals, state almshouses, state prisons, jails, or houses of correction;

Keepers of light-houses;

Conductors and engine-drivers of railroad trains;

Seamen actually employed on board of any vessel, or who have been so employed within three months next preceding the time of enrolment.

3. Every person of either of the religious denominations of Quakers or Shakers, who, on or before the first Tuesday in May, annually, produces to the assessors of the city or town in which he resides a certificate signed by two or more of the elders or overseers (as the case may be) and countersigned by the clerk of the society with which

he meets for public religious worship, shall be exempted from enrolment. The certificate shall be in form as follows : —

We, the subscribers, of the society of the people called in the       of       , in the county of       , do hereby certify that       is a member of our society, and that he frequently and usually attends religious worship with said society; and we believe he is conscientiously scrupulous of bearing arms.

E. F., *Clerk.*

A. B., } *Elders or Overseers,*
C. D., } (as the case may be.)

4. Engine men or members of the fire department in a city or town shall be exempted from military duty by forthwith filing with the assessors of the city or town in which they reside a certificate that they are engine men or members of the fire department as aforesaid, signed by the mayor and aldermen or fire commissioners of such city, or the selectmen of such town; but when a member of a volunteer company is, after his enlistment, appointed an engine man or member of the fire department, it shall not vacate his enlistment.

5. The enrolled militia shall be subject to no active duty, except in case of war, invasion, the prevention of invasion, the suppression of riots, and to aid civil officers in the execution of the laws of the commonwealth.

6. Assessors shall annually, in May or June, make a list of persons living within their respective limits liable to enrolment, and place a certified copy thereof in the hand of the clerks of their respective cities and towns, who shall place it on file with the records of such city or town, and annually, in May, June, or July, transmit returns of the militia thus enrolled to the adjutant-general.

7. Keepers of taverns or boarding houses, and masters and mistresses of dwelling houses, shall, upon application of the assessors within whose bounds their houses are situated, or of persons acting under them, give information of the names of persons residing in their houses liable to enrolment or to do military duty; and every such person shall, upon like application, give his name and age; and if such keeper, master, mistress, or person refuses to give such information, or gives false information, such keeper, master, or mistress shall forfeit and pay twenty dollars, and such person shall forfeit and pay twelve dollars, to be recovered on complaint of either of the assessors.

8. The selectmen shall provide for each regiment, battalion, corps of cadets, or portion of the volunteer militia, within the limits of their respective towns, a suitable armory for the purpose of drill, and for the safe keeping of the arms, equipments, uniforms, and other military property furnished to such portion of the volunteer militia by the state; and shall also provide suitable grounds or places for the parade, drill, and target-practice of the militia belonging to their respective towns. They shall also provide for the headquarters located within

their limits of each brigade, regiment, separate battalion, or corps of cadets, a suitable room for the keeping of books, the transaction of business, and the instruction of officers. Necessary fuel and lights, or a reasonable allowance therefor, shall be furnished by towns for each armory or headquarters located within their limits.

9. Where two or more companies of the same battalion are located within the limits of a town, the selectmen thereof shall, if practicable, provide such companies with a drill-hall, to be used by them in common, of capacity sufficient for battalion drill, together with a smaller room in the same building, for each of said companies, suitable for company meetings, and for the safe keeping of military property, as provided in the preceding section.

The headquarters of each regiment, battalion, and corps of cadets, shall be established with said commands, or portions thereof, as far as practicable.

10. Towns in which regiments, battalions, corps of cadets, or companies, or the headquarters of brigades, regiments, battalions, or corps of cadets are located, are hereby authorized to raise money, by taxation or otherwise, for the purpose of erecting suitable buildings for the armories or headquarters of such organizations.

11. When a company is formed from different places, the location of its armory shall be determined by a majority of its members, subject to the approval of the adjutant-general.

12. Armories provided for the militia shall not be used for any purpose whatever other than the legitimate uses of the commands occupying them; and no commander of any regiment, battalion, corps of cadets, or company shall allow the armory or armories of his command to be let for other than a proper military purpose, unless by approval of the commander-in-chief. And they shall be open to reasonable inspection by the selectmen.

13. The selectmen of towns shall annually, in October or November, transmit to the adjutant-general a certificate, verified by oath or affirmation of at least two of their board, showing the name of each militia organization or headquarters furnished with an armory, the amount paid for the rent thereof, and that the rent charged is fair and reasonable according to the value of real estate in their place.

14. The adjutant-general shall annually examine all certificates so returned to his office, institute any inquiries he deems expedient relative thereto, and, under the direction of the commander-in-chief, allow them, in whole or in part, to an amount not exceeding six hundred dollars for a company of artillery or cavalry, four hundred dollars for a company of infantry, and not exceeding two hundred dollars for each brigade, regimental, or separate battalion headquarters. The amount to be allowed to a corps of cadets shall be determined by the commander-in-chief, not exceeding the allowance which would be made in the aggregate to a battalion of four companies and the headquarters thereof. The adjutant-general shall, within ten days

after such examination, file in the office of the auditor his certificate, stating the sums allowed, the name of the command for whose use each sum is allowed, and the place to which it belongs; and shall thereupon notify the selectmen of the sum allowed to their place; which sum shall be paid, upon the warrant of the governor to such selectmen.

15. When there is in any town a tumult, riot, mob, or a body of men acting together by force, with attempt to commit a felony, or to offer violence to persons or property, or by force and violence to break and resist the laws of the commonwealth, or when such tumult, riot, or mob is threatened, and the fact is made to appear to the commander-in-chief, or the sheriff of the county, or the selectmen of the town, the commander-in-chief may issue his order, or such sheriff, or selectmen may issue a precept, directed to any commander of a brigade, regiment, battalion, corps of cadets, or company, directing him to order his command, or a part thereof, to appear at a time and place therein specified, to aid the civil authority in suppressing such violence, and supporting the laws; which precept shall be in substance as follows: —

————, *ss.*

### COMMONWEALTH OF MASSACHUSETTS.

L. S.

To (*insert the officer's title*) A B, commanding (*insert his command*).

Whereas it has been made to appear to (*the sheriff, mayor, or the selectmen, as the case may be*) of the (*county, city, or town*) of      , that (*here state one or more of the causes above mentioned*) in our      of      , and that military force is necessary to aid the civil authority in suppressing the same: Now, therefore, we command you that you cause (*your command, or such part thereof as may be desired*), armed and equipped with ammunition, and with proper officers, to parade at      , on      , then and there to obey such orders as may be given, according to law.   Hereof fail not at your peril, and have you there this precept, with your doings returned thereon.

This precept shall be signed and properly attested as the act of such sheriff, or selectmen, and shall be under seal, and may be varied to suit the circumstances of the case; and a copy of the same shall be immediately forwarded to the commander-in-chief.

16. The selectmen of a town, to which men so ordered out, detached, or drafted belong, when required in writing by a commander of a regiment or detachment, shall provide carriages to attend them with further supplies of provisions and to carry necessary baggage, and provide necessary camp equipage and utensils, until notified by the commanding officer to desist; and shall present their accounts for the same to the quartermaster-general.   For any neglect by such selectmen, under this section, such town shall forfeit, to the use of

the commonwealth, not less than twenty nor more than five hundred dollars.

17. Whenever it shall be necessary to call out any portion of the enrolled militia for active duty, the commander-in-chief shall direct his order to the selectmen of towns, who, upon receipt of the same, shall forthwith, by written or oral notice to each individual, or by proclamation, appoint a time and place for the assembling of the enrolled militia in their town, and shall then and there proceed to draft as many thereof, or accept as many volunteers as is required by the order of the commander-in-chief, and shall forthwith forward to the commander-in-chief a list of the persons so drafted or accepted as volunteers.

18. Every member of the enrolled militia ordered out, or who volunteers or is detached or drafted, who does not appear at the time and place designated by the selectmen, or who has not some able-bodied and proper substitute at such time and place, or does not pay to such selectmen, for the use of the commonwealth, the sum of seventy-five dollars within twenty-four hours from such time, or who does not produce a sworn certificate, from a physician in good standing, of physical disability to so appear, shall be taken to be a deserter, and dealt with accordingly.[1]

[1] Stats. 1878, ch. 265.

# CHAPTER LXI.

DUTIES OF SELECTMEN TO RETURN INDUSTRIAL STA-
TISTICS; AS TO RACE GROUNDS.   PENALTIES.

1. THE aldermen of each city and the selectmen of each town in the commonwealth shall, between the first day of May and the first day of September, in the year eighteen hundred and sixty-five, and also between the first day of May and the first day of September, in every tenth year thereafter, make to the secretary of the common-wealth the returns hereinafter specified; such returns, so far as they relate to the amount, description, and value of stock and fuel consumed, and of articles manufactured; to the produce of land, quarries, kilns, coal-beds, ore-beds, and fisheries; to wool, wood, bark, charcoal, farm products, live stock, ice, and imports; to vessels and boats built, and buildings erected, shall embrace the year ending on the first day of May in said years respectively; and in all other particulars shall state the facts as they shall exist in the respective cities and towns on said first day of May.

As the blanks furnished by the secretary will probably contain all the particular items to be returned, it is thought unnecessary to reprint them here.

2. The secretary of the commonwealth shall cause to be printed blank tables, conveniently arranged for the return of the facts aforesaid, with blank columns for the return of such facts as are not enumerated in this act, and shall furnish three copies of the same, together with one copy of this act, to the aldermen of each city and the selectmen of each town; the whole to be accompanied with such printed instructions as he shall deem proper.

3. The secretary of the commonwealth, after he shall have received the returns aforesaid, from the aldermen of the several cities and the selectmen of the several towns,

shall cause to be prepared and printed a true abstract of the same, with each column of figures of such abstract added up, for the use of the next ensuing legislature.

4. The aldermen of any city and the selectmen of any town may authorize either of their number, or some other suitable person, or persons, to collect the information required by this act.

5. If any alderman, selectman, or other person, authorized under the provisions of section four of this act, shall wilfully neglect to make the returns as required in the first section, he shall forfeit and pay a sum not exceeding two hundred dollars ; and if any person shall refuse to give the information required in said first section, he shall forfeit and pay a sum not exceeding one hundred dollars.

6. All fines and forfeitures arising under this act may be recovered in any court of this commonwealth having competent jurisdiction, in an action of debt, one moiety to the use of him or them who shall sue for the same, and the other moiety to the use of the commonwealth ; or they may be recovered by information filed by the attorney-general, in any court having competent jurisdiction, in which case they shall accrue wholly to the commonwealth.[1]

7. No land within any town or city shall be laid out or used as a race ground or trotting park, without the previous consent of and location by the selectmen or mayor and aldermen ; who may regulate and alter the terms and conditions under which the same shall be laid out, used, or continued in use ; and discontinue the same when in their judgment the public good so requires ; and no land shall be used for racing, &c. of horses for money.[2]

8. If a town, city, or county officer embezzles or fraudulently converts to his own use, or fraudulently takes or secretes with intent so to do, any effects or property belonging to or in possession of said town, city, or county, he shall be deemed guilty of larceny, and be punished by imprisonment in the state prison not exceeding ten years, or by fine not exceeding one thousand dollars, and imprisonment in the jail not exceeding two years.[3]

[1] Stats. 1865, ch. 146.  [2] Gen. Stats. ch. 167, § 10; Stats. 1864, ch. 63.
[3] Gen. Stats. ch. 161, § 37.

# CHAPTER LXII.

## PARISHES AND RELIGIOUS SOCIETIES.

1. EVERY religious society established or organized by virtue of any statute shall be and continue a body corporate with the powers given to corporations by chapter sixty-eight,[1] and the powers, privileges, liabilities, and duties set forth in this chapter; but this chapter shall not enlarge nor diminish the powers of taxation enjoyed by any religious society by virtue of a special law or act of incorporation, nor impair existing rights of property of any territorial parish.

2. Religious societies, whether corporate or unincorporate, shall continue to have and enjoy their existing rights, privileges, and immunities, except so far as the same may be limited or modified by the provisions of this chapter.

3. The respective churches connected and associated in public worship with such religious societies shall continue to have, exercise, and enjoy all their accustomed privileges and liberties respecting divine worship, church order, and discipline, and shall be encouraged in the peaceable and regular enjoyment and practice thereof.[2]

4. Where a parish or religious society is, by its constitution, limited to any place, the church of such society is equally limited, being indissolubly connected with such society; so that an adhering minority of the church, and not a seceding majority, constitutes the church of such parish or religious society, to all civil purposes.[3]

5. A religious society that is not incorporated, or which may be unable to assemble in the usual manner, if it con-

---

[1] Chapter sixty-eight of the General Statutes.

[2] Gen. Stats. ch. 30, §§ 1–3.

[3] Stebbins *v.* Jennings, 10 Pick. 172; Baker *v.* Fales, 16 Mass. 488.

tains ten or more qualified voters, may organize and become a corporation with the powers, privileges, duties, liabilities, and requirements of such societies, and may hold so much estate, real or personal, as may be necessary for the objects of such organization, and no more ; but all the powers derived from such organization may be revoked by the legislature.

6. Any justice of the peace for the county in which such society may be, upon application in writing by five or more of the qualified voters thereof, may issue his warrant directed to some one of the applicants, stating the objects, and requiring him to warn the qualified voters of the society to meet at a time and place appointed in the warrant ; and the same may be served by posting an attested copy thereof on the principal outer door of the meeting-house, or leaving such copy with or at the last and usual place of abode of such voters, seven days at least before such meeting ; and, upon due return thereof, the same justice or any other justice of the peace for the county may preside at the meeting for the choice and qualification of a clerk, who shall enter at large upon the records of the society the proceedings had in the organization thereof ; and the society may thereupon proceed to choose a moderator and do such other things as parishes are by law authorized to do at their annual meetings : *provided* the subject-matter thereof is inserted in the warrant.

7. Persons belonging to a religious society shall be held to be members until they file with the clerk a written notice declaring the dissolution of their membership, and they shall not be liable for any grant or contract thereafter made or entered into by such society. No person shall be made a member of such society without his consent in writing.[1]

8. Any parish or religious society may admit to membership women, who shall have all the rights and privileges of men.

9. Any territorial parish may admit to membership persons not residents of its territory.[2]

[1] Gen. Stats. ch. 30, §§ 4–6.      [2] Stats. 1869, ch. 346.

10. Every religious society may make by-laws not repugnant to the laws of the commonwealth, and therein prescribe the manner in which persons may become members.

11. No person shall have a right to vote in the affairs of such society unless he is a member thereof.

12. The qualified voters of every parish and incorporated religious society, and of every society organized according to the provisions of this chapter, shall hold an annual meeting in the month of March or April, or at such other time as they may prescribe by their by-laws, and if the by-laws do not otherwise determine at a time and place appointed by their assessors or standing committee ; and at such meeting shall choose a moderator, clerk, two or more assessors, a treasurer and collector, and such other officers as they think necessary, all of whom, except the moderator, shall continue in office till the next annual meeting and till others are chosen and qualified in their stead.

13. Moderators of meetings held for the choice of officers shall be elected by written ballots.   Clerks, assessors, treasurers, and collectors shall be elected by written ballot and shall be sworn.   Other officers may be elected in such mode as the society may determine.

14. The prudential affairs of such societies shall be managed by their assessors or a standing committee specially appointed for that purpose ; and the assessors or committee shall have like authority for calling meetings as selectmen have for calling town meetings.

15. If there are no assessors or committee, ·or if they unreasonably refuse to call a meeting, any justice of the peace for the county, upon the application of not less than five qualified voters, may call one in the manner provided in section five (section six above).

16. The assessors or committee shall insert in the next warrant they issue for calling a meeting any matter which not less than five qualified voters of the society in writing request.   Nothing acted upon shall have any legal operation, unless the subject-matter thereof was inserted in the warrant.

17. Meetings shall be warned in the manner provided by any by-law or vote of the society, and when no provision is made, in such manner as the assessors or standing committee in their warrant for such meeting direct.

18. The clerk, or if there is no clerk or he is absent, the assessors or the standing committee, or any one of them, shall preside in the choice of a moderator ; and a clerk may then be chosen, either *pro tempore* or to fill the vacancy, as the case may require. The moderator may administer the oath of office to the clerk ; and the clerk to the assessors and collector ; or said oaths may be administered by a justice of the peace ; and they shall be substantially the same as are required to be taken by the clerk, assessors, and collectors, of towns.[1]

The clerk may administer the oath of office to the treasurer as well as to assessors and collector.[2]

19. The moderator shall have the same power as the moderator of a town meeting ; and persons guilty of disorderly behavior at a meeting shall be subject to the penalties and punishments provided for like offences in town meetings.

20. If the person chosen collector is present and accepts the office, he shall forthwith be sworn. If not present, he shall be summoned to take the oath by a constable or any person whom the clerk or assessors may appoint for the purpose. Upon the refusal or neglect of a person present to accept the office at the time, and upon the neglect of a person so summoned, for the space of seven days, to appear and take the oath, the society shall proceed to a new choice ; and so from time to time until some person accepts and is sworn.

21. Vacancies in any of the annual offices, occurring after the annual meeting, may be filled at any other legal meeting.

22. The rector or one of the wardens of religious societies belonging to the body of Christians known as the Protestant Episcopal Church, organized under the laws of the

---

[1] Gen. Stats. ch. 30, §§ 7–15.      [2] Stats. 1865, ch. 100.

commonwealth, may, unless it is otherwise provided in some by-law, preside at their meetings with all the powers of a moderator; and the wardens or wardens and vestry may exercise all the powers of a standing committee in accordance with the usage and discipline of said church. Unless they assess or collect a tax on the polls, estates, or pews, of the members thereof, such societies need not choose a collector or assessors; and they may in their by-laws provide, that the duties of assessors shall be performed by the wardens. But the officers upon whom the duties of standing committee or assessors may devolve shall in all cases be elected by ballot.

23. The qualified voters of each religious society, at the annual meeting or at any other meeting regularly notified seven days at least before the holding thereof, may grant and vote such sums of money as they judge necessary for the settlement, maintenance, and support of ministers or public teachers of religion; for the building or repairing of houses of public worship; for sacred music; for the purchase and preservation of burial grounds; and for all other necessary parish charges; which sums shall be assessed on the polls and estates of all the members of the society, in the same manner and proportion as town taxes are by law assessed.

24. The assessors shall assess the taxes upon the property (not exempted by law from taxation) of all the members of the society, including their real estate within the state, in whatever part thereof it may be situated, and their personal estate wherever the same may be; and no citizen shall be liable to pay a tax for the support of public worship or other parish charges, to a society other than that of which he is a member.[1]

Shares in the capital stock of any corporation are not exempted from taxation for parish purposes.[2]

25. No corporation shall be taxed for any parochial purpose. Nor shall any person be taxed in a parish or

---

[1] Gen. Stats. ch. 30, §§ 16-21.    [2] Stats. 1866, ch. 196.

religious society for property held by him as guardian or trustee.

26. Every society may appoint its treasurer collector of taxes; who shall have like powers and proceed in like manner, in enforcing the collection of such taxes after the expiration of the time fixed by the society for the payment thereof, as provided in chapter twelve for the collection of taxes by collectors of towns; and any society may authorize its treasurer and collector to make an abatement of such sum as it may agree upon at its annual meeting, to those who make voluntary payment of their taxes within such periods as may be determined by the society.

The treasurer of a parish may employ an attorney to bring suit to collect a debt due to it, without express authority from the inhabitants or committee of the parish.[1]

27. Unincorporated religious societies shall have like power to manage, use, and employ, any donation, gift, or grant, made to them, according to its terms and conditions, as incorporated societies have, by law; may elect suitable trustees, agents, or officers therefor; and sue for any right which may vest in them in consequence of such donation, gift, or grant; for which purposes they shall be corporations.

28. Incorporated and unincorporated religious societies may appoint trustees, not exceeding five in number, to hold and manage trust funds for their benefit, who shall hold their offices (three[2]) years and until others are appointed in their stead. (In case of a vacancy, by death or otherwise, the parish may fill such vacancy at its next annual meeting, or at a special meeting called for that purpose.[3]) Such societies at or before the time of the first appointment of the trustees may establish rules and regulations for their government, which shall be considered as of the nature of a contract, and not subject to alteration or amendment except by all the trustees in office at the time and by a two-thirds vote of the society interested therein.

[1] Wallace *v.* First Parish of Townsend, 109 Mass. 263.
[2] Stats. 1869, ch. 248.
[3] Stats. 1870, ch. 68.

29. The terms " religious society " and " society " in the preceding sections shall include parishes.

30. Persons owning or proposing to build a house of public worship may organize themselves in the same manner as religious societies are authorized to do by the provisions of this chapter; and shall thereupon become a corporation with the powers, privileges, duties, restrictions, and liabilities, set forth in chapter sixty-eight, and in the following sections; but all the powers derived from such organization may be revoked by the legislature.

31. Every such corporation may hold so much real and personal estate, in addition to its meeting-house, as may be necessary for its objects (and no more [1]); and the annual income thereof shall be applied to parochial purposes.

32. The clerk of every such corporation shall, within ten days of such meeting, leave with the clerk of the town or city in which such house of worship is situated, or is about to be built, a true copy of the record of the proceedings. If he fails so to do, the organization shall be void. The copy shall be recorded by the clerk receiving it in a book kept for the purpose, for which he shall receive the fee of the register of deeds for like services.

33. When the proprietors deem it expedient to alter, enlarge, repair, rebuild, or remove, their house, or build a new one, they may, at a legal meeting called for that purpose, raise such sums of money as they may judge necessary for the purpose, and to purchase land necessary therefor.

Any religious society established under a special act of incorporation, shall have the powers set forth in this section, any thing contained in the act of incorporation, or any act in amendment thereof, or in section one of this chapter, to the contrary notwithstanding.[2]

34. A meeting of the proprietors for any of the purposes aforesaid, may be called in the manner prescribed in the by-laws or votes of the corporation, or by a warrant granted by a justice of the peace on application in writing by any five of said proprietors, which warrant shall be directed to

[1] Stats. 1870, ch. 63.          [2] Stats. 1876, ch. 84.

one of the applicants ; or such meeting may be called by a notification by the clerk of the proprietors, who shall warn a meeting on a like application to him ; and in either case the meeting may be warned by notification served as provided in section five (section six above).

35. Money raised may be assessed on the pews in such house, and the assessment may be committed to the treasurer of the proprietors, who shall forthwith give notice by posting up an advertisement at the principal outer door of the house, stating the completion of such assessment and the day of delivery thereof to him ; and if any part of said taxes remain unpaid for three months afterwards, the treasurer shall collect the same forthwith by sales at public auction of the pews whereon the same remains unpaid, in the manner provided in the following sections.[1]

The treasurer is the proper party to bring a suit for the purchase-money of a pew so sold.[2]

36. The treasurer shall post up a notification of the intended sale of a pew for taxes at the principal outer door of such house, at least three weeks before the time of sale, setting forth the number of the pew, if any, the name of the owner or occupant, if known, and the amount of the tax due thereon ; and if any part of said tax remains unpaid at the time, the treasurer shall sell the pew at public auction to the highest bidder, and shall execute and deliver to the purchaser a sufficient deed of conveyance. The money arising from the sale, beyond the taxes and incidental reasonable charges, shall be paid by the treasurer to the former owner of the pew, or to his assigns.

37. An affidavit annexed to an original notification or to a copy thereof, made before a justice of the peace and recorded on the proprietor's records within six months next after such sale, shall be allowed as one mode of proof of the posting up of the notifications hereinbefore required.

38. Such proprietors, for the purpose of building a new

[1] Gen. Stats. ch. 30, §§ 22–32.
[2] First Parish in West Newbury v. Dow, 3 Allen, 369.

house, or of altering, enlarging, repairing, rebuilding, or removing their house already built, may sell their house or take down any pews therein ; the pews taken being first appraised by three or more disinterested persons chosen by the proprietors for that purpose. The pews newly erected shall be sold by their treasurer at public auction to the highest bidder, and deeds thereof given in like manner as when pews are sold for the payment of taxes. The money arising from such sale shall be applied, as far as may be necessary, to paying the appraised value of the pews taken down ; and the deficiency, if any, shall be paid by the proprietors of such house, within thirty days after the sale.

39. Under the regulations of the preceding section, a parish or religious society, whenever it deems it necessary for the purpose of building a new house, or of altering, enlarging, removing, or rebuilding its house already built, may take down any pews therein or sell the house.

40. Nothing contained in the two preceding sections shall entitle a person to compensation for a pew so taken down, when such house is unfit for the purposes of public worship.[1]

Unless a meeting-house, at the time it is torn down by a vote of the proprietors, is not only unfit for public worship, but so old and ruinous as to render its entire demolition necessary, a pew-holder is entitled to indemnity for the destruction of his pew.[2]

41. Pews shall be personal estate. But this provision shall not affect any existing right of dower.

42. Corporations for religious purposes may assess upon the pews in a church or meeting-house which they have erected or procured for public worship since the twenty-fifth day of March, eighteen hundred and forty-five, according to a valuation of said pews which shall first be agreed upon and recorded by the clerk, sums of money for the support of public worship and other parochial charges, and for the repairs of the house. Such assessments may be collected in the manner provided in sections thirty-two and thirty-three.

[1] Gen. Stats. ch. 30, §§ 33-37.    [2] Gorton v. Hodsell, 9 Cush. 508.

43. A corporation which had erected or procured such house prior to the twenty-fifth day of March, eighteen hundred and forty-five, may avail itself of the provisions of the preceding section, if the consent of all the pew-owners is obtained, or two-thirds of the members present and voting at a regular meeting called for that purpose so determine.

44. A religious society which votes to avail itself of the provisions of section thirty-nine (forty-two above), shall, upon the application of a person owning one or more pews in its house, within one year after said vote, purchase the same at the appraised value. Such appraisal shall be made by three disinterested persons who may be chosen, one by the pew-owner, one by the society, and the third by the two persons thus chosen.

45. Any religious society complying with the requisitions of the two preceding sections, shall be entitled to the privileges and subject to the liabilities incident to those religious societies which have erected or procured a meeting-house for public worship since the twenty-fifth day of March in the year eighteen hundred and forty-five.

46. The trustees of any society of the Methodist Episcopal Church, or of the African Methodist Episcopal Church, appointed according to the discipline or usages thereof respectively or as such society chooses, may organize and become a corporation with powers, privileges, duties, and liabilities, of chapter sixty-eight, subject however to account to the quarterly meeting of such society according to such discipline and usages. But all powers derived from such organization may be revoked by the legislature.

47. Such trustees may receive, hold, and manage all the property, both real and personal, belonging to such society, and sell and convey the same, and hold in trust gifts, grants, bequests, or donations, made to such society for the support of public worship and other religious purposes: *provided*, that the annual income thereof, exclusive of the meeting-house, shall not exceed four thousand dollars.

48. The first meeting of such trustees may be called by

a justice of the peace upon the application of three or more
of the trustees ; at which they may choose a secretary and
other officers.   The provisions of this chapter in relation
to the warning and organization of meetings of religious
societies shall, so far as the same are applicable, be in
force in regard to meetings for the organization of such
trustees.   The secretary, before entering upon the duties
of his office, shall be sworn to the faithful discharge of the
same, and a record of such oath shall be kept in the records
of their proceedings.

49. An attested copy of the record of the proceedings
at such organization shall be left with the town or city
clerk, and recorded within the time and in the manner
prescribed in section twenty-nine (thirty-two above).   If
the secretary omits to leave such copy within the time
specified, the organization shall be void.[1]

[1] Gen. Stats. ch. 30, §§ 38–46.

32

# CHAPTER LXIII.

## DONATIONS AND CONVEYANCES FOR PIOUS AND CHARITABLE USES.

1. THE deacons, church-wardens, or other similar officers, of all churches or religious societies, if citizens of this commonwealth, shall be deemed bodies corporate, for the purpose of taking and holding in succession all grants and donations, whether of real or personal estate, made either to them and their successors, or to their respective churches, or to the poor of their churches.[1]

Other similar officers in this section means officers of similar character and with corresponding functions with those of deacons in Congregational churches, and church-wardens in Episcopal churches. Other officers, such as a treasurer, not of a character similar to that of deacons, can hold property of the church only as trustees.[2]

2. When the ministers, elders, or vestry of a church are, in the grants or donations mentioned in the preceding section, joined with such deacons or church-wardens as donees or grantees, such officers and their successors, together with the deacons or church-wardens, shall be deemed the corporation for the purposes of such grants and donations.

3. The minister of every church or religious society of whatever denomination, if a citizen of this commonwealth, shall be capable of taking in succession any parsonage land granted to the minister and his successors, or to the use of the ministers, or granted by any words of like import; and may prosecute and defend in all actions touching the same.

4. No conveyance of the lands of a church shall be effectual to pass the same, if made by the deacons without

---

[1] Gen. Stats. ch. 31, § 1.　　　[2] Weld v. May, 9 Cush. 181.

the consent of the church, or of a committee of the church appointed for that purpose, or if made by the church-wardens without the consent of the vestry.

5. No conveyance by a minister of lands held by him in succession, shall be valid any longer than he continues to be such minister, unless such conveyance is made with the consent of the town, parish, or religious society, of which he is minister, unless he is the minister of an Episcopal church and makes the conveyance with the consent of the vestry.

6. The several churches, other than those of the Episcopal denomination, may choose committees for the purpose of settling the accounts of the deacons and other church officers, and, if necessary, to commence and prosecute suits in the name of the church against the deacons or other officers touching the same.

7. The income of such grant or donation made to or for the use of a church, shall not exceed the sum of two thousand dollars a year, exclusive of the income of any parsonage lands granted to or for the use of the ministry.

8. The overseers of each monthly meeting of the people called Friends or Quakers shall be a body corporate for the purpose of taking and holding in succession grants and donations of real or personal estate made to the use of such meeting, or to the use of any preparative meeting belonging thereto ; and may aliene or manage such estate according to the terms and conditions of the grants and donations, and prosecute and defend in any action touching the same : *provided*, that the income of the grants and donations to any one of such meetings for the uses aforesaid shall not exceed the sum of five thousand dollars a year.

9. All trustees, whether incorporated or not, who hold funds given or bequeathed to a city or town for any charitable, religious, or educational purpose, shall make an annual exhibit of the condition of such funds to the board of aldermen of the city, or the selectmen of the town, to which such funds have been given or bequeathed, and all

transactions by the trustees concerning such funds shall be open to inspection by the board of aldermen of the city, or selectmen of the town, to which the returns are made.

10. The probate court for the county in which the city or town is situated to which funds have been given or bequeathed as aforesaid, may on the petition of five persons cite all parties interested to appear before the court to answer all complaints which may then and there be made ; and if a trustee has neglected or refused to render such annual exhibit, or is incapable of discharging the trust reposed, or unsuitable to manage the affairs of the same, the court may remove such trustee and supply the vacancy.[1]

[1] Gen. Stats. ch. 31, §§ 2–10.

## CHAPTER LXIV.

### ASSOCIATIONS FOR RELIGIOUS, CHARITABLE, AND EDUCATIONAL PURPOSES.

1. SEVEN or more persons within this commonwealth who shall have associated themselves together by an agreement in writing, such as is hereinafter described, with the intention to constitute a corporation for any of the purposes hereinafter specified, shall become a corporation under any name by them assumed upon complying with the provisions of section four of this act, with all powers, rights, and privileges, and subject to all duties, limitations, and restrictions, conferred by general laws upon corporations except as is hereinafter otherwise provided.

2. Such association may be entered into for any educational, charitable, benevolent, or religious purpose ; for the prosecution of any antiquarian, historical, literary, scientific, medical, artistic, monumental, or musical purposes ; for supporting any missionary enterprise having for its object the dissemination of religious or educational instruction in foreign countries, or for promoting temperance or morality in this commonwealth ; for encouraging athletic exercises and yachting ; for the association and accommodation of societies of Freemasons, Odd Fellows, Knights of Pythias, and other charitable or social bodies of a like character and purpose, and for the purpose of establishing and maintaining places for the uses of reading-rooms, libraries, or for social meeting.

3. The agreement of association shall set forth the fact that the subscribers thereto associate themselves with the intention to establish a corporation, the name by which the corporation shall be known, the purpose for which the cor-

poration is constituted, the town or city, which town or city shall be in this commonwealth, in which it is established or located, in case it shall have a capital stock the amount of its capital stock and the par value and number of its shares, and such par value may be either twenty-five, fifty, or one hundred dollars.

4. Such corporations may meet for organization, may organize, and certify their organization, in the same manner as manufacturing and other corporations are authorized to do by the ninth, tenth, and eleventh sections of chapter two hundred and twenty-four of the acts of the year eighteen hundred and seventy, and acts in amendment thereof, and the commissioner of corporations, and the secretary of the commonwealth shall, upon the payment of a fee of five dollars to the secretary of the commonwealth, do and perform in respect to corporations organized under this act, all acts required of them respectively, in respect to manufacturing corporations, by the said eleventh section of said act, and the certificate of incorporation to be issued by the secretary of the commonwealth thereupon shall be in the same form and shall have the same legal force and effect as the certificates issued to manufacturing and other corporations under the said eleventh section of said act, and the acts in addition thereto.

5. Such corporation may assume any name not previously in use by an existing corporation, which shall indicate that it is a corporation or company, and the name assumed in the agreement of association shall not be changed, but by act of the legislature.

6. Such corporations may prescribe by by-laws to be adopted by them, the manner in which and the officers and agents by whom the purpose of their incorporation may be carried out.

7. Such corporations may hold real and personal estate, and may lease, purchase, or erect suitable buildings for their accommodation, to an amount not exceeding five hundred thousand dollars, to be devoted to the purposes

and objects set forth in their agreement of association, and they may receive and hold in trust, or otherwise, funds received by gift or bequest to be by them devoted to such purposes.

8. The real and personal estate of such corporations shall not be exempt from taxation in any case where part of the income or profits of their business is divided among members or stockholders, or where any portion of such estate is used or appropriated for other than literary, educational, benevolent, charitable, scientific, or religious purposes.[1]

9. Any corporation constituted under the authority of chapter three hundred and seventy-five of the acts of the year eighteen hundred and seventy-four (preceding sections of this chapter), may have, instead of a board of directors, a board of trustees, managers, executive committee, prudential committee, wardens and vestry, or other officers having the powers of directors; and the certificate of organization of any such corporation may be made, signed, and sworn to by the presiding, financial and recording officer, and a majority of the directors, trustees, managers, executive committee, prudential committee, wardens and vestry, or other officers having the powers of directors as the case may be; and the certificate issued by the secretary of the commonwealth, under the provisions of said chapter, shall be modified to correspond with the facts in each case.

10. Nothing contained in chapter three hundred and seventy-five of the acts of the year eighteen hundred and seventy-four, entitled, " An Act concerning Associations for Religious, Charitable, Educational, and other Purposes," shall affect the existence of any association or corporation formed previously to the passage of said act, under the provisions of any statute for any of the purposes mentioned in the second section of said act, and any such corporation may, at a meeting called for the purpose, decide to adopt the provisions of this act, and upon so deciding

[1] Stats. 1874, ch. 375.

and complying with the provisions of this section shall have the powers and privileges and be subject to the duties and obligations of corporations formed under chapter three hundred and seventy-five of the acts of eighteen hundred and seventy-four. Said corporation may thereupon cause to be prepared and presented to the commissioner of corporations a certificate signed and sworn to by the presiding, financial and recording officers, and a majority of the directors, trustees, managers, executive committee, prudential committee, wardens and vestry, or other officers of whatever name, having the powers of directors, as the case may be, of said corporation, setting forth a copy of the agreement of association, of the vote hereinbefore referred to, and the date of the meeting at which the same was adopted, and may present such further evidence, if any, as the commissioner shall require of the legal existence of said corporation and its intention to adopt the provisions of this act. The commissioner of corporations shall examine the certificate submitted to him and the evidence of organization produced as aforesaid, and if it shall appear that the provisions of law have been complied with, he shall certify that fact, and his approval thereof, by indorsement thereon. The secretary of the commonwealth shall, upon the same being deposited in his office, and upon payment of the fee of five dollars, cause the same, with the indorsement thereon, to be recorded, and shall issue a certificate in the following form : —

### COMMONWEALTH OF MASSACHUSETTS.

Be it known that whereas [here the names of the original subscribers shall be inserted] have formerly associated themselves with the intention of forming a corporation, under the name of [here the name of the corporation shall be inserted], for the purpose [here the purpose declared in the articles of agreement shall be inserted], under the provisions of [here the designation of the statute under the provisions of which organization was effected shall be inserted], with a capital of [here the amount of the capital stock, as it stands fixed by the corporation at the date of the certificate, shall be inserted, or, if there is no capital stock, this clause shall be omitted], and the provisions of the statutes of this commonwealth in such case made and provided have been complied with, as appears from the certificate of the proper officers of said corporation, duly approved by the commissioner of corporations, and recorded in this office, — now therefore, I [here the name of the secretary shall be inserted], secretary of the commonwealth of Massachusetts, do hereby certify that said [here the name of the corporation shall be inserted] is legally organized and established as an existing corporation, with the powers, rights, and privileges, and subject to the limitations, duties, and restrictions, which by law appertain thereto.

Witness my official signature, hereunto subscribed, and the seal of the commonwealth of Massachusetts, hereunto affixed, this day of            , in the year of our Lord [in these blanks the day, month, and year of execution of the certificate shall be inserted].

The secretary of the commonwealth shall sign the same, and cause the seal of the commonwealth to be thereto affixed, and such certificate shall be conclusive evidence of the organization and establishment of such corporation at the date of such certificate. The secretary shall also cause a record of such certificate to be made, and a copy of such record, duly certified, may, with like effect as the original certificate, be given in evidence to prove the existence of such corporation.[1]

[1] Stats. 1875, ch. 49.

# APPENDIX.

## PARLIAMENTARY RULES FOR CONDUCTING TOWN AND OTHER MEETINGS.

1. Organization of meeting, how effected.
2. Duties of presiding officer.
3. Duties of a clerk.
4. How measures are brought before a meeting.
5. Motions: how put to vote, &c.
6. Motions before meeting cannot be withdrawn by mover: how disposed of.
7. Amendments, how made and put to vote.
8. Amendments, how amended.
9. How question is put on motion to amend by striking out, &c.
10. Privileged questions.
11. Motions to adjourn.
12. Questions of rights and privileges of members, &c.
13. Order of the day.
14. Motions to reconsider.
15. Quorum, what constitutes; effect of want of.

### *Organization of meeting, how effected.*

1. Obviously the first thing to be effected in the conduct of any deliberative assembly is *its organization;* that is, the election of a presiding officer, and a clerk or recording officer. In meetings of comparatively small numbers of people, for ordinary purposes, this is accomplished as follows : — Some one interested in the objects of the meeting, at the time appointed, requests the members to come to order for the necessary purpose of organization, and as soon as order and quiet are gained requests the company to nominate some one for chairman or presiding officer. He thereupon declares the name first heard by him as nominated, and puts the question to vote, whether this person shall act as chairman. If this is decided in the negative, another nomination must be called for ; if decided in the affirmative, such person then takes the chair, and, suggesting to the company the necessity of a clerk, requests a nomination, and proceeds as above specified in the case of the election of a chairman. If other officers are necessary, they may be elected in a similar manner. In the case of larger and more important assemblies, as for example political conventions,

it is usual to have a temporary organization as above, and a committee appointed to nominate officers for a permanent organization. In town meetings for the election of national, state, district, and county officers, the selectmen are authorized to preside, and as the town clerk acts as clerk of the meeting, the organization exists at the opening of the meeting.[1] At all other town meetings a presiding officer, called Moderator, must first be chosen. The town clerk shall call the meeting to order, and preside during the election of moderator, and if the town clerk is absent the selectmen shall preside,[2] and if the town clerk is not present to act as clerk of the meeting, the selectmen shall call upon the qualified voters present to choose a clerk *pro tempore*, in like manner as town clerks are chosen.[3]

### Duties of presiding officer.

2. The duties of a presiding officer are, in general, to preserve decorum, to announce the business before the meeting in its order, to receive all motions made by members, and put to vote all questions properly moved and seconded, and to state the result of all votes, and to inform the meeting when necessary or inquired of upon points of order. " He may speak on points of order in preference to other members." It is also his duty at an adjourned meeting to take the chair at the proper time and call the meeting to order. It is the rule that the " presiding officer may read sitting, but shall rise to state a motion, or put a question to the assembly."

### Duties of a clerk.

3. The general duties of a clerk of a meeting are to take notes of the proceedings and make the entries in his journal of " all things done and passed " in the meeting, but not of what is said or moved — simply without coming to vote. It is also his duty to read all papers which may be required to be read, to call the roll and note the answers when a question is taken by yeas or nays, notify persons of their election to office, and committees of the business referred to them, and keep the custody of papers belonging to the meeting.

### How measures are brought before a meeting.

4. It has been said to be one of the duties of the presiding officer to announce the business before the meeting in its order. This general order of business or subjects to be acted upon in town and parish meetings is found in the warrant for the meeting, which should be followed. After the presiding officer has announced to the meeting the subject to be acted upon as contained in the warrant, it is in order and usual for some member to present a proposition to the meeting in reference to such subject in the form of a motion, the

---

[1] See Ch. IV., *ante*.　　[2] See Ch. V., *ante*.　　[3] See Ch. VII., *ante*.

member rising and standing uncovered and addressing the presiding officer by his title; as, "Mr. Moderator, I move that," &c., &c. If the motion is one of any considerable length, or any but the most usual motions, it ought to be reduced to writing by the member offering it, for convenience and to avoid mistake. The presiding officer may however receive it if he choose, and reduce it to writing himself. Questions of order, such as whether or not there has been a violation of the rules of the meeting, must be decided by the presiding officer without being put to vote, and in case of dissatisfaction with his decision the party so dissatisfied may appeal to the meeting. The question is then put, Shall the decision of the chair stand as the decision of the meeting? "If the presiding officer insists upon voting on an appeal (being otherwise entitled), he cannot, on any parliamentary principle, be prevented."[1]

### Motions: how put to vote, &c.

5. All motions, except those of mere routine, and such as pass by general consent, should be seconded; that is, some member should rise, and, standing uncovered, state to the presiding officer that he seconds the motion. The motion is then in a condition to be presented to the meeting for its action, — which is done by the presiding officer stating to the assembly, "It is moved and seconded that," &c., &c. If it is one not likely to be debated, he adds, "If it be your pleasure that this motion pass, you will please to manifest it by raising the right hand," or, "in the usual manner," if there is a usual manner in which such votes are taken. After those voting in the affirmative have voted and been counted, if the vote is regarded as close enough to require a count, or the meeting has required a count, the presiding officer calls in a similar manner for the vote of those opposed to the motion; and then states to the meeting the result. If the voters are equally divided, the presiding officer may if he pleases give the casting vote. If he does not, the decision will be in the negative. "The presiding officer is justified in declining to put questions obviously frivolous or tending to disorder."

### Motions before meeting cannot be withdrawn by mover: how disposed of.

6. When a motion has been made, seconded, and stated to the meeting, it is then in the possession of the meeting, and cannot be withdrawn by the mover except by vote of the meeting granting leave.[2] It is the duty of the presiding officer to state, or cause to be read, a motion thus in possession of the assembly as often as any

---

[1] Warrington's Manual.

[2] But Mr. Robinson says the mover may withdraw it at any time before a decision, or before an amendment is moved, except a motion to reconsider. Warrington's Manual.

member requests it for his information. A motion thus before a meeting may be disposed of by indefinite postponement, or by postponement to a future day or hour, or by laying it on the table : such disposition being accomplished by motion and vote. If it be a matter of importance, and especially if it be one upon which the members require to be informed by the investigation of facts, the motion is referred to a committee with instructions to examine the subject as may be directed, and report at some future day. If it be one, on the other hand, which members are prepared to act upon, but are not satisfied with the exact form in which the motion has been made, it is in order to amend it.

### Amendments, how made and put to vote.

7. Amendments may be made by striking out certain words, by inserting or adding certain words, or by striking out and inserting or adding certain words. An amendment may itself be amended in the same manner, — but this is the limit : there can be no amendment of an amendment to an amendment, — and in putting the question to vote it must be first on the amendment to an amendment, if there be one, and next on the amendment as thus amended if the amendment to the amendment prevailed. If it is rejected, the question must then be put upon the original amendment. If this prevails, then the question is put on the original motion as amended. If it is rejected, the question is put upon the original motion. If an amendment prevails, or is rejected, it cannot be afterwards altered or amended. But if an amendment be to strike out or insert certain words and it prevails, or is rejected, an amendment may afterwards be moved to strike out or insert the same words in connection with others, if the other words so far modify the first as to make it a new amendment.

### Amendments, how amended.

8. It has been said above, that there can be no amendment to an amendment of an amendment. This object must be accomplished by rejecting the amendment to an amendment, and then moving to amend the original amendment as desired. And therefore it is well and customary for the person desiring such amendment to give notice that, if the amendment to the amendment is rejected, he shall move to amend the original amendment in such a manner, stating his amendment so that those desiring his amendment may vote to reject the other.

### How question is put on motion to amend by striking out, &c.

9. When there is a motion to amend by striking out words, the form of putting the question to vote is, *whether the words shall stand as part of the original motion*, and not whether they shall be stricken out.

The passage proposed to be amended should first be read, as it stands; then the words proposed to be stricken out; and lastly the passage as it will stand after the amendment is adopted. An amendment ought not to be something entirely opposed to the original motion, but something of the same nature, intended to make it more effectual or useful for its original purpose, *but this rule is not followed very strictly.*

### Privileged questions.

10. When a motion is regularly before the meeting it has the precedence of all other questions, except such as are termed *privileged questions.* These are motions to adjourn; questions relating to the rights and privileges of the meeting, or of individual members, and motions for the orders of the day.

### Motions to adjourn.

11. A motion to adjourn takes precedence of all other questions; but it must be a motion to adjourn, simply, without the addition of any particular time, in order to interrupt other business. It is sometimes the case therefore that a motion is made and carried early in the day, that, when the meeting adjourn, it be to some particular day, specifying it. A motion to adjourn simply, if carried, except in the case of such assemblies as have regular sitting days, has the effect to dissolve the meeting.

### Questions of rights and privileges of members, &c.

12. Questions relating to the rights and privileges of the meeting or its members are such as arise in case of the disturbance of the proceedings or quarrels between members. When these are settled, the question interrupted thereby is to be taken up at the point where it was left.

### . Order of the day.

13. When any subject has been assigned by the meeting for consideration at a particular time, it takes precedence of other questions at that time, and is called the order for the day.

### Motions to reconsider.

14. A motion to reconsider a vote already passed is usual in this country; and if it prevails, the matter of the vote to be reconsidered stands in the same condition as if the vote to be reconsidered had not passed, unless there is a rule of the assembly regulating the matter. A motion to reconsider may be made by any one, whether voting with the majority on the original question, or with the minority, unless there is a rule of the assembly to the contrary.

*Quorum, what constitutes : effect of want of.*

15. In most deliberative assemblies, it is required, either by law, or by the assembly itself, or by usage, that a certain number shall be present in order to transact business legally ; but where no rule is established in any of the ways mentioned above, a majority of the members composing the assembly is the required number.  As no business can be transacted without a quorum, the meeting should not be opened until there is a quorum present; and whenever there ceases to be, and notice is taken of the fact, there must be an adjournment; but the question under consideration must be taken up at the next meeting of the assembly at the point where it was when the adjournment was had.[1]

[1] Cushing's Manual of Parliamentary Practice.

# FORMS.

## ASSESSORS.

*Notice to bring in Lists of Polls and Estates for Taxation.*

### NOTICE.

TO THE INHABITANTS AND OTHER PERSONS LIABLE TO PAY TAXES IN THE TOWN OF B——D.

THE assessors of the town of B——d hereby give notice to the inhabitants of said town, and all other persons liable to pay taxes therein, that they will receive on and after the first day of May, instant, until and including the fifteenth day of June next, the valuation of estates, and all persons liable to be taxed in said town are hereby required to bring in to us true and perfect lists of all the polls and schedules and estimates of the real and personal estates possessed by them on the first of May, instant, for which they are liable to pay taxes in said town.

A. B. ⎫
C. D. ⎬ *Assessors of B——d.*
E. F. ⎭

B——D, May 1, 1870.

See section six, chapter ten, page eighty-six, as to omission of real estate from such schedules.

In large towns where the assessors have an office, the above may be dated at their office, and the requirement be to bring in the lists to such office.

*Form of Certificate of the Oath administered to the Person returning and subscribing a List as above required.*

Essex, ss. B——d, May, 187 . Then personally appeared the above named R. S., and made oath that the foregoing statement and list by him subscribed is true. Before me

A. B., *one of the Assessors of the town of B——d.*

*Request for Information made to Assessors of Town from which Tax-payer has removed.*

B——D, 187 .

To the Assessors of T——d.

Gentlemen, — By authority of the act of 1866, chapter 170, we require such written statement of any facts within your knowledge as will assist the assessors of this town in determining the value of the personal estate of G. K., and also the amount of personal estate on which he was last assessed in T——d.

Very respectfully, for
The Board of Assessors,
E. F., *one of the Assessors of the town of B——d.*

T——D,    187 .

To the Assessors of B——d.

Gentlemen, — G. K., a resident of T——d last year, was assessed by us as follows, viz. : —

Real Estate
Personal Estate

Very respectfully, for
The Board of Assessors,
C. D., *one of the Assessors of the town of T——d.*

### RULES FOR ASSESSING TAXES.

Divide the amount to be raised for the town tax and county tax by six, and the quotient will be the sum to be assessed upon the polls, unless it makes each poll tax more than $1.50. Divide this amount by the whole number of taxable polls, and the quotient will be the amount of each poll tax unless it exceeds $1.50. If it should, then make $1.50 the amount of each poll tax. Multiply the amount of each poll tax by the whole number of polls, and subtract the product from the whole amount to be raised. Divide the remainder by the taxable property, and the quotient will be the tax upon $1.00. Multiply the tax upon $1.00 by the taxable property of an individual; to the product add his poll tax, and the sum will be his tax.

*Warrant from Assessors to Collectors of Taxes.*

Essex, ss.

To        Collector of the town of        in the County of Essex,
Greeting :

In the name of the Commonwealth of Massachusetts you are hereby required by us, the subscribers, assessors of said town, to levy and collect of the several persons named in the list herewith committed to you, and of each one his respective proportion therein set down of the sum total of such list, the sum of        it being this town's proportion of a tax of        granted by the last General Court of said Commonwealth for defraying the necessary charges and expenses of the county aforesaid, and a tax of        voted and agreed upon by the town aforesaid at a meeting legally held for that purpose, on the        day of        last, for defraying the necessary charges and expenses thereof; together with the sum of        being the overlayings on said taxes.

And you are to complete and make up an account of the collection of the whole sum, and transmit and pay over the same as follows; to wit: to            Esq., treasurer of the county aforesaid, or his successor in that office, on or before the            day of            next, the sum of            ; to            treasurer of said town, or his successor in that office, on or before the            day of            next, the sum of

And if any person shall refuse or neglect upon demand by you made to pay the sum he is assessed in said list, you are to distrain the goods of such person to the value thereof, and the goods so distrained to keep at the expense of the owner for the space of four days at the least, and to sell the same within seven days after the seizure by public auction for the payment of the tax and the charges of keeping and of the sale; first giving notice of such sale by posting up a notification thereof, in some public place in the town, forty-eight hours at least before the sale. If the distress shall be sold for more than the tax and the charges of keeping the same and making the sale, you are to return the surplus to the owner on demand with an account in writing of the sale and charges. If any person shall refuse or neglect for fourteen days after demand thereof made to pay his tax, and you cannot find sufficient goods upon which it may be levied, besides tools or implements necessary for his trade or occupation, beasts of the plough necessary for the cultivation of his improved lands, military arms, utensils for house-keeping, necessary for upholding life, and bedding, and apparel necessary for himself and family, you are to take the body of such person and commit him to prison, there to remain until he shall pay the tax and charges of commitment and imprisonment, or be otherwise discharged by order of law.

Given under our hands by virtue of a warrant (or certificate) from the commissioners of the county aforesaid, and the vote of said town passed on the day aforesaid, this            day of            in the year eighteen hundred and

> A. B. )
> C. D. } *Assessors of B——d.*
> E. F. )

County Tax,            $
Town Tax,            $
Overlaying,            $
Highway deficiencies,            $

*The above are sold by stationers furnishing law blanks.*


*Notice of the Rates of Discount to be posted up by Assessors at the time of committing their Warrant to the Collector.*

The assessors of the town of B——d hereby give notice that they have committed to A. B., collector of taxes for said town, their warrant for the collection of taxes, and that by a vote of said town the following discounts will be allowed to all who shall voluntarily pay their taxes, viz.: —

On all taxes paid within 30 days      per cent.
    "    "   "    "  60  "      per cent.
    "    "   "    "  90  "      per cent.

E. F. &#125;
J. K. &#125; *Assessors of B——d.*
L. M. &#125;

B——D, May 1, 187 .

*Warrant from Assessors of Parish to Collector.*

E——, ss.

To A. B., treasurer and collector of taxes of the first parish of B——d in said county,

Greeting :

In the name of the commonwealth of Massachusetts you are hereby required by us the subscribers, assessors of said parish, to levy and collect of the several persons named in the list herewith committed to you, and of each one his respective proportion therein set down of the sum total of such list, the sum of      it being a tax of granted and voted by said parish, at a meeting held for that purpose on the      day of      together with the sum of      being the over-layings on said taxes.

And you are to complete and make up an account of the collection of the whole of said sums and transmit and pay over the same as follows; to wit: to      day of      on or before the      day of next.

And if any person shall refuse or neglect upon demand by you made to pay the sum he is assessed in said list, you are to distrain the goods of such person to the value thereof. [The remainder is the same as in a warrant for the collection of town taxes.]

Given under our hands by virtue of the vote of said parish passed on the day first aforesaid, this      day of      in the year eighteen hundred and

A. B. &#125;
C. D. &#125; *Assessors of the First Parish of B——d.*
E. F. &#125;

*Certificate to be placed on attested Copy of Warrant when Person is committed to Prison by Collector.*

I hereby certify that the sum which A. B. now committed to prison is to pay as his tax within mentioned is      $\frac{}{100}$ dollars, and upon his having neglected payment for fourteen days, and for want of goods whereof to make distress, I have taken his body. The cost of taking and committing him is      $\frac{}{100}$ dollars.

E. F., *Collector.*

# CONSTABLES AND COLLECTORS.

*Return on a Warrant for Town Meeting.*

E——, ss.                                          March          187 .

I have served the within warrant by posting up an attested copy of the same at the Town Hall, and also at the First Parish Meeting-house fourteen days before the said          day of March, 187 , as within directed.

A. B., Constable of T——d.

(Towns and parishes may order the manner in which their warrants shall be served, and the mode directed should be followed, and the fact set forth in the return.)

*Notice to a Person drawn as Juror.*

E——, ss.   To E. F., of T——d.   You are hereby notified that on the          day of          instant, you were drawn to serve as          juror at the          term of the Superior Court to be holden at N—— on the first Monday of          next, and to attend said court on said first Monday at          o'clock, A.M.

A. B., Constable of T——d.

*Return on a Venire for the Appointment of Jurors.*

E——, ss.   Pursuant to the within directions I notified the select-men and town clerk of said T——d, to meet as within prescribed and draw a          juror to serve at the court within named and on the          day of          instant G. H. was drawn as such juror; and on the          day of          instant I summoned him to attend said court on the first Monday of          187 .

A. B., Constable of T——d.

Fees, service, $
Travel,          miles, $

*Bond to be given by Treasurer and Collector of Town.*

### BOND.

Know all men by these presents,

That we A. B., of B——d, in the county of E—— and Common-wealth of Massachusetts, as principal, and C. D. and E. F., of said B——d, as sureties, are holden and stand firmly bound and obliged unto the said town of B——d in the full and just sum of          dollars, to be paid unto the said town; to which payment well and truly to be made, we bind ourselves, our heirs, executors, and admin-istrators, firmly by these presents.

Sealed with our seals.   Dated the          day of          in the year of our Lord one thousand eight hundred and

The condition of this obligation is such, That whereas said A. B.

has been chosen treasurer and collector of taxes for said town of B——d for the current year, and has accepted said offices, and been duly sworn to the faithful discharge of the duties thereof respectively. Now if the said A. B. shall, as treasurer and collector as aforesaid, faithfully collect, account for, and pay over all the taxes which he shall be legally required to collect, and also faithfully discharge all other legal duties of said offices, then this obligation shall be void; otherwise to remain in full force and virtue.

A. B. &rbrace; SEAL.<br>C. D. &rbrace; "<br>E. F. &rbrace; "

Signed, sealed, and delivered in presence of

*Demand for Tax on Real Estate.*

B——D, May      187 .

Mr.      I hereby demand of you the payment of      $\frac{}{100}$ dollars, that being the amount of tax assessed for the year 186 , on the real estate in this town, situated in                street, and           by you. You are hereby notified that if said amount, together with the costs thereon, is not paid within fourteen days from this date, the said estate will be sold at auction, pursuant to law.

A. B., *Collector of Taxes of the town of B——d.*

*Notice of Sale of Real Estate to be posted.   Also Form of Advertisement.*

This estate to be sold for unpaid taxes.

COLLECTOR'S NOTICE.

The owners and occupants of the following described real estate situated in the town of           county of           and commonwealth of Massachusetts, are hereby notified that the tax thereon assessed to E. D. for the year 186 , according to the list submitted to me as collector of taxes for said town by the assessors, remains unpaid, and that said parcel of real estate will be offered at public auction for sale at the Town Hall in said B——d, on August      187 , at      o'clock, P.M., for the payment of said taxes, together with the costs and charges thereon, unless the same shall be previously discharged.

[Here insert a substantially accurate description of the real estate, together with the amount of tax unpaid.]

A. B., *Treasurer and Collector of B——d.*

B——D, August 1, 187 .

*Collector's deed.*

COMMONWEALTH OF MASSACHUSETTS.

To all persons to whom these presents may come, I, A. B., collector of taxes for the town of B——d, in the county of E—— and Commonwealth of Massachusetts,

Send greeting:

Whereas the assessors of taxes of said town of B——d, in the list of assessments for taxes, which they committed to me to collect for the year one thousand eight hundred and sixty-    duly assessed C. D. as owner of the real estate in said town, which is hereinafter described, the sum of         dollars and         cents, for state, town, and county taxes thereon; and whereas, on the        day of A.D. 187 , I duly demanded of said        [If demand should be made on the mortgagee or an attorney of the non-resident owner, here insert the fact that such demand was made] the payment of said taxes, so as aforesaid assessed on said real estate, and the same were not paid; and whereas, after the expiration of fourteen days from the time of demanding payment of said taxes as aforesaid, the same still remaining unpaid, I duly advertised said real estate to be sold by public auction, for the payment of said taxes and all incidental costs and expenses, on the        day of        A.D., 187 , at        o'clock in the forenoon, at the Town Hall, in said town of B——d, by publishing an advertisement thereof, containing also a substantially accurate description, and the name of the owner of said real estate, and the amount of the taxes so as aforesaid assessed thereon, in a public newspaper published in said county, three weeks successively, the last publication whereof was one week before the time appointed for the sale, and by posting the said advertisement in three public and convenient places in said town of B——d; to wit:        and also on said real estate, three weeks before the time appointed for said sale; and whereas said taxes so as aforesaid assessed on said real estate not being paid, I proceeded, at the time and place appointed as aforesaid for the sale,[1] to sell [If a part only of the estate is sold, here insert what part] said real estate by public auction for the discharging and payment of said taxes thereon and said incidental costs and expenses,[2]

---

[1] The following is sometimes here inserted: " It being my opinion that the said land could not be conveniently divided, and a part thereof set off without injury to the residue, and judging it to be most for the public interest to sell the whole of said land."

[2] When the town is the purchaser under provisions of (§§ 47, 73, and 74, ch. 15, pages 130, 136, and 137), insert here the following in place of that in the form above, to wit: — " and no person appeared and bid for the estate thus offered for sale an amount equal to the said taxes and costs and expenses, and I thereupon, at said time and place appointed for sale, adjourned said sale until the        day of        A. D. 187 , at        o' clock in the forenoon, at the same place, and then and there made public proclamation of said adjournment; and in like manner in all respects, I adjourned said sale from day to day, to the same hour and place, being seven days (or being        days, but not more than seven days in the whole) in the whole, and then and there made public proclamation of said adjournments; and at the time and place so fixed and proclaimed for making said sale on each of said several days, I proceeded to offer for sale said real estate by public auction for the payment of said taxes, costs, and expenses, and no person appeared at either time so

and the said        was struck off to        of        in the county of
and state of        for the sum of        dollars and        cents, he being
the highest bidder therefor.

Therefore know ye, that I, the said A. B., collector of taxes aforesaid, by virtue of the power vested in me by law, and in consideration
of the said sum of        dollars and        cents to me paid by said
the receipt whereof I do hereby acknowledge, do hereby give, grant,
bargain, sell, and convey unto the said        the following described
real estate, the same being the land taxed as aforesaid, to wit:

To have and to hold the same, to the said        heirs and assigns,
to        their use and behoof for ever; subject to the right of redemption by any person legally entitled to redeem the same.

And I, the said collector, do covenant with the said        heirs and
assigns, that the sale aforesaid has, in all particulars, been conducted
according to the provisions of law.

In witness whereof, I, the said A. B., collector as aforesaid, have
hereunto set my hand and seal, this        day of        in the year
eighteen hundred and seventy.

A. B., Collector of Taxes for the town of B——d. SEAL.

Signed, sealed, and delivered in the presence of

E——, ss., August        187 .  Then personally appeared the above-
named A. B., collector of taxes for the town of B——d, and acknowledged the foregoing instrument to be his free act and deed.

Before me,                                        *Justice of the Peace.*

Entered and recorded in        registry, lib.        fol.

Summons to Delinquent Tax-payer.

B——d, March        1870.

Your tax for the year 1869, amounting to $        is now due. You
are requested to pay the same into the town treasury within ten days
from this date, with twenty cents for this summons.  At the expira-

fixed by adjournment for said sale and bid a sum equal to said taxes, costs, and expenses, and at the time and place so fixed for said sale by the last of the said adjournments, namely, on the        day of        A. D. 187 , at        o'clock in the forenoon, I made a public declaration of all the facts hereinbefore recited; and no person then appeared and bid a sum equal to said taxes, costs, and expenses; and I thereupon then and there immediately gave public notice that I should, and that I then and there did purchase on be-half of the said town of B——d, said real estate for the sum of        dollars and        cents, being the amount of said taxes and said incidental costs and expenses.

"Therefore know ye, that I, the said A. B., collector of taxes as aforesaid, by virtue of the power vested in me by law, and in consideration of the premises, hereby give, grant, bargain, sell, and convey unto the said town of B——d, the following described real estate, the same being the land taxed as aforesaid, to wit:"

tion of that period, if not paid, a warrant will issue therefor according to law, *increasing the expense by a charge for poundage and interest.*

A. B., Treasurer and Collector.

Mr.

The certificate of an abatement must be exhibited to the collector, and all costs and fees incurred before such exhibition must be paid.

### *Warrant from Collector to Sheriff or Constable.*

E——, ss.

To the sheriff 'of the county of E—— or his deputies, or the con-stables of the town of B——d, or to any or either of them,

Greeting:

In the name of the Commonwealth of Massachusetts, you are re-quired to collect of      of said      the sum of      dollars and cents, it being the amount of      taxes assessed against said      in the town of B——d in the county of E——, in said commonwealth, for the year of our Lord 18    in the lists committed to me for collec-tion by the assessors of said B——d.

And if the said      shall refuse or neglect upon demand by you made to pay the sum aforesaid, you are to distrain his goods to the value thereof, and goods so distrained to keep at the expense of the owner for the space of four days, at the least, and to sell the same within seven days after the seizure, by public auction, for the payment of the tax and charges of keeping, and of the sale ; first giving notice of such sale by posting up a notification thereof in some public place in said town, forty-eight hours at least before the sale. If the distress shall be sold for more than the tax, and the charges of keeping the same, and making the sale, you are to return the surplus to the owner, on demand, with an account in writing of the sale and charges.

If the said      shall refuse or neglect after demand by you made to pay said sum, and you cannot find sufficient goods upon which it may be levied, besides tools or implements necessary for his trade or occupation, beasts of the plough necessary for the cultivation of his improved lands, military arms, utensils for housekeeping necessary for upholding life, and bedding, and apparel necessary for himself and family, you are to take the body of such person and commit him to prison, there to remain until he shall pay the tax and charges of com-mitment and imprisonment, or be otherwise discharged by order of law.

You are to make a return of your doing on this warrant within      days from date hereof.

Given under my hand at said B——d this      day of      A. D. 187

Treasurer and Collector of B——d.

*Notice that a Warrant has been issued to Constable, &c.*

B——D, January 4, 1870.

Mr.

Sir,— The town treasurer has placed in my hands a warrant for the collection of your tax in B——d for the year 1869.

Your immediate attention to the same will much oblige

Yours respectfully,

*Constable and Deputy Collector.*

| | | |
|---|---|---|
| Tax, | | $ |
| Costs, | | $ |
| Interest from | 1869, | $ |

---

## FENCE VIEWERS.

*Complaint to the Fence Viewers by the Owner of Land that the Fence between his Land and the adjoining is insufficient.*

To A. B. and C. D., two fence viewers of the town of W——. The partition fence between my land and that of G. K., situated in W——, on the road leading from      to      which he ought to maintain, is insufficient. I hereby request you to survey the same, and direct him to repair or rebuild it.

N. O.

W——      187 .

*Notice to Adverse Party in above Complaint.*

To G. K., of W——. N. O., of said W——, has complained to us, two fence viewers of said W——, that the partition fence between your land and his adjoining situated in W——, on the road leading from      to      is insufficient, and has requested us to survey the said fence and direct you to repair the same. You are notified that we shall make the survey on Monday next at nine o'clock, A.M.

P. R. ⎫
S. T. ⎬ *Fence Viewers.*

W——,      187 .

*Award of Fence Viewers.*

To G. K., of W——. We, having surveyed the partition fence between your land and that of N. O., situated in said W——, on the road leading from      to      which you ought to maintain, and having found said fence out of repair and insufficient, hereby direct you to repair or rebuild said fence in      days from the date hereof.

P. R. ⎫ *Fence Viewers of*
S. T. ⎬ *the town of W——.*

W——,      187 .

*Certificate of the Sufficiency and Appraisal of Fence built by the Complainant when the Occupant of the adjoining Lot has neglected to comply with the Directions of the Fence Viewers.*

We hereby certify that we surveyed a certain partition fence between the land of N. O. and G. K., situated in said W——, on the road leading from          to          and adjudged the same to be insufficient and illegal, and did order and direct that the said G. K. should repair and build the same within          days from the date of said order, and the said G. K. not having complied with said order, the said N. O. at his own proper costs and charges has repaired and rebuilt the same, and we now adjudge the same to be sufficient, and appraise the said fence at the sum of          dollars.

And we certify that our fees for that service are as follows : —
For viewing said fence,   $
For appraising the same, $
      Paid us by the said N. O.,

.                                  P. R. }
                                   S. T. } *Fence Viewers of W——.*

W——,     187 .

*Notice of Fence Viewers when the right of Occupants in Partition Fence is in dispute, and their Award.*

To —— of    . M. N. has represented to us, two fence viewers of the town of W——, that a controversy has arisen between him and you about your respective rights in the partition fence between your land and his (*or* the land occupied by him and you      *as the fact may be*), situated      and has applied to us on that account; we therefore hereby notify you that we shall be at the premises on
      the ·  day of      at      o'clock in the      noon, to assign to each party his share of said fence.

                                   H. N. }
                                   N. O. } *Fence Viewers.*

Dated      18  .

Whereas a controversy has arisen between A. B. and C. D. of about their respective rights in a partition fence in the line between their lands situated at      we the subscribers, fence viewers of the town of W——, having, on the application of the said A. B. (and after having given due notice to the said C. D.) viewed the premises and duly considered the matter in dispute, do hereby assign to each of the said parties his share of said fence, as follows, viz. : —

The said A. B. shall build and keep in repair a good and sufficient fence from      to      And the said C. D. shall build and keep in repair a like fence on the other part of said line, viz., from      to

And each party is to erect (or repair) his part of said fence within
days from the date hereof.

Given under our hands at said W——, this      day of      18 .

H. N. }
N. O. } *Fence Viewers.*

*Notice issued by Fence Viewers when Lands are divided by a Brook, River,
Pond, &c.; and their Determination in such Case.*

To —— of      A. B. of      has represented to us, two fence
viewers of the town of B——, that you refuse to join with him (*or
that you and he disagree, as the fact may be*) in making a partition
fence between your land and his (*or*, between the lands occupied by
him and you), the same being bounded or divided by a pond (*river,
brook, &c., as the fact may be*), and has therefore made application to us
to view the same and determine thereupon, we therefore hereby notify
you that we shall make such view and determination on the      day
of      at      o'clock.

H. N. } *Fence Viewers of the*
M. P. }      *town of B——d.*

Dated the      day of      187 .

Whereas it has been represented to us, two fence viewers of the
town of B——, by A. B. of      whose land is bounded or divided
from the land of C. D. (*or occupied by C. D.*), that the said C. D. hath
refused to join with him (*or that they disagreed in making a partition
fence, as the fact may be*), and the said A. B. having applied to us to
view the same and determine thereupon, we have, after giving due
notice to the said C. D., performed that duty, and do determine that
the said pond (*river, brook, or creek, as the fact may be*) does not answer
the purpose of a sufficient fence, and that it is impracticable to fence
at the boundary line, we therefore determine that said fence shall be
set up as follows, viz.,      And that the said A. B. shall build and
maintain      and the said C. D. shall build and maintain

Given under our hands this      day of      18 .

H. N. }
M. P. } *Fence Viewers.*

[The other forms required by fence viewers can readily be made up
from the foregoing.]

## FIELD DRIVERS.

### *Notice to Owner of Beasts taken up and impounded.*

To A. B., of B——d. I have this day taken up and impounded in
the town pound in said town, under the care of C. D., pound-keeper,
one pair of red oxen belonging to you, found doing damage in the

enclosure of E. F. (*or running at large without a keeper on the public high-way in said town*), and for that cause I have impounded said oxen.

O. P., Field Driver of B——d.

B——D, June    187 .

[Notice to be posted up in case there is no one to receive foregoing notice, (see *ante*, p. 289,) may be as above, except the address "To A. B., of B——d," which should be omitted, and instead of "belonging to you," insert "the owner of which is unknown."]

Memorandum to be left with Pound Keeper.

To C. D., keeper of the town pound in the town of B——d.    I have this day taken up and distrained one bay horse, belonging to E. F. of said B——d, found doing damage in my enclosure, and for that reason I have impounded said horse in the town pound under your care.

The damages demanded are, $

Charges for keeping per day, $

G. H.

B——D, June    187 .

OVERSEERS OF THE POOR.

Notice to another Town that Pauper whose Settlement is in such Town is Expense chargeable to that Town, &c.    •

To the Overseers of the Poor of the town of T——,

Gentlemen, — A. B., whose legal settlement is in your town, but now residing in this town, being in needy circumstances, has applied to this board for relief, which we have granted, and charged to your town, and shall continue so to do until you remove or otherwise provide for his support.

For and in behalf of the overseers of the poor of the town of B——.

With respect, gentlemen, your obedient servant,

One of said Overseers.

Reply to foregoing.

T——,    187 .

To the Overseers of the Poor of the    of B——.

Gentlemen, — Your notice dated    informing us that    on expense as a pauper in your    and alleging that the legal settlement is in this town, is received.

Upon due inquiry, we can find no evidence that this town is the place of lawful settlement of said pauper.    We therefore decline removing said pauper    or paying any expense that has arisen, or may arise, for    support.

By order and in behalf of the overseers of the poor of the town of T——d,

Your obedient servant,

One of said Overseers.

# SURVEYORS OF HIGHWAYS.

*Notice to Tax-payer where and when he can work out his Tax, and Amount of same.*

The sum you are assessed to the highways and town ways for B——d for the year 187 , is, —

Poll, $
Personal, $
Real, $
Total,

Please take notice that I hereby appoint Monday        instant, at nine o'clock, A.M., and the road leading from the First Parish Meeting-house, &c., near the dwelling of J. R., as the time and place for providing materials and working on the highways and town ways.

E. D., *Surveyor of Highways.*

B——D, May    1870.

---

# SELECTMEN.

*Warrant for calling the Annual Town Meeting.*

E——, ss.    To either of the Constables of the town of B——, in said county                                        Greeting:

In the name of the Commonwealth of Massachusetts, you are directed to notify the inhabitants of the town of B—— qualified to vote in elections and in town affairs, to meet at the Town Hall in said B——, on    the    day of    next, at    o'clock in the forenoon, then and there to act on the following articles: —

1. To choose a moderator to preside in said meeting.
2. To choose all necessary town officers for the year ensuing.
3. To hear the annual report of the selectmen, and act thereon.
4. To raise such sums of money as may be necessary to defray town charges for the ensuing year, and make appropriations of the same.

And you are directed to serve this warrant, by posting up attested copies thereof, one at the Town Hall, and one at each of the public meeting-houses in the said town,[1] fourteen days at least before the time for holding said meeting.    The polls will open at        o'clock, A.M., and close at        o'clock, P.M.

Hereof fail not, and make due return of this warrant, with your doings thereon, to the town clerk, at the time and place of meeting as aforesaid.

Given under our hands this        day of        in the year one thousand eight hundred and

*Selectmen of B——.*

[1] Or as the town may have directed.

*Warrant for calling Town Meeting for voting for Governor, &c.*

E——, ss.  To either of the Constables of the town of B——, in said county                                                                  Greeting :

In the name of the Commonwealth of Massachusetts, you are required to notify the inhabitants of the town of B——, qualified to vote in elections, to meet at the Town Hall, in W——, on Tuesday, the       day of November next, it being the Tuesday next after the first Monday of said month, at       of the clock in       noon, to bring in their votes for a governor and lieutenant-governor of the commonwealth, and for senators, on one ballot, for the district of       for the year ensuing.  The polls will open at       o'clock, A.M., and close at       o'clock, P.M.

And you are directed, &c. (as in the foregoing form.)

*If to bring in Votes for Representative to Legislature of State.*

To bring in their votes on one ballot for a representative (*or       representatives, stating the number*) from district number       to the General Court.

*If for the choice of a Representative to Congress.*

To give their votes for a representative in the Congress of the United States, for the       district.

*Notice to Selectmen to Perambulate Boundary Lines between Towns.*

To the Selectmen of the town of F——.

Gentlemen, — The subscribers, selectmen (or two of the selectmen) of the town of B——, hereby give notice, that we shall meet at       on the       day of       at       of the clock in the       noon, to perambulate and run the lines between the said towns, and renew the marks, according to the law of the commonwealth : at which time and place you are hereby requested to attend for this service.

B——, the       day of       in the year 18  .

                                                 *Selectmen of B——.*

*Appointment of Substitute to Perambulate Boundary Lines between Towns.*

To A. B. of       We, the selectmen of the town of B——, do hereby appoint you to perambulate and run the dividing lines between said town and the town of       and renew the marks ; and you are to make returns of your proceedings into the clerk's office of the town of B—— as soon as you have completed this service.

Given under our hands this       day of       18  .

                                                 *Selectmen of B——.*

*License.*

The selectmen of B—— do hereby license C. D. to keep an intelligence office in said B—— for the year ensuing (*or as an auctioneer, inserting here all particulars required to be inserted by the statute*).

*Selectmen of B——d.*

B——D, this          day of          187 .

*Assignment of Division of Highways to Surveyor.*

To A. B., one of the surveyors of highways of the town of B——d. We hereby assign to you, to be kept in repair by you, the highways and town ways within the following limits; to wit, From the guide-post near the First Parish Meeting-house to the town line on the road leading to, &c.

J. K. ⎫<br>L. M. ⎬ Selectmen of B——d.<br>N. O. ⎭

*Notice issued by Selectmen on Petition to lay out Town Way.*

On the petition of          and others, that          be laid out as town way, the selectmen hereby give notice that they will meet at          on the          day of          at          o'clock,     M., to view the premises, and hear the parties interested.

Per order of the selectmen,

*Town Clerk.*

B——D,          187 .

(*Or signed by selectmen personally.*)

*Report to Town of laying out such Way.*

We the selectmen of the town of W——, having complied with the requirements of the law in relation to notifying the owners of land over which we were petitioned to lay out a town way, have laid out such town way as follows: Beginning at a monument on the southerly side of Ferry Street, so called, at the land of R., then through said R.'s land south twenty degrees east, one hundred and fifty rods to land of E., then continuing the same course through land of said E. fifteen rods, until it intersects the highway leading to the town of S——, the said town way to be fifty feet in width. Our agreement with the owners of the land over which said town way passes for their damages is as follows: That the said town of W—— shall pay to the said R. the sum of seventy-five dollars; and we have assessed damages of the said E. as the law directs — at twenty-five dollars. [If there are trees, fences, and other property on the land over which the town way passes, state the kind of such property, and the time allowed to remove the same.] And your selectmen hereby respectfully report said town way to the town for its acceptance.

Dated at W——, this          day of          in the year 187 .

*Selectmen of the town of W——.*

*Voting List.*

Voting List prepared by the Selectmen of the town of W——, 187 .

Names.                         Names.

N. B. The undersigned hereby give notice that they will be in session at the town officers' room in the Town Hall on      also on  ·  for the purpose of receiving evidence of the qualifications of those persons intending to vote at the coming elections, and to correct and revise the above voting list.

All those intending to vote are particularly requested to have their names registered.

*Selectmen of the town of W——.*

[It is not thought advisable to give any form of the annual report of selectmen or other town officers. So far as it is a report of the condition of the treasury, it may be in the form of a debit and credit account, so as to present intelligibly the state of the town finances during the year. Other reports should consist of a succinct statement of the doings of the officers making the reports in regard to such subjects as are of importance to the town.

They usually commence "In accordance with the requirements of law," or "In compliance with a vote of the town," and if necessary to make the matter perfectly clear insert the vote, or "In accordance with custom," as the fact may be, "we beg leave to submit the following report of our doings for the last year." And they conclude "All of which is respectfully submitted by

"*Selectmen or School Committee, or,*" *&c.*]

---

# TOWN CLERK.

*Warrant of Town Clerk to Constable to notify Town Officers to take the Oath of Office.*

To A. B., one of the Constables of the town of B——.

[L. S.]                                   Greeting :

The following is a list of those persons who were this day chosen into office, at a meeting of the inhabitants of said town, and who have not taken the oath of office required of them by law; viz. [Here designate those offices to which they were chosen.]

    ·     ·     ·     ·     ·

In the name of the Commonwealth of Massachusetts you are hereby required within three days from the date hereof to summon each of the said persons to appear before me, clerk of said town, within seven days from the service of such summons, to take the oath by law prescribed to the office unto which they are respectfully chosen.

Hereof fail not, and make return of this warrant to me with your doings thereon, within seven days from the date hereof.

*Town Clerk.*

### Certificate of Marriage.

Between      of      aged      years, by occupation a      He
was born in      and was the son of      This will be his      marriage. And      of      aged      years. She was born in      and
was the daughter of      This will be her      marriage.

The intentions of marriage, by the parties above named, were duly
entered by me in the records of the town of B—— relating to marriages, according to law.

Dated at B——, this      day of      A. D. 187 .

*Town Clerk.*

The parties above named were joined in marriage at      by me,
this      day of      A. D. 187 .

Attest,

### Intention of Marriage between

Mr.      residing in      He is      years of age, a      by occupation, was born in      Father's name (in full).      Mother's name
(in full).      This will be his      marriage.

And M      residing in      She is      years of age, was born
in      Father's name (in full).      Mother's name (in full).
This will be her      marriage.

### Return of a Birth in B—— to the Town Clerk.

Date of birth,      186 .  Full name of Child,      Sex,
Color,      Place of birth (street and number),      Christian name
of father,      Christian name of mother,      Present residence of
parents,      Occupation of the father,      Father's birthplace,
Mother's birthplace,

### Return of Death to the Town Clerk.

Date of death,      18 .  Name,      Color,      Aged
years      months      days. Place of death,
Residence,      Sex,      Single      Married
Occupation,      Wife of      Birthplace,      Widow of
Name of father,      Name of mother,      Birthplace of father,
Birthplace of mother,      Cause of death,      Primary
Duration,      Secondary      Duration,      Place of interment,
Date of interment or removal,      Undertaker or informant,

### Physician's Certificate of Death.

B——,      187 .

This certifies that      died on the      day of      187 , aged
years,      months,      days.

Cause of death,      Primary,      Duration. Secondary,
Duration.

*Physician.*

*Town Clerk's Certificate of the Registry of a Death.*

[The person to whom this Certificate is given shall deliver it to the person having charge of the interment (if other than himself), before the burial when practicable, otherwise within seven days thereafter.]

I,      town clerk of      do hereby certify that the death of who died at      street,      186 ,      aged      years, months,      days, was duly registered by me on the      day of 186 .

*Town Clerk.*

Dated this      day of      186 .

B——,      187 .

Permission is hereby given to      to remove the body of      who died at B——,      18 , aged      years,      months,      day , for inter- ment at      the particulars required by law having been duly reg- istered by me.

*Town Clerk.*

*Appointment of Persons to appraise Lost Goods or Stray Beasts.*

To A. B. and C. D., both of B——, in the county of E——, [L. S.]

Greeting :

You are hereby appointed to appraise upon oath, at their true value [here describe the goods], . . . found (*and if it be beast add*, and taken up) by E. F., of

And you are directed to make return of this warrant with your doings thereon, to the town clerk's office of said B—— within seven days from the date hereof.   Given under my hand and seal the day of      187 .

L. P., *Town Clerk of B*——

*Appointment of Persons to determine Damages done by Beasts taken up and impounded.*

To A. B. and C. D. of B——d.   You are hereby appointed to ap- praise, on oath, the damage done to the enclosure of E. F. by a pair of red oxen which for that cause have been taken up and impounded in the town pound.

B——D,      this      day of      187 .

J. H., *Clerk of the town of B*——d.

If the appointment is made at the request of the person impound- ing, add to the foregoing, " Also the costs and expenses of impound- ing, &c., including a reasonable compensation for your own services."

# ADDENDA.

[The references enclosed in parentheses are to chapters, sections, and pages of this book.]

## ELECTIONS.

1. MEETINGS in towns for the election of national, state, district, and county officers, shall be opened as early as twelve o'clock, noon, of the election day. The polls shall be kept open at least four hours, and for such longer time as a majority of the voters present shall by vote direct.

2. At any town meeting for the election of any officers, when the presiding officer shall have announced a time at which the meeting has directed the polls to be closed, the polls shall not be closed until that time has arrived, excepting that in no case shall the polls be kept open after the hour of sunset.[1] (See chapter four, page thirty-eight.)

3. (Section four of chapter four, page thirty-nine,) is amended by striking out the word "twenty," wherever the same occurs in said section, and inserting instead thereof the words "twenty-five;" also by striking out the word "fifteen," wherever the same occurs in said section, and inserting instead thereof the word "twenty."[2]

4. In all towns in this commonwealth registration of voters shall cease at ten o'clock in the afternoon on the Saturday next preceding the day of any election.[3] (See chapter four.)

## TAXES, AND COLLECTION OF SAME.

1. In making the estimate of the personal property of any assessable person as provided for in sections twenty-seven and twenty-eight of chapter eleven of the General Statutes (sections thirteen and fourteen of chapter ten of this book, pages eighty-seven and eighty-eight), the assessors shall specify the amount of each class of personal property mentioned in clauses numbered *eighth, ninth, tenth,* and *eleventh,* in section two of this act (next section), and enter the same in column number five upon the blank books furnished under the provisions of chapter one hundred and sixty-seven of the acts of the year eighteen

---

[1] Stats. 1879, ch. 2.    [2] Stats. 1879, ch. 68.    [3] Stats. 1879, ch. 37.

hundred and sixty-one (contained in chapter nine) : *provided, however,* that any error or over-estimate of any class shall not be taken into account in determining whether any person is entitled to an abatement, but only the aggregate amount of such estimate.

2. Section three of chapter one hundred and sixty-seven of the acts of the year eighteen hundred and sixty-one (section six, chapter nine, page seventy-nine) is hereby amended by striking out the clauses numbered " *Second* " to " *Twelfth* " inclusive, after the clause numbered " *First*," and inserting the following : —

" *Second.* — The tax on each poll.

" *Third.* — The total value of personal estate.

" *Fourth.* — The total value of real estate.

" *Fifth.* — The total valuation of the city or town.

" *Sixth.* — The total tax for state, county, and town purposes, including highway tax.

" *Seventh.* — The rate per cent of total tax, or rate per one thousand dollars.

" *Eighth.* — The total amount as valued for assessment of money at interest, and other debts due the persons assessed more than they are indebted or pay interest for, specifying how much of said amount is debts secured by mortgage, and how much unsecured debts.

" *Ninth.* — The amount of money on hand, including deposits taxable as valued for assessment.

" *Tenth.* — The total amount of public stocks and securities as valued for assessment.

" *Eleventh.* — The total amount of stocks in corporations without the state as valued for assessment.

" *Twelfth.* — Total number of horses assessed.

" *Thirteenth.* — Total number of cows assessed.

" *Fourteenth.* — Total number of sheep assessed.

" *Fifteenth.* — Total number of dwelling-houses assessed.

" *Sixteenth.* — The total number of acres of land assessed in the city or town."

And the secretary of the commonwealth shall cause the tables of aggregates provided for by section one of chapter one hundred and sixty-seven of the acts of the year eighteen hundred and sixty-one to be so amended as to conform to the requirements of this act.[1]

3. (Section fifty of chapter fifteen, page one hundred and thirty-one) is amended by striking out the words " provided in section eleven of this act," and inserting in place thereof the words " allowed to him when he exercises the power of taking." [2]

4. (Section seventy-two, chapter fifteen, page one hundred and thirty-six) is amended by striking out the words " one per centum per month," wherever they occur in said section, and inserting instead thereof the words " seven per centum per annum." [3]

---

[1] Stats. 1879, ch. 72.　　[2] Stats. 1879, ch. 73.　　[3] Stats. 1879, ch. 74.

5. (Section forty of chapter fifteen, page one hundred and twenty-eight) is amended by striking out the words "of the county where the real estate lies," and inserting in place thereof the words "published in the city or town where the premises to be sold for taxes are situated," and also by striking out the words "an adjacent county," and inserting in place thereof the words "the county where the real estate lies."[1]

6. (Section fifty of chapter fifteen, page one hundred and thirty-one) is amended by striking out these words, viz.: "and the sum of five dollars for examination of title," and inserting instead thereof these words, viz.: "and a sum not exceeding three dollars, for examination of title, a deed of conveyance or release, and all other necessary intervening charges."[2]

7. (Section eighteen of chapter nine, page eighty-three) is amended by striking out the words "two years from the time of its assessment," and inserting instead thereof the words "the calendar year in which the tax is assessed."[3]

---

## MISCELLANEOUS.

1. Every person having under his control a child between the ages of eight and fourteen years, who shall withhold the information in his possession and sought by the school committee or their agents as required by chapter three hundred and three of the acts of the year eighteen hundred and seventy-four (included in chapter thirty-four), or falsify in regard to the same, shall be punished by a fine not exceeding twenty dollars, or by imprisonment in the county jail for a term not exceeding thirty days.[4]

2. In cases of violation of any law, ordinance, or by-law, relating to the public health in any town, complaint may be made by any agent of the board of health of such town appointed to make sanitary inspections, as well as by the persons now authorized by law to make such complaint.[5] (See chapter on Board of Health.)

3. Section three of chapter two hundred and thirty-two of the acts of the year eighteen hundred and seventy-eight (section twenty of chapter twenty-nine, page two hundred and seventy-five and two hundred and seventy-six) is hereby amended by adding at the end thereof the following words: "*provided, however*, that in respect to any estate fronting upon such street or way which by reason of its grade or level, or for any other cause, cannot be drained into such sewer, the select-

---

[1] Stats. 1879, ch. 69.
[2] Stats. 1879, ch. 94.
[3] Stats. 1879, ch. 43.
[4] Stats. 1879, ch. 21.
[5] Stats. 1879, ch. 75.

men shall not ascertain, assess, and certify the assessment thereon, or give notice of such assessment to the owner of such estate, until the incapacity of such estate to be drained into such sewer has been removed.[1]

4. Chapter fifty of the acts of the year eighteen hundred and fifty-six is hereby amended by adding the following section: Section 4. No person shall construct or maintain any fish-weir within the tide-waters of this commonwealth unless authorized in the manner set forth in the first section of this act, or from any island within said tide-waters without authority in writing from the mayor and aldermen of every city, and the selectmen of every town, distant not over two miles from said island. Any person who shall construct or maintain any weir in violation of the provisions of this section shall forfeit the sum of ten dollars for each day he shall maintain such weir, to be recovered in any court of competent jurisdiction to the use of any cities or towns, from the mayor and aldermen or selectmen of which he ought to have obtained the authority aforesaid, and shall also be liable to be indicted therefor and to be enjoined therefrom.[2]

5. The statutes relating to the appointment of guardians to minors are so amended as to authorize the appointment of a guardian, who shall have the custody of any minor child, whose parents or surviving parent the probate court, upon a hearing after such notice to the parents or surviving parent as the court may direct, shall find to be unfit to have such custody.[3]

Upon the application of the selectmen of any town, or the overseers of the poor of any town, probate courts may, within their respective jurisdictions, pending any proceedings before them for the appointment of a guardian under the provisions of chapter three hundred and sixty-seven of the acts of the year eighteen hundred and seventy-three (preceding portion of this section), or for the removal of any guardian of any minor, appoint some suitable person to be temporary guardian of such minor during the pendency of such proceedings; and the person appointed such temporary guardian shall have the custody and control of such minor until such proceedings shall be concluded: *provided, however*, that the probate court having jurisdiction may at any time with or without notice terminate such temporary guardianship.[4]

6. The county commissioners, on application made to them in writing by any person owning property liable to destruction or damage, by the breaking of any reservoir, reservoir-dam, or mill-dam, or upon such application by the mayor and aldermen of any city, or selectmen

---

[1] Stats. 1879, ch. 55.  
[2] Stats. 1877, ch. 119.  
[3] Stats. 1873, ch. 367.  
[4] Stats. 1878, ch. 230.

of any town, on account of liability of loss of life, or damage to any road or bridges therein, from the same cause, shall, after notice to the owners of such reservoirs or dams, or their agents, of the time and place appointed therefor, view and thoroughly examine the same, with the assistance of a competent engineer.

7. If, upon such examination, in the judgment of the commissioners, the structure is not sufficiently strong and substantial to resist the action of the water under any circumstances which may reasonably be expected to occur, they, with the advice of an engineer, shall determine and direct what alterations or repairs are required to make it permanent and secure, and shall give written directions to the owners thereof to make such alterations or repairs within a reasonable time, and the results of such examination, and orders thereon, shall be duly recorded by said commissioners.

8. If the owner of a reservoir or dam thus examined and adjudged to be unsafe, refuses or neglects to make such alterations or repairs as the commissioners order, they shall cause such reservoir or dam, or such parts thereof as they may deem necessary for the safety of life or property, roads or bridges, on the stream below, to be removed, or the water drawn off ; and after such removal no structure shall be erected except in compliance with the requirements contained in the preceding sections ; and if the water has been drawn off, the reservoir shall not be filled again until the orders of the commissioners have been complied with.

9. The commissioners shall make such orders, as to the costs of all proceedings under the three preceding sections, as they may deem just : *provided*, that in all cases where the reservoir or dam is adjudged unsafe, said costs shall be paid by the owner.

10. No order, approval, request, or advice of the county commissioners shall have the effect to impair in any manner or degree the legal duties and obligations of the owners of reservoirs, reservoir-dams, or mill-dams, or their liability for the consequences of their illegal acts, or of the neglect or mismanagement of any of their agents or servants.

The supreme judicial court shall have jurisdiction in equity, and may make all judgments and decrees necessary to carry into effect the provisions of the five preceding sections.

11. No assessors of any town shall commit any tax list to the collector of taxes until the bonds of such collector and of the treasurer of said town have been given and approved as now required by law ; and the selectmen shall, upon the receipt and approval of such bonds, give written notice thereof to said assessors.

The selectmen may, if any town treasurer shall fail for ten days after his election to give his bond as required by law, declare his office vacant.[2]

[1] Stats. 1875, ch. 178.     [2] Stats. 1879, ch. 157.

12. Every town by by-law may provide regulations not inconsistent with the laws of the Commonwealth, under which the collector thereof shall exercise the powers given by (sections eighty-four and eighty-nine, chapter fifteen, pages one hundred and forty and one hundred and forty-three) ; but the passage of any such ordinance or by-law shall not render invalid any proceedings of the collector under said sections, commenced before the passage of such ordinance or by-law.[1]

13. (Section fourteen of chapter forty-eight, page four hundred and eighteen) is repealed, and the penalties imposed by chapters two hundred and nineteen and two hundred and twenty-one of the acts of the year eighteen hundred and sixty, entitled respectively "An Act concerning Contagious Diseases among Cattle," and "An Act in addition to an Act concerning Contagious Diseases among Cattle," are hereby made applicable to the diseases in horses, asses, and mules, known as farcy and glanders, and to contagious or infectious diseases in domestic animals.[2]

14. In all cases of glanders or farcy the appraisal of the animal so diseased shall be based on its value in its diseased condition, and the appraisers shall be the following persons. First, one member of the board of commissioners on contagious diseases among cattle. Second, one veterinary surgeon selected by said commissioner. Third, one reputable person who may be selected by the owner of the animal, if he chooses to do so, otherwise the two appraisers above named shall select the third.

All acts or parts of acts inconsistent herewith are repealed.[3]

15. The fees for attending as grand juror or traverse juror in any court, and the fees for attending as a juror before a sheriff, shall be three dollars a day for attendance, and eight cents a mile for travel out and home. The fees of jurors in all other cases shall remain as now fixed by law.[4]

16. Any town, either alone or jointly with any other town, may take a lease of any great pond within their limits, for the purpose of cultivating useful fishes under such conditions and restrictions as the commissioners on inland fisheries may prescribe, and may make appropriations for that purpose.[5]

17. Whoever within this commonwealth sells, offers for sale, exposes for sale, or has in his possession trout, land-locked salmon or lake trout, except alive, between the first day of October in each year and the next succeeding first day of April, shall forfeit for each fish taken, caught, or killed between said first day of October in each year

[1] Stats. 1879, ch. 169.
[2] Stats. 1879, ch. 178.
[3] Stats. 1879, ch. 160.
[4] Stats. 1879, ch. 182.
[5] Stats. 1873, ch. 195; Stats. 1874, ch. 135.

and said next succeeding first day of April, and so sold, offered for sale, exposed for sale or had in his possession, the sum of ten dollars, and in all prosecutions under this act the possession of any trout, land-locked salmon, or lake trout during the time included between the dates stated above shall be *prima facie* evidence to convict under this act (this section).

The selectmen of any town and all police officers and constables within this commonwealth shall cause the provisions of this act to be enforced in their respective cities and towns ; and all forfeitures and penalties for violations of the provisions of this act shall be paid one-half to the person making the complaint and one-half to the city or town in which the offence is committed.[1]

18. Towns may at legal meetings grant and vote such sums as they judge necessary for the purpose of keeping in repair or decorating the graves within their limits, of soldiers or sailors who have died in the military or naval service of the United States, or the monuments or other memorials erected to their memory.[2]

19. I do not find any provision for the election of an auditor in towns, but such officer is recognized in the statutes, and he is authorized to require claimants to certify, under oath, that the whole of the articles for which claim is made has been furnished, or that the whole labor or service has been performed, and that no commission, discount, bonus, reward, or present of any kind has been received, or is promised or expected on account of the same.[3]

[1] Stats. 1876, ch. 221.
[2] Stats. 1870, ch. 169.
[3] Stats. 1862, ch. 101.

# INDEX.

[Figures refer to pages. For the duties of officers upon particular subjects, see the title of those subjects in the Index.]

## A.

## E.

## H.